THE FATHERS
OF THE CHURCH

A NEW TRANSLATION

VOLUME 26

THE FATHERS OF THE CHURCH

A NEW TRANSLATION

Founded by
LUDWIG SCHOPP

EDITORIAL BOARD

ROY JOSEPH DEFERRARI
The Catholic University of America
Editorial Director

MSGR. JAMES A. MAGNER
The Catholic University of America

MARTIN R. P. McGUIRE
The Catholic University of America

ROBERT P. RUSSELL, O.S.A.
Villanova University

HERMIGILD DRESSLER, O.F.M.
The Catholic University of America

BERNARD M. PEEBLES
The Catholic University of America

REV. THOMAS HALTON
The Catholic University of America

WILLIAM R. TONGUE
The Catholic University of America

REV. PETER J. RAHILL
The Catholic University of America

SISTER M. JOSEPHINE BRENNAN, I.H.M.
Marywood College

SAINT AMBROSE

LETTERS

Translated by
SISTER MARY MELCHIOR BEYENKA, O.P.
*Edgewood College of the Sacred Heart
Madison, Wisconsin*

THE CATHOLIC UNIVERSITY OF AMERICA
Washington, D. C.

NIHIL OBSTAT:

JOHN M. A. FEARNS, S.T.D.
Censor Librorum

IMPRIMATUR:

✠ FRANCIS CARDINAL SPELLMAN
Archbishop of New York

November 13, 1954

Library of Congress Catalog Card No.: 67-28583
Copyright © 1954 by
THE CATHOLIC UNIVERSITY OF AMERICA PRESS, INC.
All rights reserved
Reprinted with corrections 1967

Reprinted 1987

First short-run reprint 2001

ISBN 978-0-8132-1091-9 (pbk.)

INTRODUCTION

ST. AMBROSE GOVERNED the Church at Milan for twenty-three years, from December 1, 373, until his death on April 4, 397. Of his correspondence, preserved in ninety-one letters, Letters 1-63 of the Benedictine edition (reprinted in Migne, *PL* 16.849-1286), can be dated with exact or approximate certitude; Letters 64-91, however, are impossible to date from either external or internal evidence. Even within the chronological limits of the traditional dates,—the years 379 to 396—scholars find discrepancies, many of which can have no definite solution. For the dates of the letters and other historical events touching their contents, J. R. Palanque, 'Essai de chronologie Ambrosienne,' *Saint Ambroise et l'empire romain* (Paris 1933) 480-556, has been followed unless otherwise noted.

Because of the wide variety of the subject matter of the letters and the unsatisfactory chronological arrangement of earlier editions and translations, the present volume offers the letters in a new order, which is an adaptation of the classification employed by Palanque.[1] The letters have been grouped according to the classes of persons addressed; namely: (1) emperors, (2) bishops, (3) priests, (4) his sister, Marcellina, and (5) laymen. Seven synodal letters, written to emperors or bishops in the name of Ambrose and other

---

*What may be a ninety-second letter, to Gratian, was published by L. Machielsen, in *Sacris erudiri* 12 (1961) 537-539 (cf. 515-532).

1 Palanque, *op. cit.* 466-479.

members of Church councils, are placed after the letters to bishops. Letters to entire congregations follow the letters to individuals within each section. Each group of letters presents the addressees in alphabetical order.

As a result of this arrangement, the letters on related subjects or those written in the same spirit to an individual are frequently found together. They range from affairs of state, problems of Church government, doctrinal disputes, exegesis, and pastoral and legal affairs, to the exchange of greetings between friends in many stations of life, letters of consolation, and the ordinary letter that attempted to bring the absent together in a world where travel and communication were extremely difficult.

The letters are a reflection of the many-sided role of St. Ambrose. His parents were Romans who were residing in Gaul at Trier in 339 when Ambrose was born. His father was praetorian prefect of the Gauls at the time. Ambrose had an older sister, Marcellina, who became a nun in 343, to whom he wrote three letters that are extant, and also an older brother, Uranius Satyrus, whom he loved dearly and over whose early death in 375 he grieved deeply.

Ambrose's education was typical of his day. He learned rhetoric, mathematics, philosophy, and science. He had a wide knowledge of Greek, by which he was able to know the works of the Greek Fathers of the fourth century, to study their writings, and to transmit them in Latin to the Western Church. Since he was desirous of following a legal career, he studied jurisprudence, and this knowledge, too, was frequently used later in the service of the Church.

Although Ambrose's family was Catholic and had a martyr among its forebears, Ambrose was not baptized in his youth. He did, however, study the truths of the Christian faith under the priest Simplicianus. This tutor came to Milan after Ambrose was made bishop and he there continued to instruct his former pupil, who, as Ambrose himself remarks, 'had to instruct before he had even learned.'² Eventually, Simplicianus succeeded Ambrose as Bishop of Milan in 397.

Ambrose's legal career began about the year 365 at Sirmium, where he practiced law in the praetorian prefect's court. About 370 he became provincial governor of Aemelia-Liguria, with Milan as his place of residence. There in November, 373,³ Ambrose was summoned to keep order at the election of a successor to Auxentius in the see of Milan upon the death of the Arian bishop. A child's cry, 'Ambrose Bishop!' brought to a unanimous decision the mixed throngs of Arians and Catholics in the cathedral and, despite the protests of Ambrose, who was only a catechumen in the Church, he was chosen by the people; the choice was seconded by the clergy, and it was approved by Emperor Valentinian I. Ambrose was duly consecrated bishop, after receiving the minor and major orders of the priesthood, on December 1, 373.⁴

As bishop of the city where the emperors had their residence, Ambrose raised Milan to recognition as the most important see of the West. He occupied a place of preeminence in the Church and contributed much to its prestige in the early years of peace when a strong pagan party still hoped to enjoy the protection of emperors not always Catholic. His religious policy was threefold: the protection of the Church against the violence of the emperors; the demand that the civil power respect the moral law; and the fostering of a close union of Church and state by which the state eventually favored only the Catholic religion and discouraged all others. Thus, without any political ambition on

---
2 *De off.* 1.1.4.
3 B. Altaner, *Patrologie* (2 ed. Freiburg 1950) 330, gives the date as 374. Palanque 483-487, 577, gives October, 373.
4 For several points of interest regarding Ambrose's election and consecration, see Dudden, *The Life and Times of St. Ambrose*, I 70-74.

his part, Ambrose gained a stronger power than the emperor in that he could exercise a moral check on him.

Ambrose's episcopacy spanned the reigns of several emperors of East and West. Valentinian I (d. 375) had sanctioned his election as bishop. Valentinian's son, Gratian, became Emperor of the West in joint rule with his half-brother, Valentinian II, in 375. The former was murdered by agents of Maximus the Usurper in 383, the latter was a victim of Arbogastes and Eugenius the Usurper in 392. Ambrose had known and corresponded with both emperors and directed their policy of refusing to provide imperial revenues for the upkeep of pagan temples. At the death of Gratian he went to Gaul to beg the body from Eugenius; he arranged the details of Valentinian's burial and delivered a consolatory funeral sermon for him.[5]

While the West had several emperors and two usurpers, the East enjoyed the long reign of Theodosius from 379 until 395. Ambrose had dealt harshly with Theodosius for the affair at Callinicum when the emperor ordered Christians to rebuild a Jewish synagogue which they had burned during a religious riot. The imperial order was rescinded. After the massacre of the Thessalonians by the command of Theodosius in 388, Ambrose exacted public penance of the emperor in the Basilica at Milan. He preached his funeral sermon, however, and praised his victories against the two usurpers of the West and his zeal in striving to unite East and West in the bond of the one faith. Two years later Ambrose died, while acting as unofficial guardian of the youthful Honorius, Emperor of the West.

The letters which Ambrose wrote to Gratian, to Valen-

---

5 Letter 4, which has not hitherto been considered among the consolatory works of Ambrose, was written to Theodosius from whom Ambrose was awaiting instructions for the burial of Valentinian. Sections 1-3 are a 'monody' wherein Ambrose expresses his great grief at the death of Valentinian.

tinian, and to Theodosius, and the synodal letters to the three conjointly, have the sustained dignity which characterized his style when addressing the highest ranking civil rulers of his day. But with all his deference to authority he pursued a relentless logic in championing the rights of God and the Church, using Scripture to illustrate the truth of God's sovereignty in matters human and divine.

Ambrose addressed more letters to bishops than to any other class of persons, and understandably so. Throughout all of Northern Italy, Ambrose acted as metropolitan, but the limits of his episcopal see never corresponded to those of his activity. He founded several bishoprics; he intervened in the election of a successor to Limenius at Vercelli, installing Honoratus; he instructed the Church at Aemelia regarding the date of Easter, having been requested by Eusebius of Bologna to do so. The provinces of Flaminia and Venetia looked to Milan rather than to their see cities; Ambrose was a sort of super-metropolitan of Italo-Illyrian bishoprics.[6]

In addition, he corresponded with the Bishops of Rome, Naples, Gaul, and Alexandria—all outside his province—and with newly elected Bishops of Thessalonica, Como, Imola, and Claterna. Several of those whom he had consecrated he continued to favor with his correspondence. The collection of letters contains six to Sabinus of Piacenza, whom Ambrose begged to criticize his writings, and for whom he wrote letters that embody commentaries of several passages of Scripture. Three letters to bishops concern legal affairs; several are mere pleasant exchanges of greeting.

Individual priests to whom Ambrose wrote are Horontianus, addressed in nine letters, and Simplicianus, addressed in four. The former appears not to have hesitated to call on

---

[6] See, in this connection, J. R. Palanque and others, *The Church in the Christian Roman Empire*, trans. E. Messenger (London 1952) II 650-655.

Ambrose for assistance in interpreting any Scriptural passage whose meaning was doubtful to him. In his replies Ambrose is generous, allowing his letters and those of Horontianus to form, as he says, 'a sort of chain' (53). Frequently, he developed the mystical and allegorical sense of Scripture with great originality and depth.[7]

The letters to these priests have a special interest in that the recipients were residents of Milan with whom the contents might have been discussed in person without recourse to writing. Undoubtedly, the letter form helped Ambrose to clarify his thought. A letter to certain members of the clergy who were discontented in the priesthood formulates in a winning manner their spiritual father's advice and encouragement. A lengthy letter to the Church at Vercelli is a veritable treatise on the duties of the clergy.

Two of the letters to Marcellina contain Ambrose's first-hand account of events of historical importance: his struggle with the Arian Empress Justina and her son Valentinian II in 386, and his conduct with Theodosius after the affair of Callinicum in 388. The third letter to his sister tells of his finding the bodies of the martyrs, Gervase and Protase, whose relics are now honored with those of Ambrose in the basilica at Milan.

Laymen to whom Ambrose wrote had in some instances requested instruction on Scripture, as a certain Clementianus did who asked the meaning of St. Paul's words: 'The law has been our tutor unto Christ, that we might be justified by faith.'[8] Others appealed for help in a family or legal difficulty, as did Paternus (86), who wished his son to marry the latter's niece, and Studius (90), who wanted to know whether the Church allowed judges who had inflicted sentences of capital punishment to receive the sacraments.

---

7 See, for example, Letter 46.
8 Gal. 3.24.

Several letters are mere exchanges of greeting when a messenger travels from Milan. A certain Irenaeus, a resident of Milan, received twelve letters from Ambrose, many of which are comparable to those addressed to Horontianus on exegetical problems. Several contain passages of great depth, and allow us to see the workings of divine grace in this spiritual guide of souls. Letters of consolation were addressed to the clergy and people of Thessalonica on the death of their bishop, Acholius, and to a certain Faustinus at the death of his sister.[9]

The letters give us a clear view of those qualities which made Ambrose the spiritul leader of his day. He was eager to propagate the faith, to defend its dogma, and, if necessary, to shed his blood for its preservation. He held firmly to his principles in dealing with the emperors. Yet, when the occasion arose, he showed great magnanimity in forgiving his enemies and in heaping benefits upon them. His care for souls was not limited to those within his official jurisdiction, but the good of the Church drew him into its concerns elsewhere and prompted him to take a leading part in Church councils at Aquileia, Rome, and Capua. His letters reveal his learning, his wisdom, his holiness, and his freedom from the least taint of worldliness. Clergy and laity alike consulted him. Men found in him the piety, charity, mercy, modesty, justice, and firmness that won their estèem. Ambrose lives as we read his letters almost 1,600 years after they were first penned.

There are details revealed by the correspondence of Ambrose which add to our knowledge of ancient epistolography. The salutations are frequently very simple, for example, 'Ambrose to Titianus,' with an occasional addition of 'greetings.' Then there are the elaborate salutations to the emperors

---

[9] For a study of these consolatory letters, see C. Favez, *La consolation latine chrétienne* (Paris 1937) 20-22.

(8), and the tenderest of greetings to his sister, 'dearer than life and eyes' (61). Many letters begin with a restatement of the difficulty proposed to him—most welcome to the reader centuries removed.

His biographer Paulinus[10] testifies to Ambrose's habit of writing with his own hand, as Ambrose himself mentions he did (24), particulary at night. He praises Gratian (1) for the letter he had penned with care to Ambrose. Ambrose wrote with his own hand to Theodosius (7) after the affair at Callinicum, so that the emperor alone might know and read his words of rebuke. Several times Ambrose speaks of letter writing as a bond between those who are apart, and, overburdened as he was with ministering to the weaknesses of men,[11] he seems to be reaching out of his loneliness toward companion souls.

That Ambrose collected some of his letters in his lifetime is evident from his words to Sabinus: 'These remarks which are a prelude to other discussions I shall put in the collection of our letters, if you are willing, and give them a number' (23). He was conscious of his style, as he speaks to the same Sabinus of 'prating like an old man . . . employing an ordinary and friendly style,' and 'savoring of older writers.'

Whatever the content of Ambrose's letters to bishops, priests, and laymen, he invariably expresses his love for his correspondents in the beautiful refrain: 'Farewell, and love us, because we love you.' The letters to emperors, however, he often concludes with great formality and by imparting a blessing. On several occasions, when he has administered a rebuke, there is no formal conclusion. Thus, the final argument lingers in the reader's consciousness.

The years 385 to 387 were those in which Augustine knew

---

10 *Vit.* 9.38, trans. John A. Lacy, in this series, Volume 15 (New York 1952).
11 Augustine, *Conf.* 6.3.3.

Ambrose as Bishop of Milan. During that time Ambrose addressed at least two letters to emperors, four to bishops, seven to priests, eight to laymen. These twenty letters are a proportionately large part of his correspondence. Unfulfilled is our longing for even one letter to Augustine at this period or in the years to come![12]

The present translation is based on the Benedictine text, reprinted in Migne, and J. Wytzes' critical text for Letters 7, 8, and 11 in *Der Streit um den Altar der Viktoria* (Amsterdam 1936). Correspondence with Rev. Otto J. Faller, S. J., of Munich, Germany, discouraged our waiting for the critical edition of the *Letters* which he is preparing for the *Corpus Scriptorum Ecclesiasticorum Latinorum*.

Eleven of the letters, considered by the editors as 'most interesting and important,' were translated by H. de Romestin in the *Nicene and Post-Nicene Fathers*, 2nd series, 10 (1896). H. Walford revised a translation by an earlier unnamed translator of all the letters (except 32 and 33) in the *Library of the Fathers* (Oxford 1881). This last-named work is the only translation of the entire correspondence of Ambrose found in any language. Rev. W. R. Waghorn's unpublished master's thesis, *Saint Ambrose: Letters to Sabinus* (Washington 1952), was also consulted.

Biblical quotations and references abound in the letters of St. Ambrose. Although at times the language is that of the Vulgate, many quotations are given in the language of the Old Latin Bible, some are from the Septuagint, and others have no counterpart in the versions which are at hand. Under these circumstances it has been necessary frequently to adapt the translation of Biblical passages to the text of Ambrose. Where possible, use was made of the New American Catholic Edition of *The Holy Bible* (New York 1950), wherein the

---
12 Evidence of their correspondence before Augustine's baptism is found in *Conf.* 9.5.13.

Old Testament is based on the Douay Version, with Psalms from the New Latin Version authorized by Pope Pius XII, and the New Testament is based on the Confraternity Edition. For the Book of Genesis the translation used was that of the Catholic Biblical Association of America for the Confraternity of Christian Doctrine (Paterson, N. J. 1948).

SELECT BIBLIOGRAPHY

Editions and Translations:

Du Frische, J., and Le Nourry, N. (Maurists), *Sancti Ambrosii Mediolanensis Episcopi Opera*, 2 vols. (Paris 1686-1690).

Migne, J.-P., *Patrologiae cursus completus*, Series latina 16 (Paris 1845) 849-1286, (Paris 1866) 913-1342 (3rd. rep. of Bened. ed.)

Romestin, H. de, in *Nicene and Post-Nicene Fathers*, ser. 2, vol. 10 (New York 1896).

Waghorn, W. R., *Saint Ambrose: Letters to Sabinus*, unpublished master's thesis, The Catholic University of America (Washington 1952).

Walford, H., *The Letters of St. Ambrose, Bishop of Milan* (Oxford 1881).

Secondary Works:

Broglie, Duc de, *Saint Ambrose*, trans. Margaret Maitland (London 1899).

Dudden, F. Homes, *The Life and Times of St. Ambrose*, 2 vols. (Oxford 1935).

Labriolle, Pierre de, *The Life and Times of St. Ambrose*, trans. Herbert Wilson (St. Louis 1928).

McGuire, Martin R. P., 'A New Study on the Political Rôle of St. Ambrose,' *Catholic Historical Review* 22 (1936-1937) 304-318.

Nagl, Maria Assunta, *Der heilige Ambrosius* (Münster 1951).

Palanque, Jean Remy, *Saint Ambroise et l'empire romain* (Paris 1933).

Paulinus, *Life of St. Ambrose*, trans. John A. Lacy, in Early *Christian Biographies*, Fathers of the Church 15 (New York 1952).

CONTENTS

Letters to Emperors   *Page*

1	*(1)* *	To Gratian	3
2	*(10)*	To Theodosius	6
3	*(51)*	To Theodosius	20
4	*(53)*	To Theodosius	26
5	*(61)*	To Theodosius	28
6	*(62)*	To Theodosius	30
7	*(17)*	To Valentinian	31
8	*(18)*	To Valentinian	37
9	*(21)*	To Valentinian	52
10	*(24)*	To Valentinian	57
11	*(57)*	To Eugenius the Usurper	62

Letters to Bishops

12	*(16)*	To Anysius	67
13	*(91)*	To Candidianus	70
14	*(50)*	To Chromatius	70

*Indicates Benedictine enumeration

Letters to Bishops *Page*

15 (2)   To Constantius 76
16 (72) To Constantius 90
17 (87) To Fegadius and Delphinus 101
18 (3)   To Felix 102
19 (4)   To Felix 102
20 (7)   To Justus 105
21 (8)   To Justus 115
22 (82) To Marcellus 120
23 (48) To Sabinus 124
24 (47) To Sabinus 127
25 (45) To Sabinus 129
26 (49) To Sabinus 134
27 (46) To Sabinus 136
28 (58) To Sabinus 144
29 (59) To Severus 149
30 (85) To Siricius 151
31 (86) To Siricius 152
32 (5)   To Syagrius 152
33 (6)   To Syagrius 163
34 (56) To Theophilus 172
35 (19) To Vigilius 174
36 (23) To the Bishops of Aemelia 189
37 (15) To the Bishops of Thessalonica 200

Synodal Letters

38 (9)   To the Bishops of Gaul 207
39 (10) To Gratian, Valentinian, and Theodosius . . 208
40 (11) To Gratian, Valentinian, and Theodosius . . 213

Synodal Letters   *Page*

41	(*12*)	To Gratian, Valentinian, and Theodosius	216
42	(*13*)	To Theodosius	219
43	(*14*)	To Theodosius	223
44	(*42*)	To Siricius, Bishop of Rome	225

Letters to Priests   *Page*

45	(*70*)	To Horontianus	231
46	(*71*)	To Horontianus	241
47	(*77*)	To Horontianus	245
48	(*78*)	To Horontianus	251
49	(*43*)	To Horontianus	254
50	(*44*)	To Horontianus	264
51	(*34*)	To Horontianus	272
52	(*35*)	To Horontianus	277
53	(*36*)	To Horontianus	283
54	(*37*)	To Simplicianus	286
55	(*38*)	To Simplicianus	303
56	(*65*)	To Simplicianus	308
57	(*67*)	To Simplicianus	311
58	(*81*)	To the Clergy of Milan	317
59	(*63*)	To the Church at Vercelli	321

Letters to His Sister

60	(*20*)	To Marcellina	365
61	(*22*)	To Marcellina	376
62	(*41*)	To Marcellina	385

Letters to Laymen   *Page*

63	*(89)*	To Alypius	399
64	*(90)*	To Antonius	399
65	*(88)*	To Atticus	400
66	*(79)*	To Bellicius	401
67	*(80)*	To Bellicius	402
68	*(74)*	To Clementianus	405
69	*(75)*	To Clementianus	410
70	*(84)*	To Cynegius	413
71	*(54)*	To Eusebius	413
72	*(55)*	To Eusebius	414
73	*(39)*	To Faustinus	416
74	*(31)*	To Irenaeus	420
75	*(32)*	To Irenaeus	425
76	*(33)*	To Irenaeus	428
77	*(64)*	To Irenaeus	432
78	*(69)*	To Irenaeus	435
79	*(29)*	To Irenaeus	437
80	*(30)*	To Irenaeus	448
81	*(28)*	To Irenaeus	454
82	*(27)*	To Irenaeus	458
83	*(73)*	To Irenaeus	464
84	*(26)*	To Irenaeus	468
85	*(76)*	To Irenaeus	475
86	*(60)*	To Paternus	481
87	*(66)*	To Romulus	484
88	*(68)*	To Romulus	488
89	*(83)*	To Sisinnius	489
90	*(25)*	To Studius	492
91	*(52)*	To Titianus	494

CROSS-REFERENCE TABLE

Bened. Ed.	This Ed.	Bened. Ed.	This Ed.	Bened. Ed.	This Ed.
1	1	31	74	61	5
2	15	32	75	62	6
3	18	33	76	63	59
4	19	34	51	64	77
5	32	35	52	65	56
6	33	36	53	66	87
7	20	37	54	67	57
8	21	38	55	68	88
9	38	39	73	69	78
10	39	40	2	70	45
11	40	41	62	71	46
12	41	42	44	72	16
13	42	43	49	73	83
14	43	44	50	74	68
15	37	45	25	75	69
16	12	46	27	76	85
17	7	47	24	77	47
18	8	48	23	78	48
19	35	49	26	79	66
20	60	50	14	80	67
21	9	51	3	81	58
22	61	52	91	82	22
23	36	53	4	83	89
24	10	54	71	84	70
25	90	55	72	85	30
26	84	56	34	86	31
27	82	57	11	87	17
28	81	58	28	88	65
29	79	59	29	89	63
30	80	60	86	90	64
				91	13

SAINT AMBROSE

LETTERS

LETTERS TO EMPERORS

1. To the most blessed Emperor Gratian, most Christian prince, Ambrose, bishop (March, 380)

DO NOT LACK affection, most Christian of princes: I have nothing more true and glorious to say than this. I am not lacking in affection, I say, but a sense of awe has kept my affection from meeting your Clemency. If I did not go on foot to meet you as you returned, I did meet you in spirit, I met you with prayer, in which lies the most important duty of a bishop. I met you, I say? When I was not with you, did I not follow with all my love you to whom I clung with mind and heart? Surely, the presence of minds is more important. I read of your journey from day to day; I put myself in your camp day and night by my concern for you and by my thought. I stretched out for you a coverlet of prayers; if I was unable to give you the attention which you deserved, yet was I unremitting in my affection.

In fact, when I showed myself solicitous for your welfare, I was acting in my own interest. Here is not flattery, which you do not want and which I consider unbefitting my office; it is merely the good grace which you have shown me. God who is our judge, He whom you profess, He in whom you piously believe, understands that my strength is refreshed by your faith, your salvation, your glory. And He knows that I give prayers which are due you not only because of your public office, but also because of my personal love for you. For you have given back to me the peace of the Church, you have closed the mouths of the wicked—ah, would that you had closed their hearts, also! You have done this not less by your faith than by the weight of your power.

What shall I say of your recent letter?[1] You wrote the entire letter with your own hand, so that the very marks of punctuation bespoke your faith and piety. In the same way with his own hand did Abraham of old slay an ox[2] to serve his guests at dinner, and in this performance of his duty did not ask the help of others. As a humble servant he ministered to the Lord and His angels, or to the Lord in His angels. O Emperor, you honor a lowly priest with royal dignity, but deference is shown to the Lord when a servant is honored, for God Himself has said: 'What you did to one of the least of these, you did unto me.'[3]

But shall I praise only the lofty humility in you, the emperor, and not rather the faith of your mind fully conscious of your deserts, that faith taught you by Him whom you do not deny? Who else could have taught you not to reproach Him for being of the created nature which you see in yourself? Nothing could be said more characteristically, nothing more clearly. For to say that the creature is Christ is to put forth an insult, not to confess reverence. Futhermore, what is so insulting as to think that He is what we are? You have instructed me, then, the one from whom

---
1 See Gratian's letter to Ambrose (*PL* 16.875-876).
2 Cf. Gen. 18.7.
3 Matt. 25.40.

you said that you wanted to learn. I have never read or heard so good an interpretation as yours.

Moreover, how pious, how admirable is the fact that you do not fear jealousy in God! From the Father you expect remuneration for your love of the Son, and by praising the Son you say that you cannot add anything to His glory, but you wish to commend yourself to the Father by praising His Son. This He alone taught you who said: 'He who loves me will be loved by my Father.'[4]

You have remarked in addition that, being weak and frail, you cannot so praise Him as to exalt the Godhead by your words. But you will preach Him according to your ability, not according to what the Godhead warrants. This weakness is more powerful in one who is in Christ, as the Apostle says: 'When I am weak, then am I strong.'[5] Humility like this does away with frailty.

To be sure, I shall come as you bid and I shall hasten to hear these words in your presence, to pick up these words in your presence when they fall from your lips. I have also sent the two books[6] you requested and, since they are approved by your Clemency, I shall not fear any damage to them. Meanwhile, I shall ask indulgence from the Holy Spirit for writing them, since I know who will be the judge of my speech.

In the meantime, your love and faith in our Lord and Saviour, drawn from the Son of God, grows into such overwhelming conviction that you also believe in the divinity of the Holy Spirit, and you do not reproach Him as being of the created nature which you see in yourself, nor think that God, the Father of our Lord Jesus Christ, is jealous of His

---
4 John 14.24.
5 2 Cor. 12.10.
6 *On Faith* (*De fide*, PL 16. 527-698).

Spirit. That which lacks all association with created nature is divine.

If the Lord grants His favor, I shall comply with the will of your Clemency; as you have received His grace, may you realize that one so pre-eminent in the glory of God has a right to our veneration in His own name.

May almighty God, the Father of our Lord Jesus Christ, deign to protect you, that you may be blessed and flourish for many years, and may He deign to confirm your reign most gloriously in peace, O lord, august Emperor, elected by divine choice, most glorious of princes.

2. To the most clement prince and blessed Emperor Theodosius Augustus, Ambrose, bishop (December, 388)

I am continually beset with almost unending cares, O most blessed Emperor, but never have I felt such anxiety as now, for I see that I must be careful not to have ascribed to me anything resembling an act of sacrilege. I beg you, therefore, give ear with patience to what I say. For, if I am not worthy of a hearing from you, I am not worthy of offering sacrifice for you, I to whom you have entrusted the offering of your vows and prayers. Will you yourself not hear one whom you wish heard when he prays in your behalf? Will you not hear one who pleads in his own defense, one whom you have heard plead for others? And do you not fear for your own decision that, if you think him unworthy to be heard by you, you will make him unworthy of being heard for you?

It is not fitting for an emperor to refuse freedom of speech, or for a bishop not to say what he thinks. There is no quality in you emperors so popular and so lovable as the cherishing of liberty even in those whom you have subdued on the battlefield. In fact, it spells the difference between good and bad emperors that the good love liberty; the bad, slavery. And there is nothing in a bishop so fraught with danger before God, so base before men, as not to declare freely what he thinks. Indeed, it is written: 'And I spoke of thy precepts in the presence of kings and I was not ashamed,'[1] and elsewhere: 'Son of man, I have made thee a watchman to the house of Israel,' in order, it is said, 'that if the just man shall turn away from his justice and shall commit iniquity, because thou hast not given him warning,' that is, not told him what to guard against, 'his righteousness shall not be remembered, and I will require his blood at thy hand. But if thou warn the righteous that he sin not, and he doth not sin, the righteous shall surely live because thou hast warned him, and thou wilt deliver thy soul.'[2]

I would rather, O Emperor, have partnership with you in good deeds than in evil. Therefore, the bishop's silence should be disagreeable to your Clemency; his freedom, agreeable. You are involved in the peril of my silence, but you are helped by the boon of my freedom. I am not, then, intruding in bothersome fashion where I have no obligation; I am not interfering in the affairs of others; I am complying with my duty; I am obeying the commands of our God. This I do, first of all, out of love for you, in gratitude to you, from a desire to preserve your well-being. If I am not believed or am forbidden a hearing, I speak, nonetheless, for fear of offending God. If my personal peril would set you free, I should offer myself patiently, though not willingly, for you, for I would rather you were acceptable to God and glorious without peril to me. But, if the guilt of silence and untruthfulness should weigh heavily upon me and set you free, I had rather that you think me too bothersome than useless and

---

[1] Ps. 118.46.
[2] Ezech. 3.17-21.

dishonest. Indeed, it is written in the words of the holy Apostle Paul, whose teaching you cannot disprove: 'Be urgent in season, out of season; reprove, entreat, rebuke with all patience and teaching.'[3]

We have one whom it is more perilous to displease, especially since even emperors are not displeased when each man performs his task, and you patiently listen to each as he makes suggestions in his own sphere; in fact, you chide him if he does not act in accordance with his rank in service. Can this seem offensive in bishops, the very thing you are willing to accept from those who are in your service, since we are saying, not what we wish, but what we are bidden to say? You know the passage: 'When you will stand before kings and governors, take no thought of what you are to speak; for what you are to speak will be given you in that hour. For it is not you who are speaking, but the Spirit of your Father who speaks through you.'[4] If I were speaking in a case involving the commonwealth (even though justice must be maintained there), I would not feel such dread if I were not given a hearing. But in a case involving God, whom will you listen to if not the bishop, who sins at a greater peril? Who will dare tell you the truth if the bishop does not?

I know that you are God-fearing, merciful, gentle, and calm, that you have the faith and fear of God in your heart, but often some things escape our notice. Some persons have zeal for God, but not according to knowledge.[5] Care must be taken, I think, lest this condition steal upon pious souls. I know your devotion to God, your leniency toward men. I myself am indebted to you for many kind favors. Therefore, I fear the more, I am the more anxious lest you condemn me later in your judgment for the fault you did not avoid,

---

3 2 Tim. 4.2.
4 Matt. 10.19,20.
5 Cf. Rom. 10.2.

because of my want of openness and my flattery of you. If I saw you sinning against me, I would not have to be silent, for it is written: 'If thy brother sin against thee, first take hold of him, then rebuke him before two or three witnesses. If he refuse to hear thee, tell the Church.'[6] Shall I, then, keep silence in the cause of God? Let us then consider wherein lies my fear.

It was reported by a count[7] of military affairs in the East that a synagogue was burned,[8] and this at the instigation of a bishop. You gave the order for those who were involved to be punished and the synagogue rebuilt at the bishop's expense. My charge is not that you should have waited for the bishop's testimony, for bishops quell disturbances and are eager for peace unless they deeply feel some wrong against God or insult to the Church. But suppose that this particular bishop was overimpetuous in burning the synagogue, and too timid at the judgment seat; are you not afraid, Emperor, that he may comply with your pronouncement and do you not fear he may become an apostate?

Are you not afraid of what will perhaps ensue, his resisting the count in so many words? Then he [the count] will have to make him either an apostate or a martyr, either alternative very different from this era of your reign, either one equivalent to persecution if he is forced to apostatize or undergo martyrdom. You see what the outcome of this case will be. If you know that the bishop is firm, beware of making him a martyr if he becomes more firm; if you consider him inconstant, have no part in the downfall of one who is frail. He incurs a heavier obligation who compels the weak to fall.

I am supposing that in the present state of affairs the

---

6 Matt. 18.15-17.
7 His name is nowhere given.
8 At Callinicum. The incident is well summarized by Gregory Figueroa, S. A., *The Church and the Synagogue in St. Ambrose* (Washington 1949) xiii-xxiv.

bishop will admit that he spread the fires, gathered the crowd, and brought the people together in order not to lose the chance of martyrdom and to present a strong individual instead of many weak ones. O happy falsehood, which wins acquittal for others and for himself grace! This, I ask, O Emperor, that you rather take your vengeance on me, and, if you consider this a crime, attribute it to me. Why pronounce judgment on those who are far away? You have someone at hand, you have someone who admits his guilt. I declare that I set fire to the synagogue, at least that I gave the orders, so that there would be no building in which Christ is denied. If the objection is raised that I did not burn the synagogue here, I answer that its burning was begun by God's judgment,[9] and my work was at an end. If you want the truth, I was really remiss, for I did not think such a deed was to be punished. Why should I have done what was to be without one to punish, and without reward? These words cause me shame but they bring me grace, lest I offend the most high God.

Let no one call the bishop to task for performing his duty: that is the request I make of your Clemency. And although I have not read that the edict was revoked, let us consider it revoked. What if other more timid persons should, through fear of death, offer to repair the synagogue at their expense, or the count, finding this previously determined, should order it to be rebuilt from the funds of Christians? Will you, O Emperor, have the count an apostate, and entrust to him the insignia of victory, or give the labarum, which is sanctified by Christ's name, to one who will rebuild a synagogue which knows not Christ? Order the labarum carried into the synagogue and let us see if they [the Jews] do not resist.

Shall a place be provided out of the spoils of the Church for the disbelief of the Jews, and shall this patrimony, given

---

9 It was probably struck by lightning.

to Christians by the favor of Christ, be transferred to the treasuries of unbelievers? We read that, of old, temples were reared for idols from the plunder taken from the Cimbrians and from the spoils of the enemy. The Jews will write on the front of their synagogue the inscription: 'The Temple of Impiety, erected from the spoils of the Christians.'

Is your motive a point of discipline, O Emperor? Which is of more importance: a demonstration of discipline or the cause of religion? The maintenance of civil law should be secondary to religion.

Have you not heard how, when Julian had ordered the Temple of Jerusalem rebuilt, those who were clearing the rubbish were burned by fire from heaven? Are you not afraid that this will also happen now? In fact, you should never have given an order such as Julian would have given.[10]

What is your motive? Is it because a public building of some sort has been burned, or because it chanced to be the synagogue there? If you are disturbed by the burning of a very unimportant building (for what could there be in so mean a town?), do you remember, O Emperor, how many homes of prefects at Rome have been burned and no one has exacted punishment? In fact, if any of the emperors wanted to punish such a deed more severely, he only aggravated the cause of all who had suffered such a great loss. If there is going to be any justice at all, which is more fitting, that a fire on some part of the building of Callinicum be avenged, or one at Rome? Some time ago the bishop's residence at Constantinople was burned, and your Clemency's son pleaded with his father, begging you not to punish the insult done to him, the emperor's son, in the burning of the episcopal residence. Do you not think, O Emperor, that if you were to

---

10 For an account of Julian's acts, see J. R. Palanque and others, *The Church in the Christian Roman Empire,* trans. E. C. Messenger (London 1949) I 234-239.

order this burning to be punished, he would again plead that it be not so? It was very suitable for your son to gain that favor from his father, for it was fitting that he first forgive what was done to him. Besides, there was a good division of grace there, since the son made the entreaty regarding his injury, and so did the father for the son's. Here is nothing for you to waive in your son's behalf; be careful, then, to derogate nothing from God.

There is really no adequate cause for all this commotion, people being punished so severely for the burning of a building, and much less so, since a synagogue has been burned, an abode of unbelief, a house of impiety, a shelter of madness under the damnation of God Himself. For we read by the mouth of Jeremias, the Lord our God speaking: 'And I will do to this house in which my name is called upon, and which you trust, and to the place which I have given you and your father, as I did to Silo. And I will cast you away from before my face, as I have cast away all your brethren, the whole seed of Ephraim. Therefore do not thou pray for this people, nor show mercy for them and do not approach me for them; for I will not hear thee. Seest thou not what they do in the cities of Juda?'[11] God forbids us to make intercession for those that you think should be vindicated.

If I were pleading according to the law of the nations, I would mention how many of the Church's basilicas the Jews burned in the time of Julian, two at Damascus—one of which is scarcely yet repaired, and that at the expense of the Church, not of the synagogue—while the other basilica is still a rough heap of unsightly ruins. Basilicas were burned at Gaza, Ascalon, Beirut, in fact, almost all over that region, and no one demanded punishment. A basilica of surpassing beauty at Alexandria was burned by heathens and Jews, but the Church was not avenged, and shall the synagogue be avenged?

---

11 Jer. 7.14-17.

Shall the burning of the temple of the Valentinians[12] also be avenged? What is it but a temple where the heathens gather? Although the heathens worship twelve gods, the Valentinians worship thirty-two Aeons, whom they call gods. I have found out that a law was passed and orders given for the punishment of some monks to whom the Valentinians denied the right of way as they sang the psalms by an ancient custom and practice, going on their way to the feast of the martyrs, the Machabees.[13] In anger at their effrontery they [the monks] burned their hurriedly built shrine in some country village.

How many can entertain such hope when they remember that in the time of Julian a man[14] who had thrown down an altar and disturbed the sacrifice was sentenced by the judge and suffered martyrdom? The judge who heard the case was never considered other than a persecutor. No one ever thought him worth meeting or saluting with a kiss. And if he were not dead, I would be afraid, O Emperor, that you would punish him, although he did not escape heaven's vengeance, for he outlived his heir.

But it is said that a trial of the judge was demanded and the decision handed down that he should not have reported the deed, but punished it; and money chests which had been taken had to be restored. I shall omit any other details. The churches' basilicas were burned by the Jews and nothing was restored, nothing was demanded in return, nothing was required. Moreover, what could a synagogue in a distant town contain, when everything there is not much, is of no value, is of no account. In fine, what could those

---

12 Cf. G. Bardy, 'Valentin,' *Dict. de théol. cath.* 15² 2497-2519.
13 The festival honoring the Machabees seems to have been universally celebrated in the Church of the fourth century on August 1.
14 Mark of Arethusa in the time of Constantius had demolished a pagan temple and was tortured under Julian for refusing to rebuild it. Cf. Sozomen 5.10; Theodoret *Eccl. hist.* 3.7.

scheming Jews have lost in this act of plunder? These are but the devices of Jews wishing to bring false charges, so that by reason of their complaints an extraordinary military inquiry may be demanded and soldiers sent who will perhaps say what was said here some time before your accession, O Emperor: 'How will Christ be able to help us who are sent to avenge Jews? They lost their own army, they wish to destroy ours.'

Futhermore, into what false charges will they not break forth, when they even falsely accused Christ with their false witnesses? Into what false charges will men not break forth when they were liars even in matters divine? Whom will they not name as the instigators of the sedition? Whom will they not attack, even though they know them not, just so that they may see countless Christians in chains, see the necks of faithful people bowed in captivity, that the servants of God may go into dark hiding places, be struck with axes, given to the flames, and delivered to the mines, so that their sufferings may not pass hurriedly?

Will you grant the Jews this triumph over God's Church? this trophy over Christ's people? these joys, O Emperor, to unbelievers? this festival to the synagogue? this grief to the Church? The Jewish people will put this solemnity among their feast days, and doubtless they will rank it with their triumphs over the Amorites and the Canaanites, or their deliverance from Pharao, the king of Egypt, or from the hand of Nabuchodonosor, the king of Babylon. They will have this solemnity marking the triumphs they have wrought over the people of Christ.

And although they refuse to be bound by the laws of Rome, thinking them outrageous, they now wish to be avenged, so to speak, by Roman laws. Where were those laws when they set fire to the domes of the sacred basilicas? If Julian did not avenge the Church, because he was an apostate, will you, O Emperor, avenge the harm done the synagogue, because you are a Christian?

And what will Christ say later to you? Do you not recall that He sent word to blessed David through Nathan the Prophet?[15] 'I have chosen you, the youngest of your brethren, and have made you an emperor from a private individual.[16] The fruits of your seed I have put upon the imperial throne. I have made barbarian nations[17] subject to you; I have given you peace; I have brought your captive enemy[18] into power. You had no grain to feed your army; I threw open the gates to you; I opened the granaries to you by the hand of the enemies themselves. Your enemy prepared provisions for themselves and gave them to you. I troubled the counsels of your enemy so that he laid himself bare. I so fettered the usurper[19] of the Empire and bound his mind that while he still had a chance to flee, as though afraid that one of his men should elude you, he shut himself in with them all. His officer[20] and forces on the other element,[21] whom I had routed earlier, so that they would not join battle against you, I brought together again to complete your victory. Your army gathered from many unruly nations I bade keep faith and peace and concord, as if of one nation. And when there was great danger that the perfidious plans of the barbarians would penetrate the Alps, in order that you might conquer and suffer no loss, I brought you victory within the very ramparts of the Alps.[22] I, then, caused you to triumph over your enemy, and are you giving my enemies a triumph over my people?'

---

15 Cf. 2 Kings 7.8-17.
16 In 382.
17 The Goths.
18 Athanaric.
19 Maximus.
20 Adragathius.
21 The sea.
22 Cf. Sozomen 4.46 and Dudden, *op. cit.* 354.

Was not Maximus undone because, when he heard that the synagogue at Rome had been burned, before the set time for his expedition, he sent an edict to Rome, as if he were the champion of public order? On this account the Christian people said: 'No good is in store for him! The king has turned Jew, we have heard he is a defender of those whom Christ soon made trial of, He who died for sinners.'[23] If this was said of his mere words, what will be said of your actual punishment? He was soon conquered by the Franks, by the Saxon nation, in Sicily, at Siscia, at Pettau; in fact, everywhere. What has the believer in common with this unbeliever? Marks of his baseness should die with the base one. The victor should not imitate, but condemn his injury of the vanquished for his offenses.

I have recounted these details for you, not through ingratitude, but I have enumerated them as rightly due to you, so that by heeding these warnings you, who have been given more, will love the more. When Simon answered in these words, the Lord Jesus said: 'Thou hast judged rightly,' and turning at once to the woman anointing His feet, setting forth an example for the Church, He said to Simon: 'Wherefore I say to thee, her sins, many as they are, shall be forgiven her, because she has loved much. But he to whom little is forgiven, loves little.'[24] This is the woman who entered the house of the Pharisee and cast off the Jew, but gained Christ, for the Church shut out the synagogue. Why is trial again being made within the household of Christ? Is it that the synagogue may shut out the Church from the bosom of faith, from the house of Christ?

These matters, O Emperor, I have gathered together in this address out of love and attachment to you. I am under obligation for your kindnesses at my requests when you

---

23 Rom. 5.6.
24 Luke 7.43,47.

released many from exile, from prisons, and from the extreme penalty of death. I am bound to prefer hurting your feelings for the sake of your welfare (for no one has greater confidence than one who loves from the heart, and certainly no one should harm one whose interests he has at heart); and I should not fear to lose in one moment the favor which other bishops and I have enjoyed for so many years. Yet it is not the loss of that favor that I would avert, but the peril to salvation.

How important it is for you, O Emperor, not to feel bound to investigate or punish a matter which no one up to now has investigated or punished! It is a serious matter to jeopardize your faith in behalf of the Jews. When Gideon had slain the sacred calf, the heathens said: 'Let the gods themselves avenge the injury done to them.'[25] Whose task is it to avenge the synagogue? Christ whom they slew, whom they denied? Or will God the Father avenge those who did not accept the Father, since they did not accept the Son? Whose task is it to avenge the heresy of the Valentinians? How can your Piety avenge them when it has given orders for them to be denied entrance and has denied them the right of assembly? If I give you the example of Josias as a king approved by God, will you condemn in them what was approved in him?[26]

Yet, if you have little faith in me, bid those bishops assemble whom you do esteem. Discuss with them, O Emperor, what ought to be done without injury to the faith. If you consult your officers on money matters, how much fairer is it to consult the Lord's priests on a religious matter!

Let your Clemency consider how many persons plot and spy on the Church. If they find a slight crack, they drive in an arrow. I speak in the manner of men, but God is more

---
25 Judges 5.32.
26 Cf. 4 Kings 22.1,2.

feared than men, for He is rightly preferred even to emperors. If someone considers it proper to show deference to a friend, or parents or relatives, I think it rightly should be shown to God and that He should be preferred to all. Consult your best interests, O Emperor, or allow me to consult mine.

What shall be my excuse later if it is found out that by authority emanating from here some Christians were slain by the sword or clubs or leaden balls? How will I justify such a deed? How will I make excuse to those bishops who sorely lament the fact that priests or other ministers of the Church who have performed their office for thirty years and more are dragged away from their sacred tasks and assigned to curial offices? If men who war for you are kept for a set time of service, how much more ought you to be considerate of those who war for God? How, I say, shall I justify this before bishops who complain about the clergy and write that the churches are being ruined by the serious attacks being made on them?

For this reason, I wanted this to come to the notice of your Clemency. You will, when it pleases you, condescend to consult and temper your wishes; but exclude and put an end to that which troubles me, and rightly so. Do yourself what you ordered to be done, even if he [the count] is not going to do it. I would rather that you be merciful than that he fail to do what he was ordered.

In return for those whom you now have, you ought to cultivate and win the Lord's mercy for the Roman Empire, for you have more for them than you hoped for yourself. Let their favor, their well-being, appeal to you in these words of mine. I fear that you will entrust your cause to another's will. You still have everything in its original state. In this I pledge myself to our God for you: Have no scruple over your oath. Can that displease God which is corrected for His honor? Alter nothing in that letter, whether it was sent or not. Order another to be written, which will be filled with faith, with piety. You can still correct yourself; I cannot hide the truth.

You forgave the people of Antioch the injury they offered you;[27] you recalled your enemy's[28] daughters and gave them to a relative to rear, and from your own treasury you sent your enemy's mother a pension. This great faith and piety toward God will be blackened by the present deed. I beg you, after sparing enemies in arms and saving personal enemies, do not presume to punish Christians with such intensity.

Now, O Emperor, I beg you not to hear me with contempt, for I fear for you and for myself, as says the holy man: 'Wherefore was I born to see the ruin of my people,'[29] that I should commit an offense against God? Indeed, I have done what I could do honorably, that you might hear me in the palace rather than make it necessary to hear me in the Church.

---

[27] The insurrection of 387 in protest against additional taxes to support a celebration honoring Arcadius.
[28] It is doubtful whether Maximus had any children except his son Victor.
[29] 1 Mach. 2.7.

3. To the most august Emperor Theodosius, Ambrose, bishop[1]

Sweet to me is the recollection of your friendship in the past, and I recall the favor of benefits which you have bestowed with supreme favor upon others at my frequent requests. Hence, you may infer that I could not have avoided meeting you through any feeling of ingratitude, for I had always heretofore ardently desired your coming. I shall briefly set forth the reason for acting as I did.

I saw that I alone of your court had been deprived of the natural right of a hearing, so that I was also shorn of the privilege of speaking. You were disturbed several times because certain decisions in your consistory came to my knowledge. I, therefore, am without a share in the common privilege, although the Lord Jesus says: 'Nothing is hidden that will not be made manifest.'[2] As far as I could, then, I reverently complied with the will of the emperor, and took heed that you yourself should have no cause for displeasure for I managed to have none of the imperial decrees brought to my knowledge. And if I am ever present, either I shall not hear out of fear of all giving me a reputation for conniving, or I shall hear in such a way that, though my ears are open, my voice is stifled so that I cannot utter what I have heard, lest I do injury to those who have incurred the suspicion of treachery.

What, therefore, could I do? Not hear? I could not stop my ears with the wax of which old fables [tell]. Should I disclose what I heard? But I had to be on my guard in what

---

1 Written from Aquileia, to Theodosius, who was in Milan to excite the emperor to repentance for ordering the massacre of the inhabitants of Thessalonica. The subsequent details are related in Ambrose's Letter 62 to Marcellina. Palanque dates this letter about September 8, 390. McGuire, following tradition and the findings of Seeck, accepts the date as *c.* April, 390; cf. *Catholic Historical Review* 22 (1936-1937) 315.
2 Luke 8.17.

I said for fear of your orders, lest a bloody deed be committed. Should I keep silence? Then would my conscience be bound, my voice snatched from me—most wretched of all conditions. And where would be the significance of the saying that if a bishop declare not to the wicked, the wicked shall die in his iniquity, and the bishop shall be guilty of punishment because he has not warned the wicked?[3]

Understand this, august Emperor! I cannot deny that you are zealous for the faith; I do not disavow that you have a fear of God—but you have a natural vehemence which you quickly change to pity when one endeavors to soothe it. When one stirs it up, you so excite it that you can hardly check it. If only no one would enkindle it, if no one would arouse it! This I gladly commend to you: Restrain yourself, and conquer by love of duty your natural impetuosity.

This vehemence I have preferred to commend privately to your own considerations rather than to rouse it publicly perchance by any action of mine. I preferred to fail somewhat in my duty rather than in submission, that others should look for priestly authority in me instead of your failing to find reverence in me, who am most devoted. The result would be that, though you restrained your vehemence, your ability to get counsel might be unimpaired. I proffered the excuse of bodily illness, truly severe, and only to be eased by men being milder. Yet I would have preferred to die rather than not await your arrival in two or three days. But that was not what I did.

The affair which took place in the city of Thessalonica and with no precedent within memory, that which I could not prevent from taking place, which I had declared would be most atrocious when I entered pleas against it so many times, and which you yourself, by revoking it too late, manifestly considered to have been very serious, this when

---
3 Cf. Ezech. 3.19,20.

done I could not extenuate. It was first heard of when the synod had met on the arrival of Gallican bishops.⁴ No one failed to lament, no one took it lightly. Your being in fellowship with Ambrose was not an excuse for your deed; blame for what had been done would have been heaped upon me even more had no one said there must needs be a reconciliation with our God.

Are you ashamed, O Emperor, to do what King David the Prophet did, the forefather of the family of Christ according to the flesh? He was told that a rich man who had many flocks had seized and killed a poor man's one ram on the arrival of a guest, and recognizing that he himself was being condemned in this tale, for he had himself done so, he said: 'I have sinned against the Lord.'⁵ Do not be impatient, O Emperor, if it is said to you: 'You have done what was declared to King David by the prophet.' For if you listen carefully to this and say: 'I have sinned against the Lord,' if you repeat the words of the royal Prophet: 'Come, let us adore and fall down before him, and weep before our Lord who made us,'⁶ it will be said also to you: 'Since you repent, the Lord forgives you your sin and you shall not die.'⁷

Again, when David had ordered the people to be numbered, he was smitten in heart and said to the Lord: 'I have sinned very much in the command I have made, and now, O Lord, take away the iniquity of thy servant, because I have sinned exceedingly.' And the Prophet Nathan was sent again to him to offer him the choice of three things, that he might select what he chose: a famine in the land for three years, flight from the face of his enemies for three months, or pestilence in the land for three days. And David answered: 'These three things are a great strait to me, yet I

---

4 It is not known to what council Ambrose refers.
5 2 Kings 12.13.
6 Ps. 94.6.
7 2 Kings 12.13.

shall fall into the hand of the Lord since his mercies are exceedingly great, and I shall not fall into the hands of men.'⁸ His fault was that he desired to know the number of all the people who were with him, and the knowledge of this he should have left to God alone.

And it is said that when the pestilence came upon the people on the first day at dinner time, when David saw the angel striking the people, he said: 'I have sinned, I, the shepherd, have done evil and this flock, what has it done? Let your hand be upon me, and upon my father's house.'⁹ So the Lord repented and He bade the angel to spare the people, but David to offer sacrifice, for sacrifices were then offered for sin, but now they are sacrifices of penance. Thus, by his humility he became more acceptable to God, for it is not strange that man sins, but it is reprehensible if he does not acknowledge that he has erred and humble himself before God.

Holy Job, also powerful in this world, says: 'I have not hid my sin, but declared it before all the people.'¹⁰ To fierce King Saul his own son Jonathan said: 'Sin not against thy servant David,' and 'Why wilt thou sin against innocent blood by killing David, who is without fault?'¹¹ Although he was a king, he sinned if he killed the innocent. Finally, even David, when he was in possession of his kingdom and had heard that an innocent man named Abner was slain by Joab, the leader of his army, said: 'I and my kingdom are innocent now and forever of the blood of Abner the son of Ner,'¹² and he fasted in sorrow.

These things I have written not to disconcert you but that the examples of kings may stir you to remove this sin from

---
8 2 Kings 24.10,14.
9 2 Kings 24.17.
10 Job 31.34 (Septuagint).
11 1 Kings 19.4,5.
12 2 Kings 3.28.

your kingdom, for you will remove it by humbling your soul before God. You are a man, you have met temptation—conquer it. Sin is not removed except by tears and penance. No angel or archangel can remove it; it is God Himself who alone can say: 'I am with you';[13] if we have sinned, He does not forgive us unless we do penance.

I urge, I ask, I beg, I warn, for my grief is that you, who were a model of unheard-of piety, who had reached the apex of clemency, who would not allow the guilty to be in peril, are not now mourning that so many guiltless have perished. Although you waged battles most successfully, and were praiseworthy also in other respects, the apex of your deeds was always your piety. The Devil envied you this, your most outstanding possession. Conquer him while you still have the means of doing so. Do not add another sin to your sin nor follow a course of action which has injured many followers.

I among all other men, a debtor to your Piety, to whom I cannot be ungrateful, this piety which I discover in many emperors and match in only one, I, I say, have no charge of arrogance against you, but I do have one of fear. I dare not offer the Holy Sacrifice if you intend to be present. Can that which is not allowable, after the blood of one man is shed, be allowable when many persons' blood was shed? I think not.

Lastly, I am writing with my own hand what you alone may read. Thus, may the Lord free me from all anxieties, for I have learned very definitely what I may not do, not from man nor through man. In my anxiety, on the very night that I was preparing to set forth you appeared [in my dreams] to have come to the church and I was not allowed to offer the Holy Sacrifice. I say nothing of the other things I could have avoided, but bore for love of you, as I believe. May the Lord make all things pass tranquilly. Our God

---

13 Matt. 28.20.

admonishes us in many ways, by heavenly signs,[14] by the warnings of the Prophets, and He wills that we understand even by the visions of sinners. So we will ask Him to remove these disturbances, to preserve peace for you who are rulers, that the faith and peace of the Church continue, for it avails much if her emperors be pious Christians.

You certainly wish to be approved by God. 'There is a time for everything,'[15] as it is written: 'It is time to act, O Lord,'[16] and 'The time of mercy, O God.'[17] You will make your offering then when you receive permission to sacrifice, when your offering has been acceptable to God. Would it not delight me to have the emperor's favor, so that I could act in accord with your will if the case allowed? Prayer by itself is sacrifice, it brings pardon when the other [sacrifice] causes offence, for the one bespeaks humility, the other contempt. We have God's word that He prefers the doing of His command to the offering of sacrifice. God proclaims this, Moses declares it to the people, Paul preaches it to the Gentiles. Do at the right moment what you know is of greater value. 'I desire mercy,' it says, 'and not sacrifice.'[18] Are they not more Christian who condemn their sin than they who hope to defend it, for 'The just is first accuser of himself.'[19] One who accuses himself when he has sinned is just, not one who praises himself.

I wish, O Emperor, that before this you had relied upon me rather than on your own habits. Since I realize that you

---

14 Palanque and others think Ambrose's reference to 'heavenly signs' refers to a comet which appeared and was visible from August 22 to September 17, 390. McGuire (*op. cit.* 316) does not think Ambrose would use a comet as a 'divine sign of warning.'
15 Eccle. 3.1.
16 Ps. 118.126.
17 Ps. 68.14.
18 Matt. 9.13.
19 Prov. 18.17 (Septuagint).

are quick to pardon, quick to retract, as you have so often done, you have now been prevented and I have not shirked what I had no need to fear. But, thanks be to the Lord who wills to chastise His servants lest He lose them. This I have in common with the Prophets and you will have it in common with the saints.

Shall I not value the father of Gratian[20] more than my eyes? Your other blessed offspring deserves pardon. I conferred a sweet name formerly on those to whom I bore a mutual love. I love, I cherish, I attend you with prayers. If you trust me, follow me; if, I say, you trust me, acknowledge what I say; if you do not trust me, pardon what I do in esteeming God more than you. May you, the most blessed and eminent Emperor Augustus, together with your holy offspring, enjoy perpetual peace.

4. Ambrose to Theodosius the Emperor (August, 392)[1]

Word from your Clemency has broken my silence,[2] for I had decided that amid so great sorrows I could do nothing better than withdraw as far as possible. Yet, being unable to hide away in some retreat or abdicate my priestly state, I at least retired within myself by my silence.

I sorrow, I confess, with bitter sorrow not only that Augustus Valentinian has died so young, but also because, instructed in the faith and molded by your teaching, he had become so devoted toward our God and clung to me with so

---

20 It is uncertain which Gratian is referred to in this passage.

1 The *Consolation on the Death of Valentinian*, translated by R. J. Defarrari in Volume 22 of this series (New York 1953), should be read in connection with this letter.
2 On the letter of Theodosius to Ambrose, see Theodoret, *H. E.* 5.15.

much affection as to love now one whom he formerly persecuted; he now esteemed as a father one whom he formerly repulsed as an enemy. I mention this, not as a reminder of his former wrong-doing, but as proof of his conversion. The first-named [wrong-doing] was learned from others; the latter was his own; and he clung so firmly to what you inspired that he was proof against the arguments of his mother. He used to say he had been reared by me; he longed for me as for a solicitous parent and when some persons made believe they had news of my arrival, he awaited it impatiently. Nay, even on the days of great mourning,[3] although he had within the territory of Gaul saintly and eminent bishops of the Lord, he felt obliged to write to me to give him the sacrament of baptism. In this way, unreasonably, but lovingly, he gave proof of his affection toward me.

Shall I not sigh for him with my inmost breath? Shall I not embrace him within the deepest recesses of my heart and soul? Shall I think that he is dead to me? Indeed, he is more than dead to me. How grateful I was to the Lord that he was so changed toward me, so improved, and had assumed a character so much more mature. How grateful was I to your Clemency, also, that you had not only restored him to power, but, what is more, had taught him your own faith and piety. Shall I not grieve that, while young in years, before he had attained as he desired the grace of the sacraments, he met with a sudden death?[4] You have comforted my soul in condescending to bear witness to my grief. I have you, O Emperor, as judge of my affections and interpreter of my thoughts.

But we shall have time to weep later; let us now attend to his burial which your Clemency has commanded to take

---
3 The days of Holy Week.
4 For the various theories of his death, cf. Deferrari, *op. cit.* 264.

place here. If he has died without baptism, I now withhold what I know. We have here a very beautiful porphyry vessel, well suited to the purpose; Maximian, the colleague of Diocletian, was so buried. There are also very precious porphyry tablets with which a cover may be made to encase the king's remains.

This was made ready but we awaited your Clemency's command; its arrival has greatly comforted your holy daughters,[5] sisters of your son Valentinian, who are deeply affected and the more so, since for a long time they received no word from you. Your message has been no small consolation to them, but while the remains are unburied they do not spare themselves, for they daily imagine that they are attending the funeral of their brother. In truth, they are never without many tears and heavy sorrow, and whenever they visit the body they return almost lifeless. It will be good for them and for the dear remains if the burial is hastened, lest the summer heat utterly dissolve them, for we have hardly passed its first tide.

Your command I observe and commend to the Lord. May the Lord love you, for you love the Lord's servants.

5. *Ambrose to Theodosius the Emperor (September, 394)*

You thought, most blessed Emperor, as I learned from your august letter, that I kept away from Milan because I believed your cause was abandoned by God. But I have not been so unwise or so unmindful of your virtue and your merits as not to know that the help of heaven would attend your Piety while you were protecting the Roman Empire

---

5 Justa and Grata, sisters of Valentinian, in whose presence Ambrose delivered the funeral speech on Valentinian.

from the ravages of the barbarian robber and from the dominion of an unworthy usurper.¹

I hastened to return here as soon as I learned that the one whom I deemed it right to avoid was now gone, for I had not abandoned the Church at Milan entrusted to me by the judgment of the Lord. I was avoiding the presence of one who had involved himself in sacrilege. I returned, therefore, about the first of August and I have been here since that day. Here, Augustus, your Clemency's letter reached me.

Thanks be to the Lord our God who has responded to your faith and piety! He has refashioned an ancient type of holiness, letting us see in our time that which we marvel at as we read the Scriptures, namely, the great presence of divine help in battles, so that mountain heights have not slowed up the course of your coming, nor were enemy arms a hindrance.

In return for these favors you realize that I should give thanks to the Lord our God. Gladly shall I do so, mindful of your merit. It is certain that the oblation offered in your name will be pleasing to God, and what a mark of great devotion and faith is this! Other emperors, immediately upon a victory, order the erection of triumphal arches or other monuments of their triumphs. Your Clemency prepares an oblation to God and desires an offering and thanksgiving to be presented by priests to the Lord.

Although I am unworthy and unequal to the great privilege, and the solemnizing of your prayers, I will describe what I have done. I took the letter of your Piety with me to the altar. I laid it on the altar. I held it in my hand when I offered the Sacrifice, so that your faith might speak through my words, and the letter of the Augustus discharge the function of the priest's offering.²

---
1 See Letter 11, below.
2 An interesting revelation of the manner of offering Mass for another's intention in the early history of the Church.

Truly is the Lord propitious to the Roman Empire when He chooses such a prince and father of princes, whose virtue and power, set upon such a triumphant pinnacle of power, rests on such humility that he surpasses emperors by his virtue and priests by his humility. What can I yet hope for? What do I yet desire? You have everything and from what is yours I shall take the full measure of prayers. You are pious, O Emperor, and you possess the utmost clemency.

Yet I hope that you will experience even more and more an increase of piety, for God can give nothing more excellent than this, that through your Clemency the Church of God, as it rejoices in the peace and tranquility of the innocent, may even so be gladdened by your pardoning of the guilty. Pardon especially those who have not offended before. May the Lord preserve your Clemency. Amen.

6. Ambrose to Theodosius the Emperor (September, 394)

Although I have written but recently to your august Clemency and have done so a second time, it did not seem to me that I had responded sufficiently to the duty of intercourse by so answering in turn, for I have been enriched so by the frequent benefits of your Clemency that I can in no way repay the services I owe, most blessed and august Emperor.

Therefore, since that first occasion was not to be lost when, through your chamberlain, I gave thanks to your Clemency and performed the duty of addressing you, lest you think that it was through negligence rather than need that I did not write you on the previous occasion, I had to find a reason for sending my dutiful greeting to your Piety.

To deliver my letter in a manner befitting you I am sending my son, the deacon Felix, that he may at one and the same time represent me and also bring the appeal of those who fled to the Church, the mother of your Piety, begging mercy. I could not bear their tears but anticipated by my entreaty the coming of your Clemency.

Ours is a great request, but we are asking it of one to whom the Lord has granted unheard-of wonders, of whose clemency we know and whose piety we have as a pledge. Hence, we confess that we hope for more in that you have conquered by your virtue and ought also conquer yourself by your piety. It is said that your victory was granted in the manner of the ancients, with ancient portents like those of blessed Moses, of blessed Josue the son of Nun, of Samuel, and of David; it was granted not by man's foresight but by the outpouring of heavenly grace. We here beg a like piety by whose excellence so great a victory has been gained.

7. Ambrose, bishop, to the most blessed prince and most Christian Emperor, Valentinian (Summer, 384)[1]

Not only are all men under the sway of Rome in the service of you, the emperors and princes of the earth, but you yourselves are also in the service of almighty God and of our holy faith. Salvation will not be assured unless each one truly worships the true God, that is, the God of the Christians, by whom all things are governed. He alone is the true God who is worshiped with the inmost being: 'For the gods of the gentiles are idols,' as Scripture says.[2]

Whoever serves this true God, receiving Him with deep affection, in order to worship Him, displays not lying and

---
1 This letter gave occasion to the *Relatio* of Symmachus. These works and Ambrose's letter to Eugenius are edited and commented upon by J. Wytzes, *Der Streit um den Altar der Viktoria* (Amsterdam 1936).
2 Ps. 95.5.

treachery, but a zeal and devotion to the faith. And if he owes not these, he at least owes no worship to idols and to profane ceremonial cults. No one deceives God to whom all things, even the secrets of the heart, are manifest.

Therefore, since you have truly shown your faith in God, most Christian Emperor, I am amazed that your zeal for the faith, your protection and devotion have given hope to some persons that you are now obligated to erect altars to the gods of the heathens and to furnish credit for the upkeep of profane sacrifices. This expense, which for a long time was charged to the revenues or to the treasury, you will appear to expend out of your own resources, rather than to be making restitution from it.

They are complaining of their losses, they who were never sparing of our blood, who ruined our church buildings. They also ask you to give them privileges, who by the recent Julian law refused to us the ordinary privilege of preaching and teaching, those privileges by which even Christians have often been made to apostatize.[3] By these privileges they have wanted to win some persons by improvidence and others through the difficulty of bearing public offices; and, since all are not found steadfast, several, even under Christian princes, have fallen from the faith.

If these privileges had not already been abolished, I would approve their being done away with by your authority. But, since these were almost universally banned and suppressed by several predecessors and annulled by rescript at Rome by your Clemency's brother, Gratian of august memory, through the logic of his true faith, do not, I beg you, repeal these measures on religion or tear up your brother's edicts. It does not occur to anyone to interfere rashly in a

---

3 Wytzes omits this passage in the Latin text, but translates it in the German.

civil matter which is a statute of law, and here you are overriding an edict on religion.

Let no one take advantage of your youth; if it is a pagan who makes these demands, he ought not ensnare your mind in the meshes of superstition, but by his zeal he should teach and instruct you how to be zealous for the true faith since he defends untruth with so much zeal. I agree that we must be respectful of the true merits of men of distinction, but it is certain that God should be preferred to all men.

If one is seeking advice on military affairs, he should await the advice of a man skilled in battle and should hold to his opinion. Now that it is a matter of religion, think of God. No one is offended when almighty God is more esteemed than he is. God has His opinion. You do not compel a man to worship what he does not wish, being unwilling. You, too, O Emperor, are allowed the same, and everyone should bear up graciously if he does not secure from the emperor what he would impatiently bear if the emperor desired to wrest it from him. The pagans themselves are wont to detest one who betrays his conscience; each one should be free to defend faithfully and keep his own principles.

But if some men, Christians in name, think such a decree should be promulgated, let not their mere words overwhelm your mind, their vain assumptions deceive you. Whoever gives this advice or whoever agrees to it is offering sacrifice. But the sacrifice of one is more tolerable than the downfall of all. In this the whole number of Christian Senators is in danger.

If today some pagan emperor—God forbid!—should set up an altar to idols and compel Christians to hold their meetings there, to be present at the sacrifices, so that the Christian's breath and nostrils would be filled with the ashes from the altar, cinders from the sacrifice, and smoke from the wood; and if he would give his opinion in the curia, where in giving their opinion they would be forced to swear at the altar of the idol (for this is how they interpret the altar erected so that, as they think, each meeting, by his oath, will be held in its midst, although the curia already has a majority number of Christians), the Christian compelled to come into the Senate would on these conditions think it a persecution. This is being done quite generally. They are forced to meet under penalties. Now that you are the emperor, will Christians be forced to take their oath on an altar? What does taking an oath mean except to put one's trust in the divine power of one who you think is the judge of your good faith? Now that you are the emperor, is this being asked for and expected? Are you bidding that an altar be raised and money allocated for profane sacrifices?

A decree like this cannot be enforced without sacrilege. I beg you not to make such a decree, nor pass a law, nor sign a decree of this sort. As a priest of Christ, I appeal to your faith. All priests would make the appeal with me if the sudden news which came to their ears were not unbelievable that such a measure was suggested in your council or demanded by the Senate. Do not let it be said that the Senate demanded this, A few pagans are usurping the name which is not theirs. When the same thing was tried about two years ago, Damasus, the holy bishop of the Roman Church, elected by God's judgment, sent me a counter-petition which the Christian senators had given him. In great numbers they protested that they had made no such demand, that they did not agree with such requests of the pagans or give their assent. In public and in private they murmured that they would not come to the Senate if such a measure were decreed. Is it dignified in your day, a Christian day, that Christian Senators be deprived of their dignity so that heathens may have deference paid to their unholy will? I sent this memorandum to the brother of your Clemency, wherein was clear evidence that the Senate had made no provision for the upkeep of superstition.

Perhaps it may be said: 'Why were they not present in the Senate when such proposals were being made?' They say clearly enough what they wish, by not being present; they have said enough by speaking to the emperor. Yet it is strange to us that they take from private individuals at Rome the liberty of resisting, while they are unwilling that you be free to withhold ordering what you do not approve and to maintain what you feel is right.

Mindful, therefore, of the commission lately laid upon me I again call upon your faith, I call upon your judgment. Do not think that you have to give an answer favorable to the pagans, nor join to your answer in such a matter the sacrilege of your signature. Refer with assurance to the father of your Piety, Emperor Theodosius, whom you have been accustomed to consult in almost all matters of great importance. Nothing is of more importance than religion; nothing is more exalted than faith.

If this were a civil case, the opposing party would be guaranteed the right of reply. It is a religious case, and I, the bishop, am using that right. Let a copy of the appeal be given me, and I will answer more fully. And may it seem fit to you to consult your faith's opinion on all these matters. Certainly, if any other decision is reached, we bishops cannot tranquilly allow it and pretend not to notice. You will be allowed to come to the church, but either you will find there no priest or you will find one who will gainsay you.

What will you answer the priest who says to you: 'The Church does not want your gifts because you have adorned the heathen temples with gifts. The altar of Christ spurns your gifts since you have made an altar for idols. Yours is the voice, yours the hand, yours the signature, yours the work. The Lord Jesus scorns and spurns your worship since you have worshiped idols, for He said to you: "You cannot serve two masters."⁴ Virgins consecrated to God have no privileges from you, and do Vestal virgins lay claim to them? Why do you ask for God's priests to whom you have brought the unholy demands of the pagans? We cannot be associated with another's error.'

What will you answer to these words? That you are but a boy who has fallen? Every age is perfect in Christ, every one full of God. Childhood is not allowed to faith; even babes have confessed Christ before persecutors with fearless words.

What will you answer your brother? Will he not say to you: 'Because I left you as emperor, I did not think I was vanquished; I did not grieve dying, because I had you as heir; I did not mourn in leaving my kingdom, because I believed that my imperial commands, especially those on divine religion, would last forever. I had set up these memorials of pious virtue, these trophies from the world, these spoils from the Devil, I offered these victories over the adversary of all in whom there is eternal victory. What more could my enemy take from me? You have annulled my decrees; even he [Maximian], who took up arms against me, did not do this. In this I am wounded by a heavier weapon in that my brother has condemned my decrees. The better part of me is imperiled with you; that was death of the body, this the death of my reputation for virtue. Now my power is annulled and, more serious, is annulled by your acts, is annulled by my own family, and that is annulled which even my enemies had praised in me. If you have acquiesced willingly, you have destroyed my faith in you; if you have yielded unwillingly, you have betrayed your own faith. And this is even more serious, the fact that I am imperiled with you.'

What will you answer your father, who will confront you with great sorrow, saying: 'Son, you have judged me very

---
4 Matt. 6.24.

ill, thinking that I would have connived with the pagans. No one ever told me that there was an altar in the Roman Senate House; I had never believed such wickedness, that in the common meeting place of Christians and pagans the pagans offered sacrifice, that is, the pagans reviled the Christians present and Christians unwillingly were forced to attend the sacrifices. When I was emperor, many kinds of crimes were committed. I punished those I detected. If some one escaped my notice, should it be said I approved what no one had appraised me? You have judged me very ill if the Gentiles' superstition and not my faith preserved the Empire.'

Wherefore, O Emperor, you see that if you decree anything of this kind you will offer injury first to God and then to your father and brother; I beg you do what you know will benefit your own salvation before God.[5]

8. Ambrose, bishop, to the most blessed prince and most clement Emperor Valentinian Augustus (Autumn, 384)

The illustrious prefect of the city, Symmachus, has made an appeal to your Clemency that the altar which was removed from the Senate House in the city of Rome be restored to its place.[1] You, O Emperor, still young in age, a new recruit

---

5 In his second letter on this subject to Valentinian, Ambrose seems to imply that Valentinian had already rejected the proposal of the Senate when he addressed this letter to him. He likewise says (*Cons. Val.* 19) that 'when all who were present in the consistory, Christians and pagans alike, said that these privileges should be restored, he alone [Valentinian] like Daniel, with the spirit of God aroused within him, denounced the Christians for lack of faith and resisted the pagans by saying: "How can you think that what my brother took away should be restored by me?" since thereby both his religion and his brother, by whom he was unwilling to be surpassed in piety, would be offended.' (Trans. Deferrari, Fathers of the Church 22, pp. 274-275). The above statement is difficult to reconcile with the general tone of reproof in this letter.

1 Symmachus, *Memorial*, ed. J. Wytzes, *op. cit.* 48-61.

without experience, but a veteran in faith, did not approve the appeal of the pagans. The very moment I learned this I presented a request in which, although I stated what seemed necessary to suggest, I asked that I be given a copy of the appeal.

Not doubtful, therefore, regarding your faith, but foreseeing the care that is necessary, and being confident of a kindly consideration, I am answering the demands of the appeal with this discourse, making this one request that you will not expect eloquence of speech but the force of facts. For, as holy Scripture teaches,[2] the tongue of the wise and studious man is golden, decked with glittering words and shining with the gleam of eloquence, as though some rich hue, capturing the eyes of the mind by the comeliness of its appearance, dazzling in its beauty. But this gold, if you examine it carefully, though outwardly precious, within is a base metal. Ponder well, I beg you, and examine the sect of the pagans. They sound weighty and grand; they support what is incapable of being true; they talk of God, but they adore a statue.

The distinguished prefect of the city has brought forth in his appeal three points which he considers of weight; namely, that (according to him) Rome is asking again for her ancient rites, that the priests and Vestal virgins should be given their stipends, and since these stipends have been refused to the priests there has been general famine.

According to the first proposal, as he says, Rome is shedding tears with sad and mournful complaints, asking again for her ancient ceremonies. The sacred objects, he says, drove Hannibal from the city and the Senones from the Capitol. But at the same time as the power of the sacred objects is proclaimed, their weakness is betrayed. Hannibal reviled the sacred objects of the Romans for a long time, and while the

---
2 Cf. Eccle. 6.11; Prov. 15.2.

gods warred against themselves the conqueror reached the city's walls. Why did they allow themselves to be besieged when the weapons of their gods did battle for them?

Why should I make mention of the Senones, whom, when they penetrated the innermost recesses of the Capitol, the Roman forces could not have withstood had not a goose (with its frightened cackling) betrayed them. See what sort of protectors guard the Roman temples. Where was Jupiter at that time? Was he making a statement through a goose?

Why do I refuse to admit that their sacred objects warred in behalf of the Romans? Hannibal, too, worshiped the same gods. Let them choose whichever they wish. If these sacred objects conquered in the Romans, then they were overcome in the Carthaginians. If they triumphed in the Carthaginians, they certainly did not help the Romans.

Let us have no more grudging complaint from the people of Rome. Rome has authorized no such complaints. She addresses them with the words: 'Why do you stain me each day with the useless blood of the harmless herd? Trophies of victory depend not on entrails of sheep but on the strength of warriors. I subdued the world by other skills. Camillus was a soldier of mine who slew those who had captured the Tarpeian rock and brought back the standards which had been taken from the Capitol. Valor laid low those whom religion had not reached. What shall I say of Attilius,[3] who bestowed the service of his death? Africanus found his triumphs not amid the altars of the Capitol but among the ranks of Hannibal. Why do you give me these examples of ancient heroes? I despise the ceremonies of the Neroes. Why mention emperors of two months' duration? And the downfall of kings coupled with their rising? Or is it something new, perhaps, for the barbarians to have overrun their territory? In those wretched and strange cases when an

---
3 Regulus.

emperor was held captive, and then a world held captive under an emperor, was it the Christians who revealed the fact that the ceremonies which promised victory were falsified? Was there then no altar of Victory? I lament my downfall. My old age is accompanied by shame over that disgraceful bloodshed. But I am not ashamed to be converted in my old age along with the whole world. Surely it is true that no age is too late to learn. Let that old age feel shame which cannot rectify itself. It is not the old age of years which is entitled to praise, but that of character.[4] There is no disgrace in going on to better things. This alone I had in common with the barbarians, that I did not know God before. Your sacrifice consists in the rite of being sprinkled with the blood of beasts. Why do you look for God's words in dead animals? Come and learn of the heavenly warfare which goes on on earth. We live here, but we war there.[5] Let God Himself, who established the mystery of heaven, teach me about it, not man who does not know himself. Whom more than God shall I believe concerning God? How can I believe you who admit that you do not know what you worship?'

So great a secret, it is said, cannot be reached by one road. We [Christians] know on God's word what you do not know. And what you know by conjecture we have discovered from the very wisdom and truth of God. Your ways do not agree with ours. You ask peace for your gods from the emperors; we beg peace for our emperors from Christ. You adore the works of your hands; we consider it wrong to think that anything which can be made is God. God does not wish to be worshiped in stones. Even your philosophers have ridiculed these ideas.

But if you say that Christ is not God because you do not

---

4 Cf. Wisd. 4.9.
5 In heaven.

believe that He died (for you do not realize that that was a death of the body not of the divinity, which has brought it about that no believer will die), why is this so senseless to you who worship with insult and disparage with honor, thinking that your god is a piece of wood? O worship most insulting! You do not believe that Christ could have died. O honorable stubborness!

But, says he, the ancient altars should be restored to the images, the ornaments to the shrines. Let these demands be made by one who shares their superstition. A Christian emperor knows how to honor the altar of Christ alone. Why do they force pious hands and faithful lips to do service to their sacrilege? Let the voice of our emperor utter the name of Christ and call on Him only whom he is conscious of, for 'the heart of the king is in the hand of God.'[6] Has any heathen emperor raised an altar to Christ? While they demand the restoration of all things which used to be, they show by their own example what great reverence Christian emperors should give to the religion which they follow, since the heathens offered everything to their superstitions.

We had our beginning long ago, and now they are following those whom they excluded. We glory in [shedding] our blood; they are disturbed by the spending of money. We think these acts take the place of victory; they reckon them a loss. Never did they confer more upon us than when they ordered Christians scourged and outlawed and put to death. Religion made a reward out of that which unbelief thought was a punishment. See these magnanimous individuals! We have increased through our losses, through want, through punishment. They do not believe that their ceremonies can continue unless donations continue.

Let the Vestal virgins, he says, keep their privileged state. Let men say this who are not able to believe what virginity

---
6 Prov. 2.1.

can do without reward. Let them derive encouragement from gainful means, having no confidence in virtue. How many virgins get the rewards promised to them? About seven Vestal virgins are accepted. Lo! that is the whole number of those attracted by fillets and chaplets for the head, or purple-dyed robes, the pomp of a litter surrounded by a group of attendants, the greatest privileges, great gains, and a set period of virginity.

Let them raise the eye of the mind and of the body and see a nation of modesty, a people of purity, an assembly of virginity. Fillets are not the adornment of the head but a veil in common use, ennobled by chastity. The finery of beauty is not sought after, it is relinquished. There are none of those purple insignia, no charming luxuries, but rather the practice of fasts, no privileges, no gains. All are such, in fine, that you would think enjoyment restrained while duties are performed. But while *they* perform their duty, enjoyment grows apace. Chastity mounts by its own sacrifices. That is not virginity which is bought for a price and not kept through a desire for the virtue. That is not purity which is paid for with money at an auction and only for a time. Chastity's chief victory is to conquer the desire for wealth because eagerness for gain is a temptation to modesty. Let us grant that bountiful provisions should be given to virgins. What amounts will overflow upon Christians! What treasury will supply such riches? Or if they think that only Vestals should be given grants, are they not ashamed that they claimed the whole for themselves under heathen emperors and do not think that under Christian princes we should have a like share?

They complain also that public support is not being duly granted to their priests and ministers. What a storm of words has sounded on this point! On the other hand, under recent laws we were denied even the inheritance of private property, and no one is complaining. We do not think that is an injury because we do not grieve over losses. If a priest seeks the privilege of declining the municipal burden, he has to give up the paternal and ancestral ownership of all his property. If the heathens suffered this, how would they urge their complaint, if the priest had to buy free time for the exercise of his ministry by the loss of his patrimony, and purchase the power of exercising his public ministry at the expense of all his private means! In addition, alleging his vigils for the common safety, he must console himself with the reward of domestic poverty, because he has not sold his service but has obtained a favor.

Compare the cases. You wish to excuse a decurion when it is not permitted the Church to excuse a priest. Wills are made out in favor of the ministers of the temples; no ordinary person is excluded, no one of the lowest condition, no one openly shameless; only the clergy are denied the common privilege, and they are the ones who offer common prayer for all men and render a common service.[7] They may have no legacy even from venerable widows, no gifts. And where no fault of character can be found a fine is imposed upon one's official capacity. A bequest made by a Christian widow to the priests of the temple is valid, but what is left to the ministers of God is invalid. I have described this not to complain but so that they will know of what I do not complain, for I prefer that we be poorer in money than in grace.

They answer that what has been given or left to the Church has not been touched. Let them say also who it is that has taken away gifts from the temples, for that is what has been done to the Christians. If this had happened to

---

7 An imperial constitution of 370 had forbidden clerics or ascetics to inherit from any woman or to receive any gift from a woman while they were both alive. In 390, Theodosius forbade deaconesses to leave their property to clerics or to the Church (*Cod. Theod.* 17.11.27).

heathens, the wrong would be rather a reprisal than an injury. Is it only now that justice is being demanded and a claim being made for fairness? Where was that feeling when they despoiled all Christians of their property, grudged them the very breath of life, and finally forbade them the privilege of burial, a privilege denied to none of the dead anywhere? The sea gave back those whom the heathens had thrown into it. This is the victory of faith, that they now reap the deeds of their ancestors. But, alas! What sense is there in seeking the favors of those whose actions were not approved by them?

No one, however, has refused gifts to the shrines or legacies to the soothsayers; only their land has been taken away because they did not use in a religious way what they claimed as a right of religion. Why did they not make use of our practice if they are using us as an example? The Church owns nothing except her faith. It furnishes her with returns, it furnishes her with increase. The property of the Church is the support of the poor. Let them take account of how many captives the temples have brought back, what food they have provided for the poor, to what exiles they have furnished the means of a livelihood. Their lands have been taken away, not their rights.

See, they say, a sad condition atoned for[8]—a public famine avenged what had taken place and that which served only the advantage of priests began being advantageous to all. For this reason, they say, the bark was stripped from the woods and carried off and the fainting men drank with their lips[9] the unsavory sap. Therefore, changing Chaonian wine for the acorn,[10] going back again to the food of cattle and to the nourishment of wretched provisions, they shook the oaks

---

8 Virgil, *Aeneid* 2.184. This is the first of numerous imitations of Virgil in this letter. See also, Sister M. D. Diederich, *Vergil in the Works of St. Ambrose* (Washington 1931).
9 Cf. *Aen.* 2.211.
10 Cf. *Georg.* 1.8.

and satisfied their dire hunger in the woods.[11] Surely, these are strange events in earth, which never happened before when the heathen superstition was fervent throughout the world! In fact, when before did the crops mock the prayers of the greedy farmer with empty stalks,[12] or the blade of corn sought in the furrows deceive the hopes of the rustic crew?[13]

And how is it that the Greeks considered their oaks oracles,[14] except that they thought that the sustenance of their sylvan food is the gift of religion? Such they believe to be the gifts of their gods. What people except heathens have worshiped the trees of Dodona when they paid honor to the sorry food of the woods? Is it not likely that their gods in anger inflicted on them as a punishment what they, when they were appeased, used to give them as a gift? What fairness would there be of grudging the food denied to a few priests if they would deny it to everybody, for the vengeance would be more unbearable than the injury? There is no real reason for bringing such suffering on a world to accomplish one man's downfall as that the full-grown hope of the year should suddenly perish while the stalks were green.

And, surely, it has been many years since the rights of temples were taken away throughout the world. Has it just now entered the mind of the heathen gods to avenge the wrong? Did the Nile fail to overflow in its accustomed course to avenge the losses of the priests of the city while it did not avenge its own?

Suppose that they think that the wrongs done to their gods were avenged last year, why have they been unnoticed this year? The country people no longer tear up roots and feed

---
11 Cf. *Georg.* 1.159.
12 Cf. *Georg.* 1.226.
13 Cf. *Georg.* 1.134.
14 Cf. *Georg.* 2.16.

upon them, nor look for refreshment from the berries of the woods,[15] nor pluck their food from thorns, but, taking joy in their prosperous labors and even marveling at their harvest themselves, they have sated their hunger with the full enjoyment of their wishes.[16] The earth gave us her fruit with interest.

Who, then, is such a stranger to men's affairs as to be astonished at the alternation of the seasons of the year? Yet we know that last year several provinces had an abundance of produce. What shall I say of the Gauls who were richer than usual? They sold the grain of Pannonia which they did not sow, and Rhaetia Secunda incurred hostility owing to her fertility, for she who was ordinarily safe in her scarcity made herself an enemy by her fertility. The fruits of autumn fed Liguria and the Venetias. Last year had no drought because of sacrilege; in fact, it flourished with the fruits of faith. Let them try to deny that the vineyards abounded with immense produce. We have received a harvest with interest and we also possess the benefit of a more abundant vintage.

The last and most important point remains, O Emperors, whether you ought to reinstate those helps which have profited you, for our opponent says: 'Let them defend you and be worshiped by us!' This, most faithful Princes, is what we cannot tolerate, that they taunt us saying that they supplicate their gods in your name and without your command commit a great sacrilege. For they interpret your suppression of feelings as consent. Let them have their guardians to themselves; let these, if they can, protect their devotees. For, if they cannot help those who worship them, how can they help you who do not worship them?

But, he says, we must keep the rites of our ancestors. What of the fact that everything has made progress later to

---

15 Cf. *Aen.* 3.650.
16 Cf. *Georg.* 1.103.

a better condition? The world itself, which at first was composed of elements in a void, in a soft mass, hardened or was clouded with the confusion of a shapeless piece of work, did it not later receive the forms of things by which it appears beautiful when the distinction between sky, sea, and earth became set? The lands shaking off their misty shadows wondered at the sun. The day does not shine at first, but as time proceeds it is bright with an increase of light and grows warm with an increase of heat.[17]

The moon herself, by which the appearance of the Church is mirrored in the sayings of the Prophets, when first rising waxes to her monthly age, but is hidden in night's shadows. Gradually filling up her horns,[18] finishing them in the region of the sun, she glows with the brightness of clear shining.

Formerly, the earth did not know how to be worked for her fruits. Later, when the careful farmer began to rule the fields and to clothe the shapeless soil with vines, she put away her wild dispositions, being softened by domestic cultivation.[19]

The first part of the year itself, stripped of growing things which have tinged our fields with a likeness to itself, springlike with flowers which will fall, grows up later on to full fruits.

We, too, the uninstructed ages, have an infancy of reasoning, but, changing over the years, we lay aside the rudiments of our faculties.

Let me say that all things should have remained in their first beginnings; the earth shrouded in darkness now displeases us because it has been illumined by the rays of the sun. And how much more pleasing is it for the shadows of the mind to have vanished than those of the body, and for the ray of faith to have shone rather than that of the sun. So, then, the

---
17 Cf. *Ecl.* 6.31.
18 Cf. *Aen.* 3.645.
19 Cf. *Georg.* 1.99.

primeval age of the world has changed just as the age of all things and in the same way the venerable old age of hoary faith may change. Let those whom this disturbs find fault with the harvest for its abundance in the late season; let them find fault with the vintage for coming at the fall of the year; let them find fault with the olive for being the last of fruits.

So, then, our harvest is the faith of souls; the grace of the Church is the vintage of merits which has flourished in the saints since the beginning of the world, but in the last age it has spread among the nations in order that all may know that the faith of Christ has not crept upon unlettered minds (for there is no crown of victory without an adversary), but, the opinion having been rejected which prevailed before, that which was true has rightly been preferred.

If the old ceremonies gave pleasure, why did Rome also take up foreign ones? I will make no mention of the ground hidden by costly buildings and the shepherds' huts glittering with ill-suited gold. Why? In order that I may refer to the very matter of which they complain. Why have they eagerly taken statues from captured cities, and conquered gods, and foreign rites of alien superstition? Whence comes the precedent for Cybele to wash her chariot in the stream of the counterfeiting Alma? Whence come the Phrygian seers and the deities of unjust Carthage ever hateful to the Romans? Whence is she whom the Africans worship as Coelestis, the Persians as Mithra,[20] and most people as Venus, according to a diversity of names, but not a variety of deity? They believed that Victory was a goddess, yet it is a gift, not a power; it is granted and it does not rule; it is the result of the legions, not of the power of religion. Is that goddess great

---

20 Ambrose wrongly makes Mithra a goddess, not a god; cf. McGuire, *op. cit.* 308.

whom a number of soldiers claim or the outcome of battle gives?

They ask to have her altar erected in the Senate House of the city of Rome, the very place where most of those who meet are Christians. There are altars in every temple and an altar even in the Temple of Victories. Since they take pleasure in numbers, they offer their sacrifices everywhere. Is it not an insult to the faith to insist upon a sacrifice on this one altar? Must we tolerate a heathen offering of sacrifice in the presence of a Christian? Let them imbibe, he says, although they are unwilling, let them imbibe the smoke with their eyes, the music with their ears, the cinders with their throats, the incense with their nostrils. And let the dust raised from our hearths cover their faces although they detest it. Are not the baths and colonnades and streets filled with enough statues for them? Will there not be a common privilege in that common meeting place? The dutiful portion of the Senate will be bound by the voices of those who call upon the gods, by the oaths of those who swear by them. If they refuse, they will appear to utter a lie; if they consent, to acknowledge what is sacrilegious.

Where, he says, shall we swear fealty to our laws and decrees? Does your mind which is contained in the laws gain assent and bind to faithfulness by the rites of heathens? Not only is the faith of those present attacked but also of those absent, and, what is more, O Emperors, your faith is attacked, for you compel if you command. Constantius of august memory, although he had not yet been admitted to the sacred mysteries, felt he would be polluted if he saw the altar. He ordered it to be removed; he did not order it to be replaced. That removal has the authority of an act; the replacing of it has not the authority of a command.

Let no one flatter himself over his absence. He is more present when he joins himself to the thoughts of others than if he gives assent before their eyes. It is more important to be drawn together by the mind than to be united with the body. The Senate has you as its presidents to convene its assembly. It meets in your behalf; it gives its conscience to you, not to the gods of the heathens. It prefers you to its children, but not to its faith. This is the affection you should seek; this is a love greater than power, provided the faith which preserves the power be safe.

Perhaps it may cause concern to some that, if this be so, a most faithful emperor has been forsaken, as if the reward of merits were to be thought of in terms of the passing value of those present. What wise man does not know that human affairs have been arranged in a kind of round and circuit, that they do not enjoy the same success, but that their state varies and they undergo changes?

Whom have the Roman temples sent forth more prosperous than Gnaeus Pompey? Yet, when he had circled the earth with three triumphs, after suffering defeat in battle, a fugitive from war, and an exile within the boundaries of his own empire, he fell by the hand of a eunuch of Canopus.

What king have the lands of all the East produced more noble than Cyrus of the Persians? He, too, after conquering extremely powerful princes who opposed him, and keeping the conquered as prisoners, was overthrown and perished by the weapons of a woman. And that king who had treated even the vanquished with honor had his head cut off and placed in a vessel full of blood, while he was bidden to be sated with the plaything of a woman's power. The mode of his own life was not repaid with similar conduct on the part of others, but far otherwise.

And whom do we find more devoted to sacrifice than Hamilcar, the leader of the Carthaginians? Although all during the battle he stood between the fighting ranks and offered sacrifice, when he saw that his side was conquered he threw himself into the very fires which he was feeding, so that he might extinguish with his own body the fires which he knew were of no avail.

What shall I say of Julian? When he foolishly trusted the responses of the soothsayers, he destroyed his own means of retreat. Therefore, in similar cases there is not a similar offense, for our promises have not deceived anyone.

I have answered those who provoked me as though I had not been provoked, for my object was to refute the appeal, not to expose superstition. But let their very appeal, O Emperor, make you more cautious. After saying that of former princes, the earlier ones practiced the cult of their fathers, and the later ones did not abolish them, it was claimed in addition that if the religious practice of older princes did not set a pattern, the act of overlooking them on the part of the later ones did. This showed plainly what you owe to your faith, that you should not follow the pattern of heathen rites, and to your affection, that you should not set aside the decrees of your brother. If in their own behalf only they have praised the permission of those princes who, although they were Christians, did not abolish the heathen decrees, how much more ought you to defer to your brotherly affection, so that you who must overlook some things, even though you do not approve them, should not abrogate your brother's decrees; you should maintain what you judge to be in agreement with your own faith and the bond of brotherhood.

9. To the most clement Emperor and most blessed Valentinian Augustus, Ambrose, bishop (February, 386)

Alleging that he was acting at your command, the tribune and notary Dalmatius came to me and asked that I choose judges just as Auxentius has done. Yet he has not indicated the names of those who have been demanded. But he adds that there will be a discussion in the consistory, and the judgment of your Piety will be the deciding factor.

To this I am making, as I think, a suitable response. No one should find that I am being insolent when I assert that your father of august memory not only gave his answer by word of mouth, but sanctioned by law this truth: In a matter of faith or of any Church regulation the decision should be given by him who is neither unsuited to the task nor disqualified by law. These are the words of his decree; in other words, he wished priests to make judgments regarding priests. In fact, if a bishop were accused of any charge and the case of his character needed to be examined, he wished these matters to belong to the judgment of bishops.

Who, then, has given your Clemency an insolent answer? One who wishes you to be like your father, or one who wishes you to be unlike him? Perhaps little importance is attached by some persons to the opinion of that great emperor, although his faith was proved by his firm confession and his wisdom was declared by his development of a better commonwealth.

O most clement Emperor, when have you heard the laity judge a bishop in a matter of faith? Are we so bent down with flattery as to forget our priestly privileges and think that we should entrust to others that which God has given to us? If a bishop has to be instructed by a layman, what next? If so, the laity will dispute and the bishop will listen; and the bishop will learn from the laity! But if we examine the context of holy Scripture or of times past, who will deny that in a matter of faith, in a matter, I say, of faith, bishops usually judge Christian emperors; not emperors, bishops.

By God's favor you will reach a ripe old age, and then you will realize what kind of a bishop subjects his priestly power to the laity. By God's favor your father, a man of ripe old age, said: 'It does not belong to me to judge between bishops';[1] your Clemency now says: 'I must be the judge.' He, although baptized, thought he was unfit for the burden of such a judgment; your Clemency, who must still earn the sacrament of baptism, takes to yourself a judgment concerning faith, although you are unacquainted with the sacraments of that faith.

We can well imagine what sort of judges he [Auxentius] will choose, for he fears to reveal their names. Of course, let them come to the church, if there are any to come. Let them listen to the people, not so that each may sit in judgment, but that each may have proof of his disposition and choose whom he will follow. The matter concerns the bishop of that church; if the people decide after hearing him that he argues a better case, let them follow the faith he teaches. I shall not be jealous.

I will not mention the fact that the people have already passed judgment. I am silent about their demand from the father of your Clemency for the one whom they have.[2] I am silent about the promise of the father of your Piety that there would be peace if the one chosen would assume the bishopric. I have kept faith in these promises.

If he boasts of the approval of some foreigners, let him be bishop there where there are people who think that he

---

1 Valentinian, who began his reign in 364, made a practice of not interfering with the bishops in matters of faith.
2 Ambrose had been promised that he would not be harassed by the Arians if he accepted the bishopric of Milan. He certainly had been unwilling to become a bishop. Cf. Paulinus, *Vita Ambrosii* 3.7-9.

should be given the name of bishop. But I neither recognize him as a bishop nor know whence he comes.

When have we ever decided a matter on which you have declared your judgment? Nay, have you not even promulgated laws and not allowed anyone freedom of judgment? When you made such a provision for others, you also made it for yourself. An emperor passes laws which he first of all keeps. Do you want me to try to see whether those who have been chosen judges will begin to go contrary to your opinion, or at least excuse themselves on the grounds that they cannot act against so severe and rigid a law of the emperor?

This, then, is the action of an insolent individual, not of a well-meaning bishop. See, O Emperor, you are rescinding your own law in part. Would that you did so, not in part, but entirely, for I would not want your law to be above the law of God. God's law teaches us what we are to follow; man's laws cannot teach us this. These alter the conduct of the timid; they are unable to inspire confidence.

What man will there be who reads that at one moment it has been decreed that one who opposes the emperor should be struck with the sword, and whoever does not hand over the temple of God is straightway slain; what man, I say, either singly or with a few could say to the emperor: 'Your law does not meet my approval'? If priests are not allowed this, are the laity permitted? And will he be the judge in a matter of faith who either hopes for favor or fears to give offence?

Shall I agree to choose laymen as judges, who, if they maintain the truth with faith, will be proscribed or killed, because a law passed about faith has so decreed? Shall I expose these men either to the denial of truth or to punishment?

Ambrose is not worth so much that he would throw away his priestly office for his own sake. The life of one man is not worth the dignity of all priests on whose advice I made these statements, since they suggested that we would perhaps surrender the triumph of Christ to some pagan or Jew, chosen by Auxentius, if we gave them judgment regarding Christ. What else do they rejoice to hear but the harm being done to Christ? What else can please them except that (God forbid!) Christ's divinity is being denied? Plainly, they agree completely with the Arians, who say that Christ is a creature, for heathens and Jews readily admit this.

This decree was made at the Synod of Ariminium and I rightfully despise that council, for I follow the rule of the Council of Nicaea from which neither death nor the sword can separate me. This is the creed which the parent of your Clemency, Theodosius most blessed emperor, follows and approves. This creed is held by the Gauls, it is held by the Spaniards, who keep it with pious profession of the Holy Spirit.

If there must be discussion, I have learned from my predecessor to have the discussion in church. If there has to be a conference about the faith, it should be a conference of bishops, as was done under Constantine, prince of august memory, who promulgated no laws until he had given free judgment to the bishops. This was also done under Constantius, emperor of august memory, heir of his father's dignity. Yet, what began well is ending otherwise. The bishops had subscribed at first to a definite creed. Then, when certain persons within the palace wished to pass judgment on the faith, they managed to alter the judgments of the bishops by surreptitious methods. The bishops at once called for resolute opinions. And, certainly, the greater number at Ariminium approved the creed of the Council of Nicaea and condemned the Arian decrees.

If Auxentius appeals to a synod to dispute the faith (please God it may not be necessary for so many bishops to be wearied on account of one man, for, even if he were an angel from heaven, he must not be esteemed above the peace of the Church), when I shall hear that the synod is gathering, I myself will not be missing. Pass the law if you want a struggle!

I would have come, O Emperor, to your Clemency's consistory to make these remarks in person if either the bishops or people had permitted me, but they said rather that discussions of the faith should be held in church in the presence of the people.

Would, O Emperor, that you had not sentenced me to go wherever I wished! I went out daily; no one guarded me. You should have dispatched me where you wished, me who offered myself for anything. Now I am told by the bishops: It makes little difference whether you willingly leave the altar of Christ or hand it over, for, when you leave it, you will be handing it over.

Would that it were clearly evident to me that the Church would not be handed over to the Arians! I would then willingly offer myself to the wishes of your Piety. But, if I am the only one guilty of making a disturbance, why is there the decree to invade all the other churches? Would that there were the assurance that no one would harm the churches! I choose that you pass on me whatever sentence you wish.

Wherefore, O Emperor, receive with dignity my reason for being unable to come to the consistory. I have not learned to take my place in a consistory except to act in your behalf,[3] and I am unable to dispute in the palace, neither seeking nor knowing the secrets of the palace.

I, Ambrose, the bishop, offer this notice to the most clement emperor and most blessed Augustus Valentinian.

---

3 Ambrose had gone twice to the Consistory of Maximus and bore many affronts while there, first in the winter of 383-384 when he pleaded for peace in behalf of the young Valentinian, and later at the beginning of 385 when he begged that the body of Gratian be returned for burial at Milan.

10. Ambrose to Emperor Valentinian (386)

You have had such confidence in my recent embassy that no report of it was demanded of me. It was sufficiently clear from my having stayed some days in Gaul that I did not accept the terms favorable to Maximus[1] or agree with those which favored his will rather than peace. Moreover, you would never have sent me on a second embassy unless you had approved the first. But, inasmuch as I was forced to the necessity of contesting with him on my arrival, I have determined to give an account of my embassy in this letter so that no one's report will confuse the false with the true before, on my return, I make a clear and trustworthy account of the truth.

The day after I arrived at Trier I went to the palace. The grand chamberlain Gallicanus, a royal eunuch,[2] came out to me. I asked the privilege of entering; he asked if I had an imperial order from your Clemency. I answered that I did. He retorted that I could be interviewed only in the consistory. I replied that this was not customary for one of episcopal rank and, in fact, that there were certain matters of which I had to speak in earnest with the prince. In short, he went and consulted him, but maintained that the conditions would have to hold, so that it became clear that even his first remarks had been prompted by the other's wishes. I remarked that it was not in keeping with my office, but that I would not fail the embassy entrusted to me. I was happy to be humbled, especially on your behalf and in the performance of a duty which involved the affection you bear your brother.

As soon as he was seated in the consistory, I entered; he arose to give me the kiss of greeting; I was standing with the

---
1 Maximus was offering peace, but only on the condition that Valentinian himself come to Trier.
2 *praepositus cubiculi.*

members of the consistory. Some began urging me to step forward; he began summoning me. I said: 'Why would you greet with a kiss one whom you do not know? If you knew me you would not see me here.' 'Bishop,' he said, 'you are greatly upset.' 'Not by the insult,' I answered, 'but by the embarrassment of standing in a place where I do not belong.' 'You came into the consistory,' he said, 'on your first embassy.' 'That was not my fault,' I said, 'but the fault of the one who summoned me; I merely came in answer to the summons.' 'Why did you come?' he asked. 'Because,' I replied, 'at that time I was asking for peace for one who was weaker than you, but I do so now for one who is your equal.' 'Equal by whose kindness?' he asked. 'That of almighty God,' said I, 'for He preserved for Valentinian the kingdom He had given him.'

At length he broke forth, saying: 'You and that Bauton have tricked me. He wanted to get the power for himself under the figurehead of a child, and he sent barbarians against me! As if I do not have just as many thousands of barbarians in my service and in my pay whom I can call upon. Had I not been restrained from doing so at your coming, who would have been able to withstand me or my forces?'

To this I replied gently: 'You need not be angry; there is no cause for alarm. Listen patiently to what I have to say to your remarks. You assert that while you trusted me I deceived you by coming and taking part in your first embassy—a glorious accusation that I was safeguarding the emperor who was a mere child. Whom are we bishops to guard if not children? It is written: "Judge for the fatherless, and defend the widow, and free the one receiving harm."[3] And elsewhere: "Defenders of widows and fathers of orphans."[4]

---
3 Isa. 1.17.
4 Ps. 67.6.

'Still, I shall not censure Valentinian for services I rendered him. To say the truth, when did I prevent your legions from streaming into Italy? With what cliffs or battlelines or troops? Or did I block the Alps with my body? Would that I had the power! I would not have feared to lie in your way nor would I have dreaded your accusations. With what promises did I trick you into making peace? Did not Count Victor[5] come to meet me near Mayence in Gaul, he whom you had sent to make peace? In what way has Valentinian played you false, for he was asked for peace before he asked it. How has Bauton played you false—by showing his loyalty to the emperor? Because he did not betray his lord?

'How have I deceived you? On my arrival you said that Valentinian should come to you like a son to his father. I said it was unreasonable to expect a boy to cross the Alps with his widowed mother during the roughest part of winter. Moreover, was he to embark on the hazards of such a journey without his mother? I was sent on an embassy of peace, not to promise his arrival. It is clear that I could not promise what was not enjoined on me. At least I made no promise; therefore you said: "Let us wait and see what reply Victor will make." It is well known that he reached Milan while I was being detained [at Trier], and his request was refused. It was said that peace was the only issue, not the return of the emperor, who was not to be moved from there. I was present when Victor returned. How, then, did he influence Valentinian? The legates who were sent again and said that he would not come met me at Valence in Gaul. I found soldiers of both sides guarding the mountain heights. What armies of yours did I turn from you? What standards have I caused to leave Italy? What barbarians has Count Bauton brought against you?

'If Bauton, who came from across the Rhine, had done so,

---

5 Son of Maximus.

would it have been strange? You yourself were threatening the power and boundaries of Rome with barbarian troops and squadrons, with men to whom the food supplies of the provinces went as tribute. Note the difference between these threats of yours and the mildness of the august child Valentinian. You were intent upon coming into Italy surrounded by troops of barbarians. Valentinian made the Huns and Alans[6] who were approaching Gaul turn back to the lands of the Germans. What harm if Bauton had set barbarians against barbarians? While you were employing Roman soldiers and he opposing those attacking him on either side, the Juthungi were laying waste the Raetias within the the very heart of the Roman Empire. For this reason he set the Huns against the Juthungi. Yet, because the Germans were already crushing and threatening Gaul with approaching ruin, he was forced to abandon his triumphs lest you have ground for fear. Compare your deeds and his. You made the Raetias subject to attack; Valentinian has bought peace for you with his own money.

'Look at the man on your right.[7] Valentinian sent him back to you in honor, although he had the opportunity of avenging a personal wrong. He had him within his own country at the very moment when his brother's death was announced, and he restrained his anger. He did not treat in the same manner one who is of different dignity but of the same relationship with you. Compare your conduct with his. You be the judge. He gave you back your brother alive; give him back his, even though dead. How can you refuse him his brother's remains when he did not refuse those forces that were used against him?

---

6 The Alemanni, a tribe of Juthungi, were at Maximus' instigation raiding Raetia. To get rid of them, Count Bauton invited Huns and Alans to raid the territory of the Alemanni.
7 Marcellinus, the brother of Maximus, who was sent back to Trier with Ambrose.

'You say you fear to arouse the sorrow of the soldiers when the remains are returned. This is your excuse. Having abandoned him alive, will they now defend him when he is dead? Why fear one who is dead, whom you slew, although you could have saved him? I killed my enemy, you say. He is not your enemy, but you are his. He no longer puts up a defense, but consider why. If someone began plotting here today to rob you of your lands, would you say, I ask, that you were his enemy or he yours? If I am not mistaken, the usurper brings war; the emperor protects his rights. Then why refuse to part with the remains of one you should not have slain? Let Emperor Valentinian have his brother's remains as a pledge of your peace. And how can you keep alleging that you did not give the order to slay him if you do not allow him to be entombed? Will people be able to believe you did not grudge him life, when you grudge him burial?

'But to get back to myself. I hear that you are charging that the people who were with Emperor Valentinian went over to Emperor Theodosius. What did you expect would happen when you demanded that refugees be punished and captives slain, while Theodosius enriched them with favors and granted them honors?' 'Whom did I put to death?' he asked. 'Vallio,' I answered. 'What a man, and warrior, besides! Was it a just cause for his murder that he was faithful to his emperor?' 'I did not order him to be killed,' he said. 'We heard,' said I, 'that such orders were given.' 'But,' said he, 'if he had not destroyed himself, I did order that he be dispatched to Châlons and there burned alive.' 'True,' said I, 'this is the reason you are thought to have killed him. Who would expect to be spared when such a vigorous warrior, so loyal a soldier, so useful a count, had thus been slain?' I then departed so that he might say he would consider the matter.

Later, when he observed that I stayed aloof from the bishops who were in his service and who were asking that certain persons, heretics, should be put to death, he became very angry and ordered me to leave at once. I went, although several thought I would not escape his ambushes. I was overwhelmed with sorrow finding that the old bishop, Hyginus, though he had but the last breath of life left in him, was being sent into exile. When I approached some of his men and begged them not to allow him to be driven forth without clothing, without a bed to lie on, I was myself driven out.

This is the account of my embassy. Farewell, O Emperor, and be on your guard against a man who is cloaking war under the mask of peace.

11. To the most clement Emperor Eugenius, Ambrose, bishop (Summer, 393)

My reason for leaving [Milan][1] was the fear of the Lord to whom I direct all my acts, as far as possible, never turning my mind from Him nor considering any man's favor of more worth than the grace of Christ. By preferring God to everyone else I harm no one, and trusting in Him I have no fear of telling your majesties, the emperors, what I feel with my own conviction. Thus I shall not refrain from saying to you, most clement Emperor, what I have never refrained from saying to other emperors. And in order to preserve the order of events I shall review one by one the facts which concern the present difficulty.

---

1 Ambrose left Milan and went to Bologna, thence to Faenza, and finally to Florence. Cf. *Vit.* 27, where a portion of this letter is quoted by Paulinus. The letter is in effect an implicit notice of excommunication served to Eugenius for his donations to the upkeep of pagan temples.

The most excellent Symmachus, when prefect of the city,[2] appealed to Emperor Valentinian the younger, of august memory, begging that he would command the restoration to the temples of what had been removed, for he fulfilled his obligations in accordance with his own wish and religious conviction. It was also fitting that I, as bishop, should know my duties. I presented two petitions[3] to the emperors in which I declared that a Christian could not contribute to the upkeep of sacrifices; that I had not proposed that they be removed; but that I did now propose they should not be decreed; and, finally, that he would seem to be giving rather than restoring contributions to the images. What he had not withdrawn he could not be said to be restoring; he seemed rather to be willingly donating money for the cost of superstition. Lastly, if he had done so, he either must not come to the church, or, if he should come, he would find no priest or one withstanding him in the church. Nor could he plead the excuse that he was only a catechumen, since even catechumens are not allowed to contribute to the upkeep of idols.

My petitions were read in the consistory in the presence of Count Bauton, a man of the highest military rank, and of Rumoridus, of the same dignity and devoted from early boyhood to the heathen religion. Valentinian then listened to my suggestion and did only what the practice of our faith demanded. The counts acquiesced to their lord.[4]

Later, I openly addressed the most clement Emperor Theodosius,[5] and did not hesitate to speak to him face to face. And when he received word of the same sort from the Senate, although it was not the whole Senate that made the demand,

---

2 In 384.
3 See the two letters to Valentinian, above.
4 Wytzes' emendation of a troublesome passage: *acquieverunt comites domino suo.*
5 In 390.

he at length gave approval to my suggestion. Then, for some days I did not go near him, nor did he take it amiss, because I was acting not for my own advantage but for his profit and that of my own soul; 'I was not ashamed to speak in the presence of the king.'[6]

Again an embassy was sent by the Senate to Emperor Valentinian, of august memory, when he was in Gaul,[7] but they could extort nothing from him. I was absent at the time and had not written anything to him.

But, when your Clemency assumed the government of the Empire,[8] these donations were found to have been made to distinguished citizens of the heathen religion. Perhaps, O august Emperor, it may be said that you yourself did not make the donations to the temples, but merely gave benefits to men who deserved well of you. But the fear of God, you know, ought to make us act firmly as do priests in the cause of liberty, and as those do who serve in your armies or hold rank among the provincials. As emperor, you asked the envoys to make restitution to the temples, but you did not. Others also made these demands and you withstood them. Yet, later, you decided to bestow gratuities on the petitioners themselves.

The imperial power is great, but consider, O Emperor, how great God is. He sees the hearts of all; He probes their inmost conscience; He knows all things before they come to pass; He knows the innermost secrets of your heart.[9] You do not allow yourself to be deceived; do you expect to hide anything from God? Has this thought not occurred to you? Although they persisted in their requests, was it not your duty, O Emperor, out of reverence for the most high, true,

---

6 Ps. 118.46.
7 In 391, following his and Theodosius' joint order, forbidding pagan sacrifices and visits to pagan temples.
8 In August, 392.
9 Cf. Acts 1.24; Dan. 13.42.

and living God, to oppose them still more persistently and to refuse what was harmful to the holy law?

Who grudges your giving to others what you choose? We do not pry into your benefactions, nor are we jealous of the privileges of others. But we are the interpreters of the faith. How will you offer your gifts to Christ? Few will respect your actions; all will respect your wishes. Whatever they did will be to your credit; what they did not do will be to theirs. You are indeed the emperor, but you must all the more submit to God. Otherwise, how will Christ's priests distribute your gifts?

There was question of this kind in former times, and then persecution itself was overcome by the faith of the patriarchs and paganism gave way. When that game, occurring every fifth year, was held at Tyre and the wicked king of Antioch had come to see it, Jason appointed and sent messengers from Jerusalem to bring 300 didrachmas of silver and give them to the sacrifice of Hercules.[10] The patriarchs would not give the money to the pagans, but, sending trusted men, they asked that it not be assigned to the sacrifice of the gods, for it was not needed, but be deputed to other expenses. And it was decided that, because Jason had stipulated that the money be sent for the sacrifice of Hercules, it must be used for that purpose. Yet, when those who brought it pleaded in opposition, in their zeal and devotion insisting that it should not be used for the sacrifice, but for other necessities, the money was given over to the building of galleys. Although they sent the money under force, they did not use it for the sacrifice but for other public expenses.

Undoubtedly, those who brought the money might have maintained silence, but they broke their trust knowing to what their action was leading. So they sent God-fearing men to use their effort to have it employed, not for the temple,

---

10 Cf. 2 Mach. 41.18-20.

but for the building of galleys. They entrusted their money to men who would plead the cause of divine law, and He who clears the conscience was made judge of the affair. If those who were under foreign power took such precautions, there is no doubt concerning what you, O Emperor, should have done. Since no one constrained you, nor had you in his power, you ought certainly to have consulted the advice of a bishop.

At least, when I withstood you, although I alone withstood you, I was not the only one to wish or advise this course of action. Being bound by my words before God and men, I knew I could not, must not, consult anyone but myself, for I could not reasonably trust you. For a long time I stifled and concealed my distress and determined to give no hint to anyone, but now I may no longer pretend, nor am I at liberty to be silent. This is why at the beginning of your reign I made no reply to your letters, foreseeing what would take place. Afterwards, when you found I was not writing and you demanded a reply, I said: 'The reason is that I think they will get it from him by force.'

Yet, when a just occasion for exercising my duty arose, I wrote and petitioned for those who were worried on their own account to show that in the cause of God I have a just fear, and I do not value flattery more than my own soul. And in matters where it is fitting to petition you I show a just deference to your authority, as it is written: 'Honor to whom honor is due; tribute to whom tribute.'[11] Since I am deeply respectful of a private individual, why should I not be so of the emperor? Just as you wish to be held in respect, allow us to respect Him from whom you would like to prove that your authority is derived.

---
11 Rom. 13.7.

LETTERS TO BISHOPS

12. Ambrose, bishop, to Brother Anysius[1] (383)

I HAVE BEEN quite sure for a long time of what I have just now read; you were mine by your deeds even though I had not laid eyes on you. I grieve over that which has happened, but I rejoice over the later happy succession of events. I did not wish that to happen while I lived, yet I did hope after his death that only one of this merit might possibly be his successor. And so we have you, the disciple for a long time of Acholius of blessed memory, now his successor and the heir of his rank and of his grace. You have been given a great recompense, brother, and I rejoice on your account that there was not a moment's doubt regarding the successor of one so great. It is also a great burden, brother, to support the weight of so great a name, of so great esteem, of so great a scale. Men are looking for Acholius in you, and as he was held in affection by you, so in the performance of his ministry there is needed a replica of his virtue, of his learning, and the vigor of mind in so aged a body.

---

1 The successor of Bishop Acholius.

I saw him, I say; and I owe it to him that I had this glimpse of him. I saw him in the body in such a way that I thought he was not of the body; I saw the image of him [Paul] who, not knowing whether in the body or out of the body, saw himself raised to paradise.² He used to travel everywhere—on frequent trips to Constantinople, to Achaia, to Epirus, to Italy—in such fashion that younger men could not keep up with him. Men of more sturdy physique yielded to him, for they knew that he was free from the hindrance of the body; he used his body only for a covering, not an instrument, surely a means of servitude, not of companionship. He had exerted such influence on his body as to crucify the world in it and himself to the world.

Blessed was the Lord, and blessed was the youth of this man spent in the tabernacle of the God of Jacob, living in a monastery where, to his parents or relatives in search of him, he used to say: ' "Who are my brethren, and who is my mother?"³ I do not know my father or mother or brethren, unless they are those who hear the Word and keep it.' Blessed also were his mature years when he was raised to the office of high priest, deemed worthy of an early recompense for virtue. He came like David to restore peace to the people; he came like the ship carrying with him pure gold, cedar woods, and precious stone,⁴ and that dove⁵ with rings of silver with which amid the lots he slept the sleep of peace and the repose of tranquility.

Sleep is the workman of the saints according to what has been written: 'I sleep and my heart watches,'⁶ and according to holy Jacob⁷ who while asleep saw divine mysteries which

---

2 Cf. 2 Cor. 12.2.
3 Matt. 12.48.
4 Cf. 2 Par. 9.21.
5 Cf. Ps. 67.14.
6 Cant. 5.2.
7 Cf. Gen. 28.13.

he had not seen when he was awake—a path in the heavens for the saints, leading from sky to earth, and the Lord looking down upon him and promising him the possession of that land. Asleep in this way for a short while, in his dream he asked and obtained what his descendants later acquired with great toil. The sleep of the saints is free from all pleasures of the body, from all disturbance of the mind; it brings calm to the mind and peace to the soul, so that, released, as it were, from the ties of the body, it raises itself aloft and clings to Christ.

This sleep is the life of the saints such as blessed Acholius lived, whose old age also was blessed, for old age is truly venerable when it grows hoary not with grey hairs but with good deeds. This hoariness is revered, hoariness of soul, gleaming with shining thoughts and deeds. What truly is old age if it is not a spotless life[8] which is measured not by days or months, but by ages whose durability knows no end, whose longevity knows no weakness? The older it is, the stronger it is, and the longer he has lived that life, the more vigorously does he grow into the perfect man.

May the Lord, therefore, set His approval upon you, his successor, not only in honor, but also in character, and may He see fit to establish you in great grace so that to you also the people may run and you may say of them: 'Who are those who fly about like clouds and like doves with their young?'[9] Let them come, too, like the ships from Tharsis[10] and bring in grain which the true Solomon gives, the twenty measures of wheat. Let them receive oil and the wisdom of Solomon, and let there be peace between you and your people, and may you guard well the covenant of peace.

Farewell, brother, and love us, because we also love you.

---
8 Cf. Wisd. 4.8,9.
9 Isa. 60.8.
10 Cf. 2 Par. 9.21.

13. Ambrose to Brother Candidianus[1]

There is in your language the utmost clarity, but it shines even more in your love for me; indeed, in your letters I behold the brilliance of your mind, dearly beloved and most blessed brother. May the Lord bless you, and give you His grace, for I see in your letters your good wishes more than my own excellence. What excellence of mine could compare with your language?

Love us, brother, because we love you.

14. Ambrose to Chromatius (c. 390)[1]

Does God tell a lie? He does not; it is impossible for God to tell a lie. Is this an impossibility because of some weakness? Certainly not! How could He be the cause of all things if there were something which He could not cause? What, then, is impossible to Him? Not what is difficult for His power, but what is contrary to His nature. It is impossible, it is said, for Him to tell a lie. The impossibility comes, not from weakness, but from His power and greatness, for truth admits of no lie, nor God's power of the fault of inconstancy, for 'God is true, and every man is a liar.'[2]

Truth, therefore, is always in Him; He remains reliable; He cannot change or deny Himself. For, if He says He is not true, He tells a lie, and to lie belongs not to power, but to weakness. Nor can He change Himself, because His nature admits of no weakness. This impossibility comes from

---

1 Undated.

1 Intended as the first of a series of letters to Chromatius, Bishop of Aquileia, of which this is the only one extant.
2 Rom. 3.4.

His fullness which cannot diminish or increase, not from weakness which is powerless in that which increases it. Hence we gather that this impossibility for God is a very powerful attribute. What is more powerful than not to know any weakness?

Yet there is a weakness in God which is stronger than men, and a foolishness in God which is wiser than men.³ The one is the foolishness of the Cross, the other of His divinity. If, then, His weakness is power, how is His power weakness? Let us keep in mind that God does not deceive.

There is no diviner in Israel, in accordance with the law of God.⁴ How, then, does Balaam say he was prevented by the oracle of God from going to curse the people of Israel? Yet he went and an angel of the Lord met him who told him to go no farther and stood in the path of the ass which he was riding. Nonetheless, the angel himself did tell him to proceed and to speak only what was put in his mouth. If there was no soothsayer in Israel, whence came the oracle of God which disclosed the future to one who was a soothsayer? If he spoke as the mouthpiece of God, whence had he derived the privilege of divine inspiration?

But do not be surprised that the diviner was inspired by the Lord what to say, since you read in the Gospel that it was granted the chief of the synagogue, one of Christ's persecutors, to prophesy that one man should die for the people.⁵ In him was not the gift of prophecy, but the statement of a truth, so that even by the witness of enemies the truth might be declared and the treachery of unbelievers refuted even by the words of their own diviners. In fact, Abraham, a Chaldean, was brought to the faith to put to

---
3 Cf. 1 Cor. 1.25.
4 Cf. Deut. 18.10.
5 Cf. John 11.50.

silence the superstition of the Chaldeans. It is not, then, the merit of the one who confesses, but the mouthpiece of the one who calls, the grace of God, who makes the revelation.

Was it not Balaam's guilt that he said one thing and planned another, whereas God demands a clean vessel, not one soiled with uncleanness? Balaam, therefore, was tried and was not found worthy, for he was full of guile and deceit. Moreover, when he inquired whether he should go to the vain people and was forbidden, he made an excuse to go. When other more honorable messengers came, asking him, he should have refused, but attracted by greater promises and more numerous gifts[6] he decided he should again inquire [of God] as if God would be influenced by money or gifts.

He received a miser's answer, not that of one seeking the truth, so that he was mocked rather than given information. He set out; an angel met him in a narrow place,[7] and revealed himself to the ass, not to the diviner. He revealed himself to the one; he scorned the other. Then, that Balaam might recognize him for some little while, the angel opened his eyes. He saw and still did not trust the plain oracle, and, though he should have trusted his eyes, he gave doubtful and confusing answers.

Then the Lord, being angry, said through the angel: ' "Go and speak what I shall command you,"[8] that is, not what you wish, but what you are forced to say. You will furnish your tongue, as an empty instrument, for my words. It is I who speak, you only echo what you hear and do not understand. You will accomplish nothing by going, for you will return without a reward of money and without the

---
6 Cf. Num. 22.19.
7 Cf. Num. 22.22,23.
8 Num. 22.35.

profit of grace.' His first words were: 'How shall I curse him whom God hath not cursed?'[9] to show that the blessing of the Hebrew people depended not on his will but on the grace of God.

'I shall see them,' he says, 'from the tops of the mountains,[10] since I cannot with my vision embrace this people which will dwell apart, marking their boundaries not by their ownership of places, but by the indwelling of virtues, and by the perfection of their character which will make them live for everlasting ages. Which of the neighboring nations will be numbered with this one, for it far surpasses their fellowship? Who can understand the nature of its foundation, for we see that the bodies of its citizens are compounded and fashioned from human seeds, but their souls spring from higher, more marvelous seeds?

' "Let my soul die with their souls,"[11] die to this bodily life that among the souls of the just it may attain the grace of that eternal life.' Herein was revealed already the excellence of the heavenly sacrament and of the holy baptism by whose operation men die to original sin and the works of the unjust, that, being transformed in newness of life into fellowship with the just, they may rise again to the just man's way of life. And why is it strange that when they die to sin they live to God?

When Balak heard this he was angry and said: 'I brought you here to curse and you are uttering a blessing.' He answered: 'I suffer insult for what I know not, for I speak not my own words, I merely utter sounds like a tinkling cymbal.'[12] When he was brought to a second and a third place, although he wished to utter a curse, he continued to

---
9 Num. 23.8.
10 Num. 23.9.
11 Num. 23.10.
12 Cf. 1 Cor. 13.1.

bless: 'There is no labor in Jacob, no sorrow.'[13] The Lord protected him. Then he commanded seven altars and sacrifices to be made ready. Surely, he should have gone his way, but his weak mind and changeable notions made him think he could alter God's will. Being in a trance, he kept desiring one thing and saying another.

'How beautiful,' he said, 'are thy dwellings, O army of Hebrews! Thy tabernacles are like wooded valleys, as a park near rivers, and as cedars by the waterside. A man will go forth from Jacob and will take many nations, and his kingdom will be lifted on high; and on earth he will spread his kingdom over Egypt. They that bless him, shall be blessed, and they that curse him, shall be cursed.'[14] What people does he mean except the people of Christ? God blesses that people into whose heart the Word of God comes down even to the division of soul and of joints and of marrow.[15] Balaam would have had the grace of God in him if he had acted according to the interest and purpose of his heart. But, because a wicked mind is bound by its counsels, and the secrets of the soul are betrayed by events, his mind was discovered by his later wicked deeds.

Therefore he received a reward in keeping with his malice, for, when he realized that, being in a trance, he was unable to utter a curse, he told the king: 'Let my utterances be of things which God has commanded; hear now my counsel against the words of God. This is a just people; it enjoys God's protection since it has not given itself to divining and augury, but to the eternal God alone, excelling others in faith. Yet sometimes even faithful minds fall prey to the enticements of the body and the blandishments of beauty. You have many women here, many of them are not un-

---
13 Cf. Num. 23.21 (Septuagint).
14 Num. 24.5,6,9.
15 Cf. Heb. 4.12.

adorned with beauty. Now the male sex is led astray and captivated by nothing more quickly than by a woman's beauty, particulary if by frequent conversation the love of their hearts is aroused, set afire as if by torches; but if it clings to the hope of enjoyment it keeps its feelings pent up. Let your women cast their fishhooks with words, let them be of easy access at first, let them roam about exposed to view, affable in speech, going everywhere about the camp. Let them draw these men so skillfully that they allow them no intercourse until they have first pledged their mutual love by participating in sacrilege. Thus will they be deprived of heaven's protection if by sacrilege they will depart from their Lord God.'

In advising fornication and sacrilege, Balaam proved himself unjust; even in the Apocalypse of John the Evangelist this is plainly written, where the Lord Jesus says to the Angel of the Church of Pergamum: 'Thou hast there some who hold the teaching of Balaam, who taught Balak to cast a stumbling block before the children of Israel, that they might eat and commit fornication. So thou hast also some who hold the teaching of the Nicolaites.'[16] Hence comes the sacrilege of the Manichaeans and of Manasse, who mingle and unite sacrilege with impiety.

God was not unjust, nor was His opinion changed, for He detected Balaam's mind and the secrets of his heart, and He tested him as a diviner, but He did not choose him as a prophet. Surely, he ought to have been converted by the grace of those great oracles and by the sublimity of the revelation, but his mind, full of wickedness, uttered words but did not attain faith, frustrating by its counsels what it had predicted. Then, because he could not gainsay the prophecy, he suggested fraudulent ideas which tempted but did not overcome the people of the Jews. By the righteousness of one

---

16 Apoc. 2.14,15.

priest all the advice of this corrupt man was undone,[17] for it was much more wonderful that our many forefathers could be delivered through one man than deceived by one.

I am sending your holy soul this little work in response to your wish that I make some compilations from the interpretations of earlier writers. I have presumed to write this letter in a friendly style, somewhat reminiscent of the manner of the patriarchs. Provided you approve their flavor, I shall not hesitate later on to send you others of this kind. I prefer to prate of heavenly matters with you, in an old man's fashion, which in Greek is called meditating. 'Isaac was gone forth into the field to meditate,'[18] seeing in Rebecca's coming the mystery of the future Church. Lest I give the impression of having lost my skill in writing—I prefer, I say, this prating with you in the words of an old man instead of uttering in vehement style words unsuited to our interests or strength.

Farewell, and love us, because we love you.

15. *Ambrose to Constantius (before Lent, 379)*

You have entered upon the office of bishop and, sitting at the helm of the Church, you are piloting the ship in the face of the waves.[1] Take firm hold of the rudder of faith so that the heavy storms of this world cannot disturb you. The sea is mighty and widespread, but do not fear, because 'He hath founded it upon the seas; and hath prepared it upon the rivers.'[2] Therefore, not without cause does the Church

---

17 Num. 25.11.
18 Gen. 24.63.

---

1 Cf. Cicero *Epist. ad fam.* 9.15.3: *sedebamus enim in puppi et clavum tenebamus.*
2 Ps. 23.2.

of the Lord, built upon the rock of the Apostles, remain unmoved amid the many storms of this world and, with her foundation unshaken, stand firm against the assaults of the seething sea.[3] She is lashed by waves, she is not shattered, and, although the elements of this world often beat upon her with loud crashing sound, she has a place where she receives those in distress, the well-guarded harbor of salvation.

Nevertheless, although she tosses on the sea, she rides on the floods; see that she rides no more upon those floods of which it is said: 'The floods have lifted up their voice.'[4] There are rivers which flow from the belly of him who drinks from Christ and partakes of the Spirit of God.[5] These rivers, therefore, when they redound with the grace of the Spirit, lift up their voice. There is also a stream which overflows upon its holy ones like a torrent.[6] Likewise, there is a stream of a river which gladdens the peaceful and tranquil soul.[7] Whoever receives of the fullness of this stream, like John the Evangelist, like Peter and Paul, lifts up his voice. Just as the Apostles with the harmony of their message spread the sound of their preaching of the Gospel to all the ends of the earth, so also does he begin to tell the good tidings of the Lord Jesus. Drink, then, from Christ so that your sound, too, may go out.

The sea is holy Scripture which has within it profound meanings and the mysterious depths of the Prophets. Into this sea many rivers have entered. Delightful and clear are these streams; these fountains are cool, springing up into life everlasting;[8] there, too, are pleasant words, like 'honey-

---

3 Cf. Matt. 16.18.
4 Ps. 92.3.
5 Cf. John 7.38.
6 Cf. Isa. 66.12.
7 Cf. Ps. 45.5.
8 Cf. John 4.14.

comb,'⁹ and courteous conversations which water souls with the sweetness of moral commands. The streams of holy Scripture are diverse; you know that which you should drink from first, second, and last.

Store up the water of Christ, that which praises the Lord.¹⁰ Store up the water from many places, the water which the clouds of prophecy pour out. He who gathers water from the mountains and draws it to himself, or drinks from the fountains, he himself also sheds dew like the clouds. Therefore, fill the center of your mind so as to have your plot of land moistened and watered by fountains from the family estate. Accordingly, he who reads much and also understands is filled; he who has been filled sheds water upon others. So Scripture says: 'If the clouds be full, they will pour out rain upon the earth.'¹¹

Therefore, let your sermons be flowing, let them be clear and lucid so that by suitable disputation you may pour sweetness into the ears of the people, and by the grace of your words may persuade the crowd to follow willingly where you lead. But if in the people, or in some persons, there is any stubbornness or any fault, let your sermons be such as to goad the listener, to sting the person with a guilty conscience. 'The words of the wise are as goads.'¹² Even the Lord Jesus goaded Saul when he was a persecutor. Consider how saltutary was the goad which made of a persecutor an apostle, saying: 'It is hard for thee to kick against the goad.'¹³

There are also sermons like milk which Paul gave to the Corinthians;¹⁴ those who cannot eat strong food develop from infancy by drinking a natural milk.

---

9 Cf. Prov. 17.24.
10 Cf. Ps. 145.5.
11 Cf. Eccle. 11.3.
12 Eccle. 12.11.
13 Acts 9.5.
14 Cf. 1 Cor. 3.2.

Let your exhortations be full of meaning. Concerning this Solomon says:[15] 'The weapons of the intellect are the lips of the wise.' And in another place: 'Thy lips have been bound for wisdom,' that is, let the revelation of your sermons shine forth, let your understanding be bright, and let your sermon by itself protect itself, as it were, with its own weapons, and let not any word of yours go out in vain and go forth without meaning. Speech is a bandage which ties up the wounds of souls, and if anyone rejects this, he shows his despair of his own salvation.[16] Likewise, with those who are vexed by a serious sore, use the oil of speech that you may soften their hardness of heart; apply a poultice; put on a bandage of salutary advice, so that you may never allow those who are astray or who are wavering regarding the faith or the observance of discipline to perish through loss of courage and a breakdown of activity.

Warn the Lord's people, therefore, and beg them to abound in good works, to renounce vice, not to enkindle the fires of passion—I shall not say on the Sabbath, but in every season. Let them not destroy their bodies; let there be no immorality and uncleanness in the servants of God, because we are the servants of the unspotted Son of God.[17] Let each one know himself and possess his vessel,[18] and when the soil of the body has been ploughed, let him wait for the fruit in due season, and let his land not bring forth thorns and thistles,[19] but let him, too, say: 'Our earth has yielded her fruit,'[20] and in the once thickly wooded frailty of passion let there flourish ingrafted virtues.

Teach and instruct them to do what is good, and let no one interrupt a laudable work whether he is being seen by

---
15 Prov. 14.3; 15.5.
16 Isa. 1.6.
17 Cf. Eph. 5.3.
18 Cf. 1 Thess. 4.4.
19 Cf. Gen. 3.18.
20 Ps. 84.13.

many or is without a witness, for conscience is a trustworthy security for him.

Let the people also shun evil deeds, even though they do not believe they can be found out. Although men are enclosed in the house, surrounded by darkness, without a witness, without an accomplice, they have the Judge of their deeds whom nothing deceives, to whom all deeds cry out.[21] Each one also has himself and his soul as a severe judge of himself, as an avenger of wickedness, a vindicator of crime. In fear and trembling Cain wandered over the earth[22] paying the penalty of the murder of his brother, so that for him death was a remedy, for it set free the wandering exile who at every moment had a dread of death. Let no one either alone or with another do anything base or wicked. And if anyone is alone, let him respect himself, rather than others, himself whom he ought especially to reverence.

Let your people not desire many things, for the reason that a few things are many to them: poverty and riches are names which imply want and satiety. He is not rich who wants anything, nor poor who does not want. Let no one spurn a widow, or cheat an orphan, or defraud his neighbor. Woe to him who has a fortune amassed by deceit, and builds in blood[23] a city, in other words, his soul. For it is this [the soul] which is built like a city.[24] Greed does not build it, but sets it on fire and burns it. Do you wish to build your city well? 'Better is a little with the fear of the Lord than great treasures without fear.'[25] The riches of a man ought to work to the redemption of his soul, not to its destruction. Wealth is redemption if one uses it well; so, too, it is a snare if one does not know how to use it.[26] For what is a

---
21 Cf. Gen. 4.10.
22 Cf. Gen. 4.14.
23 Cf. Hab. 2.6.
24 Cf. Ps. 121.3.
25 Prov. 15.16.
26 Cf. Prov. 13.8.

man's money if not provision for his journey? A great amount is a burden; a little is useful. We are wayfarers in this life; many are walking along, but a man needs to make a good passage; the Lord Jesus is with him who makes a good passage. Thus we read: 'When thou passest through the waters, I will be with thee, and the rivers shall not cover thee, nor fire burn thy garments when thou shalt walk through.'[27] But, one who keeps a fire pent up in his body, the fire of lust, the fire of immoderate desire, does not pass through but burns the covering of his soul.[28] A good name is more excellent than money, and above heaps of silver is good favor.[29] Faith itself redounds to itself, sufficiently rich and more than rich in its possession. There is nothing which is not the possession of the wise man except what is contrary to virtue, and wherever he goes he finds all things to be his. The whole world is his possession, since he uses it all as his own.

Why, therefore, is a brother cheated? Why is a hireling defrauded? The gain from the sale of a harlot is not great, he [the writer of Proverbs] says;[30] it is the gain of fleeting frailty. A harlot is not one's own possession, but a public possession; not woman alone is a harlot, but every wandering desire is a harlot. Every act of faithlessness, every lie, is a harlot, and not the one who prostitutes her body, but every soul which sells her hope, which seeks disgraceful profit and an unworthy reward. We, too, are hired men who work for a price and hope for the price of our labors from our Lord and God. If anyone wants to know how mercenary we are, let him hear the one who says: 'How many hired men in my father's house have bread in abundance, while I am perishing here with hunger!' And below: 'Make me as one of thy

---
27 Isa. 43.2.
28 Cf. Prov. 6.7.
29 Cf. Prov. 22.1.
30 Prov. 6.20.

hired men.'³¹ All are hired men, all are laborers. Let the man who is waiting for the fruit of his labor consider that he who defrauds another of his pay will himself be defrauded of his own. In lending he acts unwisely and will repay later with greater measure. Therefore, let one who does not wish to lose what endures forever, take not from another what is only for a time.

Let no one speak deceitfully to his neighbor. A snare is on our lips, and often one is not set free by his words but is ensnared.³² The mouth of one speaking ill is a great pit, a steep precipice for the innocent, but steeper for one of ill-will.³³ An innocent man, though easily credulous, falls quickly,³⁴ but when he has fallen rises again. The slanderer is thrown headlong by his own acts, from which he will never emerge or escape. Therefore, let each one weight his words without fraud and deceit: 'A deceitful balance is an abomination before the Lord.'³⁵ I do not mean that balance which weighs out another's pay (in trivial matters the flesh is deceitful). Before God that balance of words is detestable which simulates the weight of sober gravity while practicing at the same time cunning fraud. God condemns especially the man who deceives his neighbor with kind promises and overwhelms his debtor with treacherous injustice. He will have no gain from his clever skill. For, what does it profit a man if he gains the wealth of the whole world but defrauds his own soul of the payment of eternal life?³⁶

Pious souls must consider another scale by which the deeds of individuals are weighed, in which, generally, sins are overbalanced toward judgment, or deeds well done are of more weight than sins. Alas for me if my sins are heavy and

---

31 Luke 15.17,19.
32 Cf. Prov. 6.2.
33 Cf. Prov. 22.14.
34 Cf. Prov. 14.15.
35 Prov. 11.1.
36 Cf. Matt. 16.26.

incline toward a decree of death by their mortal weight! More tolerable would it be if all the things manifest to the Lord came to pass, even before my judgment; good deeds cannot be concealed nor can those be hidden which are full of offense.[37]

How happy is the man who has been able to cut out the root of vices, avarice. Surely he will not dread this balance. Avarice generally dulls men's senses and corrupts their judgments,[38] so that they think piety a gain, and money, a sort of reward for sagacity. But great is the reward of piety and the gaining of sobriety; the possession of these virtues is sufficient. For, what do superfluous riches profit in this world when they do not assist our birth or impede our dying? We are born into this world naked, we leave it without a cent, we are buried without our inheritance.

Each one will have the weight of his good deeds hung in the balance, and for a few moments of a good work or a degenerate deed the scale often inclines to this side or that. If evil inclines the scale, alas for me; if good, pardon is ready at hand. No one is free from sin, but, when good deeds prevail, the weight of sins is lessened; they are cast into the shadow and covered up. So, in the day of judgment, our works will either succor us or plunge us into the depths, like men weighted down with a millstone. Iniquity is heavy, supported, as it were, on a talent of lead;[39] avarice is hard to carry; so, too, all pride and ignoble fraud. Urge the people of the Lord to hope more in the Lord, therefore, to abound in the riches of simplicity, in which they may walk without a snare, without hindrance.[40]

The guilelessness of plain speech is also good; it is rich before God, even if it walks amid snares, for, not knowing

---
37 Cf. 1 Tim. 5.24.
38 Cf. 1 Tim. 6.10.
39 Cf. Zach. 5.7.
40 Cf. 2 Cor. 8.2.

how to weave snares or bands for another, it is not bound.

It is also very important that you persuade them to know how to be humbled, to know the true character and nature of humility. Many have the appearance of humility, but they do not have the virtue. Many make a pretense of it on the outside, yet within they fight against it. They make a display of it for pretense, yet reject the truth; they say 'no' to grace, for 'There is one who humbleth himself wickedly and his interior is full of deceit.'[41] Such a person is very far from humility. Humility does not exist except without pretense, without fraud. That is true which has a pious sincerity of soul. Great is its virtue. Finally, through the disobedience of one man death entered,[42] and through the obedience of our Lord Jesus Christ was wrought the redemption of all men.

Saintly Joseph[43] knew how to be humble. When he was sold into slavery by his brothers and purchased by merchants,[44] bound in fetters, as Scripture says,[45] he learned the strength of humility, he scorned frailty. When he was bought in Egypt by an official of the royal palace—a man in charge of the household—although he knew his noble lineage and his descent from the sons of Abraham, Joseph did not become disgusted with his lowly condition, unworthy [as he was to perform] the duties of a servant. Rather, he showed himself diligent and faithful to his master's commands, knowing by great prudence that it makes no difference in what condition of life one is found trustworthy, but that the purpose of a good man is to be approved in any condition, and, in particular, that character dignifies the position more than position the character. In fact, the lower the status, the more outstanding the virtue. He proved so earnest that his

---
41 Eccli. 19.23.
42 Cf. Rom. 5.19.
43 Cf. Gen. 39.1-12.
44 Cf. Gen. 37.28.
45 Cf. Ps. 104.18.

master entrusted to him his whole house and committed to him all his goods.

Then the wife of his master cast her eyes upon him, captivated by his comeliness. We need not be concerned whether his age or beauty is coveted by her impure glances: provided these be artless, there is no crime in comeliness; provided enticement is not present, seemliness and charm of beauty are innocent. This woman, deeply aroused and maddened, accosts the young man, and driven on by lust, overcome by the sting of passion, admits her crime. But he disowns any wickedness, saying that it is not in keeping with the custom or the laws of the Hebrews for those to violate the stranger's bed who have the duty of protecting its purity; that the chaste spouse may be joined in marriage with chaste maidens, but they are not allowed marriage with a woman who does not make use of her legitimate marriage rights. Moreover, he is bound not to be overcome with wanton intemperance or to be ungrateful for his master's kindness, nor may he bring deadly injury upon one to whom he owes obedience.

Was he ashamed to say that his owner was a despised person, and to admit that he himself was a slave? Nay, even when the woman strove to gain him, entreated him with fear of betrayal, or poured out passionate tears in order to win him by force, he was not drawn to consent to the crime through a sense of duty, nor compelled by fear, and he resisted her entreaties. He did not yield to her threats, preferring to have as his reward honor fraught with danger, a base remuneration for his chaste modesty. Again, beginning with greater inducements when she saw him inflexible and unmoved by her second attempt, wild with passion, her shamelessness furnishing strength, the woman went up to the young man, and, catching hold of his garment, dragged him to a couch, offering her embrace. And she would almost have succeeded in holding him, except that Joseph tore off the garment by which he was held, lest he tear off the cloak of humility, the garment of purity.

He knew how to be humble, for he was humbled even to prison, and while he bore this outrage he preferred to submit to a false charge rather than to bring a true one. I say he knew how to be humbled for the sake of virtue. He was humbled in the manner of Him who was humbled unto death, even to the death of the Cross.[46] He was to come to arouse this life of ours from sleep, and to show that our use of life, in which there are various sorts of vicissitudes, was a dream with nothing solid or firm therein, as in sleep we see a dream but do not see, hearing do not hear, eating are not filled, rejoicing are not made glad, running do not reach our goal. Vain are the hopes of men in this world when they think they must attain things which do not exist, as if they did exist. So the empty and vain appearances of things, just as in sleep, come and go. They stop beside us, they vanish. They are near and they disappear. They seem to be grasped but they are not. Finally, when one hears it said: 'Awake, sleeper,'[47] and he rises from his dream of this world, he knows then that everything is false. He awakes and his dream flees; he loses his concern over an inheritance, over the charm of beauty and the desire for honors. These are dreams by which those are undisturbed who watch with the heart, while those who are asleep are disturbed.

The saintly Joseph provides material for my statement that the things of this world are not everlasting or even of long duration. He who from youth was of noble lineage, rich in his possessions, is suddenly a lowly slave, and to further embitter his mean estate of servitude his purchase was paid for with the money of a degenerate master. It is considered

---
46 Cf. Phil. 2.8.
47 Eph. 5.14.

less disgraceful to be the slave of a freedman; slavery is twice servitude when one is the slave of a slave. Joseph, the slave, was nobly born, a pauper, richly sired, experiencing instead of love, hatred, instead of favor, punishment, dragged time and again from prison to palace, from criminal charge to seat of judgment. Yet he was not broken by adversity or carried away by success.[48]

That the turn of events is momentary is further proved by the constantly changing fortune of blessed David, who was an object of scorn to his father, but precious to God. Noble in triumph, cheapened by envy, called to a kingly ministry, loved as a son,[49] but later changed in appearance and features,[50] fleeing his own murderous son, he used to deplore his personal offenses and atone for those of others, more noble in winning back his heir's affection than if he had disgraced him. Having experienced all this, he fittingly remarked: 'It is good for me that thou hast humbled me.'[51]

Yet, this saying can also be referred to Him who, being God by nature, could bend the heavens without effort, but, coming down to earth and taking the nature of a slave, bore our infirmities,[52] because He foresaw that His saints would not think it fitting to claim honors due to themselves, but would submit to their equals and prefer others to themselves, He said: 'It is good for me that thou has humbled me.' It is good for me that I have brought myself down so that all things may be under me, and God may be all in all.[53] Infuse this humility into every individual soul, and show yourself an example to all, saying: 'Be imitators of me as I am of Christ.'[54]

---
48 Cf. Gen. 41.39-45.
49 Cf. 1 Kings 18.3.
50 Cf. Virgil, *Aeneid* 1.658.
51 Ps. 118.71.
52 Cf. Phil. 2.6.
53 Cf. 1 Cor. 15.27,28.
54 1 Cor. 11.1.

Let them learn to search for the riches of good works and to be rich in character. The beauty of riches is not in the purses of the rich, but in their support of the poor. In the weak and needy, riches shine brighter. Let the wealthy learn to seek not their own interests, but those which are Christ's, so that Christ may search for them to bestow His possessions upon them. He spent His blood for them;[55] He poured out His Spirit; He offers them His kingdom. What more will He give who has offered Himself? Or what is the Father not going to give, who delivered His only-begotten Son to death for us? Therefore, admonish them to serve the Lord in purity and grace, to lift up their eyes to heavenly things with all the intensity of their minds, to count nothing as gain except that which is for eternal life, because all the gain of this world is the loss of souls. Finally, the one who wished to gain Christ suffered the loss of all things,[56] and although he spoke wonderfully well, he still fell short of expressing what he had received, for he spoke of things which were not his own; but Christ has said: 'If anyone wishes to come after me, let him deny himself.'[57] In this way he becomes his own loss, that he may become Christ's gain. All such possessions are perishable, accompanied by loss and without gain. There is gain only where there is everlasting enjoyment, where eternal peace is the reward.

My son, I am giving to your care the church at Forum Cornelius,[58] so that by reason of its nearness you may visit it from time to time until a bishop is ordained for it. I cannot travel such a distance, because I am occupied with the approaching days of Lent.

You have there Illyrians, imbued with the false teaching

---
55 Cf. Rom. 8.32.
56 Cf. Phil. 3.8.
57 Luke 9.23.
58 Modern Imola.

of the Arians; beware of their cockle, do not let them come near the faithful or insidiously spread their false seeds of doctrine. Let the faithful take note of what has happened to them because of their perfidy; let them be quiet so they may follow the true faith. With difficulty can minds imbued with the poisons of infidelity be delivered from their impiety. And if the virus unfortunately is implanted in them, do not think they can be easily trusted. The strength and power of wisdom is not to be trusted rashly, especially in the matter of faith, which is rarely perfect in man.

Nevertheless, if you find one tainted with this dangerous doctrine and of doubtful disposition, who wishes to get rid of the reputation in which he is held, permit him to think that he has made satisfaction, indulge him somewhat, for if satisfaction is not allowed a person his mind is estranged. Even skilled doctors, when they notice the signs of illness, do not immediately upon naming them administer medicine, but wait for the proper time for dispensing it. They do not give up the patient, but with words or with what ointments they can use, they soothe him so that the neglected illness may not grow worse through a loss of spirit, or the patient, being sick to his stomach, spit out the medicine; if a physician inexperienced in matters of this kind treat the illness prematurely, it will never be able to come to a head. So also an unripe apple quickly rots if it is shaken from a tree.

Continuing our figure from agriculture, teach your people to keep sacred their boundary laws, to guard their fathers' boundary stones which the law will protect.[59] The good favor of a neighbor is frequently of more value than the love of one's brother.[60] A brother is often far away; a neighbor is near, a witness of a whole life, the judge of daily living.

---

59 A reference to boundary laws; cf. Daremberg-Saglio, *Dict. antiq. grecq. et rom.*, art., 'Finium regundorum actio,' II.2 1140-1141.
60 Cf. Deut. 19.14.

One should be glad to have his neighbor's flock wander freely through the nearby open spaces and lie on the green grass,[61] taking its rest without a care.[62]

Let the master also keep his slaves subdued by the law of slavery instead of by control of force, treating them as kindred souls. For he is called *paterfamilias* so that he may govern them as sons; and he himself is a slave of God and calls the Lord of heaven Father, the Ruler of all the powers.

Farewell, and love us as you do, for we love you.

16. Ambrose to Constantius[1]

Many persons are disturbed over the question, not by any means unimportant, why circumcision should have been made of obligation under the ruling of the Old Testament, and set aside as useless by the teaching of the New Testament,[2] especially since it was Abraham who first received the command to observe the rite of circumcision,[3] he who saw the day of the Lord and was glad.[4] It is certainly evident that he was considering not the physical, but the spiritual sense of the divine law, and saw in the sacrifice of the lamb the true suffering of the Lord's body.

What purpose shall we think Abraham our father intended by first instituting what his posterity would not continue? Or why are infants' bodies circumcised and imperiled at birth, and commanded thus by a divine pronouncement so that by reason of a mystery of religion their life is endangered? What does this mean? The true cause lies hidden; the

---

61 Cf. Virgil, *Ecl.* 6.59; *Aen.* 5.330.
62 Cf. Virgil, *Georg.* 3.376.

---

1 Undated.
2 Cf. Acts 15.10.
3 Cf. Gen. 17.10.
4 Cf. John 8.56.

meaning should have been disclosed by a clear mystery or enjoined by a type of mystery not so fraught with danger.

And why was the sign of the divine testament given to that member of the body which is considered unseemly to behold, or for what reason did the Creator of our body, at the very beginning of our race, choose to have His work circumcised, and wounded, and stained with blood, and a part cut off which He, who has arranged all things in order, thought proper to mold together with our other members as something necessary? This part of our body is either contrary to nature, and all men should not have what is contrary to nature, or it is according to nature, and that which was molded for the perfection of our nature ought not to be cut off, especially since those who are unfriendly, being outside the flock of the Lord our God, are wont to make this the chief subject of ridicule. Since it is God's purpose, as He has frequently declared, to bring as many as possible to the observance of holy religion, how much the more would these persons be attracted were they not deterred either by the danger of this very circumcision or disapproval of it?

But to return to my first purpose, following the order I have laid down, it seems best to speak of the exact nature of circumcision. Its defense should be twofold, since the accusation is such: the one brought forward by the Gentiles, the other raised by those belonging to the people of God. The stronger objection comes from the heathens who think that men who have been marked with circumcision are worthy even of scorn and mockery. Yet their wise men show such approval of circumcision that they think it right to circumcise those set apart to know and celebrate their mysteries.[5]

And the Egyptians, who devote themselves to geometry and the observation of the courses of the stars, consider unholy

---
5 Herodotus 2.37.

that priest who has not the distinctive mark of circumcision. For they believe that neither the wisdom of magical incantation, nor geometry, nor astronomy exert their power without the seal of circumcision. And to render their operations effective they deem it necessary to celebrate a sort of purification of their seers by a secret rite of circumcision.

We also find in ancient history that not only the Egyptians, but some of the Ethiopians and Arabs and Phoenicians used circumcision among their people. They think by this rite to maintain a custom still to be approved, for, being initiated through the first fruits of their own body and blood, they feel that by this consecration of a very small portion they can defeat the snares which the demons set for this race of ours. They think, too, that those who attempt to harm the well-being of the whole man will be crippled in their operations either by the Law or by the appearance of this sacred circumcision. I am of the opinion that in the past that Prince of devils has realized that his arts lose their baneful effects if he tries to injure one whom he finds initiated in the seal of sacred circumcision, or one who, at least in this respect, seems to be observing the divine law.

One who carefully considers the functions of each of our members will be able to realize that it was for no idle purpose that in this little portion of this member the child was not only circumcised, but circumcised on the eighth day,[6] when the child's mother begins again to have pure blood, for she is said to sit in unclean blood until the eighth day. This answer should be given those who are not joined to us in the unity of faith, yet with those who differ from us discussion is somewhat difficult.

To those who believe in the Lord Jesus the same reply must be given which we were unwilling to disclose when we argued against the notions of the Gentiles. If we were

---
6 Cf. Gen. 17.12.

redeemed not with perishable things—with silver and gold—but with the precious blood of our Lord Jesus Christ,[7] surely the one who sold us had a right to our service in the coin of a now sinful race. And, undoubtedly, to release from slavery those whom he held bound he demanded a price. The price of our freedom was the blood of the Lord Jesus, and it had to be paid necessarily to the one to whom we had been sold by our sins.

Until this price was paid for all men by the shedding of the Lord's blood for the forgiveness of all, blood was required of each man who, by the Law and the customary rite, was following the holy precepts of religion. Since the price has been paid for all after Christ the Lord suffered, there is no longer need for the blood of each individual to be shed by circumcision, for in the blood of Christ the circumcision of all has been solemnized, and in His cross we have all been crucified with Him, and buried together in His tomb, and planted together in the likeness of His death that we may no longer be slaves of sin, 'For he who is dead is acquitted of sin.'[8]

If men like Marcion and Mani think to find fault with God's judgment for having determined to publish His command about the observance of circumcision or a law directing the shedding of blood, they must also think that the Lord Jesus is to be found fault with for having shed not a little, but much, blood for the redemption of this world. Even today He bids us shed our blood in the great struggle of religion, saying: 'If anyone wishes to come after me, let him take up his cross, and follow me.'[9] If such an accusation is not just when a man offers himself completely out of love, and cleanses himself by the shedding of much blood,[10] how

---

7 Cf. 1 Peter 1.18,19.
8 Rom. 6.5-7.
9 Matt. 16.24.
10 A reference to the martyrs.

can we blame the Law for exacting a mere drop of blood, when we preach that the Lord Jesus commands the shedding of much blood and the death of the whole body?

Neither was the symbol and outward appearance of circumcision useless, by which the people of God, marked with a certain seal of the body, were set off from other nations. But, now that the name of Christ has been given them, they need no bodily sign, for they have attained the honor of a divine title. Why was it absurd for them to seem to bear some pain or labor for piety's sake, that by these difficulties their devotion might be better tried? It is also becoming that from the very cradle of life the symbol of religion should grow with us, and an older person would be ashamed not to meet labor and pain when his tender infancy had overcome them both.

Christian people now have no need of the light pain of circumcision; they bear with them the death of the Lord; in their every act they engrave on their forehead contempt of death, knowing that without the cross of the Lord they cannot be saved. Who would use a needle in battle while armed with stronger weapons?

Now, anyone knows how easy it is to refute those who maintain that more persons could have been won over to the observance of holy religion had they not been restrained through fear of pain or the sight of hardship. Could this frighten an older person when many babies endured it without peril? Granted that some Jewish babies died because they were unable to bear the pain and keen stroke of circumcision in their bodies, it did not deter others who were stronger by reason of their more advanced age, and it made more praiseworthy the man who obeyed the heavenly precepts.

If they think so slight a pain an obstacle to the confession of faith, what do they say of martyrdom? If they find fault with the pain of circumcision, let them find fault, too, with the death of martyrs by whom religion has been heightened, not diminished. So far is the pain of circumcision from being harmful to faith that pain but makes greater trial of faith, for the grace of faith is greater if one despises pain for religion's sake. Such a man has a greater reward than one who was willing to undergo the pain of circumcision, only that he might glory in the Law and win praise from men rather than from God.

It was fitting for this partial circumcision to take place before the coming of Him who was to circumcise the whole man, and for the human race to be partially prepared to believe that which is perfect. And if circumcision needed to take place, in what part of the body ought it to have been performed than in that which seems unseemly? 'So that those we think the less honorable members of the body, they surround with more abundant honor, and our uncomely parts receive a more abundant comeliness.'[11] In what part should a man have been reminded more of his blood than in that which ministers to his transgression?

Now it is time to reply also to those who say that if this part of our body is according to nature it should never have been cut off, and if it is not according to nature it should not have been part of it at birth. Since they are so subtle, let these very men tell me whether the succession of the human race, which rises by generations, is according to nature or contrary to it. If it is according to nature it should never be interrupted, and how can we praise the chastity of men, the virginity of maidens, the abstinence of widows, the restraint of spouses? No effort to promote generation ought to be neglected. But the Author of nature Himself did not pay this regard to generation for He gave us, when living in the body, His own example and exhorted His disciples to

---

11 1 Cor. 12.23.

chastity, saying: 'There are eunuchs who have made themselves so for the sake of the kingdom of heaven. Let him accept it who can.'[12]

Since man is composed of body and soul (for the present it will suffice to speak of this and not mention the spirit), he is naturally not the same in both, but what is natural to the body is contrary to the nature of the soul, and what is natural to the soul is contrary to the nature of the body, so that, if I mention what is natural to a visible object, it is contrary to the nature of what is not seen; and what is natural to what is not seen is contrary to the nature of what is seen; and what is natural to what is not seen is contrary to the nature of the visible object. It is no incongruity in the men of God if there should be some things contrary to physical nature which are in accord with the nature of the soul.

Let those who say that more persons would have believed, had circumcision not been instituted, be told in answer that more would have believed if there had not been martyrdom, but the constancy of a few is more excellent than the carelessness of many. Just as many kinds of baptisms first took place, because the true sacrament of baptism in spirit and water which would redeem the whole man was to follow, so circumcision of many first had to take place because the circumcision of the Lord's passion was to follow, which Jesus bore like the Lamb of God in order to take away the sins of the world.[13]

I have written this to show that it was right for circumcision, which is outward, to occur first so that now, after the Lord's coming, it might seem to be rightfully set aside. Now, however, there is a necessary circumcision which is in secret and in the spirit, as the Jew is more excellent when he is in secret and in the spirit, not in the letter, for there

---
12 Matt. 19.12.
13 Cf. John 1.36.

are two men in one, and of them it is said: 'Even though our outward man is decaying by reason of his desires for wrongdoing, yet our inner man is being renewed day by day,'[14] and in another passage: 'For I am delighted with the law of God according to the inner man.'[15] Our inward man is one who was according to the image and likeness of God; our outward man is fashioned of clay. Therefore, again in Genesis, He reveals to you two creations of man,[16] showing that by the second [creation] man was created.[17]

Therefore, just as there are two men, so is there a twofold life: one of the inward, the other of the outward man. Indeed, many actions of the inward man reach to the outward one, in the same way as the purity of the inward man passes over into bodily chastity. One who is free from adultery of the heart is free from bodily adultery, but it does not follow that one who has not committed adultery in the body will not have sinned in his heart, according to the saying: 'Since anyone who so much as looks with lust at a woman has already committed adultery with her in his heart.'[18] Such a man, although he is not yet an adulterer in body, is already one in desire. So there is a circumcision of the inward man, for the circumcised man has put away, like foreskin, the allurements of all his flesh, that he may be in the spirit, not in the flesh, and by the spirit may mortify the deeds of his body.

This is that circumcision in secret, for Abraham was first in uncircumcision and later in circumcision. Thus, our inward man, while it is in the flesh, is, as it were, in uncircumcision, but, when one is no longer in the flesh but in the spirit, he begins being in circumcision, not in uncir-

---
14 2 Cor. 4.16.
15 Rom. 7.22.
16 Cf. Gen. 1.27.
17 Cf. Gen. 2.7.
18 Matt. 5.28.

cumcision. And just as the circumcised man does not put away the whole flesh but only his foreskin, where corruption is more frequent, so the man who is circumcised in secret puts away the flesh of which it is written: 'All flesh is grass, and all the glory thereof as the flower of the field. The grass is withered and the flower is fallen: but the word of our Lord endureth for ever.'[19] There still remains the flesh which will see the salvation of God, as it is written: 'All flesh shall see the salvation of God.'[20] Cleanse your ears that you may understand what this flesh is.

The circumcision in secret should be such that it bears no comparison with that which is outward. Thus, one who is a Jew in secret excels; he is of Juda whose hand, like a lion crouching, rests on the neck of his enemies, and [he is] like a lion's whelp, which his brothers praise.[21] The prince does not depart from this Juda, because his words choose as princes those who are not overcome by worldly allurements or ensnared by the pleasures of this earth. And since Juda was born into this generation, many born afterwards are preferred that they may enjoy a pre-eminence in virtue. Let us have, therefore, a secret circumcision and let us have the Jew who is such in secret, that is, the spiritual one, for the spiritual man, like a prince, judges all things, and he himself is judged by no man.[22]

It was fitting for the circumcision, commanded by the prescription of the Law, to cease after He came who circumcised the whole man and fulfilled the circumcision of the Law. Who is this but the one who said: 'I have not come to destroy the Law but to fulfill it'?[23]

Yet, if you pay careful attention, the fact of the coming

---

19 Isa. 40.6-8.
20 Luke 3.6.
21 Cf. Gen. 49.8.
22 Cf. 1 Cor. 2.15.
23 Matt. 5.17.

of the fullness of the Gentiles is the reason why circumcision of the foreskin was no longer needed. Circumcision was not enjoined on the Gentiles, but on the seed of Abraham, as you have in the first promise of God: 'God also said to Abraham, "You shall keep my covenant, you and your descendants after you throughout their generations. This is my convenant, which you shall keep, between you and me and your descendants after you: Every male among you shall be circumcised, you shall circumcise the flesh of your foreskin; it shall be a token of the covenant between you and me. He that is eight days old among you shall be circumcised, every male throughout your generations, including the slave born in your house, or bought with money from any foreigner, not of your own race. My covenant shall be in your flesh as a perpetual covenant. If any male have not the flesh of his foreskin circumcised, that person shall be cut off from his people; he has broken my covenant." '[24] It is said that the Hebrew text, as Aquila suggests, does not have the words 'on the eighth day.' But all authority does not rest with Aquila who, being a Jew, passed it by in the letter and did not insert 'the eighth day.'[25]

Meanwhile, you have heard that the eighth day and circumcision were given as a sign. A sign is an indication of a greater matter, an indication of some future reality. A covenant was given Abraham and his seed to whom it was said: 'Through Isaac shall be your descendants,'[26] and circumcision was permitted a Jew, or one born in his house, or bought with his money. But we cannot extend this to a foreigner or convert unless he is born in the house of Abraham, or bought with his money, or descended from his seed. Again, He said nothing of converts, but when He

---
24 Gen. 17.9-14.
25 Evidence of Ambrose's acquaintance with Aquila's reading, which he consulted in exegetical discussions.
26 Gen. 21.12.

wished to speak of them He mentioned them expressly, as in the words: 'And the Lord spoke to Moses, saying: "Speak to Aaron and his sons, and to all the children of Israel, saying to them: If any man is of the sons of Israel and of the strangers that sojourn among you, let that man offer a holocaust." '[27] When it includes them, the Law touches on them, but when the divine pronouncement does not point to them, how can they appear bound by it? Again you have: 'Speak to the sons of Aaron,'[28] when the priests are meant, and so also regarding the Levites.

Thus it is clearly manifest that even by the letters of the Law, although the Law is spiritual, according to that letter the Gentile nations could not be obliged to observe circumcision. Circumcision was but a sign until the fullness of the Gentiles should enter and all Israel be saved through circumcision of the heart, not of a small portion of one member. Therefore, we are excused from circumcision, and the continuance of circumcision among the Jews of today is done away with.

Regarding those who say that it is objectionable now as in time past it was to the Gentiles, I would say, first of all, that they are not competent to find fault or scoff at what their other[29] fellows do. Suppose there were some cause for ridicule, why should this disturb us when the very cross of the Lord is a stumbling block to the Jews and to the Greeks foolishness, but to us the power of God and wisdom?[30] The Lord Himself said: 'Whoever disowns me before men, I in turn will disown him before my Father in heaven.'[31] He teaches us not to be disturbed by those practices which are scoffed at by men, if we observe them in the service of religion.

---

27 Gen. 17.1,2,8.
28 Lev. 17.2.
29 The Egyptians and others mentioned above.
30 Cf. 1 Cor. 1.23,24.
31 Matt. 10.32.

17. Ambrose to Fegadius and Delphinus, bishops[1]

My son Polybius, on his return from Africa where he had discharged his proconsular duties with distinction, spent some few days with us and endeared himself to my affections most favorably.

Then, when he wished to leave here and set forth on his journey, he asked me to write to both of you. I promised to do so, and, having dictated a letter, gave it to him, addressed to both of you. He asked for another, but I said that it was addressed to both of you in accordance with our usual custom, since your holy souls are delighted not by the number of letters but by the association of your names, and that, united as you are in affection, it would not be permissible to separate your names, whereas my office also demands the practice of this short cut to charity.

To be brief, he demanded another letter and I gave him one so as not to refuse him what he asked, nor to change my usual custom of acting. He, therefore, has a letter to deliver to each of you, for this was the only excuse he had, that when he had made the delivery to one of you he would have nothing for the other. This pledge of undivided affection I may render to you without any fear of reproach or scruple of division, especially since this form of writing is apostolic, and one may write to many, as Paul to the Galatians, or two may write to one, as it is written: 'Paul, a prisoner of Jesus Christ, and our brother Timothy, to Philemon.'[2]

Health to you; love us and pray for us, for I love you.

1 Undated.
2 Philem. 1.1.

18. Ambrose to Felix (c. 380)

The truffles you sent me are of extraordinary size, so large as to cause amazement. I had no desire to hide them, as they say, in the fold of my toga, but I preferred showing them also to others. As a result, I shared some with friends, some I kept for myself.

Your gift is most agreeable, but it is not weighty enough to still in me the complaints rightly caused by the fact that you never come to see me, although I have loved you so long. Take care lest later you find the growth of my distress no trifle. Growth has a double meaning: things grown may be pleasing as gifts, but growths in the body and in the affections are signs of trouble.[1] See to it that I am not troubled by your absence. I am upset by a deep longing for you. Try, if you can, to be less pleasing to me.

I have explained my statement; I have proved my case. I have to hurl at you a well-aimed weapon, no ordinary statement. Certainly you must be alarmed, but notice that, disturbed as I am, I can jest. Hereafter, don't make excuses, although your present excuse is a profitable one to me. Still, it looks bad for you, and it shows me in a bad light, too, when you think I have to be bribed to overlook your absence or bribed in being won back to you.

Farewell, and love us, who love you.

19. Ambrose to Felix, greetings (c. 380)

I was not feeling well when your message came, yet when I had read it, being of one heart with you, I received no small help toward recovery, as though I had been restored

---

1 A play on *doloris tubera*.

to health by the sweet potion of your discourse, and also because you said that an anniversary day was fast approaching, a day most solemn for both of us, when you took hold of the helm of the high-priesthood. I had been speaking of this but a moment before to my brother Bassianus. He had started talking of the dedication of the basilica which he built and named for the Apostles, and this fact turned our conversation in your direction. In fact, he had expressed a great desire to have your Holiness present for the dedication.

Then I brought up the matter of your day of consecration, which would occur at the beginning of November. In fact, I remarked that it was close at hand and would be celebrated on the morrow. After that day passed there would not be any excuse for you. So I made a promise on your behalf, just as you can do for me. I promised him; I exacted one for myself. I took for granted that you would be present because you should be. My promise will not be any more binding than the ordinary custom you have resolved upon, namely, of doing what you should. So, you see, I made the pledge to my brother, being not so bold in the promise as I was fully acquainted with you. Come, therefore, so that you will not disappoint two priests—yourself, who would not be present, and myself, who made the promise so readily.

We shall attend your anniversary day with prayers, and may you not forget us in your prayers. Our spirit will accompany you. And when you enter the second tabernacle which is called the Holy of Holies,[1] do as we do, that you may take us with you. When, in spirit, you burn incense in the golden censer, do not pass us by, for incense is to be found in the second tabernacle and from this your prayer becomes full of wisdom, like incense directed to heaven.

In that place is the Ark of the Testament all covered

---

[1] Cf. Exod. 26.55. A reference to the second anniversary of Felix's elevation to the episcopacy.

with gold, that is, with the teaching of Christ, with the teaching of the Wisdom of God. There is the golden vessel containing manna, the vessel of spiritual nourishment, the storehouse of divine knowledge. There is the rod of Aaron, symbol of the grace of the priesthood. In the past it withered, but it has budded anew in Christ. There are the cherubim above the tablets of the Testament, the knowledge of holy Scripture. There is the propitiatory,[2] and high aloft is God the Word, the image of the invisible God,[3] who says to you: 'I will speak to thee over the propitiatory, and from the midst of the two cherubim.'[4] He speaks to us in such a way that we may understand His speech. Then, because He speaks not of worldly matters but of those of the soul, He says: 'I shall open my mouth in parables.'[5] Where Christ is, there are all things, there is His teaching, there forgiveness of sins, there grace, there the separation of the dead and the living.

Indeed, Aaron once stood in the midst of these furnishings of the temple, exposing himself to danger so that death would not pass over to the hosts of the living from the heaps of the dead.[6] In the Holy of Holies, moreover, like the Word, He whom we do not see stands within each one of us, separating the faculty of reasoning from the lifeless bodies of our deadly passions and plague-ridden thoughts. He stands as one who has come into this world to dull the sting of death, to close its devouring jaws, to give everlasting grace to the living, to grant resurrection to the dead.[7]

For Him you fight the good fight,[8] you guard His treasure, you lend His money, as it is written: 'Thou shalt lend to nations.'[9] The profit from spiritual grace is a good thing.

---
2 The mercy seat or seat of judgment.
3 Cf. Col. 1.15.
4 Exod. 25.22.
5 Ps. 77.2.
6 Cf. Num. 16.47,48.
7 Heb. 2.14,15.
8 Cf. 1 Tim. 6.12.
9 Deut. 15.16.

The Lord when He comes will demand it with interest, and when He finds that you have managed His affairs well He will give you more in return for less. It will be a very sweet delight to me that my confidence in you is warranted. Your ordination, which you received through the laying on of my hands, and through the blessing in the name of the Lord Jesus,[10] will not be censured. Perform your task well, therefore, so that you may find a reward on that day and we may be in peace—I in you, and you in me.

The harvest of Christ is great, but the laborers are few, and it is hard to find helpers. This is an old truth. Yet the Lord is able to send laborers into His vineyard.[11] Certainly, among the people of Como several have begun now to believe your teaching and they have received the word of God through your instruction. He who gave followers will also give helpers, so that your need to apologize for seldom coming to see us will be removed, and we shall again have the oft-repeated favor of your company.

Farewell, and love us as you do.

20. Ambrose to Justus, greetings (before 381)

You make a very good suggestion, brother, that we should devote our correspondence and our conversation at a distance to the interpretation of Heaven's words, asking me as you did what is signified by that didrachma, a half of which the Hebrew is told to offer for the redemption of his soul.[1] What brings us together so closely as the weaving together of conversation on holy subjects?

---

10 Cf. 2 Tim. 1.16.
11 Cf. Matt. 9.37.

---

1 Cf. Exod. 30.12-16.

A half-didrachma is a drachma. Now, the price of the soul is faith. Faith, therefore, is that lost drachma which the woman in the Gospel seeks diligently, as we read, lighting a candle and sweeping her house, and after finding it, she calls together her friends and neighbors, bidding them rejoice with her because she has found the drachma which she had lost.[2] Great is the damage to the soul if one has lost the faith or the grace which he has gained for himself at the price of faith. Therefore, light your lamp: 'Your lamp is your eye,'[3] namely, the interior eye of the soul. Light the lamp which feeds upon the oil of the spirit and shines throughout your whole house. Seek the drachma, the redemption of your soul, for, if a man loses this, he is troubled, and if he finds it, he rejoices.

Mercy is also the ransom of the soul, for the saving of a man's soul is his riches by which, assuredly, mercy is done, gladdening the poor by this expenditure.[4] Therefore, faith and grace and mercy are the ransom of the soul; these are bought by the full payment of a drachma, that is, a large sum. So it is written in the Scriptures that the Lord said to Moses: 'When thou shalt take the sum of the children of Israel according to their number, every one of them shall give a price for souls to the Lord: and there shall be no scourge among them, when they shall be reckoned. And this shall every one give that passeth at the naming, half a didrachma according to the standard of the temple. A didrachma hath twenty obols. Half a didrachma shall be the tax to the Lord. He that is counted in the number from twenty years and upwards, shall give the tax. The rich man shall not add, and the poor man shall diminish nothing from the half-didrachma. When they begin to give an offering

---

2 Cf. Luke 15.8,9.
3 Matt. 6.22.
4 Cf. Prov. 13.8.

to the Lord and to pray for their souls, the money received from the tax on the children of Israel, thou shalt receive and deliver unto the uses of the tabernacle of the testimony and it will be a reminder of them before the Lord to be merciful to your souls.'[5]

Was not the offering made, therefore, when a rich man offered more or a poor man less, even though the half-didrachma consisted only of money and not of virtue? So we must realize that the drachma is not a material thing but a spiritual one, which is known to be contributed equally by all.

Finally, in regard to the heavenly food (for heavenly wisdom is food and delightful nourishment, which those in paradise feed upon, the unfailing food of the soul, called by the mouth of God, manna), we read that distribution was made to each soul so that there might be an equal share. They gathered it according to the direction of Moses, both those who gathered much and those who gathered little. Each man measured a gomor and the amount did not abound or remain over and above for him who had gathered much, nor was it less for him who had gathered less.[6] Each one, in accordance with the number of souls which dwelt with him in the tent, gathered a gomor for each—that is, a measure of wine as the interpretation goes.

There is a measure of wisdom, too, which harms if it is above measure, because it has been written: 'Do not be very wise.'[7] Paul, too, taught that a division of graces is given according to measure, when he says: 'Now the manifestation of the Spirit is given to everyone for profit, to one the utterance of wisdom, to another the utterance of knowledge, to another the faith of wisdom according to the same Spirit,

---
5 Exod. 30.12-16.
6 Cf. Exod. 16.17,18.
7 Eccle. 7.17.

faith in the same Spirit,'[8] and according to the will of the Spirit this grace is apportioned. It belongs to His justice that He divides; it belongs to His power that He divides according to His will, or because He wishes to give to each what He knows will be of profit.

A gomor is a measure, a measure of wine which gladdens the heart of man.[9] Can anything but a draught of wisdom be the joy of the heart? This is the wine which Wisdom has mixed in the bowl,[10] and offers to us to drink so that we may receive temperance and prudence, which should be carried to our feeling and thoughts and all the movements in this house of ours in such equal measure that we shall know how to abound in all things, to fail in none.

This truth is more fully understood regarding the blood of Christ, for its power is not lessened, is not increased. Whether we partake of a little or whether we drink much, the same measure of redemption is accomplished for all.

The patriarchs are also commanded to eat the Pasch of the Lord, that is, the lamb, that they may eat in accordance with the numbers of souls, not too many, not too few. Some are not to be given more and others less, but in accordance with the number of each. Thus, the strong may not take more, nor the weak less. An equal grace is given to each, redemption is given, a gift is given. There should not be too many persons, either, for then someone may go away deprived of his hope and redemption. There are too many when there are some beyond the number, since the saints are all numbered, and the hairs of their head. The Lord knows who are His. There should not be too few lest by reason of the great amount of grace someone be too weak to receive it.

He teaches all to bring equal devotion and faith to the

---

8 1 Cor. 12.7-11.
9 Cf. Ps. 103.15.
10 Cf. Prov. 9.2.

Pasch of the Lord, that is, to the 'passage,' for it is the Pasch when the soul lays away unreasonable passion, but takes up a goodly compassion, that she may share Christ's passion and await His passage into her, that He may dwell in the soul, and walk with her and become her God. Grace itself is equal in all, but virtue varies in each. Let each person, then, receive grace proportioned to his strength, so that the strong man does not feel need or the weak man a burden.

You have this truth in the Gospel,[11] since the same wages were given to all who worked in the vineyard. Few reach the goal, few the crown. Few say: 'There is laid up for me a crown of justice.'[12] The gift of liberality and grace is one thing; the reward of virtue, the remuneration of labor, is another.

The didrachma is our redemption, nay, a half-didrachma. It has redeemed us from death, it has redeemed us from slavery, lest we be subject to the world which we have renounced. Our Lord in the Gospel, therefore, tells Peter to go to the sea, to let down his fishhook and to take the stater he finds in the mouth of a fish and give it to the tax collector for the Lord and himself.[13] This is the didrachma which was demanded according to law. Yet it was not the king's son who owed it, but the foreigner. For, why should Christ pay to ransom Himself from this world, He who had come to take away the sin of the world?[14] Why should He pay the price of ransom from sin, He who had come down to forgive the sins of all?[15] Why should He redeem Himself from slavery, He who had emptied Himself to give liberty to all?[16] Why should He redeem Himself from death, He who

---
11 Cf. Matt. 20.10.
12 2 Tim. 4.8.
13 Cf. Matt. 17.26.
14 Cf. Matt. 17.24.
15 Cf. John 1.29.
16 Cf. Phil. 2.7.

had become incarnate to give the resurrection to all by His death?

Surely, the Redeemer of all had no need of redemption, but, just as He had received circumcision in order to fulfill the Law,[17] and had come to baptism to fulfill justice,[18] so also He did not refuse the payment of the didrachma to the tax collectors, but at once ordered a stater to be given, instead of a didrachma, for Himself and for Peter.[19] He preferred to pay beyond what was required by Law rather than to refuse to give what belonged to the Law. At the same time He showed that the Jews acted contrary to the Law by exacting a didrachma from each man, whereas Moses had prescribed that a half-didrachma should be exacted. Christ, therefore, bade a drachma apiece to be paid in the stater for Himself and for Peter. The tribute of Christ is good since it is paid in a stater, because justice is a stater and justice is above the Law. Besides, 'Christ is the consummation of the Law unto justice for everyone who believes.'[20] This stater is found in the mouth of a fish, of that fish which the fishers of men catch, of that Fish[21] which weighs its words so that He may bring forth words tried by fire.[22]

The Jews did not know the stater which they gave to the betrayer. The Law exacts a half-didrachma for the redemption of a soul, and vows this to God, being unable to claim the whole didrachma. One does not find any amount of prayer in a Jew. But the true man is free, the true Hebrew belongs entirely to God—everything which he has partakes of this freedom. But whoever refuses freedom, saying: 'I love my master and my wife and children, I will not go out

---
17 Cf. Luke 2.22.
18 Cf. Matt. 3.15.
19 Cf. Matt. 17.26.
20 Rom. 10.4.
21 *Ichthús*, a symbol of Christ.
22 Cf. Ps. 17.31.

free,'²³ has none of God. This refers not only to the Lord but also to the weakness of a man who subjects himself to the world, because he loves the world as his own soul, that is, his *noûs*, the source of his will. This refers not only to one's wife but also to the delight one has in the affairs of the house while he cares not for those which are eternal. At his doorway and on his threshold his master punctures the servant's ear²⁴ so that he will remember the words by which he chose slavery.

And you, O Christian, do not imitate such a person as this; because it is written for you that if you wish to be perfect you should offer to God not a half-didrachma, but that you should sell all that you have and give it to the poor.²⁵ Nor should you keep a part of your service for the world; you should deny yourself completely, and take up the cross of the Lord and follow Him.

We know that a half-didrachma is demanded by the Law, because half is kept for the generation of this world—that is, for worldly affairs and use in the home and for posterity, to whomever a portion from the inheritance needs to be transmitted. The Lord, therefore, responded to the Pharisees testing Him with that crafty question whether He thought tribute should be given to Caesar: 'Why do you test me, you hypocrites? Show me the coin of the tribute.'²⁶ And they offered Him a denarius on which was the image of Caesar. He then said to them: 'Render, therefore, to Caesar the things that are Caesar's, and to God the things that are God's,'²⁷ showing them how imperfect they were, although they seemed perfect in their own eyes, for they paid their debt to Caesar before they did so to God. Those who are

---

23 Exod. 21.5.
24 A mark of servitude, for earrings.
25 Cf. Matt. 19.21.
26 Matt. 22.18,19.
27 Matt. 22.21.

concerned first with this world must first make payment to that which is of this world. For this reason He also said: 'Render,' that is, you yourself, 'give back those things which belong to Caesar,' you, in whom the figure and image of Caesar is found.

The Hebrew youths—Ananias, Azarias, and Misael[28]—and Daniel, too, the wise man[29] who did not adore the image of the king, who did not believe it, or accept anything from the king's table, were not bound to the payment of tribute. They possessed none of the things which are subject to an earthly king.[30] Their imitators, too, whose inheritance is God, do not pay tribute. The Lord therefore says: 'Render,' that is, do you yourselves give back, you who have brought forward the image of Caesar, you with whom it is found. But I owe nothing to Caesar becauses I have no part in this world: 'The prince of the world is coming, and in me he has nothing.'[31] Peter owes nothing, My Apostles owe nothing, because they are not of this world although they are in this world. I have sent them into this world but they are no longer of this world, because they are with Me above the world.

Payment is demanded for those things which are of the divine law, not those of Caesar. The perfect man, that is, the preacher of the Gospel, because he had preached more, no longer owed that payment. The Son of God did not owe the tribute, nor did Peter owe tribute, who had been admitted by grace to adoption by the Father. 'But that we may not give offense to them, go to the sea and cast a hook, and take the fish that comes up. And opening its mouth thou wilt find a stater; take that and give it to them for me and

---

28 Cf. Dan. 2.17.
29 Cf. Dan. 3.18.
30 Cf. Dan. 1.8.
31 John 14.30.

for thee.'³² O great mysteries! He gives a half-didrachma because the Law bade Him, and He did not refuse what is of the Law, as He was born of a woman, born under the Law. I have said 'He was born' according to the Incarnation, but 'of a woman' according to sex. Womankind is the sex, virgin is the species; the sex has to do with nature, a virgin with integrity. In so far as He was born of a woman, that is, in a body, He came under the Law. And so He ordered the didrachma to be paid for Himself and Peter because they were both born under the Law. He bids it to be paid according to the Law so that He might redeem those who were under the Law.³³

Nevertheless, He orders a stater to be given, clamping shut their mouths so that out of much talking they may not admit their sin. And He bids that to be given which was found in a fish's mouth so that they might know the Word. They exacted what was of the Law; why did they not know what was of the Law? They ought not to have been ignorant of the Word of God, because it was written: 'The Word is near on your lips and in your heart.'³⁴ Therefore, a whole didrachma is paid to God by Him who kept nothing for this world. Justice is paid to God, which is soberness of the mind; guarded speech is paid to God, which is moderation in speech: 'With the heart a man believes unto justice, and with the mouth profession of faith is made unto salvation.'³⁵

Moreover, a drachma can be interpreted as the Old Testament, a didrachma as the price of both Testaments. Because, according to the Law, each one was redeemed by the Law, but he who is redeemed according to the Gospel pays a drachma according to the Law, he is redeemed by

---
32 Matt. 17.26.
33 Cf. Gal. 4.4,5.
34 Deut. 30.14.
35 Rom. 10.10.

the blood of Christ according to grace, having a double redemption, both of vow and of blood. Faith alone is not sufficient for perfection unless one also obtains the grace of baptism and, being redeemed, receives the blood of Christ. For this reason, the drachma which is paid to God is good.

A drachma is not a denarius, but something different. On a denarius there is the image of Caesar; on a drachma, the image of God. It is the image of the one God for the imitation of this one. It begins from One and is diffused endlessly. And later, from the Infinite, all things return to this One, as to their end, because God is both the beginning and end of all. Thus mathematicians do not call a unit 'a number' but the 'element' of a number. We said this, too, since it has been written: 'I am the Alpha and the Omega, the beginning and the end,'[36] and 'Hear, O Israel, the Lord thy God is one God.'[37]

You, therefore, be one and the same as the image of God, not sober today but drunk tomorrow; today peaceable, on the morrow litigious; today virtuous, on the morrow incontinent. Each one is changed by variation of his habits and becomes someone else; in this condition he is not recognized for what he was, and he begins to be what he was not, not his genuine self. It is a serious matter to be changed for the worse. Be like the image on the drachma, unchangeable, keeping the same habits every day. When you see the drachma, see the image; when you see the Law, see Christ, the image of God, in the Law. And because He Himself is the image of the invisible and incorruptible God, let Him shine for you as in the mirror of the Law.[38] Confess Him in the Law that you may acknowledge Him in the Gospel.

---
36 Apoc. 1.8.
37 Deut. 6.4.
38 Cf. Col. 1.15.

If you have known Him through His commands, acknowledge Him in His works.

Farewell, and if you think it was not fruitless to question me about the didrachma, and if you need anything later on, do not hesitate to call on me.

21. Ambrose to Justus (c. 381)

Many persons say that our sacred writers did not write in accordance with the rules of rhetoric. We do not take issue with them: the sacred writers wrote not in accord with rules, but in accord with grace, which is above all rules of rhetoric. They wrote what the Holy Spirit gave them to speak.[1] Yet, writers on rhetoric have found rhetoric in their writings and have made use of their writings to compose commentaries and rules.

In rhetoric, these qualities in particular are demanded: a cause (*aítion*), a subject (*húlē*), and an end or purpose (*apotélesma*). Now, when we read that blessed Isaac said to his father: 'Behold, you have the fire and the wood, but where is the victim,' are these qualities lacking? The one asking the question is in doubt; the one who answers the question gives the answer and removes the doubt. The fire is the cause; the wood is the subject, called *materia* in Latin; the third item, the purpose, is that which the child sought and which the father showed him when he asked: 'Where is the victim?' 'God himself,' he said, 'will provide the sacrifice, my son.'[2]

Let us discuss the meaning of the mystery for a little while. God showed a ram sticking fast with its horns;[3] the

---
1 Cf. Acts 2.4.
2 Gen. 22.7,8.
3 Cf. Gen. 22.13.

ram is the Word, full of tranquility and restraint and patience. By this is shown that wisdom is a good sacrifice and belongs to one who is duly wise and making atonement to understand the purpose of an action. The Prophet David therefore says: 'Offer up the sacrifice of justice.'[4] Sacrifice belongs to justice as it does to wisdom.

Note, therefore, that the mind which is working is aglow and warm like fire. Note the thing known to the intelligence, the subject matter. Where is the third ingredient, the understanding of the purpose? You see color, but where is 'seeing'? You perceive objects, but where is 'perceiving'? All men do not see 'matter,' and therefore God gives the gift of understanding and perceiving and seeing.

Therefore, the Word of God is our purpose, that is, the end and fulfillment of all our questioning. This Word is infused into the wise and puts an end to doubt. Yet, even men who refuse to believe in the coming of Christ refute themselves very aptly with the result that they profess what they think they should not profess. They say that the 'ram' is the Word of God, yet they do not believe in the mystery of the Passion, although the Word of God is, in that mystery, the very one in whom the sacrifice has been fulfilled.

Let us first enkindle in us the fire of the mind, so that it will be at work in us. Let us seek the subject matter, which gives us that which feeds the soul, as if seeking it in darkness, for the patriarchs did not know what manna was, yet they found it, Scripture says, and they called it the speech and Word of God.[5] From this continual and ever-flowing source all learning flows and streams.

This is a heavenly food. It is signified by the person of the one speaking: 'Behold I will rain bread from heaven for you.' This is the cause, for God works, watering minds with

---
4 Ps. 4.6.
5 Cf. Exod. 16.16.

the dew of wisdom; the subject matter is that which delights souls seeing and tasting it and asking whence comes that which is more splendid than light and sweeter than honey. They are given the answer in the Scripture narrative: 'This is the bread which the Lord hath given you to eat.'[6] And this is the Word of God which God has set in orderly array. By it the souls of the prudent are fed and delighted; it is clear and sweet, shining with the splendor of truth, and softening with the sweetness of virtue the souls of those who hear it.

The Prophet [Moses] learned the cause of what he had to accomplish. When he was sent to the king of Egypt to free the people of God, he said: 'Who am I that I should go and should bring forth the people from the power of the king?' The Lord answered: 'I will be with thee.' Again Moses asked: 'What shall I say to them if they ask me: "Who is the Lord who sent thee, what is his name?"' The Lord said: 'I AM WHO AM. You will say: HE WHO IS hath sent me.'[7] This is the true name of God, 'Eternal Being.' Therefore, the Apostle says of Christ: 'For the Son of God, Jesus Christ, who is in you, who was preached among you by us—by me and Sylvanus and Timothy—was not now "Yes" and now "No," but only "Yes" was in him.'[8] Moses answered: 'If they will not believe me, nor hear my voice, but they will say: "The Lord hath not appeared to thee," what shall I say to them?' God gave him signs to perform so that it would be believed that he was sent by the Lord. A third time Moses said: 'I am not worthy and I have a weak voice, and a slow tongue, how will Pharao hear me?' He was told: 'Go, I will open thy mouth and I will teach thee what thou shalt speak.'[9]

The questions in the middle of the passage and the answers

---

6 Exod. 16.4,15.
7 Exod. 3.11-14.
8 2 Cor. 1.19.
9 Exod. 4.1,10,14.

contain the seeds and science of wisdom. And the end, too, is pleasing, because God says: 'I will be with thee.'[10] Although He gave him certain signs to use, when Moses doubted, so that you might know that the signs were for those who would not believe, but the promise for believers, God gave an answer, taking into consideration the frailty of his merit or of his devotion: 'I will open thy mouth, and I will teach thee what thou shalt speak.' Thus a perfect end or purpose was kept.

You have this also in the Gospel: 'Ask, and it shall be given you; seek, and you shall find; knock, and it shall be opened to you.'[11] Ask from the cause, that is, seek from the Author. You have as the subject matter spiritual qualities by which you seek; knock, and God discloses the Word to you. The mind is that which seeks, which works like fire; the vigor of the mind works upon spiritual qualities as fire does upon wood; and God discloses the Word to you—this is the end or purpose. Elsewhere, too, in the Gospel we have the words: 'But when they deliver you up, do not be anxious how or what you are to speak; for what you are to speak will be given you in that hour. For it is not you who are speaking, but the Spirit of your Father who speaks through you.'[12]

You have this, too, in Genesis when Isaac says: 'How did you find it so quickly, my son?' He answered: 'The Lord your God let me come upon it.'[13] God is the end. He who seeks in the Lord finds; Laban was a man who did not seek in the Lord; because he sought idols, he did not find.[14]

He [Isaac] observed very well what are called the rules and distinctions of speech. The first distinction is: 'Set your

---
10 Excd. 3.12.
11 Matt. 7.7.
12 Matt. 10.19.
13 Gen. 27.20.
14 Cf. Gen. 31.33.

game near me, my son, that I may eat.'¹⁵ He arouses and enkindles his son's mind by a sort of fire of exhortation so that he will work and go in search. The second distinction is: 'How did you find it so quickly, my son?' This is in the form of a question. The third distinction is an answer: 'The Lord your God let me come upon it.'¹⁶ The end or purpose is God who accomplishes and perfects all things; about this there must be no doubt.

There is also a distinction about things which spring up of their own accord: 'You do not sow, you will not reap,'¹⁷ for, although cultivation stimulates the growth of seeds, nature works in them by a certain power so that they do spring up.

Thus, the Apostle says: 'I have planted, Apollo watered, but God has given growth. So then neither he who plants is anything, nor he who waters, but God who gives the growth.'¹⁸ God makes His gift to you in the spirit, and the Lord grows in your heart. Act, therefore, so that He may breathe upon you and grow. Then you may reap. But if you do not sow you will not reap. You are warned, as it were, that you should sow; you have not sowed, you will not reap—it is a proverb. The final action is included in the first act. Sowing is the beginning; reaping is the end.

Learn from me, nature says. She is a help to the learner. God is the Author of nature. It is also through God that we learn well, because it belongs to nature to learn by the heart. The hard of heart do not learn. There is growth in the nature which has the divine gift of grace. God gives to it full accomplishment and perfection, that is, the most excellent and divine nature and substance of the Trinity.

Farewell, and love us as you do, because we love you.

15 Gen. 27.25.
16 Gen. 27.20.
17 Lev. 25.11.
18 1 Cor. 3.6,7.

22. Ambrose to Marcellus[1]

There has devolved upon me the business of your lawsuit, which you did not initiate but only carried on from a sense of duty and a desire to prove your generosity toward the poor. I had to take cognizance of it because of the imperial enactment[2] and because I was obligated by the authority of the blessed Apostle and the nature and conduct of your learning and life. Since I myself rebuked you for keeping alive your age-long quarrel, the parties in question put upon me the obligation of hearing the case.

I was ashamed to refuse, I admit, especially since the lawyers for each party challenged one another, saying that it would be clear from my investigation to which party the decision of law and right would incline the more. In short, the days had almost drawn to a close—only a few hours remained while the prefect was hearing other cases—when the lawyers in the suit asked an adjournment of a few days so that I might preside as judge. These Christian men were most eager that the prefect should not be the judge of a matter under the jurisdiction of a bishop. They said, also, that certain things had been done in an unseemly fashion and each party according to his own inclination doubted what fell to a bishop's jurisdiction, what to a prefect's.

Overwhelmed by these events and reminded of the Apostle's precept which reproves and says: 'Is it not those inside whom you judge?'[3] and 'If, therefore, you have cases about worldly matters to be judged, appoint those who are rated as nothing in the Church to judge. To shame you I say it. Can it be that there is no wise man among you competent to settle a case in his brother's behalf? But brother

1 Undated.
2 Cf. Sozomen 1.9.
3 1 Cor. 5.12.

goes to law with brother and that before unbelievers?"[4]—I accepted the hearing on condition that I might be the judge of a compromise. I saw that, if I handed down a decision in your favor, the other party might not acquiesce; while, if the sentence was carried in his favor, your defense and that of your sister might break down. The rendering of a decision was very difficult. The favor resulting from our priestly relationship might have seemed suspect to them, too, for when does a defeated man ever think his opponent more righteous than himself? Truly, the costs of this long-standing suit would have been unbearable to each if its outcome failed to provide some gain or, at least, the comforting thought that one had acted generously.

I saw that the issue was doubtful, that the law was subject to dispute, while numerous pleas were being entered by each party and petitions of an invidious sort presented to the emperor which contained, in addition, charges of tampering with his decrees. Perceiving, also, that if your opponent won the case he would sue for double the mesne profits and for the costs of the protracted suit, while it was unbecoming your office to demand the costs of the case, and that it was not suitable for you to claim any of the profits which as owner you had received, I preferred to settle the case by compromise rather than aggravate the situation by a decision. In addition, there is the serious consideration that, although the dispute were settled, ill-will would remain and be destructive of good-feeling.

Involved in these difficulties and feeling that the office of the priest, the sex of the defendant and the serious state of widowhood, and regard for a friend having a threefold and weighty claim on me, I thought I should be sure to desire no one's defeat, but everyone's success. And my wishes did not fail; you all were victors in keeping with your

---

4 1 Cor. 6.4-6.

kinship, with nature, and with the saying of Scripture: 'Why not rather suffer wrong? Why not rather be defrauded?'[5]

Perhaps you feel you are in a worse state because of the loss of the suit and the money costs. But, indeed, for bishops the losses of this world are better than its gains: 'It is more blessed to give than to receive.'[6] Perhaps you will say I ought not to have been exposed to fraud, to have suffered injury, to have undergone loss. Well? Would you have inflicted these? And even though you did no such things, the other party would have complained of suffering them. Consider, therefore, what the Apostle says: 'Why not rather suffer wrong?' It almost seems as though one who does not suffer wrong inflicts it, for the stronger one should bear it.

Why am I discussing this with you as if it were my concern, not yours? You made the offer, acting as an arbiter of the case, suggesting that your sister own part of the estate during her lifetime, but that after her death the entire property go to your brother. Nor must anyone sue him in your name or in that of the Church, but, if he chooses, he may hold it without giving anything to the Church. When I announced this and acclaimed the great flood of generosity thus manifest in your heart, your brother declared that the offer suited him, provided there remained no fear of injury to the property. How, he asked, could a woman, a widow besides, manage taxable property? What would be the advantage to him if you yielded the right of ownership while he thought greater losses would accrue to him from the poor tending of the farm?

The lawyers on both sides were influenced by his remarks; so, with the consent of all, it was determined that the honorable Laetus should receive the farm and pay yearly to your sister a fixed quantity of grain, wine, and oil. Your

---

[5] 1 Cor. 6.7.
[6] Acts 20.35.

sister thus lost no rights, but only her anxiety; she relinquished not the fruits but the labor, not the revenues but the gamble, as it is often called, on an uncertain return. If violent wind storms destroy the harvest, your sister will still have the yield that is hers. If crops wither during an excessive drought, your sister will still have her crops undiminished. Laetus will assume the conditions of his offer, and, should pressure of necessity or extraordinary taxes become severe, your sister, by reason of your kindness, will be clear of Laetus' losses, while Laetus will console himself with the management of the estate.

Thus you have all been winners: Laetus in gaining a right over the property which he did not have; your sister by now enjoying the yearly profits without dispute or strife; but no one won so completely and gloriously as yourself, for, in addition to your wish to assure your sister of your generosity, you have brought her to a share in your fraternal union. You conceded to your brother the property, to your sister the use and enjoyment of it. Nothing is lost to the Church which is gained for piety; charity is not a loss but a gain for Christ; the fruit of the Holy Spirit is charity.[7] The case, then, has been concluded in the manner prescribed by the Apostle. We lamented formerly that you were engaged in this lawsuit, but the strife has enabled you to clothe yourself in the form of the apostolic life and precept. The one was unbecoming your priesthood; this transaction meets the requirements even of the Apostle.

Fear not that the Church will be rendered destitute and out of reach of your generosity. She partakes of your fruits, fruits even more plentiful, for she has the fruits of your teaching, the service of your life. She has a richness which you have watered with your discipline. Rich in these returns she seeks no temporal ones, for she has those which are

---

7 Cf. Gal. 5.22.

eternal. You have added not only the fruits mentioned by the Apostle, but those found in the Gospels, for the Lord said: 'Make friends for yourselves with the mammon of wickedness.'[8] You have made friends, even more marvelously, of your opponents. You made brothers return to the laws of kindred, and you assure them by this charity and grace that they will be received into eternal dwellings.

Thus, under the guidance of Christ and the direction of two bishops, namely, yourself who first supplied the pattern outline, and myself who passed sentence, the peace which we reached will not fail; for where so many vowed their faith infidelity cannot but be punished.

Laetus will plow the land for his sister, whereas formerly he grudged her the services of others. Laetus will gather the harvest for his sister, though before he could not bear the gifts of others; he will bear the fruits to his sister's barns and do so gladly,[9] renewing now the meaning of his name.

Meanwhile, being conformed to the Apostle of Christ, and assuming the prophetic authority, you shall say to the Lord: 'You have possessed my reins.'[10] This possession is more fitting for Christ, that He possess the virtues of His priest, that He receive the fruits of purity and continency, and, what is more, of charity and peace.

Farewell, and love us, because we love you.

23. Ambrose to Sabinus (c. 390)

You sent back my little books which I shall esteem more highly owing to your criticism of them. In fact, I am sending you others, not to be delighted with your favorable criticism,

---
8 Luke 16.9.
9 A play on his name, Laetus, meaning glad.'
10 Ps. 138.13.

but lured by the frank appraisal which I asked of you and which you promised to give. I much prefer that if something puzzles you it be corrected by your criticism before it gets abroad beyond recall, rather than for you to praise what others will censure. Therefore, I am asking you to be the judge of the works you requested, not so much wanting you to read the things I sometimes make available to all, but to submit them to the weight of your opinion. This criticism, as was said of old,[1] will not need long sittings and delay. It is easy for you to pass judgment on my writings.

I thought that at your invitation I should have recourse to you; it is now your turn to discern clearly and consider carefully the corrections so that you may not be guilty of the faults which have crept upon me unawares. For some reason or other, [in my case] because of a mist of ignorance which envelops me, one's own writings are deceptive and escape the notice of the ear, and as one delights in his children, even though they be deformed, so the writer's discourses, however inelegant, flatter him. Frequently, a remark is made unguardedly, or taken in a bad sense, or expressed with ambiguity. Thoughts which are to be subjected to another's criticism should be weighed and sifted of every grain of evil, not for our own benefit, but to facilitate the other person's judgment.

Accordingly, kindly lend an attentive ear, study all the details, test the remarks, see if there is any vain flattery and persuasiveness instead of sincere faith and sobriety of expression. Note the words of doubtful value or false connotation, that an adversary may not take any of them in his favor. Let it be toned down if it begins to be argumentative. That book is in a bad way which is defended only by its champion. The book which goes forth without a mediator speaks for itself. But this book of ours will not leave us

---
1 Cf. Cicero, *Epist. ad fam.* 9.3.

unless it has your authority. When you bid it go with your approval it will be trusted on its own.

However, since the 'kingdom of God is not in word, but in power,'[2] if a word troubles you consider the force of the expression. The expression is the opinion on faith which we hold against the Sabellians and Arians, an opinion handed down to us from our elders; namely, that we venerate God the Father and His only-begotten Son and the Holy Spirit; that this Trinity is of one substance and majesty and divinity; that in this name of Father, Son and Holy Spirit we baptize,[3] as it is written that the Son, though co-eternal with the Father, took flesh, was born of the Holy Spirit and of the Virgin Mary, equal to the Father in divinity, having the nature of God, that is, in all the fullness of the divinity which dwells in Him, as the Apostle says,[4] corporeally, and that in the person of man He took the nature of a slave and humbled Himself even to death.[5]

This, then, is our statement also against Photinus; against Apollinaris this is a lawful safeguard, the expression that just as in His nature as God He lacked nothing of the divine nature and fullness, so in the form of man He lacked nothing that would cause Him to be judged an imperfect man, for He came to save the whole man. It was not fitting that He who completed a good work in others should allow this to be imperfect in Himself. If He lacked anything as man, then He did not redeem all; and if He did not redeem all, He deceived us, since He said that He had come to save all men. But, since it is impossible for God to deceive,[6] He did not deceive us. Therefore, since He came to redeem all

---

2 1 Cor. 4.20.
3 Cf. Matt. 27.19.
4 Cf. 2 Cor. 2.9.
5 Cf. Phil. 2.8.
6 Cf. Heb. 6.18.

men and save them, He certainly took upon Himself the whole of man's perfection.

This, as you remember, is our stand. If the words are at all disturbing they do not harm the faith, for the mind which continues steadfast guards against doubtful meanings and preserves one from error.

These remarks which are a prelude to other discussions I shall put in the collection of our letters, if you are willing, and give them a number.[7] Thus they will be commended because of your name and through our letters to one another our mutual love in the Lord will be increased. Read in order to criticize and tell me what displeases you, for true love is proved by constancy. I am following the custom of old men, writing letters in an ordinary and friendly style, weaving in any words of holy Scripture that come to me.

Farewell, my brother, and love one who loves you, for I love you very much.

24. Ambrose to Sabinus (c. 390)

I have sent you the volume you asked for, written more clearly and neatly than the one I forwarded some time ago, so that by ease in reading it your judgment will in no way be hindered. The original book was written not for appearance's sake but out of necessity. For I do not dictate all my writings,[1] particulary at night, when I do not wish to trouble and burden others. Then, too, words which are

---

[7] Evidence that Ambrose collected some of his letters during his lifetime.

[1] Paulinus (*Vit.* 38) says he did not decline the task of writing books with his own hand unless his body was kept from so doing by some infirmity.

dictated need to roll out with a certain impetuosity and in a rapid flow.

But I who am desirous of selecting with nicety the words I use in my old age, employing a familiar style and proceeding at a slow pace, feel it is more suitable that I put my own hand to the stylus, not to appear to be lustily pouring forth words, but concealing them, so that I will not have to be ashamed in the presence of another who is doing the writing, but conscious only of myself, without a witness, and weighing with the ear and also with the eye the things I write. For, the tongue is swifter than the hand, as Scripture says: 'My tongue is the pen of a ready scribe.'[2]

Perhaps you will say this refers to the speed of the writer. You are not mistaken in the meaning that only the speed of the ready scribe can catch the words of prophetic language. The Apostle Paul also used to write with his own hand, as he himself says: 'I am writing to you with my own hand.'[3] He said this for reasons of honor, but we [say so] because of shame.

However, now that you have my opinion about the books, let us interchange letters, for they serve us who are widely apart to unite with one another in affection, and the image of their presence is vivid between the absent, and written discourse unites those who are apart. By this means, too, we join heart with our friend and pour out our thoughts to him.

If, as you suggest, there is a savor of older writers in my letters, not only do our hearts seem united by this progress toward true learning, but our conversation is expressed in a freer and fuller form, with the result that mutual inquiry and reply will seem to unite us for battle and in this activity we shall stimulate and encourage one another as friends.

---

2 Ps. 44.2.
3 Gal. 6.11.

Need I cite examples of our forebears, who by their letters instilled faith into the hearts of the people and wrote to whole nations together, showing themselves present though writing far away, as did the holy Apostle[4] who says that he was absent in body but present in spirit, not only when he was writing but also when passing judgment? Finally, he while absent condemned and absolved by letter. For Paul's letter was a kind of image of his presence and a pattern of his work.

His letters, he says, were not like the letters of others, 'weighty and telling,' but 'their bodily appearance weak and speech of no account.' Such was his letter, such the pattern of his preaching as was the reality of the worker. 'What we are by letters, when absent, such are we also in deed when bodily present.'[5] In his letters he expressed the likeness of his presence and in his work he stamped the fulfillment of his promise.

Farewell, and love us, as you do, because we also love you.

25. Ambrose to Sabinus (Spring, 387)

After reading my *Hexaemeron*[1] you determined to ask me if I have added anything on paradise, and indicated that you are very anxious to learn my ideas about it. I wrote on this subject a long time ago when I was not yet an experienced bishop.

I have found that most persons' opinions about this are

---
4 Cf. 1 Cor. 5.3.
5 2 Cor. 10.10,11.

1 A series of nine sermons on the creation, delivered on six consecutive days in April, 387 (*PL* 14.123-274).

divided. Josephus,[2] simply as a historian, says the place was planted with trees and many shrubs and watered, moreover, by a river which branched into four streams. After its waters were gathered into one, this earth was not drained entirely nor did its springs become dry. Even today it breaks forth into fountains and sends streams of water with which, like a loving mother, from full udders it nourishes its young.

Some hold one opinion, others another, yet all agree that in paradise[3] were planted the tree of life and the tree of knowledge which distinguishes good and evil, together with other trees, full of strength, full of life-giving powers, breathing and rational creatures. Wherefore one concludes that the real paradise cannot be considered earthly, nor planted in any particular spot, but situated in the principal part of our nature, which is animated and vivified by the virtues of the soul and the infusion of the spirit of God.

Moreover, Solomon, by inspiration, clearly declared that paradise is within man. And because he expresses mysteries of the soul and the word, or of Christ and the Church, he says of the virgin soul, or of the Church which he desired to present a chaste virgin to Christ:[4] 'My sister, my spouse, is a garden enclosed, a garden enclosed, a fount sealed up.'[5]

The word 'paradise' in Greek is rendered 'garden' in Latin. Susanna was in a paradise (orchard),[6] as we read also in Latin. And Adam was in a paradise,[7] which is also our reading. Do not be disturbed if some Latin texts have the reading *'garden'* and others *'paradise.'*

Where the virgin is, there, too, is the chaste wife. The chosen virgin holds her seal and enclosures, both in a

---

2 Josephus, *Antiq.* 1.1.2.
3 Cf. Gen. 2.9.
4 Cf. 2 Cor. 11.2.
5 Cant. 4.12.
6 Cf. Dan. 13.7.
7 Cf. Gen. 2.8.

paradise, so that in the shady bowers of virtues she may be shielded from the fevers of the body and the passions of the flesh.

Therefore, paradise is in the higher part of our nature, luxuriant with the growths of many opinions, where God in the beginning put the tree of life, that is, the root of piety, for this is the very substance of our life, if we give due homage to our Lord and God.

He has planted in us, too, a nursery of the knowledge of good and evil, for man alone among other living creatures of earth has the knowledge of good and evil. There are also many other plants whose fruits are virtues.

Now, since God knew that man's affection, capable of grasping knowledge, would incline more quickly toward cunning than the perfection of wisdom (for the quality of His handiwork could not be hidden from the Judge who had set down definite boundaries in our souls), He wished to eliminate cunning from paradise and, as the provident Author of our salvation, to put therein the zest for life and for the practice of virtue. So He ordered man to eat of every tree in paradise, but not of the tree of the knowledge of good and evil.[8]

Since every creature, however, is subject to passion, lust stole into man's affections with the stealth of a serpent. Moses was quite right in representing pleasure in the likeness of a serpent: it is prone on its belly like a serpent, not walking on feet or raised on legs, but it glides along, so to speak, with the slippery folded curves of its whole body. Earth is its food, as it is the serpent's, for it has no comprehension of heavenly food. It feeds on things of the body and it is changed into many sorts of pleasures, and bends to and fro in twisting wreathes. It has venom in its fangs, and with these the dissolute individual is disemboweled, the

---

8 Cf. Gen. 3.2,3.

glutton destroys himself, the spendthrift is undone. How many men has wine wrecked, drunkenness destroyed, gluttony bloated?

Now I know why the Lord God breathed into the face of man.[9] There is the seat and abode and enticement of lust—in the eyes, the ears, the nostrils, the mouth—[breathed there] in order to fortify our senses against such lust. These things He infused into us as the serpent did cunning. For it is not pleasure, but labor and continuous meditation, along with the grace of God, which give perfect wisdom.

Yet, because the posterity of the human race is involved in the snares of the serpent, let us imitate the cunning in him so as not to run our head into danger, but guard it unharmed above all else, 'For our head is Christ.'[10] Let it remain unharmed so that the serpent's venom may not have power to harm us, for 'Wisdom with riches is good,'[11] that is, with faith, for those who believe in the Lord have riches.

But if the first man, who was placed in paradise and talked with God,[12] could fall so easily, though made from virgin clay, but lately formed at God's word and created, not yet clotted with the gore of homicide and slaughter, not polluted with shameful and unbecoming deeds, not yet condemned in our flesh to the curse of a tainted heredity—how much more easily later on has the slippery road to sin brought the human race to a greater precipice, since one generation in turn succeeds another, a generation more base succeeding one less wicked?

We see how a magnet has such natural force as to attract iron and communicate itself thereto, as some persons, desirous of experimenting, have applied iron rings to the magnet so

---

9 Cf. Gen. 2.7.
10 1 Cor. 11.3.
11 Eccle. 7.12.
12 Cf. Gen. 2.15.

that it holds all of them in the same way. Then, if to the ring to which the magnet clings they add another ring and so on in succession, although it penetrates each by its natural strength, it holds the first with a stronger, the last with a weaker grasp. How much truer it is that the condition and nature of the human race has fallen from a purer into a less pure state when it reaches the more wicked?

If the natural law is weakened in substances which are incapable of sin, how much more is its vigor dulled by souls and bodies tainted with evil! For, when evil had appeared and innocence been destroyed, there was no one to do good, not even one.[13] The Lord came to restore grace to nature, in fact, to give it increase, that where sin abounded grace might more abound.[14] It is clear, then, that God is the Author of man, and that there is one God, not many gods—One who made the world, and one world only, not many, as the philosophers maintain.

First, therefore, He created the world and then the inhabitants of the world for whom all the world was to be a fatherland. Even today, if, wherever the wise man goes, he is a citizen and knows his own, nowhere considering himself a mere pilgrim or a foreigner, how much more was that first man an inhabitant of all the world, and as the Greeks say, a 'cosmopolite,' for he was the final work of God, continually talking with God, a fellow citizen of the saints, a groundbed of virtues? Placed over all creatures of earth, sea, and sky, he considered the whole world his dominion; God guarded him as His handiwork, and as a good parent and maker never abandoned him. In fine, He so cherished this creature that He redeemed him when he had been lost, He received him back when he had been banished, and when he died He brought him back to life through the Passion of His

13 Cf. Ps. 13.11.
14 Cf. Rom. 5.20.

only-begotten Son. God, then, is man's Author, and as a good artisan He loves His own handiwork; as a kind father He does not abandon one He has redeemed, but like a good householder reinstates him in the riches of His own possessions.

Let us beware of having that man, our understanding, enervated by woman, that is, by passion, for she was deceived and beguiled by the pleasures of the senses. Let her not enslave and drag him over to her laws and purposes. Let us flee from sensual delight as from a serpent. It has many allurements, particularly in man. Other living things are wooed by the desire for food, but man, in so far as he has more varied senses of eyes and ears, has so much the greater dangers.

Farewell, and love us as you do, because we love you.

26. *Ambrose to Sabinus (c. 390)*

Since our practice of writing letters gives you pleasure, too, whereby those who are far apart indulge in conversation as though they were near, I shall continue often addressing my writings to you, even when I am alone.[1] For I am never less alone than when I appear to be alone, nor less at leisure than when I am at leisure. Then, at least, I summon at will those whom I will, and I bring to my side those whom I love more dearly or whom I think more suited to me. No one speaks, no one interrupts our talk. Then do I have you more and I talk about the Scriptures and we chat together at great length.

Mary was alone when she spoke with an angel.[2] She was alone when the Holy Spirit came to her and the power of

---
1 A familiar saying of Cato, found in Cicero, *Off.* 3.1.1.
2 Cf. Luke 1.28.

the Most High overshadowed her. She was alone and she worked the salvation of the world and conceived the redemption of all men. Peter was alone and learned the mysteries about the Gentiles who were to be sanctified throughout the world.³ Adam was alone and he was not an offender because his heart clung to God.⁴ But, after the woman was united to him, he was unable to cling to the commands of heaven and so he hid himself when God walked in paradise.

Now, when I read the sacred Scriptures, God walks in paradise.⁵ The Book of Genesis is a paradise where the virtues of the patriarchs blossom forth. Deuteronomy is a paradise where the commandments of the Law flourish. The Gospel is a paradise where the tree of life brings forth good fruits and pours upon all men the teachings of everlasting hope.

When I hear: 'Love your enemies' and 'Sell what you have and follow me'⁶ and 'To him who strikes thee on one cheek, offer the other also,'⁷ and I am not doing these things, and scarcely love one who loves me, and do not sell what I have, and wish to avenge a wrong which I have received, and to get back by force what has been taken from me—when Scripture says that I must give more than was asked of me or taken from me—I realize that I am acting contrary to the commands of God. And opening the eyes of conscience, I see that God is present, walking up to me. I want to hide, to cover myself, but I am naked before God before whom all things are naked and open.⁸ In shame I desire to cover up my sinful deeds like the limbs of my body, but because God sees everything and because I am shaded by leaves or hidden under cover, I think I am

---

3 Cf. Acts 10.9-16.
4 Cf. Gen. 2.8.
5 Cf. Gen. 3.8.
6 Matt. 5.44; 19.21.
7 Luke 6.29.
8 Cf. Heb. 4.13.

in hiding, just because I am covered with a body. It is just the same garment of skin which Adam had when he was cast out of paradise,[9] not protected from the cold, or saved from reproach, but exposed to harm and blame.

From these words it is clear that when we are alone we offer ourselves to God, then we lay open to Him our hearts, then we lay aside the cloak of deceit. Adam was alone when he was placed in paradise; he was alone, too, when he was made to the image of God, but he was not alone when he was cast out of paradise. The Lord Jesus was alone when He redeemed the world,[10] for no ambassador or messenger, but the Lord Himself alone, saved His people. Yet, He is never alone in whom the Father always dwells. So let us also be alone, that the Lord may be with us.

Farewell, and love us, because we love you.

27. *Ambrose to Sabinus (c. 389)*

The man whom you describe as a sower of slanderous speech is of very little consequence and has already received the reward of his venomous remarks. He has been answered in public and has reaped openly what he sowed secretly. I thought him a vain and envious person before, and when his remarks reached my ears I at once stated that he had been infected with the poison of Apollinaris, who cannot tolerate the doctrine that our Lord Jesus Christ became a servant for our sake in taking a body, although the Apostle declares that He took the nature of a servant.[1] This is the bulwark, this is the hedge, of our faith. One who destroys this will

---

9 Cf. Gen. 3.23.
10 Cf. John 16.32.

1 Cf. Phil. 2.7.

himself be destroyed, as it is written: 'For the serpent will gnaw him who breaketh a hedge.'²

At first I sent a mild dispatch to him, saying: 'Why do you perform a good act with evil purpose?' For I count it a blessing if anyone reads my writings and tells me what disturbs him, first of all, because I can be deceived in what I know, and many things escape the ear, many sound different to certain individuals. It is fine, if possible, to avoid such things. Then I must not be annoyed if things are found in my writing which many consider disputable, since many questions are asked about the words of the Apostles, in the Gospels, and the words of our Lord. Persons thus indulge their own humor, especially the man who encompassed the world to find someone to censure, not to imitate.

In order to cavil at something in my writings he found plenty of room for himself, for in that passage where the Lord Jesus said: 'I praise thee, Father, Lord of heaven and earth,'³ I stated that it was intended to show that God is the Father of the Son, and the Lord of creation. [This he criticized] although in the psalm the Son very plainly calls His Father 'Lord,' saying: 'Seeing me, they shake their head. Help me, O Lord, my God.'⁴ Speaking as a servant, He called Him Lord who He knew was His Father, being the equal of God in form, yet proclaiming Himself a slave in the substance of His flesh, for servitude belongs to the flesh, dominion to the Godhead.

With admirable wisdom you note that those things which are said in the Gospel have reference to the time of the Gospel when the Lord Jesus lived among men in human form. Now we no longer know Christ as man.⁵ He was

---
2 Eccle. 10.8.
3 Matt. 11.25.
4 Ps. 108.25,26.
5 Cf. 2 Cor. 5.16.

seen and known thus to men of former times, but 'now the former things have passed away, and all things are made new.'⁶ All things are from God who reconciled us to Himself through Christ, for we were dead, but one became a slave for all.⁷ What shall I say: [only] 'a slave'? He became sin, a reproach, a curse. The Apostle said: 'For our sakes he made him to be sin,'⁸ that the Lord Jesus 'was become a curse.'⁹ He said that when He has subjected all things to Himself, then He, too, will be subject. Peter, also, in the Acts of the Apostles, said: 'In the name of Jesus of Nazareth arise and walk.' He also said there that 'He glorified His Son Jesus,'¹⁰ and no one took issue with him in regard to the time. Moreover, in the Apocalypse, He is also called by John 'the Lamb.'¹¹ And He is called in the psalm 'a worm and no man.'¹² He became all these things so that He might dull the sting of our death, that He might take away our state of slavery, that He might wipe away our curses, sins, and reproaches.¹³

Since Scripture contains these and other divine things, and many more which you have brought up, and which you pointed out to one who made inquiry, how can anyone hesitate to say that these were piously written, since they are directed to the glory of Christ, not to His disparagement? If it was said of His gift, that is, the manna, that 'he did not find less that had provided less, neither had he more that had gathered more,'¹⁴ could He Himself be either diminished or increased? For, what in Him was diminished when He took

---

6 2 Cor. 5.17.
7 Cf. Phil. 2.7.
8 2 Cor. 5.21.
9 Gal. 3.13.
10 Acts 3.6,13.
11 Apoc. 5.12.
12 Ps. 21.7.
13 Cf. 1 Cor. 15.55.
14 Exod. 16.18.

upon Himself our servitude, our weakness? He was humbled, indeed, by being in the form of a slave, but He remained unchanged in the glory of God the Father. He was a worm on the cross, but He forgave the sins even of His persecutors. He was a reproach but at the same time also the Majesty of the Lord, as it is written: 'And the glory of the Lord shall be revealed: and all flesh together shall see the salvation of God.'[15] What had He lost if He had nothing less? He had neither comeliness nor beauty, but He had the fullness of divinity. He was considered weak, but He had not ceased to be the power of God. He appeared a man, but the divine majesty and glory of the Father shone on earth.

Very aptly, then, the Apostle repeats the same expression, saying of the Lord Jesus: 'who though he was by nature God, did not think being equal to God a thing to be clung to, but emptied himself, taking the nature of a slave.'[16] What is the meaning of 'by nature God' except the fullness of the Godhead, the expression of His divine perfection? Although He was in the fullness of the Godhead, He emptied Himself and received the fullness of nature and human perfection. Just as He lacked nothing as God, so He did not lack anything for His completeness as man, and as a result He was perfect in each nature. Thus, David says He was 'beautiful above the sons of men.'[17]

The Apollinarist is refuted; he has nowhere to turn; he is caught in his own nets. He Himself said: He took the nature of a slave, He was not a slave. Again, I ask, what is the meaning of 'by nature God'? He answers: 'in the reality of God.'[18] 'There are,' says the Apostle, 'those who are not

---
15 Isa. 40.5.
16 Phil. 2.6,7.
17 Ps. 44.3.
18 Phil. 2.7.

gods in reality.' I ask you what is the meaning of 'taking the nature of a slave'? Without doubt, it means the perfection of nature and the human condition, in order that He might be in the likeness of men. And well did he say: 'the likeness' not of the flesh but 'of men,' because He was in the same flesh. But, because He alone was without sin, whereas all men are in sin, He was seen in the appearance of man. So the Prophet says too: 'He is a man and who can know it?'[19]— a man, indeed, according to the flesh; more than man according to the divine operation. When He touched a leper,[20] He seemed a man, but more than man when He cleansed him. And when He wept for Lazarus who had died He wept as a man, but He was superior to man when He bade the dead to come forth with feet bound.[21] He seemed a man when He hung on the cross, but more than man when He unsealed the tombs and brought the dead to life.[22]

Let not the venom of Apollinaris flatter itself because it is written: 'And in appearance he was found as a man,'[23] for the manhood of Jesus is not thereby denied, but confirmed, since elsewhere Paul himself says of Him: 'Mediator of God and men, himself man, Christ Jesus.'[24] It is the customary manner of Scripture so to express itself as we also read in the Gospel: 'And we saw his glory—glory as of the only-begotten of the Father.'[25] As He is there called only-begotten and it is not denied that He is the only-begotten Son of God, so He is said to be man, and the perfection of man that was in Him is not denied.

Since, therefore, He was in the likeness of a servant, He was humbled even unto death, yet He remained in the glory

---

19 Jer. 17.9.
20 Cf. Matt. 8.3.
21 Cf. John 11.33.34.
22 Cf. Matt. 27.52.
23 Phil. 2.7.
24 1 Tim. 2.5.
25 John 1.14.

of God. In what way was His slavery prejudicial to Him? We read that He became a slave because we read that He was made of a virgin and created in the flesh. Now, every creature is a servant, as the Prophet says: 'For all things serve thee.'[26] Therefore, God the Father also says: 'I have found David, my servant: with my holy oil I have anointed him, He shall cry unto me: "Thou art my Father, the God of my salvation." And I will make him my firstborn.'[27] And in another psalm: 'Preserve my soul, because I am holy to thee; save thy servant,' and further on in the same psalm: 'Give thy strength to thy servant, and save the son of thy handmaid.'[28] I have gathered together the words of the Father and of the Son that this man receive a reply, not from human arguments, but from the words of God.

Elsewhere, He says: 'Into thy hands I commend my spirit,' and 'Thou hast set my feet in a spacious place,' and 'I have become a reproach for all my enemies,' and in the same psalm: 'Make thy face to shine upon thy servant.'[29] And through Isaias, too, the Son of God Himself says: 'From the womb of my mother the Lord hath called my name. And he hath made my mouth like a sharp sword. In the cover of his hand he hath protected me. He hath made me like a chosen arrow, and in his quiver he hath covered me. And he said to me: "Thou art my servant, Israel." '[30] The Son of God is also called Israel, as [we read] elsewhere: 'O Jacob, my servant, Israel my beloved.'[31] He alone not only truly saw God the Father, but has also revealed Him.[32]

And there follows: 'In thee I shall be glorified. And I said: I have worked in vain, I have spent my strength

---

26 Ps. 118.91.
27 Ps. 118.21,27,28.
28 Ps. 85.2,16.
29 Ps. 30.6,9,12,17.
30 Isa. 49.1-3.
31 Isa. 44.1.
32 Cf. John 1.18.

without cause. Therefore my judgment is with the Lord and my sorrow before God.' And now speaks the Lord 'that formed me from the womb to be his servant that I may bring back Jacob unto him [and Israel will not be gathered together].' Who but Christ has gathered together the people of God? Who has been glorified before the Lord? Who is the Power of God? To whom did the Father say: 'Is it a great thing for you to be called my servant?' And to whom does He say: 'Behold I have given thee to be the covenant of my generation, the light of the gentiles, and thou mayst be my salvation even to the farthermost parts of the earth'?[33] Of Him He speaks also through the mouth of Ezechiel, saying: 'And I will set up one shepherd over them, and my servant David will rule them, and he will be their shepherd: And I the Lord will be their God: and my servant David the prince in the midst of them.'[34] Of course, David the king was already dead, but the true David, the truly humble one, the truly meek, the true Son of God, strong of hand, is foretold by this name. He also is pointed out in the book of the Prophet Zacharias, God the Father saying: 'I will bring my servant, the Orient is his name.'[35] Although He wore sin-soiled garments, was not the Sun of Justice clothed with the splendor of His divinity?

What more can I say? Shall we consider servitude a state of greater weakness than sin or than a curse or a reproach—more degraded than the infirmities which He took for our sake in order to turn them from us? He became all things so that He might annul them all. But they [our enemies] will not admit that He was made a slave, a reproach, sin, a curse, because they affirm that the Word and Flesh are of one substance, and they say: 'Because He redeemed us He

---
33 Isa. 49.4-6.
34 Ezech. 34.23,24.
35 Zach. 3.8.

is called a servant, and ought to be called sin.' And they do not advert to the fact that this is the glory of Christ, that He took the state of slavery in His body, to restore liberty to us all; He bore our sins that He might take away the sins of the world.

He became a slave, sin, a curse that you might cease to be a slave of sin, and to free you from the curse of the divine judgment. He therefore took upon Him your curse, for 'Cursed is everyone who hangs on a gibbet.'[36] He became a curse on the cross so that you might be blessed in the kingdom of God. He was dishonored and disregarded and esteemed of no worth. He kept saying: 'I have labored in vain.'[37] Through Him Paul merited to say: 'Not in vain have I labored,'[38] so that he might bring to His servants the first fruits of good works and the glory of preaching the Gospel, by which all men are freed from the burden of toil.

After hearing these words, the partridge is abandoned in the midst of its days, the partridge which claimed to have hatched eggs which she did not lay,[39] and has been overwhelmed by the voice of the Lord Jesus. At last, she is making preparation to flee.

Farewell, and love us, because we love you.

---
36 Gal. 3.13.
37 Isa. 49.4.
38 Phil. 2.16.
39 Cf. Jer. 17.11.

28. Ambrose to Sabinus, bishop (c. 395)

I have learned that Paulinus, second to none of the Aquitanians in luster of birth, has sold his and his wife's possessions, and has taken up these practices of faith that he is giving his property to the poor by changing it into money, while he, poor now instead of rich, as if relieved of a heavy burden, has said farewell to home, country, and kindred in order to serve God with greater zeal. Word has it that he has chosen a retreat in the city of Nola where he will pass his days out of reach of the tumult of the world.

His wife,[1] too, closely followed the example of his zeal and virtue, not objecting to her husband's resolve. She has transferred her property to the jurisdiction of others and is following her husband, where, perfectly content with his little patch of ground, she will comfort herself with the riches of religion and charity. They have no children,[2] but their desire is a posterity of good deeds.

What will our leading citizens say when they hear this? It is unthinkable that a man of such family, such background, such genius, gifted with such eloquence, should retire from the Senate and that the succession of so noble a family should be broken. Although in performing the rites of Isis they shave their heads and eyebrows, they yet call it a shameful thing for a Christian out of devotion to his holy religion to change his apparel.

I regret that falsehood is so respected while truth is so neglected, that, as a result, many persons are ashamed to appear devoted to their holy religion, not considering the voice of the One who says: 'Whoever is ashamed of me before men, of him will I be ashamed before my Father who is in heaven.'[3] Moses was not ashamed, and when he was

---
1 The saintly Therasia.
2 A child, born in Spain, died after eight days.
3 Matt. 10.32.

summoned to the palace he preferred to be reproached as one of Christ's own ráther than to have the treasures of the Egyptians.⁴ David was not ashamed when he danced before the Ark of the Covenant in the presence of all the people.⁵ Isaias was not ashamed, for he went naked and barefoot through the crowd, proclaiming heavenly prophecies.

As a matter of fact, what is actually so embarrassing as the gestures of actors and the twining of their limbs in womanly fashion? Lewd dancing is the companion of wantonness and the pastime of riotous living. What did he [David] mean by singing: 'Clap your hands, all ye people'?⁶ Obviously, if we consider his bodily actions, we realize that he clapped his hands, dancing with women and stamping with unbecoming sounds. Of Ezechiel, too, it was said: 'Strike with the hand and stamp with the foot.'⁷

Yet, these actions of the body, though unseemly when viewed in themselves, become reverential under the aspect of holy religion, so that those who censure them drag their own souls into the net of censure. Thus, Michol censured David for dancing and said: 'How glorious was the king of Israel today, for he uncovered himself today before the eyes of his handmaids.' And David answered her: 'I will play before the Lord who chose me rather than my father, and than all his house, and commanded me to be ruler over his people of Israel. And I will play before the Lord and I will thus be uncovered and I will be mean in thy eyes, and with the handmaids, to whom you said I was uncovered, I shall be honored.'⁸

David did not blush at a woman's censure, nor was he ashamed to meet with reproach, becauses of his devotion to

---

4 Cf. Heb. 11.26.
5 Cf. 2 Kings 6.20.
6 Ps. 46.2.
7 Ezech. 6.11.
8 2 Kings 6.20-22.

religion. He played before the Lord as His servant and pleased Him the more in so humbling himself before God and laying aside his royal dignity, performing the humblest tasks for God like a servant. She who censured such dancing was condemned to barrenness and had no children by the king lest she should beget the proud. In truth, she had no continuance of posterity nor of good deeds.

Let one who still doubts hear the testimony of the Gospel, for the Son of God said: 'We have played for you, and you have not danced.'[9] The Jews who did not dance and knew not how to clap their hands were abandoned, but the Gentiles were called and applauded God in spirit. 'The fool foldeth his hands together, and eateth his own flesh,'[10] that is, he becomes involved in the concerns of the body and eats his own flesh, just as does all-powerful death. And such a man will not find eternal life. But the wise man who lifts up his works that they may shine before his Father who is in heaven[11] has not consumed his flesh; instead, he has raised it to the grace of the resurrection. This is the wise man's honorable dance which David danced, mounting by the loftiness of his spiritual dance to the throne of Christ that he may see and hear the Lord saying to His Lord: 'Sit thou at my right hand.'[12]

If you think we are not foolish in using this interpretation of the dance, do not spare yourself the trouble of reading further, that you may review with me the well-known case of Isaias, how he was naked before the people, not in mockery but gloriously, as one who uttered with his mouth the words of the Lord.

Someone perhaps will say: 'Was it not disgraceful for a

---

9 Matt. 11.17.
10 Eccle. 4.5.
11 Cf. Matt. 5.16.
12 Ps. 109.1.

man to walk naked among the people since he must meet both men and women? Must not his appearance have shocked the gaze of all, but especially that of women? Do we not ourselves generally abhor the sight of naked men? And are not men's genital parts covered with clothing that they may not offend the gaze of onlookers by their unsightliness?'

I agree, but you must consider what this act represented and what was the reason for this outward show; it was that the young Jewish youths and maidens would be led away into exile and walk naked, 'As my servant Isaias hath walked,' he says, 'naked and barefoot.'[13] This might have been expressed in words, but God chose to enforce it by an example that the very sight might strike more terror, and what they shrank from in the body of the Prophet they might utterly dread for themselves. Wherein lay the greater abhorrence: in the body of the Prophet or in the sins of the disbelievers who deserved by their deeds that calamity of captivity?

Why was there no ground for reproach in the body of the Prophet? He was intent not upon bodily but spiritual affairs, for in his ecstacy he did not say: 'I shall listen to what I say' but 'what God will say to me.'[14] He paid no attention to whether he was naked or clothed. Adam was naked before his sin,[15] but he did not know that he was naked, for he was clothed with virtues, but after he committed sin he knew that he was naked and covered himself. Noe was naked,[16] but he was not ashamed, for he was filled with joy and spiritual gladness, while the one who mocked him for being naked remained exposed to the reproach of everlasting disgrace. Joseph, too, that he might not be shamefully stripped bare, left his cloak and fled naked. Which of them was

---
13 Isa. 22.3.
14 Ps. 84.9.
15 Cf. Gen. 2.25.
16 Cf. Gen. 9.21.

dishonored here, she who held another's garment or he who threw off his own?

That it may be more fully clear that Prophets look not to themselves, nor what lies at their feet, but to heavenly things, Stephen, when he was being stoned, saw the heavens open and Jesus standing at the right hand of God;[17] then he did not feel the blows of the stones, he did not heed the wounds of his body, but, fastening his eyes on Christ, he clung to Him. So, too, Isaias did not notice his nakedness, but made himself the instrument of God's voice,[18] that he might proclaim what God spoke within him.

Suppose he did see himself, was it possible for him not to do what he was bidden? Could he believe that God ordered a shameful act? Sara was accused of disbelief for laughing,[19] but Abraham was praised for not doubting God's word, and he was given a great reward for believing at God's bidding that he could devoutly become his son's slayer.[20]

Why should the Prophet feel shame when one thing is being enacted, but another prefigured? The Jews, who were abandoned by the Lord God because of their wickedness and were soon overwhelmed by their enemies, would have liked to align themselves with the Egyptians as a protection against the Assyrians, whereas they might have returned to the faith had they consulted their own good. The Lord in anger showed them that they indulged a vain hope of lessening one outrage against the Lord with a greater sin, for the very persons whose help the Jews trusted were themselves to be conquered. This is a matter of history.

Figuratively, he trusted the Egyptians, he who was given

---

17 Cf. Acts 7.55.
18 Cf. Isa. 22.2.
19 Cf. Gen. 18.12.
20 Cf. Gen. 22.1-19.

to wantonness and enslaved to pleasure. No man becomes engrossed in excess unless he departs from the commands of the true God. As soon as he begins to take pleasure in luxury, he begins wandering from the true faith. Then he commits two grevious crimes: an outrage of the body and profanation of the mind. One who does not follow the Lord his God is engulfed in extravagance and pleasure, those death-dealing passions of the body. One who is absorbed and plunged into this sort of mire falls into the meshes of evil, for 'The people sat down to eat, and drink,'[21] and then demanded that gods be made for them. In this the Lord teaches us that the person who gives his soul to these two kinds of vices is stripped of his clothing, not of a woolen garment, but of living virtue, a cloak not of time but of eternity.

Farewell, and love us, because we love you.

29. Ambrose to Severus, bishop (c. 392)

James, our brother and fellow priest, has come from distant Persia and chosen to find rest for himself in your fair countryside on the coast of Campania. Notice in what spot he hopes to enjoy a haven, as it were, from the storms of this world, where, after long toils, he may spend the remainder of his life.

That shore of yours, far removed from dangers and every disturbance, fills one's emotions with peace and draws the mind from frightening and raging seas of trouble to a beautiful repose, so that the words that David said of the Church and which apply to all in common appear to be especially suited and applicable to you: 'He has founded it upon the seas, and

---

21 Exod. 32.6.

has made it firm upon the waters.'¹ The mind that is free of onslaughts of barbarians and the bitterness of war has time for prayer, is devoted to the service of God, cares for the things of the Lord, and cherishes the interests of peace and tranquility.

However, we who are exposed to the outbreaks of barbarians and the storms of war, are tossed in the midst of a sea of many troubles and can only infer from these labors and trials more grievous trials in the future. The saying of the Prophet seems to be in accord with our condition: 'I saw the tents of the Ethiopians for their labors.'²

Having now lived fifty-three years in the body, amid the shadows of this world which obscure the reality of the future perfection, and having already endured such heavy sorrows, am I not encamping in the tents of the Ethiopians and dwelling with the inhabitants of Madian?³ They, owing to their knowledge of the works of darkness, fear to be judged even by mortal men,⁴ 'For the spiritual man judges all things, and he himself is judged by no man.'⁵

Farewell, brother, and love us as you do, for we love you.

---

1 Ps. 23.2.
2 Hab. 3.7.
3 The troubled events he mentions are thought to refer to a barbarian outbreak which greatly terrified the people of Milan in 392. This event and the reference to his fifty-three years help to date Ambrose's birth in 339. Cf. Dudden, *op. cit.* 2. McGuire (*op. cit.* 312) does not accept this date as determined by Palanque.
4 Cf. Ps. 119.5.
5 1 Cor. 2.15.

30. Ambrose to Siricius[1]

I am always pleased to receive a letter from you. But when you delegate those of our fellow servants and entrust letters to our brother and fellow priest Syrus, my joy is redoubled. Would that the pleasure had been longer-lasting! As soon as he came he decided he must return. This then made my regret less and increased my esteem for him.

I dearly love those priests and deacons who, once they have finished a duty, do not allow themselves to remain away any longer. As the Prophet says: 'I am not weary, following thee.'[2] Who can be weary following Jesus, for He Himself says: 'Come to me, all you who labor and are burdened, and I will give you rest.'[3] Let us, then, always follow Jesus and never falter, for if we follow Him we never fail, because He gives His strength to His followers. The nearer you are to this strength, the stronger you will be.

Sometimes, while we follow Him, our adversaries say to us: 'Where is the word of the Lord? Let it come.'[4] Let us not grow weary of following Him and let us not be turned aside by meeting with a crafty question. It was said to the Prophet when he was being sent to prison and cast into a pit of mire: 'Where is the word of the Lord? Let it come.' But he followed it the more and therefore reached the goal and received the crown, because he was not weary following Jesus: 'There is no weariness in Jacob nor will sorrow be seen in Israel.'[5]

Farewell, and love us, for we love as a parent one who loves us.

---
1 Undated; this may be Pope Siricius, to whom the joint letter of several bishops was directed after the Synod of Milan.
2 Jer. 17.16.
3 Matt. 11.28.
4 Jer. 17.15.
5 Num. 23.21 (Septuagint).

31. Ambrose to Siricius[1]

When Priscus came—he who is my friend and of the same age as I am—you gave him a letter for me. Now that he is returning, I am also replying as I should for duty's and love's sake. By this service he has enriched us both, bringing me your letter and you mine. May the recompense of this be the attainment of an increase of grace.

Farewell, brother, and love us, because we love you.

32. Ambrose to Syagrius[1]

You have intimated in your letter our need to be careful that the beloved people of Verona do not dispute our decision. I do not think that they will do so; such, certainly, is not their custom. There is no shred of doubt that, if they do dispute, it will be of an ordinary matter. If they are provoked to come here, let them return to you with their grievances settled, especially since we have reached our decision jointly with our brethren and fellow priests. People know that you had to make your judgment without the helping advice of any brother. Yet you made your decision before the trial with the result that a virgin, who had been highly esteemed

---
1 Undated.

1 Written to the Bishop of Verona regarding the case of a virgin Indicia, who was brought to trial at the instigation of Maximus, her brother-in-law, at whose home she lived a retired life, and subjected to an examination by a midwife in order to establish her innocence. For a complete study of the case, cf. F. Martroye, 'L'Affaire *Indicia*: une sentence de saint Ambroise,' *Mélanges Paul Fournier* (Paris 1929) 503-510. The firm attitude which Ambrose assumes in this case leads Palanque and others to date it later than 380, the traditional date. Mention of Nicensis, the tribune and notary who testified to a miracle of restored health by Ambrose (*Vit.* 9.44), also leads to the assigning of this letter toward Ambrose's closing years.

by blessed Zeno and consecrated by his blessing, was many years later subjected to the danger of imprisonment, although she knew neither the author of the charge, nor the accuser, nor the avowed informer. Envy was stirred up against her by liars and heretics, as they choose, by degraded individuals seeking, because of their wickedness, avarice, and intemperance, a liberty for their own wantonness, and, finally, by those who had been cast out and debarred from her home, who by their works of a different color concealed the pretense of their first appearance.

You set up in your court accusers of the same sort and witnesses who did not dare make a charge or bind themselves with the informer's role. So you decided to judge the virgin by an examination, a virgin whom no one censured, no one brought to trial. Where is the formality of inquiry, where is there provision for such a trial? If we consult the state laws, they demand an accuser; if the Church laws, we find: 'On the word of two or three witnesses every word stands.'[2] Take as witnesses those who were not enemies two or three days ago, so that men in anger may not desire to harm the accused or, being harmed themselves, wish for vengeance.

The disposition of the witnesses needs to be unhampered, yet in such a way that the accuser may first come into the midst of the case. Those priests of the Jews[3] first put their hands on the head of Susanna and pronounced the accusation, adding at the same time the weight of proof which the people unwisely accepted, for they had been led into error. But by a divine judgment through the Prophet, almighty God laid bare the true state of affairs and showed that the testimony was false. As a result, it became clear to all that those who failed to prove the accusation and to establish

---
2 Matt. 18.16.
3 Cf. Dan. 13.34-60.

the proof wished to sow envy to the peril of the innocent, confident that, if ill-will assaulted the mind of the crowd, whose ears were filled beforehand, prejudice might enter into the examination of the truth. For, when unfounded rumor enters, it blocks the ears, seizes the mind, and, if proof be wanting, rumor is accepted in place of the real charge.

For these reasons we examined into the accuser and determined that the instigator of the whole scene, Maximus, should get our full attention. But in his statement he abandoned the charge which he had formed with eagerness and had brought forward by word. However, he kept pressing with effect and followed up his demands with skilled eloquence. At the same time he kept running away from his responsibility, for he lacked the substance of proof, knowing that he was at fault. Finally, after spreading rumors and even composing and sending letters, he sought to aggravate the ill-will toward the charge, but integrity was not to be oppressed and tricked. For, had the judgment had proof, an inspection would never have been demanded.

I cannot imagine what he wants and how he will make the test while you believe that you must have recourse to the service of a midwife. Will it then become permissible to accuse all persons, and, when the accusations are without proof, will it be allowable to demand an inspection of the private parts, and will holy virgins always be handed over to sport of this sort, which is horribly shocking to the eye and ear? Even in your letter you attempt the utmost delicacy of expression. Can those matters which cannot sound in another's ears without loss of shame be tried in a virgin without embarrassment?

You have located a cheap slave, a shameless home-born slave. How may you not misuse her shameless services and prostitute the other's modesty, especially since there is nothing more holy in a maiden than her sense of modesty?

Does one not seek out a holy maiden, provided only that her modesty remains uninjured? The virgin of the Lord is weighed on her own scales in giving proof of herself and needs no borrowed dowry to prove herself a virgin. And no inspection of hidden and secret parts, but modesty, evident to all, gives proof of her integrity. She does not please God unless the soberness of her manner sets approval upon her. She is not approved by the Lord if she needs the testimony of a midwife, which is usually secured at a price. Does she appear to you to abound in fidelity if she can be bought and deceived, so that she excuses the guilty, covers up crime, or does not know and cannot detect disgrace?

Nor do I consider that statement of your letter a just one, namely, that unless she is inspected her integrity is imperiled and she will be disquieted by uncertainty regarding herself. Have all those who were not inspected put peril in the path of their modesty? Are those about to marry to be inspected beforehand so that they may marry with greater approval? Are those about to take the veil to be first subjected to a handling of this sort? For they are not visited but handled, and according to your opinion one unapproved is more lawfully inspected than a consecrated person.

What of the fact that medical experts say that the trustworthiness of an inspection is not clearly understood and this has been the opinion of older doctors of medicine? We know from former experience that between midwives a difference arises and a question is raised with the result that there is more doubt regarding the one who has given herself over to an inspection than of one who has not. In fact, we found this to be so in a recent case when a slave girl from Altinum, having been inspected and charged with wrong, later at Milan—not by my command but by that of Nicensis, a tribune and a notary—at the wish of her master and patron, was visited by one of the most skillful and wealthy women of this profession. And although these qualifications were found in her, so that neither the midwife's poverty made her trustworthiness suspect nor lack of training made her ignorant, a question still remains.

What advantage was it for her to be inspected when she still is under a cloud of disapproval? For, as each person wished, he asserted that the woman physician was either ignorant or had been bribed. Thus, the harm of undergoing inspection is without effect. What will be done next? Shall a girl be examined as often as someone appears who does not trust her? If she ever refuses to be visited, she will, according to your assertion, confess her crime. And it is easier to refute what one never did than what one did. The midwives will be at odds, fearing that some favor once granted will not be granted again. She will be only one of several, although even in large cities this practice of doctoring is found among few women. She will, I say, be either bad-willed or unskilled, whom the barriers of modesty leave unpracticed and through lack of skill she will put a mark on unblemished modesty. You see into what danger you bring a maiden's profession when you decide to have recourse to a midwife, so that now she is not only imperiled by the loss of her sense of modesty but also by the uncertainty of the midwife.

Let us now consider just what is the duty of a midwife, for we read of midwives even in the Old Testament, but not of inspectresses. They came to women in labor, not to virgins; they came to receive the child, not to put modesty to the test. They are called midwives that they may stand midway in pain, or at least that the child may not fall to the ground when the walls of the uterus are relaxed. In a second and a third place in Scripture we find midwives on hand, always for a birth, not for an inspection—first of all, when Rachel was in labor,[4] then when Thomar was giving

---

[4] Cf. Gen. 35.16.

birth,⁵ and third when Pharao ordered the killing of all the male Hebrews by the midwives,⁶ the time when they answered that the Hebrew women did not give birth in the manner of the Egyptians but were delivered before the midwives reached them. The reason mentioned above proved advantageous for the salvation of the Hebrews; for others it proved damaging to their reliance on midwives who knew how to lie for their own safety and to deceive for an excuse.

Why should we take suspect and doubtful measures when there are greater documents and proofs for testing the truth, where the marks are clearer that modesty has been violated? What is more public than harm done to modesty and the deflowering of virginity? Surely, nothing so proclaims itself as does the loss of chastity. The belly swells, the burden of the fetus makes the person's gait heavy—to omit other signs through which it is betrayed although the knowledge is kept secret.

Perhaps, on a pretext of sterility, some can cover up vice, but when the child is delivered and disposed of or slain (when ill-will rather than proof suggests this), and when this is circulated in the ears of all, if one has given birth, freedom from calumny is absolutely impossible. The virgin of whom we are speaking was, to be sure, at Verona; she had frequent visits from girls and women; she was always held in honor. Priests visited her because of her modesty, a mirror of dignity. How, then, could she have concealed a crime which would reveal itself by her appearance? How did she cover herself? How has she not tried to flee the gaze of women, the eyes of all who greeted her? How, when in labor, did she check her cries? The pain does not permit this, for even Scripture says that those pains which a woman has

---

5 Cf. Gen. 38.27.
6 Cf. Exod. 1.15-22.

in labor are very great.⁷ The day of the Lord comes suddenly, it says, and in an unexpected way like the pains of childbirth, which forestall all one's efforts to hide them.⁸

Evidence of these signs, which even women feel ashamed of, are of greater reliability. In fact, Elizabeth secluded herself for five months because, having been barren, she had conceived in her old age.⁹ By these signs the very virginity of Mary was under suspicion to those ignorant of the mystery. And even Joseph, to whom the Virgin was espoused, held the signs in suspicion while he still did not know the mystery of the Lord taking flesh.¹⁰

Why, then, do we maintain that virgins should not be inspected? I do not consent to what I have never read; surely, I cannot believe it true. Yet, because we do many things for appearance's sake and not for the sake of truth, and through error we frequently make many assertions (for there are many persons who do not know how to act rightly except through fear of punishment), let us leave this task to those whom shame does not deter but fear of harm alone keeps from evil, those in whom there is no regard for modesty, no charm of chastity, but only fear of penalty. Let us leave this to slaves whose fear is to be caught rather than to have sinned. Far be it that a holy virgin should make the acquaintance of a midwife, for then there comes to mind not an examination of modesty but delivery and the seeking of a remedy for pain. Let us leave this to those who have recourse to it when they have been pursued with insults, overwhelmed by witnesses, choked by arguments—let them then present themselves for inspection when they are maintaining custody of their body, provided this can be detected in those in whom the charm of modesty and training in

---

7 Cf. Gen. 3.16.
8 Cf. Isa. 13.8,9.
9 Cf. Luke 1.24.
10 Cf. Matt. 1.18.

chastity is faltering. The case is going badly when the body has to be consulted for stronger proof than the mind. I prefer virginity made manifest by works of character rather than in the body's enclosure.

Now, it is strange your writing that this was revealed to you by certain persons who never talked with you, and your believing that she should be under suspicion unless she has been visited [by a midwife]. You have seized upon a formula for coming to a decision, but what sort of persons are they who try to tell us priests what to do? But we have freed you from need of making a most serious decision, so that you do not have to follow up the prescribed formula. What difference will it be for us if we have not obeyed their wishes?

I know that there are several persons there who are god-fearing. At times we have observed and learned that there are some who regret this calumny having been devised. Although they are very hostile, they still have not favored Maximus, because the virgin in question does not visit their homes or salute or solicit their women. What will happen? How shall we free her of this charge? It becomes a serious crime for a maiden to be within the secrecy of her own home, to be shut in her own chamber! Yet the passage in Scripture reveals that Mary was found at home like this when the archangel Gabriel came to her.[11] Susanna withdrew inside to escape the crowd.[12] And when she bathed she had the orchard closed. What is more excellent (especially in a maiden whose private parts demand modesty) than this retirement? What is safer than retirement and what is more liberating to all one's actions? Such a maiden assumes the tasks of modesty, not of anxiety. I have discussed the cases of others; I must now answer your letter.

I am surprised, my brother, that you were not the accuser,

---
11 Cf. Luke 1.28.
12 Cf. Dan. 13.7.

for it is you who are making a great defense of Maximus. Yet, you have grieved with a parent's sorrow over the ill-will which has arisen from the rumor that spread abroad when that fellow was unable to deny that he was a hostile and opposing party to the lawsuit and, after the strife was already aroused, obtained charges against the holy virgin. Then, after he had built a wall and made separate entrances for his wife and the virgin, the association between blood sisters was rent, and in other ways, too, the girl had cause to regret that she had asked to live with her relatives in the country. How is that person not the accuser, who has already shown the feelings of an accuser, who has by his statement introduced the accusation, has filled your ears with cries, and having brought in persons[13] who bear witness to the crime, now demands an investigation.

You argued you could not deny that you had written to Indicia, for Maximus, on the advice of others or through personal grievances, had made a very serious charge. This letter alone is proof enough of the charge. Yet I have thought I should not press you regarding the letter you sent to me, although I have noticed that the one you gave the girl was different from that which you wrote to me. And since your letters were not consistent, I decided to consult you, not blame you. What gain could the testimony expect from the fact that it differed from what you wrote to me, namely, that she had been charged with a heinous crime? Is it to imply that a child was said to have been delivered and buried? Almost as though you would write this to Indicia and not to me! When she heard in your letter that Maximus was being introduced for the accusation, she produced your letter in which she proved that he was the instigator of the

---

13 *testes auditiones*: witnesses from hearsay, not eye-witnesses.

charge. She had not read those given to me nor did she know what they contained.

I have been horrified from the first at the calumny, for I realized that no verdict was intended, but that they wanted harm done to a girl, demanding the inspection and visitation of a maiden and not removing a charge of any sort. Who would not realize that a case fraudulently framed from the first was to remain inconsistent and not in conformity with itself? Cheap women went to the monastery, and it reached the ears of a new neighbor, Maximus. He informed the bishop; those who were said to have maintained this were gone and had been forced to flight, as was patent to us. Those who said that they had heard the rumor were called to the church, whereupon they betrayed Renatus and Leontius,[14] those two men of iniquity whom Jezabel opposed,[15] Daniel convicted,[16] and the Jewish people suborned, so that by false testimony they assailed the very author of their life. Yet, at the same time as they devised the crime and set out (to omit no details) according to Leontius, they had joined Maximus and those others who spread the rumor. Yet, when they stood in my court and I questioned them on the history of the case from the beginning, they related different discordant details, being divided not by space but by falsehood.

Then, when they did not agree with one another and had removed Mercurius and Lea, persons of the cheapest sort and of detestable character, and she had fled to Teudule, not knowing the charge thrown at her—how before she had been alone on the couch of Renatus—another slave also

---

14 The two who originated the charge which Maximus brought to Bishop Syagrius.
15 Cf. 3 Kings 21.10.
16 Cf. Dan. 13.45-61.

appeared to say that she was tainted with lewdness with this same Renatus. On the very day set for the investigation they went to the bishop's court although on the day previous this same Renatus had suddenly asserted that they would leave.

For these reasons I set a day for the trial, but when no one made an accusation and no witness came forward, I intimated to my holy sister that you were asking the inspection and visitation of the aforementioned virgin in her presence. She piously objected to the inspection and said in defense of the virgin that she had observed in Indicia nothing except a maidenly modesty and holiness. She had lived at Rome in our house when I was not there, she had been given to no frequenting of sinfulness, and she hoped that with her a share in the kingdom of God was being saved for her by the Lord Jesus.

I also mentioned our daughter Paterna, for she never leaves her, her love being proof of her life. What she says without oath must be compared to a pledge of faith. Calling God to witness, she maintained that the virgin was a stranger to the crime for which she was being sought out, nor did anything in her conduct show that she was failing to live a good life.

We also questioned a free-born nurse, whose status, in no way harmed or degenerate, would permit the liberty of speaking the truth, and whose faith and age were a guarantee to the truth, while her capacity as a nurse implied knowledge of what is secret. She also said that she had seen nothing unbecoming in the maiden, no action seemed reprehensible to her, even had she been her parent.

Moved by these considerations, we declared that Indicia had never failed in her duties as a virgin. The sentence so involved Maximus and Renatus and Leontius that hope of their return [to the sacraments] was held out only for

Maximus if he corrected his error; and Renatus and Leontius remained excommunicated unless, perhaps, proving their remorse and daily deploring their deed, they showed themselves worthy of mercy.[17]

Farewell, brother, and love us, because we love you.

33. *Ambrose to Syagrius (c. 380)*

After you found out what transpired in our court, you kept to yourself; therefore, I now summon, as it were, a part of my own soul, for I have a friendly yet sorrowful complaint against you for the outrage done to chastity. Was it necessary for an unsurpassed, unheard-of case of virginity to be subjected to a sentence? Could it not have been dismissed? In other words, unless with injury to herself she had been handed over from honored modesty to an indecent surrender of her body, though she offered strong proof regarding herself, she would be exposed to ridicule and marked out as a wanton individual! You have tendered this privilege to virginity, honor of a sort, to which they are pleased to be summoned and invited who plan to recover this boon! Thus, they lose the liberty of a common reputation, nor do they protect themselves by the statutes of sacred or public law; they may not ask their accuser, or oppose an informer, but may only put on shamelessness and expose themselves to harm.

Our ancestors did not think chastity so to be despised; rather, they showed it such reverence that they would wage war on violators of modesty. In fact, so great was their desire for revenge that all the tribe of Benjamin would

---

[17] Roman law punished calumny with exile or banishment. Ambrose administered a spiritual penalty—excommunication.

have been destroyed[1] unless the 600 who remained out of the war had been protected by a natural hill. This is the expression found in the account of the sacred lesson whose tenor it is profitable to consider.

A Levite,[2] more courageous than wealthy, lived in the region of Mount Ephrem, for to this tribe was allotted a landed possession far removed, in place of the right of inheritance. He took a wife for himself from the tribe of Bethlehem of Juda. And as they felt deeply the first attraction of their love, he burned with unbounded love for his wife. But her ways were different, and he was more and more desirous of having her, and inwardly seethed with desire. Yet, because there was a difference in their ages, and because he felt, either through the lightness or her love or the violence of his pain, that she did not consider him of equal worth with herself, he used to chide her. Frequent quarreling followed, and the offended wife gave back the keys of the house and went home.

Her husband, overwhelmed with love and having nothing else to hope for, when he saw the fourth month slip by, went to her, trusting that the young girl's heart would be softened on the advice of her parents. His father-in-law met him at the door and brought him into the house. He reconciled his daughter and, in order that he might send them away more joyous, kept them three days while he prepared a sort of nuptial banquet. Although the man wanted to depart, he kept him also a fourth day, offering him excuses of civility, devising delays. In his desire to add a fifth day as well, he found new reasons for delaying them, while the husband, unwilling to thwart the father's affection of its desire to keep his daughter, though he was at last promised an opportunity for setting forth, postponed it

---

1 Cf. Judges 20.1-48.
2 Cf. Judges 19.

to midday so that they would start out well fortified with food. Even after dinner, the father wished to find some delay, saying that evening was now approching. At last he acquiesced, though reluctantly, to the entreaties of his son-in-law.

He set out on his jouney in happy spirits because he had recovered his dearly beloved wife. One servant was with him, and as day was already declining they sped on their way with swift steps. The woman rode on an ass; her husband felt no weariness, taking joy in his desire and lightening his journey with talk at times with the woman, at times with the slave. When at length they neared Jerusalem, about thirty stades[3] away, a place inhabited then by Jebusites, the servant boy suggested that they turn into the city, especially since night makes even safe places suspect and one must guard against the uncertainties of darkness, and particulary since the inhabitants of this locality were not of the children of Israel. They should beware lest treachery be done with hostile design, for the night's darkness is opportune enough for any tricksters to perpetrate evil. But his master did not care for the servant's idea of seeking lodging among foreigners, since Gaba and Rama, cities of Benjamin, were not far distant. His strong will overrode the servant's suggestion, as though advice takes its value from one's condition [of birth] rather than that through advice a lowly condition may be raised. The sun was now setting and he agreed reluctantly to go into the city [Gaba], for he was overtaken by evening.

The Gabanites lived there, unfriendly, harsh, unbearable people, who could stand anything but to receive people hospitably. Indeed, it would have been much more suitable had the Levite not sought hospitality in Gaba. That his treatment be utterly offensive, he found on entering the city

---

3 About four miles.

that there was no inn. And when he sat on the road imploring the mercy of these strangers, an old man from the fields happened to stumble on him, for evening had compelled him to leave his work in the fields at night. Seeing him, he asked where he was from and where he was going. He answered: 'I came from Bethlehem of Juda, I am going to Mount Ephrem, and my wife is here with me. But I have learned that there is no one here to give hospitality and provide us a chance to rest.' He needed no food or drink for himself nor food for his flock, but the hospitality of shelter was refused them. They had everything; only a bare lodging was needed. To this the old man kindly and calmly said: 'Peace to you! Come in as my guest and fellow citizen, for I am also from the region of Mount Ephrem and here is a lodging place; someone who lived here a long time laid its foundations.' Having received them into his home, he attentively and carefully provided for his guests and entertained them.

The old man kept urging them to be glad and kept inviting them to drink more wine so that they would forget their cares, when all of a sudden they were surrounded by young men of Gaba, given to lust, all lacking esteem for[4] moderation. The woman's beauty had bewitched them and thrown them into utter folly. They were captivated by her beauty and because of the old man's age and lack of help, with high hope of getting her, they demanded the woman and kept pounding at the door.

The old man, going out, begged them not to defile his guest's stay with a base crime, contemplating violation of a privilege reverenced even by savage nations of barbarous peoples; they could not insultingly mistreat a fellow tribesman of his, legitimately born, a married man, without causing wrath in their heavenly judge. When he saw that

---

4 Reading *ad*, not *ac*.

he was making little headway, he added that he had a maiden daughter and he offered her to them, with great sorrow, since he was her parent, but with less damage to the favor he owed his guest. He considered a public crime more tolerable than private disgrace. Driven by a wave of fury and inflamed by the incentive of lust, they desired the more the beauty of the young woman the more she was denied them. Deprived of all righteousness, they mocked his fair words, considering the old man's daughter an object of contempt in that she was offered with less feeling of ill-will toward the crime.

Then, when pious entreaties availed nothing and the aged hands were hopelessly extended in vain, the woman was seized and all that night was subjected to violence. When day brought an end to the outrage, she went back to the door of their lodging, where she would not ask to see her husband, whom she thought she must now forego, ashamed at her pitiable condition. Yet, to show her love for her husband, she who had lost her chastity lay down at the door of the lodging, and there in pitiable circumstance came an end to her disgrace. The Levite, coming out, found her lying there and thought that she dared not lift her head for shame. He began comforting her, since she had succumbed to such injury not willingly but unwillingly. He bade her rise and go home with him. Then, as no answer came, he called her loudly as though to rouse her from sleep.

When he realized that she was dead, he lifted her onto the mule and brought her home; then, dividing her limbs into twelve parts, he sent one to each of the tribes of Israel. In great distress over this,[5] all the people met at Maspha, and there, learning of the abominable deed from the Levite, desired to go to war, deciding that it was unlawful for anyone to go to his tent until vengeance was taken on the authors

---

5 Cf. Judges 20, with many modifications.

of this deed. With courage they rushed into battle, but the advice of wiser men changed their purpose not to engage the citizens in war, but to put the charge to the test first with words and to determine the conditions for the guilty. Nor did it seem fair that the cost of a few men's crimes should fall on all, and that the private sins of young men should make the safety of the citizenry fall. So they sent men to demand that the Gabanites give up those guilty of this crime, and, if they did not do so, let them know that to have defended such a crime was not less than to have committed it.

A proud retort was made and plans for peace were changed to war. In the first and second encounters, when many were harmed by a few, the Israelites considered yielding, since the battles were so unfavorable. There were 400,000 men warring against 25,000 of the tribe of Benjamin, and they strove with 700 Gabanites experienced in war. When two battles were unfavorable, Israel with eager spirit did not lose hope of victory nor of vengeance for the hope they had built up.

Superior in cause and number they yet fell back worsted in the battle's outcome, and, feeling that God was offended, they tried with fasting and much weeping to gain a reconciliation of heaven's favor. Begging the Lord's peace, they returned more boldly to war and they to whom prayer had given courage and who had entertained much hope were now able to do what they planned. On a pretext of withdrawing their front lines, setting ambushes at night in the rear of the city, where a segment of the enemy was located, they followed as some retired and thus were provided with an opportunity for invading the unprotected city. Fires were quickly set and flared up while raging flames and waves of heat revealed the sight of the taken city. Their spirits broken, they faced the enemy. The men of Benjamin who thought they were shut in and surrounded, even before they were invaded from the rear, began scattering and fleeing to the desert, while Israel pressed after with doubled force and pursued them as they wandered in rout.

About 25,000 were slain, therefore, that is, almost all the men of Benjamin except 600 who seized a fortification on a rough cliff and by virtue of its situation and with the help of nature and partly through fear were a terror to their victors. Success advises caution; in adversity, revenge is esteemed rather than victory. Not even a minority of the women stayed clear of that struggle, but all the women of the tribe of Benjamin, along with boys and girls of every age, were wiped out by sword or fire, and an oath was taken that no one would give his daughter to a man of that tribe in marriage, so that all chance of repairing the name was abolished.

The end of the war was also the end of their wrath,[6] and anger turned to sorrow. Then, putting off their armor, the men of Israel met together and wept much and celebrated a fast, grieving that one tribe of their brethren had perished and a strong band of people had been wiped out. Rightly had they warred against the authors of the crime because of the cost of the sin, but unhappily had the people turned against their own flesh and each was afflicted with civil war. The outpouring of tears moved their minds to compassion and stirred their feelings; the plan conceived in anger was gone. Sending legates to the 600 men of Benjamin, who for four months guarded themselves on the top of sheer rocks and by the desert's barrenness, which was dangerous for a mass of attackers, they lamented their common hardship in losing their fellow tribesmen, relatives, and allies. Yet the hope of renewing the tribe was not utterly destroyed and they consulted together how they might agree on a pledge of faith and one tribe not perish, severed from the body.

After setting up an altar they offered a sacrifice of recon-

---
6 Cf. Judges 21.

ciliation and peace. But, since the men of Jabes Galaad were obliged to the penalty and oath (for all Israel had bound herself with an oath that, if anyone did not join her in punishing the crime, he should die the death), 12,000 warriors had been sent, but that all the men and women be destroyed by the sword they spared only young maidens who had not known the bed of a man. Thus, all Jabes Galaad was killed and only 400 maidens remained. Israel took them and decided that the men of Benjamin should put away fear of war and wed the innocent girls close to them in age and honor. The men had a stronger reason, in that none of them had warred against them and they owed them the favor of charity, since through them they had been snatched from death. In this way was a marriage union sought for the 400 youths.

Yet, because 200 remained without wives, we learn that they also took counsel for them without violating their oaths. Yearly, a festival was held in Silo. There maidens used to dance or lead choruses for the honor of religion. Some went ahead of the matrons, and filled the whole road with their traveling troop. One of the elders said: 'If the two hundred men of the tribe of Benjamin would keep watch from the vineyard until the troop of women comes out, and coming from the vineyard each one would claim as wife whom he chances upon, there would be no treachery, for the people favor remedying the continuation of the tribe, but because of their oath they are unable to ask for marriage for their daughters. Nor would it seem a· violation of their oath if they did not think to stop them, for by the oath no need of forcing or stopping seems imposed: they ought to look to their advantage without fear. But if the girls' parents demand punishment, by entreaty and by reminding them of the fault of unwilling custody of them, they will gainsay them, and when they know that the men of Benjamin are unmarried they will themselves come forth with their daughters. The tribe is now worthy not of penalty but of mercy. Harsh enough has been their treatment and part of the body has been vanquished. Too immoderately did the people desire to wipe out the continuation of the family, to kill some of theirs. God is not pleased that a tribe of people perish, nor that they act so bitterly over one woman.'

The Israelites approved the plan; the men of Benjamin went out and hid in the vineyard at a favorable spot and at a favorable moment swooped down upon the roads filled with crowds of women. The solemnizing of their religion furnished them a nuptial festival. Daughters were torn from the embrace of fathers, as though being given to the band of youths by their parents, and you would think each had agreed not to be drawn from her mother's arms but to leave them. Thus did the tribe of Benjamin, which had almost been annihilated and destroyed, shortly flourish, proving how the punishment of shamelessness and revenge for injured chastity mean great harm to the proud.

Scripture proves this not only here, but in many places. In Genesis, too, we read that Pharao, king of Egypt, was scourged with many torments for having loved Sara, although he did not know she was another's wife.[7]

It is the Lord's will to guard chastity; how much more, to defend purity! Hence, no harm ought to be inflicted upon holy virgins, for those who do not marry and men who do not take to wife are accounted as the angels of God in heaven.[8] So, let us not bring bodily insult to heavenly grace, since God is powerful whom no transgression escapes, who is moved by a harsh and heavy insult to consecrated virginity, a gift reserved to Him.

Farewell, brother, and love us, because we love you.

---
7 Cf. Gen. 20.2-18.
8 Cf. Luke 20.36.

34. Ambrose to Theophilus (392)

Evagrius[1] has no ground for complaint; Flavian[2] has reason to fear, and so avoids the trial. Let our brethren pardon our righteous grief; because of these men the whole world is disturbed, yet they do not share our sorrow. Let them at least calmly allow themselves to be censured by those whom they have seen harassed for a long time by their obstinacy. Because these two have refused to agree on anything which pertains to the peace of Christ, serious discord has arisen and spread throughout the world.

To this shipwreck of holy peace the holy Synod of Capua had at last offered a haven of tranquility, namely, that communion should be offered to all those in the East who profess the Catholic faith, and that the trial of these two men should be decided by your Holiness at a session of our brethren and fellow bishops of Egypt. We felt that your judgment would be a true one, since you have embraced the communion of neither party and thus would be inclined to favor neither side.

When we had begun to hope that these most equitable decrees of the synod had provided a solution and put an end to discord, your Holiness wrote to say that our brother Flavian had again sought help from entreaties and from the support of imperial rescripts.[3] The toil of so many bishops has been spent in vain; we must have recourse again to civil tribunals, to imperial rescripts; once more must they [bishops] cross the seas; once more, though weak in body, must they exchange their native land for foreign soil; once more must

---

1 Evagrius was consecrated Bishop of Antioch by Paulinus when the latter was on his deathbed.
2 Flavian, a rival claimant for the see of Antioch, was in the favor of the emperor for his success in quieting the insurrection of the people of Antioch in 387. He pleaded ill health when summoned to Capua. Cf. Theodoret, *H. E.* 5.23.
3 An imperial order had undone the work of the Synod of Capua.

holy altars be abandoned that we may travel to distant places; once more a crowd of impoverished bishops, whose poverty was not burdensome before but who now need money for travel, will be forced to bewail their poor state or at least to use for their journey what might have fed the poor.

Flavian alone, exempt from the laws, as it appears to him, does not attend when we others all assemble. The moneylender and borrower meet each other; they cannot meet him. Flavian, in keeping with his own wishes, alone shuns the fellowship of bishops and will not appear in person at the bidding of the emperor or the summons of the bishops.

Moved as we are by this sorrow, we still do not grant that our brother Evagrius has evidence of a good case, thinking he is more in the right because Flavian avoids him, or concluding that his opponent is in no better situation than himself, each of them relying more on the defects of the other's ordination than on the validity of his own.

Yet we call them to a better course so that we prefer them to be defended by their own merits rather than by the other's defects. Since you have implied in your letter that some point can be found whereby the brother's discord will be removed, and since the holy synod has given the right of trial to your Unanimity and our fellow bishops of Egypt, it is fitting that you again summon our brother Flavian so that, if he continues to choose not to appear, you may, without prejudice to the decrees of the Council of Nicaea and the statutes of the Synod of Capua, so provide for the preservation of general peace that we may not seem to tear down what has been built up: 'For if I destroy what I have built, I make myself a sinner, and if I reconstruct the things that I have destroyed.'[4] Only let the grace of the peace we have obtained be preserved by all, and the refusal of the one

---
4 Gal. 2.18.

party to appear will not cause all our actions to be in vain.

We think, too, that you should consult our holy brother, Bishop of the Church at Rome, for we presume that what you determine will in no wise displease him. As the decision will be of great advantage, so also will the security of peace and harmony, provided the decision made by your judgment is such that it will not bring discord to our communion. And we, upon receiving the statutes of your decrees and learning that the Church at Rome undoubtedly approves what has been done, shall gladly partake of the good results of this trial.

35. Ambrose to Vigilius (385)

You have asked me what should be the chief points of your teaching now that you are newly ordained to the office of bishop. Because you have built up your spirit so fittingly you have been deemed worthy of this great office; it is now your duty to build up others.

Realize, first of all, that you have been entrusted with the Church of the Lord, and therefore you must prevent any scandal from intruding and causing her body to become common by contamination with heathens. For this reason, Scripture says to you: 'Do not marry any Chanaanite woman but go into Mesopotamia, to the house of Bathuel, that is, the house of wisdom, and choose there a wife for you.'[1] Mesopotamia is a region in the East bounded by the two largest rivers in that area, the Euphrates and the Tigris, which have their rise in Armenia and flow by different courses into the Red Sea. Now, the Church is signified by the word Mesopotamia, for she waters the minds of the faithful

---

1 Gen. 28.1,2.

with the great streams of wisdom and justice, pouring on them the grace of holy baptism, typified by the Red Sea, and washing away sin. Teach the people, therefore, to seek ties of marriage not with strangers but from the households of Christians.

Let no one defraud a hireling of his wages, because we, too, are hired men of God, hoping for the reward of our labors from Him.[2] You, too [you must say], O merchant, whoever you are, are refusing the hireling the wages in money, a cheap and passing thing. But to you the reward of heavenly promises will be refused, as the Law says: 'Thou shalt not refuse the hire of the hireling.'[3]

Do not lend your money for interest, since Scripture says that he who does not lend his money at usury will dwell in the tabernacle of God,[4] because one who takes the gain of usury is overthrown. Therefore, if a Christian man has money, let him lend it as if he were not to receive it back, or at least only to receive the principal which he lent. By so doing he receives no small profit of grace. Otherwise his actions would be deception, not assistance. For, what is more cruel than to lend money to one who has none and then to exact double the amount? If one cannot pay the simple amount, how will he pay double?

Let us take Tobias as an example, for until the end of his life he never asked back the money which he had lent,[5] and then he did so more because he did not want to cheat his heir than to exact and recover the money which he had lent out. Nations have often failed because of usury and this has been the cause of public calamity. So it is especially up

---

2 Cf. Lev. 19.13.
3 Cf. Deut. 24.14.
4 Cf. Ps. 14.5.
5 Cf. Tob. 4.21.

to us bishops to root out these vices which seem to entangle most men.

Teach them to welcome strangers willingly rather than to do what they ought merely from necessity. Thus, in offering hospitality they will not reveal an inhospitable state of mind and in the very giving of welcome to a guest spoil their favor by wrong-doing. Rather, let hospitality be fostered by the practice of social duties and by services of kindness. Rich gifts are not asked of you, but a willing performance of duty, full of peace and harmonious agreement. A dinner of herbs is better with friendship and love than a banquet adorned with choice victuals, if sentiments of love are not there. We read that nations have been destroyed with utter loss because they violated the oath of hospitality,[6] and dreadful wars have arisen because of lust.[7]

There is hardly anything more deadly than being married to one who is a stranger to the faith, where the passions of lust and dissension and the evils of sacrilege are inflamed. Since the marriage ceremony ought to be sanctified by the priestly veiling and blessing, how can that be called a marriage ceremony where there is no agreement in faith? Since spouses should pray in common, how can there be love of their common wedlock between those differing in religion? Many have betrayed their faith when lured by women's charms, as did the people of the patriarchs at Beelphegor. This is why Phineas lost his sword and killed the Hebrew and the Madianite woman,[8] and soothed God's wrath so that all of the people would not be destroyed.

Why should I mention many examples? Of the many, I shall set forth one, and by the mention of this one it may be clear how dangerous it is to marry a woman who is a

---
6 Cf Judges 20.44; cf. Letter 33, above.
7 Cf. Gen. 34.25.
8 Cf. Num. 25.8.

stranger [to the faith]. Who more than the Nazarite, Samson, ever was mightier and from the cradle more endowed with strength by the Spirit of God? Yet he was betrayed by a woman and because of her he was unable to stay in God's good favor.[9] I shall tell you the events of his birth and his entire life, arranging it in the manner of a story, not word for word, but in substance, according to the account of the sacred book which goes as follows:

For many years the Philistines held the Hebrews in subjection after their surrender, for they had lost the prestige of faith by which their fathers had gained victory. Yet the mark of their election and the ties of their heritage had not been entirely obliterated by their Creator. But, because they were often puffed up by success, He delivered them for the most part into the power of the enemy, so that with manly dignity they would seek from heaven the remedy of their ills. We submit to God at a time when we are overwhelmed by other reverses; success puffs up the mind. This is proved not only in other matters but especially in that change of fortune by which success returned again from the Philistines to the Hebrews.

When the spirit of the Hebrews had been so crushed by long and injurious subjection that no one with manly vigor dared to encourage them to freedom, there arose in their behalf a great hero, Samson, whose destiny was ordained by God's words. He was not numbered with the many, but outstanding among the few; he was without question easily reckoned as surpassing all in bodily strength. We must regard him with great admiration from the very beginning, not because he gave great evidence of temperance and sobriety from boyhood by abstaining from wine, nor because as a Nazarite he was ever faithful to guard his sacred trust, with locks unshorn, but because from his youth—a period of soft-

---

9 Cf. Judges 16.18-21.

ness in others, but truly remarkable in him—he worked amazing deeds of strength, perfect beyond the measure of human nature. By his deeds he soon gained credence for that divine prophecy. For no slight cause had such great graces preceded him that an angel came down to foretell to his parents his unexpected birth, the leadership he would hold, and the protection he would give his people who had been tormented so long by the oppressive rule of the Philistines.

His godfearing father was of the tribe of Dan,[10] of no mean station in life, pre-eminent among others. His mother, a barren woman, was not unfruitful in the virtues of the soul. She was worthy to receive into the dwelling of her soul the vision of an angel, whose command she obeyed and whose words she fulfilled. She did not permit herself to know even the secrets of God without her husband's sharing of them; she told him that a man of God had appeared to her, of wondrous beauty, bringing her a prophecy that a child would be born. Because she trusted his promises she shared with her husband her trust in these heavenly pledges. When he learned them, he devoutly begged God in prayer that he might also be granted the favor of a vision, saying: 'O Lord, let thy angel come to me.'[11]

I do not think, as a certain author has supposed,[12] that he did this out of jealousy for his wife, who was remarkable for her beauty, but rather because he was moved by a desire for a favor from heaven and wished to share the benefit of the heavenly vision. One depraved by vices of the soul would not have found such favor with the Lord that an angel would return to his house, give the admonition which the fulfilling of the prophecy entailed, be suddenly raised in

---
10 Cf. Judges 13.2-23.
11 Judges 13.8.
12 Josephus, *Antiq.* 5.8.3.

the form of a glowing flame, and depart. This vision, which so frightened the husband, the wife interpreted more auspiciously, turning it to joy and removing his anxiety. She said that to see God was a proof of favor, not of ill-will.

Samson, then graced by such favors from heaven, turned his thoughts to marriage as soon as he reached manhood, whether because he detested in his mind the free and familiar manner of deceitful lust in the young, or because he was seeking a reason for loosing from the necks of his people the power and harsh tyranny of the Philistines. Going down, therefore, to Thamnatha[13] (this is the name of a city in that country which then was inhabited by the Philistines), he saw a maiden of pleasing appearance and beautiful countenance. He asked his parents, who were guiding him on his way, to ask her in marriage for him. They did not realize that his purpose was so set that, if the Philistines refused her to him, he would become very angry, nor that they, if they gave their consent, would be bringing an end to the wrong treatment of the conquered. Since from intercourse a sense of equality and kindness grows apace, and, if offense is given, the desire for revenge becomes deeper, his parents thought that he should avoid her because she was a stranger. In vain did they try to change his purpose by lawful objections; finally, then, they gave their consent to the wishes of their son.

Samson obtained his request and upon his return to visit his promised bride he turned off the road for a short while; there a lion came out of the woods to meet him, a truly fierce beast, because released from the forest. No comrade, no weapon was ready at hand; the shame of fleeing and an inner sense of power gave him courage. As the lion rushed upon him he caught it in his arms and killed it with his grasp, leaving it lying there beside the road on a heap of

---
13 Cf. Judges 14.1.

forest wood. The spot was thick with the grassy growth of fodder and planted, too, with vineyards. He felt sure that the spoils of a savage beast would be of little importance to his beloved spouse, because the times of such events [as marriage] are made charming not by savage trophies but by genteel joys and festal garlands. Later, upon his return along the same road, he stumbled upon a honeycomb in the lion's belly, and carried it off as a gift to his parents and the maiden, for such gifts suit a bride. After he had tasted the honey, he gave them the honeycomb to eat, but he did not disclose where it came from.

By chance one day, during a nuptial feast, the young people at the banquet challenged one another to a game of question and answer. And while one caught up the other with spicy banter, as is the custom on such occasions, the contest, which had begun in fun, grew heated. Then Samson proposed the question to his fellow guests: 'Out of the eater came forth meat, and out of the strong came forth sweetness.'[14] He promised as the reward for their wisdom that those who guessed it should have thirty shirts and the same number of coats, for that was the number of men present, but if they did not solve it they should pay a forfeit.

Since they could not untie the knot and solve the riddle, they prevailed upon his bride, using repeated threats and constant entreaty, that she ask her husband for the answer to the question as a mark of his devotion in return for her love. Truly terrified in mind, or perhaps in the plaintive manner of a woman, she began her supposedly loving complaints, pretending that she was sorely grieved that her husband did not love her: she who was his life partner and confidant did not know her husband's secret and was treated like the rest of his friends and not entrusted with her hus-

---

14 Judges 14.14.

band's secret. She even said: 'Thou hatest me and dost not love me whom until now you have deceived.'[15]

These and other remarks overcame him and, weakened by her womanly charms, he revealed to his beloved the riddle which he had proposed. She in turn revealed it to her countrymen. Seven days later, before sunset, which was the time agreed for the solving of the riddle, they gave the answer which they had learned and which they expressed thus: 'What is stronger than a lion? What is sweeter than honey?' And he answered that nothing is more treacherous than woman, saying: 'If you had not ploughed with my heifer, you had not found out my riddle.'[16] Immediately he went down to Ascalon, slew thirty men, stripped off their garments and gave them as the reward he had promised to those who had solved the riddle.

Moreover, he did not live with the girl whose treachery he had learned, but, instead, returned home to his own country. But the maid, in fear and dread of the wrath of one so wronged, afraid lest his wrath be vented on her, agreed to marry another man, one whom Samson considered a friend of his, a bridal companion on his wedding day. Even though their union was offered as an excuse, she did not escape the peril of his hatred.[17] When this became known and he was denied an opportunity of going to his wife, for her father said that she had married someone else, but that he might, if he wished, marry her sister, sorely stung with wrong, he made plans to wreak public revenge in anger over his personal affront. He caught three hundred foxes and, at the end of summer when the grain was ripe in the fields, coupled them tail to tail and fastened torches between

---

15 Judges 14.16.
16 Judges 14.18.
17 Cf. Judges 15.1.

their tails, tying them with unbreakable knots. Then, to avenge the affront, he sent them into the standing corn fields which the Philistines had cut. The foxes, driven mad by the fire, spread the blaze wherever they ran and burned the corn stalks. Greatly disturbed by their loss, for their entire harvest had perished, the owners went and told their leaders. They dispatched men to the Thamnathite woman, who had given her troth to more than one husband, and also to her house and parents. They said that she was the cause of her own destruction and harm, but that it was not right for the husband who was wronged to avenge himself by injuring the whole people.

Samson still did not content himself with this wrong against the Philistines, nor was he content with what he had done in revenge. He slaughtered them in a great orgy of bloodshed and many died by the sword. He then went to Elam to a stream in the desert. The rock there was a fortification belonging to the tribe of Juda. The Philistines, who did not dare attack him or to climb the steep and hazardous fortification, denounced the tribe of Juda and rose up, urging the tribe to battle. They saw that justice would be done otherwise, if the men, who were their subjects and paid tribute, seemed about to lose a rightful and fair treatment in public affairs just because of another's crime. In consulation, they demanded that they hand over the perpetrator of such a crime and on this condition they would be unharmed.

The men of the tribe of Juda, hearing this stipulation, gathered 3,000 of their men and went up to him, maintaining that they were the subjects of the Philistines and had to obey them, not from choice but through fear of danger. They put the blame for their deed upon those who had the right to force them. Then he said: 'And what form of justice is it, O race of the sons of Abraham, that the wrong of first betrothing and then stealing my spouse should be my punishment, and that one may not avenge with impunity a wrong done to one's home? Are you stooping in submission to little domestic slaves? Will you make yourselves agents of another's insolence and turn your own hands upon yourselves? If I must die for the sorrow which is understandably mine, I will gladly die at the hands of the Philistines. My home has been assailed, my wife has been harassed. If I may not live without their evil deeds, at least I may die without crimes being committed by my people. Have I not returned an injury which I received? Have I inflicted it? Consider whether the exchange was a fitting one. They complain of damage to their crops; I, the loss of my wife. Compare sheaves of wheat and the marital union. They have themselves seen proof of my pain, the injuries which they have avenged. See what service they consider you worthy of. They want the one put to death whom they thought should be avenged, whom they injured, and to whom they gave the weapon of revenge. If you bring my neck to bend to the proud, hand me over to the enemy, but do not yourselves kill me. I do not shrink from death, but I dread your being contaminated. If you yield to those insolent men through fear, bind my hands with cords. Defenseless though they be, they will find their weapons in the knotted cords. Surely, the enemy must think you have made sufficient payment of your promise if you deliver me alive into their power.'

In answer, the 3,000 who had climbed up the mountain gave him an oath that they would not use force against his life provided he would wear chains, so that they could hand him over and free themselves of the crime with which they were charged.

When he had received their pledge, he left the cave and abandoned his rocky fortification. When he saw the strong

Philistines approaching to take him, although he was bound with double cords, he groaned in spirit and broke his bonds. Then, seizing the jawbone of an ass lying there, he struck a thousand men and put the rest to flight in a magnificent display of strength, while battle lines of armed men fell back before a single defenseless man. Any and all who dared to approach him were slain with easy effort. Flight staved off death for the rest. Thus, even today, the place is called Agon, because there Samson won a great victory by his overwhelming strength.

I wish that he had been as controlled in victory as he was strong against the enemy! But, as usually happens, a soul unused to good fortune, which ought to have attributed the outcome of the engagement to God's favor and protection, attributed it to himself, saying: 'With the jawbone of an ass I have destroyed . . . a thousand men.'[18] He neither erected an altar nor sacrificed a victim to God, but, failing to sacrifice and taking glory to himself, he called the place 'the killing of the jawbone' to immortalize his triumph with an everlasting name.

Soon he began to feel a fierce thirst; there was no water and he could no longer stand to bear his thirst. Knowing that to attain human help would not be easy and that it would be difficult without divine aid, he called upon and begged almighty God, who he thought would not help him because of his offense against Him, and because he had unwisely and carefully attributed any success to himself. Nay, he even assigned the victory to almighty God, saying: 'Thou hast given this very great deliverance into the hand of thy servant, and it has been my help. And behold! because I die of thirst, I am placed by my need of water into the power of those over whom thou gavest me a great

---
18 Judges 15.16.

triumph.'[19] Then God's mercy opened the earth when he threw down the jawbone, and a stream issued from it and Samson drank and resumed his spirit and called the place 'the invoking of the spring.' Thus, by his prayer, he atoned for his vaunting of victory. Men expressed different opinions, noticing how arrogance might speedily bring harm and humility make atonement without offense.

When in the course of events he had brought an end to the war with the Philistines, despising his people's cowardice and scorning the enemy bands, he went off to Gaza. This city was in the territory of the Philistines, and he lived there in a certain lodging house. The people of Gaza immediately took note and hastily surrounded his lodging place, putting a guard at all the doorways so that he could not plan to flee by night. When Samson became aware of their preparations he anticipated the plot they had laid for the nighttime, and taking hold of the columns of the house, lifting all the wood framework and the weight of the tower on his strong shoulders, he carried them up to the top of a high mountain which faced Hebron, where the Hebrew people dwelled.

But when with free and untrammeled gait he passed not only beyond the limits of his home country, but also the boundaries which his ancestors had been taught to observe by custom, he soon found that he was playing with death. With small faith he contracted a marriage with a foreign-born wife and should have been cautious then or later. But he did not refrain from again forming a union, this time with Delila, who was a prostitute. Out of love for her he caused her to tempt him with the wiles of an enemy. For the Philistines came to her and each man promised her eleven hundred pieces of silver if she would find out in what lay

---

19 Judges 15.18.

the source of his strength. If they but possessed this secret he could be surrounded and taken.

She who had once prostituted herself for money,[20] cleverly and craftily amid the banquet cups and the charms of her love, in admiration, as it were, of his pre-eminent bravery, began to question him about it and to ask him how it was he so excelled others in strength. Then, too, as though she were fearful and anxious, she begged him to tell his beloved what bond precisely would put him in the power of another. But he was still prudent and strong-willed and he countered deceit with deceit against the harlot's treachery, saying that if he were bound with supple green boughs he would be as weak as other men. When they learned this, the Philistines had Delila put boughs on him like chains while he slept. Then, as if suddenly awakened, the hero felt his famed and customary strength, broke his bonds, and fought back against the many who had their strength untrammelled.

After a short time, Delila, like one who had been made fun of, began to complain passionately and to ask again and again what his real skill was, demanding proof of his affection for her. Samson, still strong of purpose, laughed at her tricks and suggested to her that if he were bound with seven brand-new ropes he would come into the power of his enemy. This also was tried, in vain. The third time he pretended that she had drawn him out regarding the mystery, but in reality, being nearer to a fall, he said that his strength would leave him if seven hairs of his head were cut and woven into a coverlet. This, too, deceived the tricksters.

Later, when the woman boldly deplored the fact that he mocked her so many times and when she lamented that she was unworthy to be entrusted with her lover's secret and begged as a remedy that which she saw was likely to mean

---

20 Cf. Judges 16.6-18.

a betrayal, she gained his confidence by her tears. And just as it was due that a man of bravery who had been invincible all this time, should pay the price, he opened up the wounded recesses of his soul: the strength of God was in him; he was holy to the Lord and by His command he let his hair grow, for, if he cut it, he would cease to be a Nazarene and would lose the use of his strength! When the Philistines discovered his weakness, through the woman, they gave her, the slave of their price, the reward for the treachery and thus concluded the affair.

Next, by her charms as a harlot she drew the weary lover to sleep and, summoning a barber, she cut seven hairs of his head with a razor. At once his strength was reduced by the treachery of the forbidden act. At length, awaking from sleep, he said: 'I shall do as before and shall shake myself over my enemies.'[21] But he knew neither swiftness of soul nor strength. Force was not his, and grace had left him. Chiding himself further for having put his trust in women, he thought he would make further trial of the effect of his infirmity, so he allowed his eyes to be blinded, his hands bound, and his feet chained as he entered the prison which throughout his many vicissitudes he had never known.

With the passage of time[22] his hair began to grow; then, during a crowded banquet of the Philistines, Samson was brought from prison and shown before the people. About 3,000 men and women were there. They taunted him with cruel remarks, they surrounded him with mocking jests which he bore with greater stamina and beyond what his blind appearance suggested, for he was a man of great native strength. To live and to die are functions of nature, but mockery belongs to the base-born. The wish arose in him,

---
21 Judges 16.20.
22 Cf. Judges 16.22.

therefore, either to compensate for such insults by revenge or preclude any more insults by death. He pretended that he could no longer support himself, because of the weakness of his body and the knots of his shackles, and he asked a servant boy, who was guiding his steps, to put him near the pillars which supported the house. Placed there, he grasped with both hands the support of the entire building and, while the Philistines were intent upon the sacrifices of the feast in honor of their god Dagon, through whom they thought the adversary had come into their hands, accounting the woman's treachery among the benefits of heaven, he called to the Lord, saying: 'Lord, once more remember your servant so that I may revenge myself on the Gentiles for my two eyes. Let them not give glory to their gods, because with their help they have gotten me in their power. I count my life as of no worth. Let my soul die with the Philistines, so that they may know that my weakness no less than my strength is deadly.'[23]

So he shook the columns with mighty force and he loosened and shattered them. The crash of the roof came next and fell on him and hurled headlong all those who were looking on from above. There in great confusion lay heaps of lifeless men and women, and, though slain, he attained his wished-for triumph, greater than all his former victories, and a death not inglorious or lacking luster. Although he was inviolable here and hereafter, and was not to be compared in his life to men who experienced war, in his death he conquered himself and made his invincible soul despise death, giving no thought to the end of life which all men fear.

Through his valor he ended his days with numerous victories and found the captive not undone but triumphing. The fact that he was outwitted by a woman must be

---

23 Judges 16.28-30.

attributed to his nature, not to his person; his condition was human rather than his fault less. He was overwhelmed, and yielded to the enticements of sin. And when Scripture bears witness that he slew more in death than when he had the light of life, it seems that he was made a captive more to work the ruin of his adversaries than to become cast down or counted less. He never experienced degradation, for his grave was more famous than had been his power. Finally, he was overwhelmed and buried not by weapons but by the dead bodies of his enemies, covered with his own triumph, leaving to posterity a glorious renown. Those people of his, whom he had found captive, he ruled in liberty for twenty years and then, entombed in the soil of his native land, he left behind the heritage of liberty.

Because of this example, men should avoid marriage with those outside the faith,[24] lest, instead of love of one's spouse, there be treachery.

Farewell, and love us, because we love you.

36. To our lords the bishops, beloved brethren of Aemelia, Ambrose, bishop (386)[1]

Holy Scripture and the tradition of the Fathers teach us that it requires more than ordinary wisdom to determine the day for the celebration of Easter. Those who met at the Council of Nicaea, in addition to their decrees, true and admirable,

---

24 A law of Theodosius in 388 forbade marriage with Jews, but it does not antedate this letter. Ambrose mentions such an imperial prohibition in 2 *Abr.* 9.84; *Expos. in Ps. 118,* serm. 20.48; 2 *In Luc.* 8.

1 The authenticity of this letter is sometimes doubted by scholars, because of the condition of the text. Cf. F. Dekkers, O. S. B., *Clavis Patrum Latinorum* (Bruges 1951) 26, and C. W. Jones, *Bedae opera de temporibus* (Cambridge, Mass. 1943) 35 n. 3.

regarding the faith, using the help of men skilled in calculations, formulated for the above-mentioned celebration a scheme of nineteen years, and set up a sort of cycle on which might be patterned subsequent years. They called this the 'nineteen-years' cycle,'[2] and, if we follow it, we should not waver amid foolish ideas regarding a celebration of this kind. Having found a true method of calculating, let everyone be of one opinion, so that the Sacrifice [of the Mass] for the Resurrection of the Lord may be offered everywhere on one night.

Dearly beloved brethren of the Lord, we ought not deviate from the truth, nor dissent with varying opinions on the obligation of this celebration imposed on all Christians. The Lord Himself chose that day to celebrate the Passover which agreed with the method of the true observance. Scripture says: 'And the day came when it was necesary to sacrifice the Passover, and he sent Peter and John, saying: "Go and prepare for us the Passover that we may eat it!" But they said, "Whère dost thou want us to prepare it?" And he said to them: "Behold on your entering the city there will meet you a man carrying a pitcher of water: follow him into the house into which he goes, and you will say to the master of the house: 'The Master says to thee, "Where is the guest chamber, that I may eat the Passover there with my disciples?"' And he will show you a large upper room; there make ready."'[3]

We observe, therefore, that we should not descend to earthly things but seek a large furnished upper room for celebrating the Lord's Passover. When we cleanse our senses in a kind of spiritual water of the eternal fountain and

---

2 Gr., *enneakaidekaetēris*; Lat., *enneadecaeteris*, the decennovenal cycle. For a history of the reckoning of the date of Easter, cf. Jones, *op. cit.* 6-33. Its use in the Church of Milan is discussed on pp. 35-37.
3 Luke 22.7-12.

keep the rule of a devout celebration, and do not follow common opinions, looking for certain days according to the moon, since the Apostle says: 'You are observing days and months and seasons and years. I fear for you, lest perhaps I have labored among you in vain,'[4] a beginning of another sort is in effect.

It is one thing to keep the observance like the heathens, judging on what day something should be begun, as you think: 'avoid the fifth day,'[5] and that you ought begin nothing on it, trusting also various stages in the course of the moon for undertaking business, or avoiding certain days, as some persons habitually shy away from 'following' days or 'Egyptian' days.[6] It is quite another thing to keep a pious attitude toward that day of which Scripture says: 'This is the day which the Lord has made.'[7] Now, although it is written that the Lord's Passover should be celebrated on the fourteenth day of the first month, and we ought to look for the fourteenth moon[8] in spring for celebrating the course of the Lord's Passion, we should understand from this that for a solemnity of this kind we must have either the perfection of the Church or the fullness of clear faith, as the Prophet said when he spoke of the Son of God that 'His throne shall be as the sun in my sight, and as the full moon, it will last forever.'[9]

So it is that the Lord, having done wonderful works on earth, having deepened, as it were, the faith of men's minds, observed that it was the time of His Passion, saying: 'Father, the hour has come! Glorify thy son, that thy son may

---
4 Gal. 4.10,11.
5 Virgil, *Georg.* 1.276.
6 A reference to current suspicions about days, as recorded by Gellius 5.7.
7 Ps. 117.24.
8 *quartamdecimam lunam.*
9 Ps. 88.37,38.

glorify thee.'¹⁰ He explains elsewhere that He wanted special renown in celebrating His Passion, saying: 'Go and say to that fox, "Behold, I cast out devils and perform cures today and tomorrow, and the following day I am to end my course." '¹¹ Let Jesus end His course in those who are beginning to be perfect, so that through their faith they may believe the fullness of His divinity and redemption.

This is why we are seeking the day and the hour, as Scripture bids us. Even the Prophet David says: 'It is the time for thee to work, O Lord,'¹² as he begs for understanding to know the Lord's testimonies. And Ecclesiastes also says: 'All things have their season.'¹³ Jeremias cries: 'The turtle and the swallow and the sparrows of the field have known the times of their coming.'¹⁴ What is more evident than that it is said of the Passion of the Lord: 'The ox knoweth his owner and the ass his master's crib.'¹⁵ Let us, then, know the Lord's crib where we are nourished, fed, and refreshed.

We should know in particular the time when the harmonious prayer of the sacred night is poured forth throughout the whole world, because prayers are made acceptable in time, as Scripture says: 'In an acceptable time I heard thee and in the day of salvation I have helped thee.'¹⁶ This is the time of which the Apostle said: 'Behold now is the acceptable time; behold now is the day of salvation.'¹⁷

Accordingly, it is necessary, even after the calculations of the Egyptians, and the definitions of the Church at Alexandria and of the bishop¹⁸ of the Church at Rome,

---

10 John 17.1.
11 Luke 13.32.
12 Ps. 118.126.
13 Eccle. 3.1.
14 Jer. 8.7.
15 Isa. 1.3.
16 Isa. 49.8.
17 2 Cor. 6.3.
18 *episcopi* is ambiguous here; our reading is '*post . . . definitiones episcopi* [genitive] *quoque Romanae Ecclesiae.*'

since several are still awaiting my opinion by letter, to write what I think regarding the day of the Passover. Granted that it is a question concerning the coming day of the Passover, we are stating what we feel should be maintained in the future, if such a question should ever arise.

Two observances are necessary in solemnizing the Passover: the fourteenth moon and the first month, called the month of new fruits.[19] Now, that we may not seem to depart from the Old Testament, let us review the very chapter which concerns the day for celebrating the Passover. Moses tells the people to keep the month of new fruits, specifying that it be the first month, saying: 'This will be the beginning of months for you, it will be the first of the months of the year; and thou shalt offer the Passover to the Lord thy God on the fourteenth day of the first month.'[20]

To be sure, the Law 'was given through Moses; grace and truth came through Jesus Christ.'[21] He who spoke the Law, coming later Himself through a virgin in later times, accomplished the fulfillment of the Law, because He came not to destroy the Law but to fulfill it.[22] He celebrated the Passover in a week when the fourteenth of the month fell on the fifth day [of the new moon]. In fact, on that very day, as the above indicates, He ate the Passover with His disciples; on the following day, that is, the sixth day [of the new moon] and the fifteenth day [of the month] He was crucified; the sixteenth was on the great Sabbath, and therefore He arose from the dead on the seventeenth.

We must keep the law regarding Easter in such a way that we do not observe the fourteenth as the day of the Resurrection; that day or one very close to it is the day of

---

19 *novorum.*
20 Exod. 12.1,6. These are the words of God to Moses who transmitted them to the Israelites.
21 John 1.7.
22 Cf. Matt. 5.17.

the Passion, because the feast of the Resurrection is kept on the Lord's day. Moreover, we cannot fast on the Lord's day; fasting on this day is what we criticize in the Manichaeans. One shows disbelief in the Resurrection of Christ if he proposes a law of fast on the day of the Resurrection, since the Law says that the Passover should be eaten with bitterness, that is, with sorrow because the Author of our salvation was slain by mankind's great sacrilege. On the Lord's day the Prophet bids us rejoice, saying: 'This is the day which the Lord has made, let us be glad and rejoice at it.'[23]

Consequently, we must observe both the day of the Passion and of the Resurrection, to have a day of bitterness and one of joy, fasting on one day, being refreshed on the other. If it happens, however, as will occur next time, that the fourteenth day of the first month is the Lord's day, since we should not fast on that day nor break our fast on the thirteenth which falls on the Sabbath, for it is a day of special observance as the day of the Passion, the celebration of Easter should be postponed to the following week. Otherwise, it happens that the fifteenth when Christ suffered will be on the second day of the week, the third day will be the sixteenth when the Lord's body rested in the tomb, and the fourth day will be on the seventeenth when the Lord arose.

Therefore, when, as will happen next time, the three holy days run into the following week, the three days within which He suffered, lay in the tomb, and arose, the three days of which He said: 'Destroy this temple and in three days I will raise it up,'[24] what can cause troublesome doubt in us? If we scruple because we do not celebrate the day of the Passion or the Resurrection on the fourteenth, recall that the Lord Himself suffered not on the fourteenth, but

---

23 Ps. 117.24.
24 John 2.19.

on the fifteenth, and arose on the seventeenth. If our difficulty is in our failing to observe the fourteenth of the month which falls on the Lord's day, that is, April 18, and we tell you to celebrate the following Lord's day, there is authority for this practice, too.

A short while ago, when the fourteenth of the first month fell on the Lord's day, the solemnity was observed on the following Lord's day. And in the eighty-ninth year of the era of Diocletian[25] when the fourteenth day of the first month fell on March 24, we celebrated Easter on the last day of March. So, too, did the people of Alexandria and Egypt. They wrote to say that when the fourteenth fell on the twenty-eighth day of the month of Phamenoth[26] they celebrated Easter on the fifth day of Pharmuth,[27] which is the last day of March. Thus, they agreed perfectly with us. Again, in the ninety-third year of the era of Diocletian[28] when the fourteenth fell on the fourteenth of Pharmuth, which is April 9 and happened to be the Lord's day, they celebrated Easter on the Lord's day, the twenty-first of Pharmuth, or, according to us, April 16. Since we are supplied with a method of calculating as well as precedent, we should have no more trouble on this point.

Here something else demands explanation, the fact that some think we will be celebrating Easter in the second month, whereas Scripture says: 'Keep the first month of new fruits.'[29] Yet it will not happen that we celebrate the Passover outside

---

25 A. D. 373.
26 Phamenoth, the month before Pharmuth, i. e., the seventh month.
27 Pharmuth, so called in honor of the serpent Renenutet (later pronounced Remute[t]), 'the raising goddess.' She was worshiped as a more special harvest goddess than Osiris and the month Pharmuth was dedicated to her evidently because the harvest once fell in that month. Cf. *Mythology of All Races* ed. L. H. Gray, Vol. 12 (Boston 1918) 66.
28 A. D. 377.
29 Deut. 16.1.

of the month of new fruits unless the fourteenth is kept exactly to the letter, and is not celebrated on any but the very day. Now, the Jews are planning to celebrate on the twelfth, that is, March 20 according to us, and it will be not the first month. However, according to the Egyptians it will be the twenty-fourth day of Phamenoth, which is not the first month, but the twelfth month. The Egyptians call the first month Pharmuth; it begins March 27 and ends April 25. Thus, in accord with the reckoning of the Egyptians, we will be celebrating Easter Sunday in the first month, that is, April 25, the thirtieth day of Pharmuth.

I do not think we are unreasonable in borrowing, from the country where the first Passover was celebrated, an example for observing the month. Our predecessors, too, in the ordinance of the Council of Nicaea thought that the very same nineteen-years' cycle should be decided upon. If one carefully considers the matter [he will see] that they preserved the month of the new fruits, because in Egypt grain is cut in this month. This month is not only the first as far as the crops of the Egyptians are concerned, but first according to the Law, and it is the eighth month with us, since the indiction[30] begins in September. April 1 is in the eighth month, yet the month begins—according to the experts, although not according to common usage—with the equinox, March 21, and ends April 21. That is why the Passover has usually been celebrated within these thirty-one days.

Six years ago we celebrated Easter on April 21, which was the thirtieth day of the month, as we reckon it; therefore, we must not be disturbed to be soon celebrating Easter on the

---

30 Ambrose is the first of the Latin Fathers to mention the indiction. He is here probably referring to the Constantinian or Constantinopolitan indiction which was used principally in the Greek East. It began September 1, 312, as the schedule of rate of tax to be raised on *capita* and *iuga* for a period of fifteen years; cf. art. 'Indictio,' *Oxford Classical Dictionary* (Oxford 1949) 452.

thirtieth day of Pharmuth. If anyone says it is in the second month, since Easter will occur three days after the completed month, which appears to end on April 21, he should realize that our concern is with the fourteenth day, which occurs on April 18, well within the month's count. The Law only requires that the day of the Passion be celebrated within the first month of new fruits.

This reckoning is satisfactory as far as the full month is concerned, since it still has three days remaining for its completion. Easter does not pass into a different month when it is celebrated within the same month, the first. And, too, we should not be bound to the letter if the custom of the celebration of Easter is our guide. The Apostle, too, teaches us, saying: 'Christ, our passover, has been sacrificed.'[31] The passage just read teaches us not to follow the letter, for you have the words: 'You will perform the Pasch to the Lord your God on the fourteenth day of the first month.'[32] He uses the word 'day' instead of 'month'; consequently, those skilled in the Law compute the month by the course of the moon. Since the course of the moon, that is, its first day, may begin on more than one of the nones, you see that the nones of May can still be reckoned within the first month of new fruits. According to the judgment of the Law, therefore, this is the first month. Finally, the Greeks call the moon *mēnē* and so call the months *mēnas,* in Greek, while the natural practice of foreign peoples uses the term 'month' in place of 'days.'

Yet, the writings of the Old Testament show that we must celebrate the Passion one day and the Resurrection another. You have the words: 'And it will be a lamb without blemish, clean, perfect, of one year, a male; you will take it from the sheep and goats, and it will be for the observing

---
31 1 Cor. 5.7.
32 Exod. 12.18.

until the fourteenth day of this month, and the whole multitude of the sons of the synagogue of Israel will slay it at evening and take of its blood and put it on both the side posts, and on the upper doorpost of the house in which they will eat it together, and they shall eat the flesh that night roasted at the fire.'[33] And further on: 'And you will eat it with care, for it is the Phase [Passage] of the Lord and I will pass through the land of the Egyptians that night and will kill every first-born in Egypt of man and beast, and I will execute judgment on all the land of Egypt. I am the Lord. And the blood shall be unto you for a sign in the houses where you shall be; and I shall see the blood and I shall protect you, and the plague of destruction will not be upon you. And I shall crush the land of Egypt and this day will be a memorial and solemnity for you, and you will keep it a feast of the Lord in your generations, an everlasting covenant, you will keep that festival day.'[34]

We note, too, that the day of the Passion is appointed on a fast day because the lamb is to be slain toward evening, although we can understand 'the last time' instead of 'evening' according to John who says: 'Children, it is the last hour.'[35] But, according to the mystery, it is certain that the slaying took place in the evening when the shadows were falling quickly, and the fast should be kept on that day, for then you will eat it with anxiety, since those fasting have anxiety. On the day of the Resurrection there is the joy of refreshment and happiness, for it appears that the people left Egypt on that day, after the first-born of the Egyptians had been slain. Later details indicate this more clearly where Scripture says that, after the Jews performed the Passover as Moses commanded, 'it came to pass at midnight the Lord struck

---
33 Exod. 12.5-8.
34 Exod. 12.11-14.
35 1 John 2.18.

every first-born in the land of Egypt, from the first-born of Pharao. And Pharao called Moses and Aaron in the night and said to them: "Arise and go forth from among my people, you and your children, go and serve the Lord your God." '[36] The Egyptians even urged the people to go, hurrying to drive them out as quickly as possible. Whereupon, the Israelites departed in such fashion that they had no chance to leaven their dough, for the Egyptians drove them out and they could not take what they had prepared for their journey.

It is evident, then, that the day of the Resurrection should be kept after the day of the Passion, and the former should not be on the fourteenth of the month, but later, as the Old Testament says. The day of the Resurrection is that on which the people departing from Egypt were baptized in the sea and in the cloud, as the Apostle says,[37] and overcame death, receiving a spiritual food and drinking a spiritual drink from the rock. Again, the Lord's Passion cannot be celebrated on the Lord's day. And, if the fourteenth day falls on the Lord's day, another week should be added, as was done in the seventy-sixth year of the era of Diocletian.[38] Then, with no hesitancy on the part of our predecessors, we celebrated the Lord's day of Passover on the twenty-eighth of Pharmuth, April 23. The course of the moon and careful calculation support this plan to celebrate the next Easter on the twenty-first day, because the month is commonly extended to the twenty-first.

Since we have so much evidence of the truth, combined with the example of our predecessors, let us keep the feast of the people's salvation with joy and gladness, and color our doorposts where is hung the door of the Word, which

---

36 Exod. 12.29-31.
37 Cf. 1 Cor. 10.2-4.
38 A. D. 360.

the Apostle wishes to be opened to Him with faith in the Lord's Passion.³⁹ Of this door David also speaks, saying: 'Set a watch, O Lord, before my mouth, and a guard at the door of my lips,'⁴⁰ so that we will speak of nothing but the blood of Christ, by which we overcame death, by which we were redeemed. Let the sweet odor of Christ burn in us. Let us listen to Him, let us direct the eyes of our soul and body to Him, and marvel at His works and proclaim His goodness. Over the threshold of our door let the praise of His holy Redemption gleam. Let us take the Sacrament with fervent soul in the azymes of sincerity and truth, chanting together with holy wisdom the glory of the Father and Son, and the undivided majesty of the Holy Spirit.

37. Ambrose to Anatolius, Numerius, Severus, Philippus, Macedonius, Ammianus, Theodosius, Eutropius, Clarus, Eusebius, and Timotheus, priests of the Lord, and to all the beloved clergy and people of Thessalonica, greetings (383)[1]

While I had a deep longing to keep always in mind the saintly man and to scrutinize his acts, stationed, as it were, on a watchtower, with ever-enveloping anxiety I drank the bitter draught of that too sudden message and learned what I would prefer still to be unacquainted with, that the one we were ever seeking on earth is already at rest in heaven.

You ask who brought this message, since the letter of your Holiness had not yet arrived. I do not recall the

---
39 Cf. Col. 4.3.
40 Ps. 140.3.

1 Written to console the people of Macedonia after the death of their bishop, the saintly Acholius.

bearer of the message; we generally do not willingly remember the messenger of sorrow. And although at that time the sea was closed and our lands held fast by invading barbarians, although there was no one who could come, there was not lacking one to bring that message. It seems to me that the saint himself was his own messenger to us, because, having received the everlasting reward of his labors, and being set free from the chains of the body, fast by the side of Christ amid the ministry of angels, he wished to dispel the cloud of doubt of one who loved him, lest we should pray for long life for one to whom the rewards of eternal life were already being given.

He departed, he did not die; this veteran soldier of Jesus Christ left us, exchanging the soil of this earth for heaven. Beating his wings, the oarage of his spirit, he says: 'Lo, I have gone far off flying away.'[2] In the spirit of the Apostle he wanted long ago to leave this earth, but he was detained by the prayers of all, as we read of the Apostle,[3] because the Church had need of his abiding longer in the flesh. He lived not for his own interests but for those of all, and he was to his people the dispenser of eternal life, experiencing the enjoyment of it in others before knowing it in himself.

Now he is an inhabitant of the regions above, an occupant of the eternal city Jerusalem, which is in heaven. He sees there that city's boundless boundary,[4] its pure gold, its precious stone, and its perpetual light which knows no sun. Seeing all these, known to him for a long time, but now revealed face to face, he says: 'As we have heard, so have we seen, in the city of the Lord of hosts, in the city of our God.'[5] Stationed there, he addresses the people of God, say-

---
2 Ps. 54.8.
3 Cf. Phil. 1.23,24.
4 *mensuram immensam*.
5 Ps. 47.9.

ing: 'O Israel, how great is the house of God, and how vast is the place of his possession! It is great and hath no end.'⁶

But what is happening? While I am pondering the merits of the man, and, as it were, following him in spirit as he departs, and mingling with the choirs of the saints who are escorting him—not by any virtue of mine, but by my affection—I am almost forgetful of myself. Has there not been taken from us a wall of faith, of grace, and of sanctity? Often, although troops of Goths besieged this wall,⁷ their barbarian weapons have never been able to penetrate, nor has the warlike fury of many nations been able to take it by storm. In other lands they sought plunder, but in your land peace. And when men wonder what brings them to a halt without benefit of a soldier, the wise suggest that a man who resembles Eliseus is within, like him in age, not unlike him in spirit; let them beware [they say] lest blindness overwhelm them as it did the Syrian ranks.⁸

Yet around Christ's disciples are His various gifts. Eliseus led the captive lines of the Syrians into Samaria, while the saintly Acholius by his prayers drove the victors from Macedonia. Do we not see it was by a higher power that from where there was no soldier they were routed without a soldier? Is it not blindness for them to have fled whom no one pursued? Truly the saintly Acholius was attacking and engaging them, not with swords but with prayers, not with spears but by his merits.

Or do we not know that the saints keep up the struggle even when they are unoccupied? Was not Eliseus enjoying quiet? Yes, his body was quiet but his spirit was all aquiver,

---

6 Bar. 3.24,25.
7 A reference to the guerilla warfare which Theodosius waged against the Goths from Thessalonica. A pestilence which Ambrose here attributes to the prayers of Acholius eventually caused a severe though temporary setback for the Goths.
8 Cf. 4 Kings 7.

and he did battle by his prayers when the cry of horsemen was heard in the Syrian camp along with the cry of a great host. In fact, the Syrians thought that the armies of other kings were coming upon them to aid the people of Israel. For this reason they fled in great fear, and four lepers who had come forth, longing for death, contaminated the camp of the enemy. Did not the Lord work similar or almost greater miracles in Macedonia by the prayers of the saintly Acholius? For, not by vain fear or vague suspicion, but by a raging plague and burning pestilence, were the Goths routed and terrorized. In fact, they fled at first to escape, but later came back and sued for peace to live.

In the deeds of this great man we have seen ages past and we have witnessed the works of those Prophets of which we used to read. Like Eliseus, while he lived, Acholius spent his days amid armies and battles, bringing wars to an end by his good deeds. At last, when peace was restored to his countrymen, he gave up his holy spirit, a misfortune harsher than the war itself. Like Elias he has been taken up to heaven,[9] not in a fiery chariot, or by fiery steeds—unless, perchance, we did not see them—or in a fiery whirlwind, but by the will and favor of our God, and with the joy of all the holy angels who rejoiced that one so great had come to them.

Certainly we cannot doubt these facts since other details agree so well. At the very moment when he was being taken up, letting his garment fall, as it were, he put it on blessed Anysius,[10] his own disciple, and vested him with the miter of the episcopal office. I am not hearing of his deeds and favor now for the first time, nor did I learn of them in letters from you, but I recalled them from your letters. Knowing beforehand that he would be his successor, Acholius kept

---

9 Cf. 4 Kings 2.11.
10 To whom Ambrose addressed a letter of encouragement.

assuring him by promises, marking him with special tokens, speaking of the help he had received through his care and labor and ministry. He seemed already to declare him his coadjutor so that he might come not like a tyro to the high office of the episcopate, but like a veteran and an accomplished performer of the priestly office. To him is applied very beautifully that saying of the Gospel: 'Well done, good and faithful servant; because thou hast been faithful over a few things, I will set thee over many.'[11]

These thoughts about the saintly Acholius you and I have in common. I have a special attachment to this man of blessed memory, since he made it possible for me to know him. For, when he came to Italy and I was confined by an illness so serious that I could not go to meet him, he himself came and visited me.[12] With what fondness and affection did we rush into each other's embrace! With what groans did we deplore the evils of our age and the events taking place here so that we moistened our garments with a stream of tears all the while we two enjoyed this hoped-for meeting and I clung to the embrace of one so long desired. Thus did his kindness make possible my prayer to see him, and although in the soul, the seat of love, the greater share and deeper knowledge of others reside, we also desire to see our friends in person. Therefore, in times past the kings of the earth sought to see the face of Solomon and to hear his wisdom.[13]

But Acholius has gone from us and left us on this sea. An event which is beneficial to him is harder upon many than was the fury of the barbarians. He used to drive them off; but who will be able to take his place for us? The Lord takes his place and in his disciple he succeeds himself. Your decisions re-

---

11 Matt. 25.23.
12 This probably took place at the Council of Rome in 382 when Ambrose fell ill soon after his arrival and was confined to his bed at his sister's home.
13 Cf. 3 Kings 10.24.

present him whereby it has been said: 'Grant to Levi those who are manifest as his, and his truth in the holy man.'[14] You have chosen one who is manifestly his, inasmuch as he was grounded in his teaching; you have chosen an imitator of that man who said to his father and mother: 'I do not know you.'[15] This man, too, has not acknowledged his brothers and did not know his sons; he has kept the word of the Lord and observed His Testament. The people will declare his justice.[16]

Such was this man's life, such his heritage, his way of life, his succession. As a youth he entered a monastery; he was enclosed in a narrow cell in Achaia while by grace he wandered over the space of many lands. Having been called to the fullness of the priesthood by the people of Macedonia, he was elected by the clergy; and where formerly the faith was weakened[17] through its priest, there, later, through a priest the foundation walls of faith were made firm.

Imitating no one else, he is a disciple of him 'who said to his father and mother: "I have not seen you." '[18] He saw them not with longing or with affection, and he did not know his brethren because he desired to know the Lord. He observed the word of the Lord and kept His Testament, and he will always lay honor upon His altar. O Lord, bless his faith, his holiness, his zeal! May Thy blessings come upon his head and his shoulders! May he be like the bull in the herd; may he toss the hearts of his enemy and melt the souls of the saints, and may the judgment of Thy priests flourish in him like a lily.[19]

Farewell, brethren, and love me as I also love you.

---

14 Cf. Deut. 33.8.
15 Deut. 33.9.
16 Cf. Eccli. 44.15.
17 Several mss. read *claudebat* ('closed'), but this is no less difficult to construe than *claudebatur*. The Benedictines suggest *claudicabat* ('was lame'), which agrees well with the sense of the following phrase.
18 Cf. Deut. 33.9.
19 Cf. Deut. 33.16,17; Eccli. 39.19.

SYNODAL LETTERS

38. To the beloved brethren, the Bishops of Vienne and Narbonne in Gaul, the Council which met at Aquileia (May, 381)

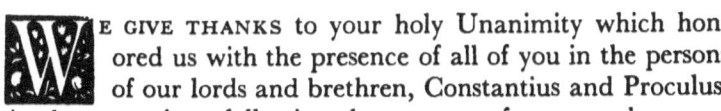E GIVE THANKS to your holy Unanimity which honored us with the presence of all of you in the persons of our lords and brethren, Constantius and Proculus. At the same time, following the customs of your predecessors, you added no slight weight to our deliberations when your Holiness agreed to our statements, dearly beloved lords and brethren. Therefore, as we gladly welcomed those revered men of your assembly and ours, so are we sending them away with a rich testimony of thanks.

How necessary was a meeting such as we held is evident from the very events which took place, namely, that our adversaries, enemies of God, those defenders of the Arian sect and heresy, Palladius and Secundianus, the only two who dared come to the council, received their due sentence, and were convicted of impiety.

Farewell. May our God omnipotent keep you safe and prosperous, our lords, most beloved brethren. Amen.

39. To the most clement and most Christian Emperors and most blessed princes Gratian, Valentinian, and Theodosius, the holy Council which met at Aquileia (May, 381)

Blessed be God the Father of our Lord Jesus Christ who gave you the Roman Empire, and blessed be our Lord Jesus Christ, the only-begotten Son of God, who guards your rule with His love, in whom we give thanks to you, most gracious Princes. You have proven the zeal of your faith, being zealous to assemble a council of bishops[1] for the removal of discord, and by your favor you granted honor to the bishops so that no one who wished to attend was absent, and no one was forced to attend against his will.

Therefore, in accord with the order of your Mildness we met without unpleasantness of crowds and with the intention of debating the issues. No heretical bishops were found in attendance except Palladius and Secundianus, names of long-standing disloyalty, on whose account men from the farthest reaches of the Roman world asked that a council be summoned. No one burdened with the years of old age and with grey hairs, which in themselves are venerable, was forced to come from distant shores of the ocean. Nevertheless, the council lacked nothing. No one dragging a weak body burdened with the rigors of fasting was forced by the difficulty of the journey to lament the hardships laid upon his ruined strength. Finally, no one groaned if destitute of the means of coming because of poverty so laudable in bishops. That which holy Scripture has praised was fulfilled

---

[1] For the date, see J. Zeller, 'La date du concile d'Aquilée,' *Revue d'histoire ecclésiastique* 33 (1937) 39-45. The authentic official account of the Council (*Gesta concilii Aquiliensis*: *PL* 16.939-949) is supplemented by four synodal letters included in Ambrose's correspondence, since he probably drew them up. See also *Dissertatio Maximini contra Ambrosium*, an Arian pamphlet published a little later; ed. F. Kaufmann, *Aus der Schule des Wulfila* (Strassburg 1899) 67-90.

in you, most clement of princes, Gratian: 'Blessed is he that takes thought for the needy and poor.'[2]

How truly serious it would have been if, because of only two priests withering away with disloyalty, the churches over the whole world were deprived of their greatest bishops? Although some from the western provinces were unable to come in person because of the length of the journey, almost all from the western provinces were present in the delegates they sent, and gave evident proofs that they held what we assert and that they were in harmony with the proceeding of the Council of Nicaea as their documents declared. Everywhere now the prayers of nations are raised in concert for the welfare of your empire, and the defenders of the faith have not failed your wishes. Although our predecessors' decrees, from which it is unholy and sacrilegious to deviate, were plain, we made it possible to discuss even these.

First we examined the root of the matter under investigation and decided to read the letter of Arius, who is found to be the author of the Arian heresy, and from whom the heresy gets its name. Then, those who had always maintained that they were not Arians could, by censuring the contents of the letter, condemn the blasphemies of Arius, or defend them by additional arguments, or, at least, not refuse the name of him whose irreligion and disloyalty they followed. Inasmuch as they could not condemn and were unwilling to give approval to their own founder, and three days previously had challenged us to a discussion at a fixed place and time, not waiting for the assembly to begin, those who had said they would readily prove that they were Christians (which we heard with joy and hoped they would prove) suddenly began to leave the meeting and to refuse to debate further.

---

2 Ps. 40.2.

Nevertheless, we had already had a great deal of discussion with them; the holy Scriptures were brought into our midst; the opportunity for patient discussion was offered from dawn until the seventh hour. Would that they had spoken on only a few matters or that we were able to forget all we heard! Since Arius says in sacrilegious phrases that only the Father is eternal, only He is good, only He is true God, only He has immortality, only He is wise, only He is powerful, and by impious inference wishes the Son to be thought of as not partaking of these attributes, these men preferred to follow Arius rather than admit that the Son of God was the eternal God, the true God, the good God, wise, powerful, and possessing immortality. We spent many hours in vain. Their impiety mounted and could in no way be checked.

Finally, when they realized that they were hard pressed by the sacrileges contained in Arius' letter (which we have appended so that your Clemency may also realize the pain it caused) they jumped up in the midst of the reading of the letter and demanded that we answer their proposals. Although it was not consonant with the order of the day or with reason that we interrupt the agenda, and we had said that in reply they should condemn Arius' heresies, and in due order and in a set place we would reply to their charges, notwithstanding, we agreed to their preposterous wish. Then, falsely interpreting the reading of the Gospel, they proposed to us that the Lord had said: 'He who sent me is greater than I,' although the context of Scripture teaches otherwise.

They were made to admit the falsehood, although they still were not corrected by reason. For, when we said that the Son was said to be less than the Father in His taking of a body, but that in His divinity He is proved by the testimony of Scripture to be like and equal to the Father, and that there could be no difference in degree of rank or greatness, where there was unity of power, they not only refused to correct their error, but even began to be more enraged and to say that the Son was subject in His divinity, as if there could be any subjection of God in His divinity and majesty. Finally, they attributed His death not to the mystery of our salvation but to some weakness of His divinity.

We shudder to think, most clement Princes, of these dreadful sacrileges, these corrupt teachers. And that they may not further deceive the people whom they govern, we have decided that they should be deprived of their priestly power, since they agreed to the impiety in the document presented to them. It is not fitting that they claim for themselves the priesthood of One whom they deny. We beg your faith and glory to manifest the reverence of your authority to Him who is its source, and determine that these proclaimers of impiety and corrupters of the truth, by a rescript of your Clemency to competent authority, be barred from the doors of the Church, and that, in place of the guilty ones, holy priests be delegated through the legates of our Littleness.

The same opinion was held by Attalus, a priest who admitted his collusion with and adherence to the sacrilegious teachings of Palladius. Why should we speak of his master Julian Valens? Although he lived close by, he refused to attend the council of bishops, fearing he would be compelled to explain before the bishops the ruin of his country and the betrayal of his citizens. He, desecrated by the impiety of the Goths, is said to have even dared like a heathen, wearing necklace and bracelets, to make his appearance before the Roman army. Such conduct is obviously sacrilegious, not only in a bishop but in any Christian whatsoever. It is also alien to Roman custom, although the idolatrous worshipers of the Goths are accustomed to appear thus.

May the name of bishop move your Holiness, a name

which that unholy person disgraces. He is convicted of unspeakable wickedness by the statements of his people who still survive. Let him at least return to his own home, let him not befoul the cities of a very flourishing Italy. At present, by illegal ordinations he associates with himself men like himself and through certain reprobate persons seeks to leave the seeds of his impiety and treachery. He has not even begun to be a bishop. First of all, he replaced the saintly Mark at Pettau, a priest of holy memory. Being unable to stay at Pettau, he is now at Milan after the overthrow, or, let us say, 'betrayal,' of his country.

May your Piety, therefore, deign to counsel us on all these matters, so we will not appear to have met in vain when we complied with the ordinances of your Tranquility. Care must be taken not only that our decrees but also yours be not held in dishonor. Therefore, we beg your Clemency to hear with all indulgence the delegates of the council, holy men, and bid them return as soon as possible with those things accomplished which we ask. Thus may you receive a reward from the Lord God, Christ, whose Church you have rid of all stain of sacrilege.

You have also removed the Photinians,[3] who by a former law you had decreed should hold no assemblies, revoking, too, that law which was passed regarding the meeting of a council of bishops. We ask your Clemency, knowing that their assemblies are still being held in Sirmium, though these

---

[3] Followers of Photinus, a heretic, a native of Ancyra and bishop of Sirmium. Reviving Sabellianism, he denied the plurality of Persons in the Trinity. He was condemned at Antioch (344), at Milan (347), and deposed by the first Synod of Sirmium. His condemnation was confirmed by the second Ecumenical Council. He died in 366. Cf. J. Thein, *Ecclesiastical Dictionary* (New York 1900).
[4] Gratian complied with the request of the bishops; cf. Letter 42, below.

assemblies have been put under interdict, that you give orders to have reverence shown first to the Catholic Church and then to your laws, so that, with God as your patron, you may triumph, while you provide for the peace and tranquility of the churches.⁴

40. To the most clement Emperors and most Christian Princes, most glorious and most blessed Gratian, Valentinian, and Theodosius, the Council which met at Aquileia (May, 381)

Provision has been made, most clement Princes, by the enactments of your Tranquility, that the disbelief of the Arians may not be further hidden or spread abroad, for we do not anticipate the decrees of the council being without effect. As regards the West, only two individuals have been found to dare oppose the council with profane and blasphemous remarks, men who had previously thrown into confusion only a small corner of southern Dacia.¹

There is another reason which distresses us more, which we had to treat when we assembled, lest it spread over the whole body of the Church scattered thoughout the world, and thus throw everything into confusion. Although we generally agreed that Ursinus² could not have deceived your Piety (although he allows no tranquility and, amid the countless exigencies of war, attempts an ill-timed deceit), yet, that your holy mind and tranquility of soul, which delight in

---
1 On the Danube.
2 Ursinus, antipope, was elected in 366 by jealous adherents of Liberius after the election by a large majority of Pope Damasus. Eventually, Ursinus came to Milan where he found adherents among the Arians there.

taking thought for all, may not be swayed by the false adulation of that unreasonable man, we think it right, if you condescendingly allow it, to pray and beseech you, not only to guard against future events, but also to be alarmed over that which has been achieved by his temerity. For, if he found any avenue for his boldness, what would he not put into confusion?

If pity for a single person can influence you, let the prayer of all the bishops move you much more. Who of us will be joined in fellowship with him, when he has tried to usurp a position not due to him, and to which he could not rightfully attain, and tries to regain most unreasonably what he has unreasonably sought? As often as he has been found guilty of disturbances, he still goes on, as though undeterred by past experiences. Generally (as we ascertained and saw in the present council), he was in union and combination with the Arians, when, in company with Valens,[3] he tried to throw into confusion the Church at Milan, holding secret assemblies, sometimes before the doors of the synagogue, sometimes in the homes of Arians, and getting his friends to join them. Then, since he himself could not openly enter their assemblies, teaching and informing them how the peace of the Church might be disturbed, he drew fresh courage from their madness when he was able to earn the favor of their supporters and allies.

Since it is written: 'A factious man avoid after a first admonition,'[4] and since another who spoke by the Holy Spirit said that beasts of this sort should be spurned and not received with greeting or welcome,[5] how can we not

---

3 Julian Valens of Pettau had the assistance of the antipope Ursinus, who bore a grudge against Ambrose because the latter supported Pope Damasus.
4 Tit. 3.10.
5 Cf. 2 John 10.

judge the person whom we have seen united to their society to be also an exponent of disbelief? Even if he were not there, we would nevertheless have besought your Clemency not to allow disturbance to reach the Roman Church, head of the whole Roman world, and that sacred trust of the Apostles, whence flow all the rights of venerable communion upon all persons. We therefore beg and beseech you to deprive him of the means of stealing advantage from you.

We know your Clemency's holy modesty. Let him not press upon you words unfit for your hearing, or give his noisy utterance to what is foreign to the office and name of priest, or say to you what is unseemly. Since he must have a good reputation at least with those who are outside,[6] may your Clemency condescend to recall what is his reputation among his own fellow citizens. It is shameful to say and immodest to repeat how disgraceful is the rumor which does him harm. Shame over this should have kept him silent, and, if he had some of a bishop's conscience, he would prefer the Church's peace and concord to his own ambition and inclination. But, far removed from all embarrassment, sending letters through Paschasius, an excommunicated individual, the standard-bearer of his madness, he sows confusion, and tries to excite even heathens and abandoned characters.

We therefore beg that through the removal of this very troublesome person you will restore peace to us bishops and to the Roman people whose security has been interrupted and whose condition at present keeps them in uncertainty and suspense, now that the city prefect has made an appeal. Attaining this, let us in continual accord offer thanks to God the almighty Father and Christ, also the Lord God.

---

6 Cf. 1 Tim. 3.7.

216 SAINT AMBROSE

41. To the most clement and most Christian Emperors and the most glorious and most blessed Princes, Gratian, Valentinian, and Theodosius, the holy Council which met at Aquileia (June, 381)

We are unable, even with the most overflowing return of thanks, to match the benefits of your Piety, most clement Emperors, most blessed and glorious Princes, Gratian, Valentinian, and Theodosius, beloved of God the Father and of His Son our Lord Jesus Christ. After many seasons and various persecutions which the Arians brought upon all Catholics, and especially Lucius,[1] who attacked monks and virgins with unholy slaughter, and Demophilus,[2] too, a dread source of impiety, all the churches of God, particularly in the East, have been restored to the Catholics; and in the West just two heretics have been found to oppose the holy council. Who, then, would feel able to make acknowledgment adequate to your favors?

Although we cannot express your favors in words, we still desire to compensate them by the prayers of the council. Although in all of our several churches we celebrate vigils each day before God for your Empire, yet assembled together, thinking no service more glorious, we offer thanks to

---

1 Lucius was forced upon the Church at Alexandria by Palladius, governor of the province, in place of Peter, the duly elected successor of Athanasius. He was later expelled from the see he had usurped. Cf. Theodoret, *H. E.* 4.19; Socrates, *H. E.* 4.37.

2 Demophilus, originally Bishop of Boaea (probably in Thrace), was deposed for his Arianism. In 370 he was elected bishop of Constantinople by the Arian party and was supported by the Emperor Valens, who banished Evagrius. In 380, at the accession of Theodosius, he was asked to subscribe to the Nicene Creed if he wished to maintain his see. He refused, and along with Lucius and others he conducted Arian worship outside the walls of Constantinople until his death in 386. Cf. Socrates, *H. E.* 4.37; Ambrose, *De fide* 1.6.45.

our almighty God for the Empire and for your peace and well-being, because through you peace and concord have been shed upon us.

In only two small corners of the West, that is, on the borders of southern Dacia and in Moesia, did there appear to be murmurs against the faith. Now, after the vote of the council, we feel that these should at once be allowed the indulgence of your Clemency. Throughout all territories and districts and village departments as far as the ocean, the communion of the faithful remains one and unsullied. And Arians in the East who had violently laid hold of churches have, we learn with great joy and happiness, been ejected, and the sacred temples of God are attended by Catholics alone.

But, since the envy of the Devil never subsides, word comes to our ears that there are among the Catholics themselves frequent dissensions and restless discord. All our feelings are stirred at learning that many new [disturbances] have taken place, and that persons are now molested, who should have been relieved, men who remained always in communion with us. In fact, Timothy,[3] Bishop of the Church at Alexandria, and Paulinus of Antioch,[4] who always maintained an unbroken concord of communion with us, are said to be distressed by the dissensions of others, whose faith was

---
3 The nature of the difficulty with Timothy is uncertain. Tillemont (*Mémories* 10.139) says the question probably concerns the successor to the see of Antioch. The members of the Council of Aquileia who addressed themselves to the emperor seem not to have heard of the outcome of the recent Council of Constantinople, when the death of Meletius was followed by the consecration of the presbyter Flavian and the irregular consecration of Maximus. Cf. Dudden, *op. cit.* I 206-212.
4 A reference to the long schism of Antioch, which lasted from the deposition of Eustathius by the Arians in 331 until 415. Cf. Theodoret, *H. E.* 3.2.

steadfast in former times. If it is possible, and if these people are recommended by the fullness of their faith, we should like to have them added to our fellowship, on the condition that our associates in the ancient communion may keep their privilege. Our concern for them is not unnecessary, first, because the fellowship of communion ought to be without offense, and second, because we have long received letters from both parties, and especially from those in the Church at Antioch who were heretics.

Indeed, if hostile interference had not been a hindrance, we should have arranged to send some of our own number to act as mediators and judges in restoring peace, if possible. But, since our desires could not take effect at that time, because of the troubles of the state, we feel that we should offer your Piety our prayers, asking that by mutual agreement, when a bishop dies, the rights of the Church should belong to the survivor, and no other consecration be forcibly attempted. Therefore, we request you, O most clement and Christian Princes, to permit a council of all Catholic bishops at Alexandria, where they may more fully discuss together and decide to what persons communion is to be granted and with whom it is to be maintained.

Although we have always upheld the direction and order of the Church at Alexandria, and in accord with the manner and custom of our predecessors have maintained communion with it in indissoluble fellowship even down to the present time, yet, that others may not seem less esteemed, who have sought our communion by an agreement which we desire to continue, or lest we neglect a short-cut to peace and fellowship with the faithful, we entreat you that, when they have discussed these matters in a full assembly, the decrees of the bishops may be furthered by the help of your Piety. Allow us to be notified, that our minds may not waver in uncertainty, but that joyously and peacefully we may give thanks before almighty God for your Piety, not only that disbelief has been eliminated but faith and harmony restored to Catholics. This the Churches of Africa and Gaul beg you through their legates, that you may make the bishops of the whole world your debtors, although the debt already due your Virtue is by no means slight.

To entreat your Clemency and, to obtain our requests, we have sent as legates our brethren and fellow priests whom we ask you to condescend to hear graciously and allow to return speedily.

42. To the most blessed Emperor Theodosius, most clement prince, Ambrose and the other bishops of Italy (Autumn, 381)

We are aware that your saintly mind has been dedicated to the service of almighty God with unblemished and pure faith. But through your latest good offices you have perfected your dedication by bringing back to the churches the Catholics, O Emperor Augustus. Would that you had brought back the Catholics to their old sense of reverence, so that they would make no changes contrary to the regulations of their predecessors, neither rashly doing away with customs that should be preserved, nor preserving what should be abolished. More grievously, perhaps, than ill-advisedly have we lamented, revered Emperor, the fact that it has been easier to drive out the heretics than to establish concord among the Catholics. It is impossible to explain how great confusion has recently prevailed.

Some time ago we wrote to you regarding the city of Antioch, which had two bishops, Paulinus and Meletius, who we knew were in agreement on faith.[1] Therefore, we thought that peace and concord between them would protect the interests of Church discipline, or, at least, that if either of them died and the other survived, there would be no substitution of another person in the place of the deceased. Now, however, upon the death of Meletius, while Paulinus is still living—a man who has remained in communion with us by the peaceful rule of his congregation under our predecessors—contrary to what is right, and contrary to Church discipline, someone is being planted in Meletius' place, one is being imposed rather than installed.

This is being carried out, moreover, with the consent and agreement of Nectarius,[2] whose ordination does not appear to us to be regular. In the council recently held,[3] Bishop Maximus[4] revealed by letters from Peter, of holy memory, that the members of the Church of Alexandria were in communion with him, and he proved that he had retired for the ceremony of his ordination to his own home because

---

[1] Two rival bishops were in Antioch: Euzoius, installed by Constantius' orders, and Meletius, legitimately elected by his colleagues. But a group of persons openly separated from these two and put themselves under a certain Paulinus. The Council of Alexandria had decided regarding the doctrine of the contending parties that Paulinus' and Meletius' adherents were in agreement, although the former, following the terminology of Nicaea, accepted the perfected synonymity of *ousía* and *hypostásis*. They refused to recognize or accept the Meletian formula, 'Three hypostases in the Trinity.' Cf. Palanque and others, *op. cit.* 305.

[2] Nectarius, a nobleman of Tarsus, was, like Ambrose, unbaptized when he was elected Bishop of Constantinople in 381 at the resignation of Gregory Nazianzen.

[3] The Council of Aquileia (381).

[4] Maximus of Alexandria had been irregularly consecrated in 380 by some Egyptian bishops, who brought the authorization of the consecration from Peter of Alexandria during the illness of Gregory.

the Arians still had possession of the basilicas of the church. We had no occasion, best of princes, to question his episcopacy, since he proved that he resisted violence brought to bear on him by several of the laity and the clergy.[5]

Nevertheless, we thought that your Clemency should be informed so that we would not seem to have presumed to pronounce finally upon an affair when the parties concerned were not present. Consultation should be held for the sake of public peace and concord. Actually, we have observed that Gregory [when he abdicated his see], in accord with the tradition of the Fathers, laid no claim to the office of priest of the Church at Constantinople. In the synod, therefore, whose attendance seemed binding upon the bishops of the whole world, we agreed to decide nothing with haste. Yet, those who refused to attend the general council are said to have met at the same time at Constantinople. When this assembly learned that Maximus had come to their synod to plead his case (although the council had not been lawfully proclaimed in the manner of our predecessors, like Athanasius, of holy memory, and like Peter, earlier—both bishops of the Church at Alexandria—and as several of the Eastern bishops had done before, appearing to have recourse to the judgment of Rome, of Italy, and of all the West), when they, as we said, found Maximus wanting to make trial against those who had refused him a bishopric, they surely should have waited for our opinion. We do not challenge the right of an examination into such a matter, but there should have been a meeting for a united decision.

Finally, there should have been an agreement as to whether it seemed necessary to recall him before transferring the office of priest to another. The procedure was important especially to those by whom Maximus claimed he had been

---

5 In favoring Maximus, Ambrose and the Western bishops were not in possession of the full facts of the matter.

deserted or harmfully attacked. Since our assembly had received Bishop Maximus into communion, agreeing that he had been ordained by Catholic bishops, we did not think that he should be removed from his claim to the bishopric of Constantinople. We thought that his claim should be weighed by the parties present. However, since our people recently learned that Nectarius was ordained at Constantinople, we do not see how we can unite our communion with the Eastern countries, especially since it is said that Nectarius left there, deprived of the fellowship of communion by the same persons by whom he had been ordained.[6]

This is no mean difficulty. The trouble causes us anguish not out of any personal interest and ambition, but we are disturbed over the tearing and rending asunder of the union of the faithful. We do not see how agreement can be reached unless either he is returned to Constantinople who was first ordained, or there is at least a joint council in Rome of the East and West regarding the ordination of the two persons in question.

It does not seem unfitting, O Augustus, that a treatise be drawn up by the head of the Roman Church and the neighboring and Italian bishops, who thought that the judgment of the one bishop, Acholius, was so worth waiting for that they presumed to summon him to Constantinople from the West. If protection was provided for this one man alone, how much more is it to be provided for many persons?

Yet, having been advised to write to the power of your Clemency by our most excellent Prince, the brother of your Piety,[7] we ask that where there is one communion you may wish a judgment in common and agreement in perfect accord.

---

6 This was a false rumor.
7 Gratian.

43. To the blessed Emperor Theodosius, most clement prince, Ambrose and the other bishops of Italy (381)

The knowledge of your faith, spread throughout the world, has won the deep affection of our hearts. And now, to enhance even more the glory of your reign, since it seems you have brought back unity to the Churches of East and West, we have thought that your Clemency should be petitioned by our letters and instructed also regarding the affairs of the Church, O Emperor most serene and faithful! There has been cause for sorrow between Eastern and Western people because the sacred communion of their congregations has been interrupted.

We pass over in silence those whose error and sin caused this, that we may not appear to be weaving tales and idle talk. We are not sorry to have tried a course of action the neglect of which might have been cause for censure. We are often blamed for seeming not to value highly unison with the Eastern brethren, and for seeming to refuse their good will.

As a matter of fact, however, we have thought that our endeavors should be publicly recognized as being concerned not for Italy, which has been at peace for a long time and free from the Arians, and is not disturbed by any trouble with any other heretics—not, we repeat, for ourselves. We do not look for that which concerns us, but that which concerns all, not for the interests of Gaul and Africa, which possess a united friendship of all their bishops, but we are anxious that these matters which pertain to the East and have troubled our communion may be discussed before a synod and every difficulty removed from our midst.

Some matters pertain to those persons of whom your Clemency has deigned to write; others, to those who are trying to introduce some sort of dogma into the Church, said to be the teaching of Apollinaris; and these items, which should have been cut out by the roots while both parties were present, greatly distress us. Then, if a person is spreading a new dogma and is found guilty of error, he should not hide himself under the general name of the faith, but, immediately, because he does not have title to it through his teaching authority, he should lay aside his priestly office and title, and no materials or devices for treachery should remain for those who, in the future, wish to deceive others. If one is not found guilty when the parties are present, for by your august and princely response your Clemency has defined [the limits of discussion for us], he will seize upon some loophole of complaint which will have to be reckoned with.

For these reasons, therefore, we have asked for a council of bishops so that no one can allege falsehood while members are absent, and that whatever is true may be discussed in the council. Thus, no suspicion of intention or willingness falls on those who have done everything in the presence of all parties.

We have prepared this rescript not by way of definition, but of instruction, and in asking for a judgment we do not advance a pre-judgment. Nor must any disapproval of those parties be presumed when the bishops, whose absence has been noted frequently, are summoned to the council, because now the common good is being consulted. We ourselves have never thought there was any disapproval expressed when a bishop of the Church at Constantinople, one Paulus by name, called for a synod of Eastern and Western bishops in Achaia.

Your Clemency notices that this is not an unreasonable demand, for it has been asked for by the Eastern bishops. But, because there is a disturbance in Illyricum, safer places have been sought on the coast. Plainly, we do not, as it were, start something out of the ordinary, but we are keeping the pattern established for councils by Athanasius, of holy memory, who was like a pillar of faith, and by the ancient fathers of times past. We have not torn up boundary stones which our Fathers laid down, we do not violate the laws of the communion to which we are heirs, but, preserving the honor due your power, we merely show ourselves zealous for peace and repose.

44. To our lord, dearly beloved Brother Pope Siricius, Ambrose, Sabinus, Bassianus, and others (c. 389)[1]

In the letter of your Holiness we recognize the vigilance of the good shepherd, for you carefully keep the door which has been entrusted to you, and with holy anxiety you guard the sheepfold of Christ, worthy to have the Lord's sheep hear and follow you. Since you know so well the sheep of Christ, you will readily catch the wolves and meet them like a wary shepherd that they may not scatter the Lord's flock by their habitual unbelief and mournful barking.

This we praise and heartily commend, our Lord and dearly beloved Brother. We are not surprised that the Lord's flock was frightened by the raving of wolves in whom they did not recognize the voice of Christ. For it is brutish barking to show no favor for virginity or claim for chastity, to wish to group all deeds indiscriminately, to abolish the different degrees of merit, and to intimate a certain poverty in heavenly rewards, as if Christ had but one palm to give, as if countless claims to reward did not exist in great numbers.

They pretend that they are giving honor to marriage. What praise is possible to marriage if virginity receives no distinction? We do not say that marriage was not sanctified

---

[1] Written at the Synod of Milan as a defense of virginity against Jovinian.

by Christ, since the Word of God says: 'The two shall become one flesh'² and one spirit. But we are born before we are brought to our final goal, and the mystery of God's operation is more excellent than the remedy for human weakness. Quite rightly is a good wife praised, but a pious virgin is more rightly preferred, for the Apostle says: 'He who gives his daughter in marriage does well, and he who does not give her does better. The one thinks about the things of God, the other about the things of the world.'³ The one is bound by marriage bonds, the other is free from bonds; one is under the law, the other under grace. Marriage is good: through it the means of human continuity are found. But virginity is better: through it are attained the inheritance of a heavenly kingdom and a continuity of heavenly rewards. Through a woman distress entered the world; through a virgin salvation came upon it. Lastly, Christ chose for Himself the special privilege of virginity and set forth the benefit of chastity, manifesting in Himself what He had chosen in His mother.

How great is the madness of their mournful barking when the same persons say that Christ could not have been born of a virgin and also assert that virgins remain among womankind which has given birth to human offspring! Does Christ grant to others what they say He cannot grant to Himself? Although He took a body, although He became man to redeem man and recall him from death, still, being God, He came to earth in an unusual way so that, as He had said: 'Behold I make all things new,'⁴ He might thus be born from the womb of an immaculate virgin, and be believed to be, as it is written: 'God with us.'⁵ Those on

---

2 Matt. 19.5.
3 1 Cor. 7.38.
4 Isa. 43.19.
5 Matt. 1.23.

the path of evil are known to say: 'She conceived as a virgin but she did not bring forth as a virgin.' How could she conceive as a virgin but be unable to bring forth as a virgin? Conception always precedes; bringing forth follows.

If they do not believe the teaching of the clergy, let them believe the words of Christ. Let them believe the instruction of the angels saying: 'For nothing will be impossible with God.'[6] Let them believe the creed of the Apostles which the Church of Rome keeps and guards in its entirety. Mary heard the words of the angel, and she who had said before: 'How shall this be?' not questioning faith in the generation, later replied: 'Behold the handmaid of the Lord; be it done to me according to thy word.'[7] This is the virgin who conceived in the womb, the virgin who brought forth a son. Thus Scripture says: 'Behold a virgin shall conceive and bear a son,'[8] and it declares not only that a virgin shall conceive, but also that a virgin shall bring forth.

What is that gate of the sanctuary, that outer gate facing the East and remaining closed: 'And no man,' it says, 'shall pass through it except the God of Israel'?[9] Is not Mary the gate through whom the Redeemer entered this world? This is the gate of justice, as He Himself said: 'Permit us to fulfill all justice.'[10] Holy Mary is the gate of which it is written: 'The Lord will pass through it, and it will be shut,'[11] after birth, for as a virgin she conceived and gave birth.

Why is it hard to believe that Mary gave birth in a way contrary to the law of natural birth and remained a virgin, when contrary to the law of nature the sea looked at Him and fled, and the waters of the Jordan returned to their

---

6 Luke 1.37.
7 Luke 34.7,38.
8 Isa. 7.14.
9 Ezech. 44.20.
10 Matt. 3.15.
11 Ezech. 44.20.

source.[12] It is not past belief that a virgin gave birth when we read that a rock issued water,[13] and the waves of the sea were made solid as a wall.[14] It is not past belief that a man came from a virgin when a rock bubbled forth a flowing stream,[15] iron floated on water,[16] a man walked upon the waters.[17] If the waters bore a man, could not a virgin give birth to a man? What man? Him of whom we read: 'The Lord will send them a man, who will save them, and the Lord will be known in Egypt.'[18] In the Old Testament a Hebrew virgin led an army through the sea;[19] in the New Testament a king's daughter was chosen to be the heavenly entrance to salvation.

What more? Let us add further praises of widowhood, since, after relating the miraculous birth from a virgin, the Gospel has the story of the widow Anna, 'who lived with her husband seven years from her maidenhood, and by herself as a widow to eighty-four years. She never left the temple, with fasting and prayers worshiping day and night.'[20]

Quite rightly do some persons look with contempt upon widowhood, which observes fasts, while they deplore the fact that at some time or other they were mortified by fasts; they take revenge for the injury they did themselves, being anxious through constant feasts and habits of luxury to keep away the pain of abstinence. They do nothing more than condemn themselves out of their own mouth.

Such persons even fear that their former fasting will be

---

12 Cf. Ps. 113.3.
13 Cf. Exod. 17.6.
14 Cf. Exod. 14.22.
15 Cf. Num. 20.11.
16 Cf. 4 Kings 6.6.
17 Cf. Matt. 14.26.
18 Isa. 19.20.
19 Cf. Exod. 14.21.
20 Luke 2.36,37.

charged to them. Let them have their choice. If they have ever fasted, let them suffer the hardship of their good deed; if never, let them admit their intemperance and wantonness. So they say that Paul was a teacher of wantonness. Pray, who will be a teacher of sobriety if he taught wantonness, for he chastized his body and brought it to subjection[21] and by many fasts said that he had rendered the worship which is due to Christ. He did so not to praise himself and his deeds, but to teach us what example we must follow. Did he give us instruction in wantonness when he said: 'Why, as if still living do you lay down the rules: "Do not touch; nor handle; nor taste!" things that must all perish in their use'?[22] And he also said that we must live 'Not in indulgence of the body, not in any honor to the satisfying and love of the flesh, not in the lusts of error; but in the Spirit by whom we are renewed.'[23]

If the Apostle said too little, let them hear the Prophet saying: 'I afflicted my soul with fasting.'[24] He who does not fast is uncovered and naked and exposed to wounds. Finally, if Adam had covered himself with fasting he would not have become naked.[25] Nineve freed herself from death by fasting.[26] The Lord Himself said: 'But this kind of demon will be cast out only by prayer and fasting.'[27]

Why should we say more to [you] our master and teacher, since those very persons have paid a price befitting their disloyalty, having even come here so that there might be no place where they were not condemned. And they proved that they were Manichaeans in truth by not believing that

---

21 Cf. 1 Cor. 9.27.
22 Col. 2.20-22.
23 Cf. Tit. 3.3-5.
24 Ps. 68.11.
25 Cf. Gen. 3.7.
26 Cf. Jonas 3.5.
27 Matt. 17.20.

He came forth from a virgin. What madness, pray tell, is this, equal almost to that of the present-day Jews? If they do not believe that He came, neither do they believe that He took a body. Thus, He was seen only in imagination, in imagination He was crucified. But He was crucified for us in truth; in truth He is our Redeemer.

A Manichaean is one who denies the truth, who denies Christ's Incarnation. To such there is no remission of sins. It is the impiety of the Manichaeans which the most clement emperor has abominated and all who have met them run from them as from a plague. Witnesses of this are our brethren and fellow priests, Crescens, Leopardus, and Alexander, men imbued with the Holy Spirit, men who brought upon them the condemnation of all and drove them as fugitives from the city of Milan.

Therefore, may your Holiness know that those whom you condemned—Jovinian, Auxentius, Germinator, Felix, Plotinus, Genial, Martian, Januarius, and Ingeniosus—have also been condemned by us in accord with your judgment.

May our almighty God keep you safe and prosperous, O Lord, dearly beloved Brother.

Signed:

I, Eventius, Bishop, greet your Holiness in the Lord and sign this letter.

Maximus, Bishop

Felix, Bishop

Theodorus, Bishop

Constantius, Bishop

By order of my lord Geminianus, Bishop, in his presence, I, Aper, Presbyter, sign.

Eustasius, Bishop, and all the Orders sign.

LETTERS TO PRIESTS

45. Ambrose to Horontianus[1] (c. 387)

THE PROPHETS foretold the gathering of the Gentiles and the future rearing of the Church, yet in the Church there is not only the continual progress of courageous souls, but also the failure of the weak and their conversion anew. Therefore, we can conclude from the prophetic books that the fair and strong soul proceeds without stumbling, but the weak one falls and recovers from her falls and amends her way.

As we read in the Canticle of Canticles of the continual progress of the blessed soul, so let us consider in Micheas the conversion of the fallen soul of which we began to speak. Not without good reason have the Prophet's words, 'And thou, Bethlehem, house of Ephrata,'[2] disturbed you. How can Christ's birthplace be a house of wrath? Though the name of the place expresses this, certain mysterious operations are being illustrated.

---

1 For the letters to Horontianus, a priest of Milan, probably Syrian in origin, and those to Irenaeus, a layman, the sequence given by J. Palanque, 'Deux correspondents de S. Ambroise,' *Revue des études latines* 11 (1933) 152-163 has been followed. He groups all the letters to Horontianus around the year 387.
2 Mich. 5.2.

Let us first consider what meaning Micheas has in Latin. It means 'Who is from God,' or, as we find elsewhere: 'Who is he, the son of the Morasthite,'³ in other words [son of] the heir.⁴ Who is the heir but the Son of God who says: 'All things have been delivered to me by my Father,'⁵ who, being the heir, wished us to be co-heirs? It is well [to ask]: 'Who is he?' for He is not one of the people, but one chosen to receive the grace of God, in whom speaks the Holy Spirit, who began to prophesy in the days of Joathan, Achaz, and Ezekias, kings of Juda.'⁶ By this order is signified the progress of the vision, for it goes from the times of evil kings to those of the good king.

Since the afflicted soul was first oppressed under evil kings, it seems best to consider what progress in conversion she experienced. In her weakness she was overthrown, and all her fences became a path for passers-by and for the inroads of passion. Spent with luxury and pleasure, she was trodden down and banished from the presence of the Lord: 'Her tower was decayed,'⁷ that tower which, as we read in the song of Isaias, was placed in the midst of a choice vineyard.⁸ For the tower is desolate when the vine withers and her flock wanders, but when the verdure of the vine returns or the sheep come back, it grows bright, for nothing is more desolate than iniquity, nothing more bright than justice.

To this tower the sheep is recalled when the soul is recalled from her downfall, and in that sheep returns the reign of Christ which is the beginning, for He is the beginning and the end, and the beginning of salvation.⁹ The soul is first

---

3 Mich. 1.1.
4 Ambrose here agrees with the interpretation of Jerome (*Prol. in Mich.*, PL 25.1151-1154) that Micheas means *humilis*, and Morasthi means *coheres*.
5 Matt. 11.27.
6 Mich. 1.1.
7 Mich. 4.8.
8 Cf. Isa. 5.2.
9 Cf. Apoc. 1.8.

rebuked for having grievously transgressed, and she is asked: 'Why hast thou known evil? Hast thou no king in thee?'[10] In other words, you had a king to rule and guard you; you should not have strayed from the path of justice, or left the ways of the Lord, for He imparted to you sense and reason. Where were your thoughts and counsels with which you could have by your own power guarded against unrighteousness and warded off iniquity? 'Why have your sorrows overwhelmed you like a woman that is in labor,'[11] that you might bring forth iniquity and conceive injustice? There is no greater sorrow than to have a man wound his conscience with the sword of sin; there is no heavier burden than the load of sin and the weight of transgression. It bows down the soul, it bends it to the ground, so that it cannot raise itself. Heavy, my son, exceedingly heavy are the burdens of sin. Thus that woman in the Gospel who had been bent over, giving the semblance of a heavily laden soul, could be raised up only by Christ.[12]

To such a soul it is said: 'Act manfully, and approach, O daughter of Sion, that you may bring forth,'[13] for the pains of childbirth work tribulation, and tribulation endurance, and endurance tried virtue, and tried virtue hope. And hope does not disappoint forever.'[14] At one and the same time all that is opposed to virtue is plucked up and cast forth, lest the seeds remain behind and revive, budding forth again into new fruits.

Not without reason was she given horns and hoofs, to bruise all the sheaves of the threshing floor, like the calf of Libanus,[15] for, unless the sheaves are bruised and the straw winnowed, the corn within cannot appear and be separated.

---
10 Mich. 4.9.
11 *Ibid.*
12 Cf. Luke 13.11.
13 Mich. 4.10.
14 Rom. 5.3,4.
15 Cf. Mich. 4.13.

Let the soul that would advance in virtue first bruise and thresh out its superfluous passions that at the harvest it may have its fruits to show. How many weeds choke the good seed! These first must be rooted out, so that they will not destroy the fruitful crop of the soul.

The careful guardian of the soul then sees how he may restrain her in her pleasures, and cut off her desires, to prevent her being overwhelmed with delight in them. The correction of the father who does not spare the rod is useful, that he may render his son's soul obedient to the precepts of salvation.[16] He punishes with a rod, as we read: 'I shall punish their offenses with a rod.'[17] Therefore, one who with a rod strikes an Israelite's soul on the cheek instructs her by the Lord's punishment in the discipline of patience. No one who is chastened and corrected need lose hope, for one who loves his son chastises him.[18] No one should despair of a remedy.

Lo! where you had the house 'of one seeing wrath,'[19] there is the house of bread;[20] in the place of cruelty, there is now piety; where there was the slaughter of the Innocents, there is the redemption of all, as it is written: 'And thou, Bethlehem Ephrata, art not the least among the princes of Juda: out of thee shall he come forth the ruler in Israel.'[21] Bethlehem is the house of bread, Ephrata the house of one seeing wrath, for this is the meaning of those names. In Bethlehem Christ was born of Mary, but Bethlehem is the same as Ephrata.[22] Christ, therefore, was born in the house of wrath, yet it is no longer a house of wrath, but a house of bread, because it has received Him, the Bread which

---

16 Cf. Prov. 13.24.
17 Ps. 88.33.
18 Cf. Eccli. 30.1.
19 Ephrata.
20 Bethlehem.
21 Mich. 5.2.
22 Cf. Luke 2.6.

came down from heaven.²³ But Ephrata is the house of one seeing wrath, because while Herod searched there for Christ he ordered the Innocents slain; therefore: 'A voice was heard in Rama, Rachel weeping for her children.'²⁴

Let no one be afraid now, because that repose which David sought has been heard of in Ephrata, and it has been found in the fields of the woods.²⁵ The nations met in the woods, but, after they believed in Christ, it became fruitful, for it received the fruit of the blessed womb.²⁶ And Rachel died in childbirth because, even then, as the patriarch's wife, she saw Herod's wrath which spared not the tenderest years. Likewise, in Ephrata she gave birth to that Benjamin of surpassing beauty, the last in the order of mystery, namely, Paul, who caused no small grief to his mother before his birth, for he persecuted her sons. She died and was buried there, that we, dying and being buried with Christ, may rise in the Church. Hence, according to another interpretation Ephrata means 'enriched' or 'filled with fruits.'

Now, here in the book of the Prophet we find the words: 'Thou art *oligostós*,' that is, 'thou art among the few,' but in Matthew: 'And thou, Bethlehem, house of Juda, are not among the few.' In one expression is 'house of Juda,' in this, 'house of Ephrata,' and a difference only of words, not of meaning, for inwardly Judea saw the wrath and outwardly she suffered it. She is among the few, for there are who enter the house of bread by the narrow way. But she who knows not Christ is not among the few, among those who make progress. Nor is she the least, she who is the house of benediction, the recipient of divine grace. Yet in this she is the least, that what one offers to Christ he seems to offer to

---

23 Cf. John 6.50.
24 Matt. 2.18.
25 Cf. Ps. 131.3-6.
26 Cf. Luke 1.42.

her. One who seeks the Church seeks Christ, and He is either despised or honored in every least one, for He says Himself: 'What you have done to the least of these my brethren, you did for me.'[27]

That Bethlehem is the very same as Ephrata a passage in Genesis makes clear, when it says: 'So Rachel died, and was buried on the way to Ephrata, that is, Bethlehem.'[28] The tomb of holy Rachel is on the road, for she is a type of the Church so that passers-by may say: 'The blessing of the Lord be upon you!'[29] and 'Coming they shall come with rejoicing.'[30]

Thus, every soul which receives the bread which comes down from heaven is a house of bread, the bread of Christ, being nourished and having its heart strengthened by the support of that heavenly bread which dwells within it. Hence, Paul says: 'We are all one bread.'[31] Every faithful soul is Bethlehem, just as that is called Jerusalem which has the peace and tranquility of the Jerusalem on high which is in heaven. That is the true bread which, after it was broken into bits, has fed all men.

The fifth version[32] has 'house of bread,' because Beth means 'a house,' and 'leem' means 'bread.' The words were omitted from the other versions, I imagine, because of the unbelief of the Jews who feared to convict themselves, or possibly they were removed by others.

We learn also that Bethlehem is of the tribe of Juda from the reading in the Book of Judges where the Levite took a concubine from Bethlehem of Juda, and the concubine was angry with him and returned to her father's house in Bethlehem of Juda.

---

27 Matt. 25.40.
28 Gen. 35.19.
29 Ps. 128.8.
30 Ps. 126.6.
31 1 Cor. 10.17.
32 Ambrose here appears to be using a copy of Origen's *Hexapla*.

Christ's going forth is from the days of eternity,[33] for eternity commenced for us when He went forth to run His course and gave to Israel the days of salvation.[34] When Christ comes to a soul there is fruitfulness and childbearing. So she came to the Church, she who brought forth more than she who had sons,[35] bringing forth seven who are law-abiding, tranquil, peacemakers. That soul begins to conceive and Christ is formed in her if she welcomes His arrival and feeds on His riches. As a result, she has no needs, and other souls, seeing her, return to the path of salvation.

'She shall have peace,'[36] but it is tried only by temptations. Then only will her peace and tranquility be proved when she has shut out or repulsed vain thoughts, when she has subdued all the emotions of rising passion, when distress, persecution, hunger, peril, the sword beset her. 'Then,' it says, 'there will be peace,' because in the midst of all these we overcome through Him who loved us, for we trust in Him that neither death nor the power of temptations shall tear and separate us from His love.[37] Then He will send temptation that the just may be tried. The Lord wills to send temptation, not to beguile anyone, but because many who are weak are vanquished by temptation and those who are strong are tried.

Then will come the dew from the Lord,[38] then repose, then will the soul of the just be like 'the young lion among the flocks of sheep.'[39] I have no doubt that on the model of the Gospel this refers to Christ, for He Himself said: 'Then the just will shine forth like the sun in the kingdom of

---
33 Cf. Mich. 5.2.
34 Cf. Ps. 18.6.
35 Cf. Isa. 54.1.
36 Mich. 5.5.
37 Cf. Rom. 8.35.
38 Cf. Mich. 5.7.
39 Mich. 5.8.

their Father.'[40] Then shall be tamed the chariot car, that is, the wild coursing and the motions of his body;[41] there will be an end of 'Conflicts without and anxieties within';[42] everywhere, within and without, there shall be calm; no one shall feel repugnance or resist this good will, when the intervening wall is broken down, when both are made one,[43] for the obedience of the flesh will end all discord.

But, if a weak soul, such as Israel according to the flesh, stumbles and is shaken by persecutions and separates herself any distance at all from the charity of Christ, she is caught up and reproved as faithless, as ungrateful, as unbelieving, for, after being freed from the vanities of this world, she has looked back and suffered a relapse. Yet, she was not required to offer gifts or sacrifice bulls, but only to know the good and to act justly: 'It was shown thee, O man,' [he says] 'what is good and what the Lord requireth of thee. Only do judgment and justice, love mercy, and be prepared to walk with thy Lord.'[44] But, since the weak soul has not kept these commands, the Lord says: 'Woe is me, for I am become as one who gathers the straw at harvest time, and like a grape in vintage time.' When the Prophet hears these words by which God has spoken, he says to the soul: 'Alas for me, O soul, that the man full of fear has gone from the earth.'[45] These are as the words of the Lord pitying the punishment which will come upon sin, and weeping over our transgressions.

Then the soul who hears that she will not gather the fruit of her seeds, and, in losing the harvest, will find no strength for herself; that she will press the olive but will not find the oil of gladness or drink the wine of pleasure; finding, also,

---

40 Matt. 13.43.
41 Cf. Mich. 5.10.
42 2 Cor. 7.5.
43 Eph. 2.14.
44 Mich. 6.8.
45 Mich. 7.1,2.

that the deeds of the flesh are full of blood, full of deception, cheating, and fraud, empty shows of affection and calculated guile, and all those of her own house her enemies; that she must guard the movements of her companion body, for they are grievous enemies of the soul—is converted and begins to hope in God, and, knowing that the flesh is truly her enemy, she says to it: 'Rejoice not thou, my enemy, over me, because I have fallen. I shall arise. When I sit in darkness, the Lord shall enlighten me.'[46]

When she finds that some power mocks her to prevent her following a better path, and tramples her to deliver her to the destruction of the flesh,[47] that she may be afflicted with diverse evils, which are decreed either by the Lord in satisfaction for her sins or by the Evil One out of jealousy at her conversion, to afflict and call her back to himself, she still says: 'I will bear the wrath of the Lord,' for either He chastizes me in my fall or has given you the power of afflicting me, 'because I have sinned,' yet I will bear this, 'until he justify my cause.'[48] Unless I confess and pay the price of my iniquities, I cannot be justified. But, when I am justified and have paid double for my sins, 'He will execute judgment for me,' and lay aside His wrath since the sentence against me is satisfied. 'He will bring me forth into the light that I may see his justice' and behold His delight. My enemy, the iniquity of the Devil, will see the light of my reconciliation, and 'shall be covered with shame,' who saith to me: 'Where is the Lord thy God?'[49] He will see in me His mercy, he will see His love.

Let us not listen to him when we are in the troubles of the world, whether of bodily pain, or the loss of children, or of other necessities. Let us, I say, not listen to him as he

---
46 Mich. 7.8.
47 Cf. 1 Cor. 5.5.
48 Mich. 7.9.
49 Mich. 5.10.

says: 'Where is the Lord thy God?' When we suffer severe pain we must then beware of his temptations, for then he is trying to lead astray the weary soul.

That soul which has not heeded his snares, seeing later the wonderful works of God, seeing herself in heaven, and the Devil creeping like a snake on the earth, will congratulate herself, saying: 'Who is a God like to thee, who takest away iniquity and passest by the wickedness?'[50] You have not been mindful of Your wrath, but have cast all our iniquities into the sea, like Egyptian lead, and graciously have restored us to mercy which You gave with twofold generosity, forgiving and hiding our sins, according to that which has been written: 'Blessed are those whose iniquities are forgiven, and whose sins are covered!'[51] Some sins You have washed away by the Blood of Your Son, others You have remitted for us, that by doing good and rendering praise we may cover up our mistakes. The expression, 'pardoning sins,' applies to their forgiveness, for He takes them away altogether, and what He remembers not are as though they did not exist. But the words 'passest by the wickedness' mean that, by confessing our failings and covering them with good deeds, they become charged to the author of our fault, the instigator of our sin. Does he not do this who confesses his fault, proving that he was beguiled by the malice and craft of that spiritual wickedness opposing him?

For this that soul gives thanks, that the Lord pardons sin, passes over and plunges iniquity into the depths of the sea. This may also refer to baptism in which the Egyptian is drowned, and the Hebrew rises again, wherein by the depths of wisdom and a multitude of good works her former sins are

---
50 Mich. 7.18.
51 Ps. 31.1.

covered up by the riches of the mercy of our God, who is mindful of the promise which He made to Abraham, and allows no soul which is an heir to Abraham to perish.

By these a soul is called back. But do you, my son, from the first flower of your youth an heir of the Church, which bore and sustains you, persevere in your purpose, remembering God's grace and His gift which you received by the imposition of my hands. Thus, in this office, too, as in the sacred ministry, you may reveal your faith and diligence and look for the recompense of the Lord Jesus.

Farewell, and love us as a son, for we love you.

46. Ambrose to Horontianus[1]

In my last letter I spoke of the soul which journeys through certain devious and winding roads, wavering as did Israel of old in the flesh. But Israel herself will be set free through the grace of our Lord Jesus Christ, 'when the full number of the Gentiles shall enter,'[2] for, her sin being lighter, she has renewed herself by repentance. Let us speak in this letter of the daughter of the Church and let us consider how the Lord Jesus first took her under His care, instructed her, and led her to perfection in His Gospel.

Now, it was when she lay in distress that He first took her under His care—how but in distress can the soul of anyone live an exile from paradise?[3]—and He brought her to Bethlehem.[4] The progress of that soul which He has taken in hand is signified in her going up to the 'house of bread' where she will not experience dearth or sterility of faith. I

---
1 Undated.
2 Rom. 11.25.
3 Cf. Gen. 3.25.
4 Cf. Matt. 2.1.

am speaking of souls in general, the souls by which we live and move, and not of any soul in particular, for it is not of the individual or particular soul of anyone, but of souls in general, as I said, that I intend to discourse.

Christ went down into Egypt,[5] assuming the protection and guidance of our soul, and then He returned to Judea. He was in the desert;[6] He was in Capharnaum; He was near the borders of Zabulon; He was by the sea coast; He passed through cornfields; He was in Bethphage, in Ephraim, in Bethany. Then He went into the garden where He gave Himself up; He suffered on Golgotha.

These are all steps in the progress of our soul through which by practice she receives the grace of a holy life. For, when the human race, in the person of Adam and Eve, was excluded from paradise and banished to a little town, she began wandering here and there, tracing her misguided steps without any delight. But in His own good time the Lord Jesus emptied Himself[7] that He might take upon Himself this state of exile and bring back the soul to her former state of grace. When He found her, and she had retraced her devious course of error, He called her back to paradise, as the Gospel reading explains.

He led her through the cornfields in order to feed one who was fasting; next into the desert, then into Capharnaum, a dwelling in the country, not in the city. Next, He brought her to the borders of Zabulon, near the floods of the night, those dark riddles of the Prophets, so that she might learn to find her way to the land of the Gentiles where all men meet, and that she might not fear the storms and billows of this world. Christ owns ships from Tharsis,[8] mystical

---

5 Cf. Matt. 2.14.
6 Cf. Matt. 4.1.
7 Cf. Phil. 2.8.
8 Cf. 3 Kings 10.22.

ships, of course, which traverse the sea and bring pious offerings for the construction of the temple. In ships like these Christ sets sail, and, like a good pilot, rests in the stern when the sea is calm. But when it is disturbed He awakes and rebukes the winds that He may flood His disciples with peace.[9] By going to the Gentiles, too, He sets free the soul which was held fast by the chains of the Law, so that she may not go to the company of heathens.

He came to Bethany, 'to the place of obedience,' where a dead man is raised to life, for, when the flesh is subdued by the soul, human nature no longer lies as if dead in its tomb, but is raised up by the grace of Christ. There, too, she learns to offer to suffer in the name of God.[10] As John teaches,[11] she is led from the 'place of obedience' to Ephraim, that is, to the richness of good fruits. From there she is brought to Bethany, that is, to obedience, for, once she has tasted the fruit of holy obedience, she is never unwilling to preserve it and to be called into its service.

When at last she was found pleasing, she came to Jerusalem, being worthy to be made into the temple of God where Christ dwelt. Here it is that the Lord Jesus sits upon the foal of an ass and is welcomed with the joy and gladness of an age that does no harm.[12]

Later, the words of eternal life are explained there in the garden where the Lord even allowed Himself to be seized, as John the Evangelist writes,[13] signifying that our soul, or rather, human nature, after the bonds of error are loosed, returns through Christ to the place from which in Adam she was expelled. Therefore, even to the thief who confessed his guilt

---

9 Cf. Matt. 8.26.
10 Cf. John 11.17-44.
11 Cf. John 12.1.
12 Cf. John 12.14.
13 Cf. John 18.8.

it was said: 'Amen I say to thee, this day thou shalt be with me in paradise.' He had said: 'Remember me when thou comest into thy kingdom.'[14] In answering him, Christ did not speak of His kingdom, yet for this reason [He said]: 'This day thou shalt be with me in paradise,' that what was lost should first be formed anew, and then must be increased. Thus a way is provided through paradise to the kingdom, not through the kingdom to paradise.

It is reserved for the disciples to receive more in proportion to their labors. That is why He only promised the thief a dwelling, but He reserved the kingdom for a later time. Let the man who is converted at the stroke of death and confesses the Lord Jesus merit an abode in paradise, but he who disciplined himself long before and has been a soldier for Christ, won souls, and offered himself for Christ should have the kingdom of God for his wages and should rejoice to receive the full reward of his deeds. So it is said to Peter: 'I will give thee the keys of the kingdom of heaven.'[15] Thus, the one converted from robbery obtains rest, the one tried in the apostleship receives authority.

This is the soul trained by the Gospel, the soul of the Gentiles, the daughter of the Church. She is far better after her journeying than the soul cast out of Judea, for she has mounted up to the Lord Jesus and to higher things by her good counsels and good works, and Christ has acknowledged her as His own on Golgotha. There was the burial place of Adam so that there through His cross Christ might raise the dead to life. And where in Adam all have death, there in Christ all have the resurrection.

Farewell, son, and love us, because we love you.

---
14 Luke 23.42,43.
15 Matt. 16.19.

47. Ambrose to Horontianus[1]

Not in vain have you decided to inquire about the nature of the inheritance of a divine legacy and the reason why it is esteemed of such value that many even offer up their death for its sake. But if you realize that even among men the advantage of inheriting money gives an additional sanctity to the laws of filial affection, and that parents are given greater respect lest the slighted love of a father may wreak its vengeance by disinheriting or repudiating a rebellious child, you will cease wondering why there is so great desire of the divine inheritance.

Now, there is an inheritance offered to all Christians, as Isaias says: 'This is the inheritance of those who believe in the Lord,'[2] and it is hoped for by promise, not by the Law. This is proved by the parable of the Old Testament in the words of Sara: 'Cast out this slave-girl with her son; for the son of this slave-girl shall not be heir with my son Isaac.'[3] Sara's son was Isaac, the slave-girl's son was Ismael; since they antedated the Law, the promise was older than the Law. We, in comparison with Isaac, are sons by promise; the Jews, in comparison with the flesh, are sons of the slave-girl.[4] We have a free woman as our mother, she who was barren and later begot and bore a son of promise. Their mother is Agar, she who brings children to bondage. Whoever is promised grace is free; whoever is given the yoke of the Law is enslaved. Therefore, the promise was ours before they had the Law, and by nature freedom is more ancient than bondage. Freedom is by promise; bondage, by the Law. But, although the promise is before the Law, as we have said,

---

1 Undated.
2 Isa. 54.17.
3 Gen. 21.10.
4 Cf. Gal. 4.28.

and freedom is the promise, love is in freedom; love is according to the Law and love is greater than freedom.

Are we not, then, servants? Why is it written: 'Praise the Lord, ye servants'?[5] Why does the Apostle say: 'But as slaves of Christ, doing the will of God from your heart, with good will'?[6] Truly, this service is free and willing, of which the Apostle says: 'A freeman who has been called is a slave of Christ.'[7] This is service of the heart, not of necessity. Thus, we are the servants of our Creator, but we enjoy the freedom which we have received through the grace of Christ, being born of the promise by faith. And as those born of a free woman, let us make an offering of our freedom, for we have been signed on the forehead as befits the free, so that we will not be confounded, but rejoice, being signed in the spirit, not in the flesh. To these is it properly said: 'Stand fast, and do not be caught again under the yoke of slavery.'[8] He did not say: 'Do not be slaves,' but 'do not be caught by the yoke of slavery,' for the yoke of slavery is heavier than slavery.

Isaac also says to his son Esau, when he asks his blessing: 'Behold, without the fruitfulness of the earth shall your dwelling be; without the dew of the heavens above. By your sword shall you live, you shall serve your brother. But there will be a time when you shall take and shake his yoke from your neck.'[9] How does his being a slave fit in with his casting from his neck his brother's yoke, unless we realize the difference that exists in slavery? Let Scripture itself explain this difference to us: Isaac is good, and he is good to us who are born after him into freedom; he is a good father to both his sons. He proved that he loved them both by affection

---

5 Ps. 134.1.
6 Eph. 6.6.
7 1 Cor. 7.22.
8 Gal. 5.1.
9 Gen. 27.39,40.

for the one, by a blessing for the other, for he bade the older son bring him food and receive his blessing, but while he delayed and went in search of wild game from afar, the younger brother brought him a kid from his own fold.

The good food of all is Christ, the good food is faith; the sweet food is mercy; the pleasing food is grace, foods which the people of holy Church feed upon. The good food is the Spirit of God; the good food is the remission of sins. But very hard food is the severity of the Law, the fear of penalty; and coarse food is the observance of the letter in place of the grace of pardon. Those people are under a curse, but we in blessing. A ready food is faith: 'But the word is nigh in thy mouth and in thy heart.'[10] The food of the Law is slower, for while they awaited the Law the people went astray.

Therefore, the father gave his blessing to his alert and faithful son, but, being a good father, he also saved his blessing for his older son in order to make him his brother's servant. This he did, not because he wished to debase his family to slavery, but because he who is incapable of ruling and governing himself must be a slave and be in the service of one more wise, so that he will be guided by his wisdom, and not fall through his own folly or stumble through his want of caution. Such a state of slavery is given instead of a blessing. Moreover, it is numbered among benefits, along with the fatness of the earth and the dew of heaven from above. But, having said: 'By your sword you shall live,'[11] lest he be harmed by confidence arising from strength or power, he added: 'You shall serve your brother,' in order that you may obtain the rich fruits of the body, and the dew of divine grace, and may follow him who will guide you by his leadership.

---

10 Deut. 30.14.
11 Gen. 27.40.

There will be a time when you shall shake off his yoke from your neck that you may have the reward of a willing slavery and not undergo the evil of compulsory bondage. That slavery is dishonorable which is compelled by necessity, but that is honorable which is offered in affection. Hence the Apostle's words: 'If I do this willingly, I have a reward. But if unwillingly, it is a stewardship that has been entrusted to me.'[12] Surely, it is better to merit a reward then to serve as a steward. Let us, then, not be bound by the yoke of slavery, but let us serve in charity of spirit, since the Apostle says: 'By charity of spirit serve ye one another.'[13] Fear of the Law is the charity of the Gospel. 'The fear of the Lord is the beginning of wisdom, but the fulness of the Law is charity.'[14] Yet the Law itself says: 'But the whole Law is fulfilled in one word,'[15] and it is summed up in this: 'Thou shalt love thy neighbor.'[16]

This, then, is what we asserted, for, although bondage is of the Law, freedom is in accord with the Law, for love belongs to freedom, fear to bondage. There is, therefore, a love of the Law and a bondage of love; and the Law is the forerunner of love, and the love of the Gospel is a free donation of loving service.

The Law, then, is not unneeded, for like a tutor it attends the weak.[17] I mean weakness of character, not of body, for there are children who do not know how to utter God's word, who do not receive His works, for, if a spotless life is old age,[18] surely a life full of stains is the time of youth. The Law, therefore, was a tutor, that is, *nómos*, until faith came, 'And,' he says, 'like weaklings we were kept imprisoned

---
12 1 Cor. 9.17.
13 Gal. 5.13.
14 Eccli. 1.16.
15 Gal. 5.14.
16 Rom. 13.9.
17 Cf. Gal. 3.24.
18 Cf. Wisd. 4.9.

by the Law, shut up for the faith that was to be revealed.'[19] Later came faith; he does not mean the Gospel, but faith, for that is only faith which is the Gospel, for in it the justice of God is revealed which is from faith unto faith,[20] yet this of the Law is faith if the fullness of faith reaches it. Rightly, therefore, is faith spoken of as a single thing, for that [law] without this [faith] is not faith, it is confirmed in this [faith]. When faith came, there arrived, too, the fullness, there arrived the adoption of sons, weakness departed, childhood left, we rose to perfect manhood, we put on Christ. How can one be weak and small in whom is Christ, the power of God? Thus have we arrived at perfection and we have received the teachings of perfection.

Today you have heard the reading: 'Of myself I can do nothing. As I hear, I judge.' You have also heard: 'I do not accuse you, I do not judge.' I do not accuse: 'Moses accuses you, in whom you hope.' And you have heard: 'If I bear witness concerning myself, my witness is not true.'[21] I have been taught what sort of judge, what sort of witness I should be. For it is not as a weakling that He says: 'Of myself I can do nothing,' but one who hears this is the weakling. Indeed, the Son does nothing without the Father, because in them are community of operation and unity of power. Here He speaks like a judge, so that we may know in judging men that we must form our opinion equitably, not according to our own will and power.

Choose some criminal who has been charged and found guilty of a crime, one who does not persist in excuses, but begs pardon, falling at the knees of the judge. He answers him: 'Of myself I can do nothing; justice, not power, is in the pronouncement of judgment. I do not judge; your own deeds judge you. They charge and accuse you. The laws

---
19 Gal 3.23.
20 Cf. Rom. 1.17.

condemn you; I as judge do not charge but only guard them. Of myself I produce nothing, but from you proceeds the sentence of judgment against you. As I hear, I judge, not as I wish, and my judgment is true because I favor not my wish but fairness.'

Let us next consider the divine rule of judging. The Lord of heaven and earth, the Judge of all, says: 'Of myself I can do nothing. As I hear, I judge,' and man says to his Lord: 'Dost thou not know that I have power to release thee, and I have power to crucify thee?'[22] Why is the Lord not able? 'Because,' He says, 'my judgment is true, because I seek not my own will, but the will of him who sent me,'[23] that is, not the will of man whom you see, not the choice of man whom you judge only as man, not the will of the flesh, for the spirit is willing, but the flesh is weak,[24] but the divine will which is the source of law and the rule of judgment. Likewise is that witness true who bears witness not of himself, but of another, for it is written: 'Let another praise thee, and not thy own mouth.'[25]

In a mystical sense it is well said to the Jews: 'I do not judge you. I, the redemption of all, I, the remission of sins, I do not judge you because you have not received me. I do not judge; I freely pardon. I do not judge; I redeem sinners with my blood. I do not judge; I blot out iniquities and I will not remember.[26] I do not judge; I prefer the life rather than the death of the sinner.[27] I do not judge, I do not condemn you, but I justify those who confess. Moses accuses you; he has blamed you, in whom you hope. He accuses you, because he has not the power of judging; this is reserved for

---

21 John 5.30,45,31.
22 John 19.10.
23 John 5.30.
24 Cf. Matt. 26.41.
25 Prov. 27.2.
26 Cf. Isa. 43.25.
27 Cf. Ezech. 18.23.

his Maker.' He, then, in whom you trust is accusing you, while the One in whom you willed not to hope has forgiven you.

O great folly of the Jews! Rightly are they accused of their crimes, for they have chosen an accuser and refused a good judge; pardon, therefore, is not for them; punishment surely reaches them.

It is right for you, my son, to have begun with the Law and to have been confirmed in the Gospel, from faith to faith, as it is written: 'He who is just lives by faith.'[28]

Farewell, and love us, because we love you.

48. Ambrose to Horontianus[1]

If 'Abraham believed the Lord, who credited the act to him as justice'[2] and his act was considered just, taking him from unbelief to faith, surely we are justified by faith, not by the works of the Law. But Abraham had two sons, Ismael and Isaac, one of a slave-girl, the other of a free woman.[3] But he was told to cast out the slave-girl and her son, for the son of the slave-girl would not be his heir. We, therefore, are not sons of the slave-girl but of the free woman by whose freedom Christ has set us free. Hence it follows that they are sons of Abraham who are so by faith, for heirs of faith surpass heirs by birth. The Law is a tutor; faith is a free woman. Let us, then, cast out the works of bondage; let us keep the grace of freedom; let us leave the shade, following the sun; let us break with Jewish rites.

The circumcision of one member is of no avail, for the

---

28 Rom. 1.17.

1 Undated.
2 Gen. 15.6.
3 Cf. Gal. 4.22.

Apostle says: 'Behold, I, Paul, tell you that if you be circumcised, Christ will be of no advantage to you,'[4] not because He is powerless, but because He does not consider those worthy of His benefits who desert His paths.

Sephora of old circumcised her son and warded off a threatening danger.[5] Even then Christ was of advantage, although perfection was still deferred. While the group of believers was small, the Lord Jesus came, not small, but perfect in all things. He was circumcised first in accordance with the Law so as not to destroy the Law, and later through the Cross in order to fulfill the Law.[6] That which is only partial has ended, because that which is perfect has come, for in Christ the Cross circumcised not one member but the useless pleasures of the whole body.

Perhaps it is still being asked why one who had come to show a perfect circumcision wished to be circumcised partially. On this I do not think we need ponder further, for, if He became sin in order to cleanse our sins,[7] if He became a curse for us in order to make void the curse of the Law,[8] for this reason He was also circumcised for us in order to remove the circumcision of the Law, for He was about to give us the salvation of the Cross.

In the spirit we must wait for the hope of justice by faith, as the Apostle tells us, and we who are called to freedom must not use our liberty as an occasion for sensuality. Indeed, 'neither circumcision is of any avail, nor uncircumcision, but faith which works through charity.'[9] Therefore, it is written: 'Thou shalt love the Lord thy God.'[10] One who loves surely

---

[4] Gal. 5.2.
[5] Cf. Exod. 4.25.
[6] Cf. 1 Cor. 13.10.
[7] Cf. 2 Cor. 5.21.
[8] Cf Gal. 3.13.
[9] Cf. Gal. 5.5,13,6.
[10] Deut. 6.5.

believes and in believing each man begins to love. Abraham believed and so began to love, and believed not in part, but entirely; otherwise, he could not have perfect charity, because it has been written: 'Charity believes all things.'[11] Unless charity believes all things it does not appear perfect. Therefore, perfect charity has all faith.

Yet, I would not lightly assert that all faith at once has perfect charity, for the Apostle says: 'If I have all faith so as to remove mountains, yet do not have charity, I am nothing.'[12] In a Christian man there are three virtues in particular, hope, faith, and charity, but the greatest of these is charity.[13]

I suppose the Apostle said this for the sake of his argument, for it hardly seems possible that one who had all faith so as to remove mountains would not have charity, or how if he had all mysteries and all knowledge he would not have charity, especially since John says: 'Everyone who believes that Jesus is the Christ is born of God,'[14] and he has said above: 'Whoever is born of God does not commit sin.'[15] Hence it is understood that if one who believes that Jesus is the Christ is born of God, and one who is born of God does not sin, then surely one who believes that Jesus is the Christ does not sin. If a man sins, he does not believe; one who does not believe does not love; one who does not love is guilty of sin. Therefore, he does not love who sins, for charity covers a multitude of sins.[16] But charity precludes the love of sin and, since it also casts out fear, charity surely is full of perfect faith.

The Apostles, who were to be His friends, said as they asked the good Physician to heal their weak faith: 'Increase

---
11 1 Cor. 13.7.
12 1 Cor. 13.2.
13 Cf. 1 Cor. 13.13.
14 1 John 4.7.
15 1 John 3.9.
16 Cf. 1 Peter 4.8.

our faith.'[17] Their faith was still weak, since even Peter heard: 'O thou of little faith, why didst thou doubt?'[18] Thus does faith as the forerunner of charity take hold of the soul and prepare the way for love that is to come. And there is all faith where there is the perfection of charity.

I believe it is said that charity believes all things,[19] that is, she makes faith believe all things and such a soul has all faith. Consequently, where charity is perfect there is all faith, and where charity is perfect there is all hope. As it believes all things so it is said to hope all things. It is the greater in that it embraces hope and faith.

A man with this charity fears nothing, for charity casts out fear; when fear is banished and cast out, charity endures all things, bears all things. One who bears all things through love cannot fear martyrdom. For this reason, like a conqueror at the end of his course, he [Paul] says elsewhere: 'The world is crucified to me, and I to the world.'[20]

Farewell, son, and love us, for we love you.

49. Ambrose to Horontianus (c. 387)

After reading the *Hexaemeron* which I wrote, you told me that you were disturbed in the course of the sacred narrative and in my discussion of it because more was bestowed upon man than upon any living creature on earth, yet the earth and water produced all those things that fly or are on land or in water before man was produced for whose sake everything was made. You are asking me the reason for this: Moses was silent on this point and I dared not touch on it.

---

17 Luke 17.5.
18 Matt. 14.31.
19 Cf. 1 Cor. 13.7.
20 Gal. 6.14.

That spokesman of the divine decrees perhaps could have been purposely silent so as not to seem to set himself up as the judge and adviser of heaven's plans. It is one thing to utter what is inspired by the Spirit of God; it is another to interpret God's will. I think that we, speaking not as interpreters of God, but gathering, as it were, the seeds of reason from human usage, can give an opinion as to why it was becoming for man to be created last. For we have the example which men give us themselves and we also realize that God Himself has instilled into other creatures those practices which man may take as an example for himself.

One who sets out a banquet, as did the rich man in the Gospel (for we must compare divine things with divine things the better to be able to gather our arguments), prepares everything beforehand, kills his bulls and fatlings, and only then invites his friends to dinner. The trifles are first made ready, then the honored guest is summoned. In this way, too, the Lord first prepared for man the food of all animals, then summoned him like a friend to His banquet. Truly is that man a friend, a partaker of divine love, an heir of glory. To man himself He says: 'Friend, how didst thou come in here to the banquet?'[1] Those things which precede are furnishings, the friend is the one who is asked last.

Take another example. What is the world but an arena full of fighting? Therefore the Lord says in the Apocalypse: 'To the victor I shall give the crown of life,'[2] and Paul says: 'I have fought the good fight,'[3] and elsewhere: 'No one is crowned unless he has competed according to the rules.'[4] He who initiated this contest is actually Almighty God. When one initiates a contest in this world, does he not prepare all

---

1 Matt. 22.12.
2 Apoc. 2.10.
3 2 Tim. 4.7.
4 2 Tim. 2.5.

that is necessary for the contest, and only after he has made ready the wreaths for rewards call those who are to contend for the crown, so that the winner may not meet with delay but depart after being given his reward? The rewards of man are the fruits of the earth and the lights of heaven. The former are for his use in the present life; the latter, for his hope of life eternal.

Like an athlete, then, he comes last into the arena; he lifts his eyes to heaven; he sees that the heavenly creation was made subject to vanity not by its own will, but by reason of Him who made it subject in hope.[5] He sees that all creation groaned awaiting redemption. He sees that his whole task awaits him. He lifts his eyes, he sees the crowns of lights, he studies the spheres of moon and stars; 'But the just who have conquered will be like the stars in heaven.'[6] He chastises his body so that it will not defeat him in the contest; he anoints it with the oil of mercy; he practices daily exhibitions of virtue; he smears himself with dust; he runs with assurance to the goal of the course; he aims his blows, he darts his arms, but not at empty spaces; he strikes the adversary whom he does not see, because he is watching Him alone to whom all give way, even those who are not seen, at whose name spiritual powers were turned aside. It is he who poises the blow, it is Christ who strikes; he lifts his heel, Christ directs it to the wound. Lastly, although Paul did not see those whom he struck, he struck not as at the air,[7] because in preaching Christ he dealt wounds to all those spiritual evils which were His enemies. Not undeservedly, then, did man enter the stadium last, and a crown was prepared for him so that heaven might go before him as being his reward.

---

5 Cf. Rom. 8.20.
6 Dan. 12.3.
7 Cf. 1 Cor. 9.26.

But our struggle is not only against the spirits of evil, which are in heaven, but also against flesh and blood.[8] We struggle with satiety, we struggle with the fruits of the earth, we struggle with wine, by which even the just man was made drunk,[9] by which the whole army of the Jews was thrown back. We struggle with wild beasts; there is a struggle with the birds of the air, for our flesh, made fat with these, is not put in our service; we struggle with perils of journeying, with perils of waters, as Paul says;[10] we struggle with rods from trees by which the Apostles were beaten.[11] You see what great fights these are. Earth is man's training ground; heaven his crown. Therefore, as courtesies precede the friend, so do rewards precede the athlete.

Consider another example. In all things the beginning and the end are the most important. If you observe a house, the foundation and roof are most important; if it be a field, it is the sowing and harvest, the planting and the vintage. How pleasant are the graftings of trees, how desirable the fruits! So, too, heaven was formed first, man last, as being a heavenly creature on earth. Although he is compared in body with the beasts, in mind he is counted among celestial beings, for, even as we have borne the likeness of the earthly, so we bear the likeness of the heavenly.[12] How is he not heavenly who was made to the image and likeness of God?[13]

Rightly is heaven first and last in the creation of the world, for in heaven there is what is beyond heaven, there is the God of heaven. Lastly, of him it is understood: 'Heaven is my throne,'[14] for God does not sit above the element of heaven but in the heart of man. For this reason the Lord

---
8 Cf. Eph. 6.12.
9 Cf. Gen. 9.21.
10 Cf. 2 Cor. 11.29.
11 Cf. Acts 16.22.
12 Cf. 1 Cor. 15.49.
13 Cf. Gen. 1.26.
14 Isa. 66.1.

also says: 'We will come to him and make our abode with him.'[15] Heaven, therefore, is the first of the works on earth; man is the close or end or last.

Heaven is of the world, man above the world; the one is part of the world, the other an inhabitant of paradise, Christ's possession. Heaven is considered incorruptible, yet it passes away; man is regarded as corruptible and is clothed with incorruption; the figure of the one perishes, the other rises as being immortal. Yet, according to the authority of Scripture, the hands of the Lord fashioned both. We read of the heavens: 'The heavens are the works of thy hands.'[16] Man, too, says: 'Thy hands have made me and formed me,'[17] and 'The heavens declare the glory of God.'[18] As heaven is lighted with the splendor of the stars so do men shine with the light of their good works, and their deeds shine before their Father in heaven.[19] The one is the firmament of heaven on high, the other is a similar firmament of which it is said: 'Upon this rock I will build my Church';[20] the one is a firmament of the elements, the other of virtues, and this last is more excellent. They sucked oil out of the hard stone,[21] for the rock is Christ's body which redeemed heaven and the entire world.[22]

Why should I weave these details further and, as it were, take you over the whole course? The fact is that God made man a partaker of the divine nature, as we read in the Epistle of Peter.[23] Hence, someone says not without cause: 'For we

---

15 John 14.23.
16 Ps. 101.26.
17 Ps. 118.73.
18 Ps. 17.1.
19 Cf. Matt. 5.16.
20 Matt. 16.18.
21 Cf. Deut. 32.13.
22 Cf. 1 Cor. 10.4.
23 Cf. 2 Peter 1.4.

are also his offspring.'[24] He granted us a relationship with Himself, and we are of a rational nature so that we may seek that which is divine, which is not far from each one of us, in whom we live and are and move.

When He had bestowed the greatest of graces on man, as though he were His dearest and nearest friend, He gave him everything in the world,[25] so that no one would be without the necessities of life and the good life. One of these is the means of providing pleasure—the abundance of the earth's fruits; another is the knowledge of the secrets of heaven, which inflames the mind with love for his fellow men and longing for virtue by which we can reach the summit of divine mysteries. Both are most excellent—to have, as a king of the elements, the use of the sea, and to have all the world's wealth subject to him—creatures of air, land and water; to abound in all things without labor or want in the image and likeness of the adorable Creator, living in the greatest plenty, opening a way and advancing along a path by which to reach the palace of heaven.

You will discover quite early that the traveler on this difficult road is the man who has been so fashioned in purpose of heart and will that he has little association with his body, who enters into no fellowship with vice and is not impressed by flattering words. When he rides the chariot of prosperity he does not scorn the humble, or flee sorrows, or shake off and make light of the praises of the saints, or by desire for glory and bold gain expend all the eagerness of his hope. Sadness does not bow down his mind; wrong-dealing does not break it; suspicion does not arouse it; lust does not stir it. The body's passions do not overwhelm it; desire for vain objects and the allurements of pleasure do not disquiet it.

---

24 Acts 17.28. The words quoted by St. Paul are from the Greek poet Aratus of Cilicia, a fellow countryman of Paul.
25 Cf. Gen. 1.28.

If you add to these the virtues of chastity, soberness, and temperance, he is easily able to rein in the unruly drives of fickle passions, he sets bounds to his pleasures and desires, he puts an end to irresolution with fairness, he settles doubts with tranquility of mind and body, and, like a good judge, he keeps a harmless peace between the exterior and interior man, stilling each within himself. And if he is in distress, no evil counselor turns him back through fear from the crown of suffering; plainly, he will be brought in not only as a friend but as a son by a father, so that he may enjoy the riches of glory and His inheritance.

Quite rightly is he the last, as it were, the consummation of nature fashioned for righteousness, the judge of right among other living creatures. For example, as among men Christ is the consummation of the law for all who believe justice,[26] and we are, as it were, beasts in God's sight, so the Prophet says: 'I became as a brute beast before thee.'[27] Yet, what is the comparison when He redeemed those who were perishing, and we put them to death—He called slaves to liberty and we put the free into captivity? But who is equal to God?[28]

Man, therefore, came the last of all creatures, attractive in appearance, lofty in mind, so that he would be admirable to every creature, having in him, after the image of the eternal God, an invisible intelligence,[29] clothed in human form. This is the intelligence, the power of the soul, claiming for itself like a ruler the direction of soul and body. Other creatures fear this, although they do not see it, as we fear God whom we do not see, and fear the more because we do not see Him.

---

26 Cf. Rom. 10.4.
27 Ps. 72.22.
28 Cf. Ps. 88.9.
29 Gr.: *noûs*.

Since we are in His image and likeness, as Scripture says,[30] let us presume to speak, just as He expresses Himself in the fullness of His majesty, and sees all things—sky, air, earth, sea—embracing all and penetrating each one, so that nothing passes His notice and nothing exists unless it exists in Him and depends on Him and is full of Him, as He Himself says: 'I fill heaven and earth, saith the Lord.'[31] In the same way man's intelligence sees all, and is not seen, and has an invisible nature of its own. Through learning and judgment and perception the mind understands hidden matters, penetrates the secrets of the sea and the deep recesses of all the earth. She searches both parts of nature, in the likeness of the high God whom she imitates and follows, whose image is mirrored in each individual in proportionately small particles. She raises herself into the air and treads above the regions of the clouds; she soars to the heights of heaven by her desire for knowledge and her longing for wisdom; there, held fast for a while by wonder at the stars of heaven, delighted by their brilliant light, she gazes down on the things of the world. She betakes herself to Hesperus and Arcturus and the other unerring planets, and she sees that their wandering is not waywardness, that in order to visit all regions they appear to weave about and wander in and out unerringly. She soars with greater longing to the very embrace of the Father in whom is the only-begotten Son of God telling secrets of God, which will be revealed face to face in a later time.[32] Now, He reveals in part and in mystery to those who are worthy, and He sheds forth the Spirit and from His countenance, like a torrent, a resplendent light, so that man who has been illumined may say: 'And there was in my bones a flaming fire, and I am melted on all sides and cannot

---

30 Cf. Gen. 1.26.
31 Jer. 23.24.
32 Cf. John 1.18.

bear it.'³³ And David says: 'Let my sentence come forth from thy presence.'³⁴

After this digression let me now speak of that vigor of mind through which she governs all outside her, gazes at scattered and far-distant things, subdues animals of greater strength, inspires in others such great respect for herself that they vie with one another in obeying her, as though she were a king, and heed her words. Though irrational, they recognize reason and they are impressed with that learning which nature did not give them. Even wild beasts, seeing her gentleness, grow gentle at her command. They often close their jaws when the sound of a man's voice restrains them. We see hares caught without injury by the harmless teeth of dogs, and lions will let go their prey if a man's voice is heard; leopards, too, and bears are driven on or called off by men's words; horses neigh at men's applause and slacken their pace because of [men's] silence, and often, although not whipped, they outstrip those which are lashed, so much more powerfully does the whip of the tongue drive them on.

What shall I say of gifts [of creation]? In order to please man the ram nourishes his fleece and plunges into the stream in order to increase his sheen. Sheep chew richer grasses³⁵ in order to distend their filled udders³⁶ with the sweeter juice of milk; they suffer the pains of travail in order to give their gifts to man. Bulls groan all day under the plow which is pressed into the furrows.³⁷ Camels, besides the task of carrying loads, allow themselves to be sheared like sheep. The various animals make their offering as to a king and pay an annual tax. The horse, taking delight in his rider, prances proudly and, arching his back when his master

---

33 Jer. 20.9.
34 Ps. 16.2.
35 Cf. Virgil, *Aen.* 12.475.
36 Cf. Virgil, *Ecl.* 4.21.
37 Cf. Virgil, *Georg.* 1.45.
38 *Ibid.* 3.117.

mounts, offers his back as the rider's seat.[38] If it still puzzles you why man was made last, let that horse teach us that man was delayed not as a slight, but as an honor. A horse carries one who came after him; he does not despise but fears him; he takes him everywhere with pain to himself. In a moment man reaches distant places, traverses long distances, now on a single horse, now in a triumphal chariot.

Since I have mentioned triumphal chariots, I must refer to the chariot of Elias in which he was carried through the air,[39] and those chariots of elephants on which man the conqueror sits and rules those before him, although he is the last. So, too, the ship's helmsman sits in the stern, yet he guides the whole ship. That is why, I suppose, it is said, not without purpose in the Gospel, that the Lord Jesus was asleep in the stern, and when He was awakened He commanded the wind and the sea and calmed the storm,[40] showing that He came last because He came as the helmsman. Therefore, the Apostle says: ' "The first man, Adam, became a living soul"; the last Adam became a life-giving spirit. But it is not the spiritual that comes first but the physical, and then the spiritual,' and he added: 'The first man was of the earth, earthy: the second man is from heaven, heavenly.'[41]

Rightly, then, is the last one like the sum of the whole work. It is he alone who, like the cause of the world for which were made all things, dwells, so to speak, in all the elements—lives amid beasts, swims with fish, flies above the birds, talks with angels, dwells on earth, wars in heaven, ploughs the sea, feeds in the air, is a tiller of the soil, a traveler on the deep, a fisherman in streams, a fowler in the air, an heir in heaven, a joint-heir with Christ.[42] This he does by his energy.

---

39 Cf. 4 Kings 2.11.
40 Cf. Matt. 8.24.
41 1 Cor. 15.45-47.
42 Cf. Rom. 8.17.

Learn, too, man's supernatural powers. Moses walked along the bottom of the sea,[43] the Apostles upon it,[44] Habacuc flew without wings,[45] Elias conquered on earth and had his triumph in heaven.[46]

Farewell, son, and love us, because we love you.

50. Ambrose to Horontianus (Spring, 387)

You have noted remarkably well the distinction drawn by the Prophet, or, rather, by God, for Moses did not write by his own power; he wrote by inspiration and revelation, particularly in what concerns the creation of the world. This distinction sets apart worker and works.[1] Since the one was incapable of suffering and the other susceptible of suffering, he attributed that which is incapable of suffering to God the worker, and to the world that which is susceptible of suffering, having no life or motion of its own, receiving from its Creator motion, life, and form. The world, once it was made, was not to be left unguarded, without a pilot and father. Hence, he relates very clearly that the unseen God is the guide and protector of this visible world. The invisible, then, is everlasting; the visible is temporal.[2]

He states that the world was made in six days, not because God had need of time to set it up, since a moment suffices for Him to do what He wishes, for 'he spoke and they were made,'[3] but things which are made require an order and order generally requires both time and number. For this

---
43 Cf. Exod. 14.29.
44 Cf. John 21.8.
45 Cf. Dan. 14.35.
46 Cf. 4 Kings 2.11,

---
1 Cf. Gen. 1.1.
2 Cf. 2 Cor. 4.18.
3 Ps. 148.5.

reason, being about to give us a pattern for our work, He observed a number of days and seasons. We, too, need time to do something well, so as not to hurry our plans and works, or fail to keep a proper order. But when we read, as Scripture shows,[4] that God did all things with wisdom and certain foresight and purpose and order, it is consonant with reason that He first made heaven which is most beautiful. This must be so that we may lift our eyes there first and realize that we must arrive there, and esteem that abode preferable to all things of earth.

Hence, 'He created the world in six days and on the seventh He rested from His works.'[5] The number seven is good; we shall treat it, not as do the Pythagoreans or other philosophers, but according to the form and divisions of spiritual grace, since the Prophet Isaias has included seven principal virtues of the Holy Spirit.[6] This sevenfold number, like that of the adorable Trinity of the Father and Son and Holy Spirit, without time or order, is the origin of number, being not bound by the law of number. And as the sky, the earth, and the sea were formed for the sake of the Trinity, as well as the sun, the moon, and the stars, so, too, do we note that for the sevenfold path and orbit of spiritual virtues, driven on by the vigor of a divine operation, a sevenfold ministry of planets was created for the illumination of the world. Their services are said to agree with their number, being called fixed stars or, as the Greeks say *aplaneîs*.[7] The north has also received its Latin name, *septemtrio*,[8] because a gleam of seven stars shines in it and pilots are said to keep it before their gaze as a guide.

---

4 Cf. Ps. 103.24.
5 Cf. Gen. 2.2.
6 Cf. Isa. 11.2.
7 Literally, 'not wanderers.'
8 *septemtrio*, also called the Wain and the Great and Little Bear.

This particular dignity of rank has come down from heaven to earth, not to mention the sevenfold gift of head, two eyes, two ears and nostrils, and the mouth by which we partake of great sweetness. How wonderful it is that for most men their genuine beginning is formed in the seventh month,[9] and one who will issue forth at a later time begins the course of his life's generation. But we see that nature itself prohibits the eighth month as the season for bringing forth children; if some grave necessity perchance opens the barrier of the womb[10] at that time, peril is advanced for the mother and child.[11]

A child, born at seven months, though born well, is born for hardships; but one who begins the mystery of regeneration on the eighth day is sanctified by grace and called to the inheritance of the kingdom of heaven. Great in the power of the Holy Spirit is the grace of seven, yet the same grace echoes in response to seven and consecrates the number eight. In the one is the name; in the other, the enjoyed. Thus, the grace of the Spirit which was bestowed on the eighth day brought back to paradise those whom sin had made outcasts.

The Old Testament took note of this number eight, called by us in Latin an octave, for Ecclesiastes says: 'Give a portion to those seven, and also to those eight.'[12] The seven of the Old Testament is the eight of the New, since Christ arose and the day of the new salvation has shed light upon all. It is the day of which the Prophet says: 'This is the day which the Lord has made; let us be glad and rejoice at it.'[13] On that day there comes the splendor of a full and

---

9 *I.e.*, the seventh month from conception.
10 Cf. Virgil, *Aen.* 2.259.
11 Here the Benedictine edition repeats sections 3 and 4 between sections 4 and 5. The paragraphing is made consecutive here.
12 Eccle. 11.2.
13 Ps. 117.24.

perfect circumcision to the hearts of men. On this account the Old Testament gave the number eight a share in the ceremony of circumcision. But it still lay hidden in darkness. Then came the Sun of justice[14] and in the accomplishment of His passion He revealed the rays of His light, showing them to all, disclosing the brightness of eternal life.

Those are the seven and eight of which Osee says that with this number he bought and took to himself the fullness of faith, for you read: 'And I went and bought her to me for fifteen pieces of silver and for a core of barley and for a half core of barley and a measure of wine.'[15] The Lord had told him previously to buy a harlot, and it is proof that he bought her since he declares how much he paid. The fifteen pieces of silver consist of seven and eight and symbolize the number seven and the number eight. By the price of the two Testaments, that is, of the fullness of faith, the prophecy received the consummation of faith, the Church received the fullness. By the first Testament the people of Israel were gained; by the second, the heathens and Gentiles. By the plenitude of faith the harlot is bought who seeks union with the Gentiles or with adulterous people of the Jews who left their Lord and the author of their virginal faith, spreading their assemblies all over the world.

When he said 'a core and a half core of barley,' understand that in a core there is full measure, in a half core half measure. The fullness is in the Gospel, only semi-perfection is in the Law, as we read when the Lord said: 'I have not come to destroy the law, but to fulfill.'[16] Elsewhere, too, we have the Lord saying through the Prophet Micheas: 'Then this man will be our peace in the land of Israel, when the Assyrian shall come into his land, and seven shepherds and

---

14 Cf. Mal. 4.2.
15 Osee 3.2.
16 Matt. 5.17.

eight jaws of men have risen against him.'[17] The faithful people then will enjoy perfect peace and freedom from all temptation and vanity, for peace and grace will shut out of their hearts the vanity of this world. Peace is of the Old Testament; grace, of the New.

The seven shepherds are the commandments of the Law which in the rod of Moses guided and governed the flock through the desert.[18] The eight jaws of men are the commandments of the Gospel and the words of the Lord's mouth: 'With the heart a man believes unto justice, and with the mouth profession of faith is made unto salvation.'[19] Those jaws are good by which we have tasted the gift of eternal life, devouring the remission of sins in the Body of Christ. In the Old Testament the jaw of death is bitter, since it is said: 'Strong death is all devouring.'[20] In the New Testament the jaw of death is sweet, for it has swallowed death, as the Apostle says: 'Death is swallowed up in victory! O death, where is thy victory? O death, where is thy sting?'[21]

To use, in addition, the Apostle's evidence: when God made man He rested the seventh day from all His works.[22] But because the Jewish people through contempt refused to obey the commands of their God, the Lord said: 'If they shall enter into my rest.'[23] God appointed another day and said of it: 'O that you may hear My voice today.'[24] The words of Scripture include all days in two days, yesterday and today, as in the words: 'Imitate their faith in Jesus Christ, He is the same yesterday and today, yes, and forever.'[25] The promise is made the first day; the following day

---

17 Mich. 5.5.
18 Cf. Exod. 4.20.
19 Rom. 10.10.
20 Isa. 25.8 (Septuagint).
21 1 Cor. 15.54,55.
22 Cf. Gen. 2.2.
23 Ps. 94.11.
24 Ps. 94.7.
25 Heb. 13.7,8.

it is fulfilled. Since neither Moses nor Josue, the son of Nun, brought the people to their rest yesterday, Christ brought them today to whom His Father said: 'This day I have begotten thee.'[26] Through His resurrection Jesus has purchased rest for His people. Our rest is the Lord Jesus, who says: 'This day thou shalt be with me in paradise.'[27] Rest is in heaven; it is not on earth.

What need have I to study the rising and the setting of the stars,[28] and at their rising plough up and pierce the fallow ground with hard ploughshares, or at their setting cut the fruitful crop?[29] One star means more to me than all the others, 'the bright morning star'[30] at whose rising was sown not the seed of grain but the seed of martyrs, that time when Rachel wept for her children[31] to offer for Christ her babes washed with her tears.[32] The setting of that star brought back in triumph from the tomb not the unfeeling relics of funeral piles, but bands of the living, who had been dead.

The number seven should be esteemed because the life of man passes through seven stages to old age, as Hippocrates,[33] the master of medicine, has explained in his writings. The first age is infancy; the second, boyhood; the third, youth; fourth, adulthood; fifth, manhood; sixth, maturity; seventh, old age. So there is the infant, the child, the youth, the young man, the man, the man of experience, and the aged.

Solon imagined that there were ten periods of life, each of seven years' duration.[34] The first period of infancy extends to the time when he cuts his teeth, which he uses in chewing

---

26 Ps. 2.7.
27 Luke 23.43.
28 Cf. Virgil, *Ecl.* 9.46.
29 Cf. Virgil, *Georg.* 1.71.
30 Apoc. 22.16.
31 Cf. Jer. 31.15.
32 The Holy Innocents.
33 Ambrose here makes use of Philo Judaeus, ed. L. Cohn (Berlin 1896). *De mundi opificio* 36.105 contains the reference to Hippocrates.
34 *Ibid.* 35.104 contains the reference to Solon.

his food and articulating his speech so that it is distinct; boyhood extends to the time of puberty and carnal temptations; youth to the growth of the beard; adulthood to attaining of perfect manliness; the fifth age is manhood—during its seven-year period it is fully adapted to marriage; the sixth period, too, is assigned to manhood, which is well-suited to display prudence and is vigorous in its action; the seventh period and the eighth show man ripe in years, vigorous in his faculties, and his speech endowed with a quality of delivery not unpleasant; the ninth period still has some strength left, while in speech and wisdom it is more mellow; the tenth period of seven years completes the span, and one who reaches this period will after the full course of time finally knock at the gate of death.

Both Hippocrates and Solon admitted either seven ages or seven-year periods. In these the number seven should prevail. The eighth period introduces one continual period in which we grow up into a perfect man, knowing God, possessing the fullness of faith, wherein the measure of genuine life is fulfilled.[35]

Even in the organs of our body the number seven is favored. They say that we have seven organs within us: stomach, heart, lungs, spleen, liver, and the two kidneys. These are also seven outwardly: head, hind parts, abdomen, two hands, and two feet.

These are very excellent, but they are subject to pain. Would anyone doubt that the number eight has a greater task, for it renews the whole man and makes him unable to suffer? Now that the seventh age of the world has been concluded, the grace of the eighth has dawned, and made man no longer of this world but above it. No longer do we live our life, but we live Christ: 'For me to live is Christ and to die is gain. . . . I no longer live in the flesh, but in the faith

---

35 Cf. Eph. 4.13.

of Christ.'³⁶ The Apostle has spoken and we know from this that the day of the world has drawn to a close. At the last hour, the Lord Jesus came and died for us. And we are all dead in Him so that we may live to God.³⁷ We who were do not live, but Christ lives in us.³⁸

The number seven has gone; the number eight has come. Yesterday is gone; today has come. That is the promised day on which we have been warned to hear and follow God's word. The day of the Old Testament is gone; the new day has come wherein the New Testament is made perfect, of which he [Paul] says: 'Behold the days are coming, says the Lord, when I will make a new covenant with the house of Israel and with the house of Juda, not according to the covenant which I made with their fathers, in that day that I took them by the hand to lead them out of the land of Egypt.'³⁹ He adds the reason why the covenant was changed: 'They did not abide by my covenant, and I did not regard them, says the Lord.'⁴⁰

The priests of the Law and the sanctuaries of the Law have gone. Let us draw near our new High Priest,⁴¹ to the throne of grace,⁴² the Guest of our souls, the Priest, made not according to the law of the carnal commandment, but chosen by the power [of the command] which cannot end.⁴³ He did not take the honor to Himself,⁴⁴ but He was chosen by the Father, as the Father Himself says: Thou art a priest forever according to the order of Melchisedech.'⁴⁵ We see what the

---

36 Phil. 1.20.
37 Cf. 1 John 2.18.
38 Cf. 2 Cor. 5.15.
39 Jer. 31.31,32.
40 Heb. 8.9.
41 Cf. Heb. 4.14.
42 Heb. 4.16.
43 Cf. Heb. 7.16.
44 Cf. Heb. 5.4.
45 Ps. 109.4; Heb. 7.17.

new Priest has offered. Other priests make offerings for themselves and their people. This one, having no sin of His own for which He should make offerings, offered Himself for the world and by His own Blood entered the Holy of Holies.

He, then, is the new Priest and the new Victim, not of the Law but above it, the Advocate of the world, the Light of time, who said: 'Behold I come, and he came.'[46] Let us approach Him to adore Him in the fullness of faith and to hope in Him whom we do not see with our eyes, but whom we have in our heart. To Him is all honor always and glory.

Farewell, son, and love us, because we love you.

51. Ambrose to Horontianus, greetings (c. 387)

You asked me whether the soul is in all likelihood a heavy substance, for you do not believe that the soul is blood or fire or a harmony of nerves, as ordinary philosophers teach. Again, it seems to you that the soul is that which moves itself and is moved by no other, for this is the teaching of the ancient line of followers of Plato. You feel at least, since Aristotle inferred with remarkable originality some sort of fifth element, that there is an element, *entelechia,* from which you would derive or form the substance of the soul.[1]

I suggest that you read the Book of Esdras,[2] for he has his back on those little nothings of the philosophers and with that deeper wisdom which he gathered from revelation has shown quite briefly that souls are of a superior substance.

---

46 Apoc. 32.7.

1 Cf. Plato, *Laws* 10.891, where he takes issue with Aristotle for saying that 'the first cause of the generation and destruction of all things is not the first but the last.' But Cicero (*Tusc.* 1.10.22) calls *entelechia* 'continuum.'

2 Cf. 4 Esd. *passim.*

The Apostle, too, if not expressly, at least like a good teacher and spiritual farmer, quickening the souls of his disciples with hidden seeds of doctrine, leaves us to understand that our souls are of a higher order of creation and a most excellent nature. When he says that 'creation was made subject to vanity—not by its own will but by reason of him who made it subject—in hope, because creation itself will also be delivered from its slavery to corruption into the freedom of the glory of the sons of God,'[3] he shows that the grace of the soul is no small thing, for by its strength and power the human race rises to the adoption of sons of God, having in itself that which was given to it in the image and likeness of God. Souls are grasped by no touch, they are seen not with bodily eyes, and they have a likeness to that incorporeal and invisible nature, surpassing with their substance the corporeal and sensible character of things. Objects which are seen are temporal, they indicate the temporal, they are bound up with the temporal; those which are not seen cling to that eternal and highest good, and in it they live and are and move.[4] Good men, if they take thought, do not let themselves be separated or drawn away from this [good].

Every soul, then, since it is enclosed within the hovel of the body, if it has not debased itself by partnership with this earthly habitation, sighs under the weight of union with the body,[5] because the corruptible body is a load upon the soul and the earthly habitation presses down the mind which muses on many things.[6] At the same time, realizing that it walks by faith and not by vision, it wishes to be exiled from the body and to be at home with the Lord.[7]

Let us notice how the creature has been made subject to

---
3 Rom. 8.20,21.
4 Cf. Acts 17.28.
5 Cf. 2 Cor. 5.4.
6 Cf. Wis. 9.15.
7 Cf. 2 Cor. 5.7,8.

vanity,[8] not by its own wish, but by the divine will which has arranged that souls must be joined to a body in hope, so that while hoping for good things they may prepare themselves to be worthy of a heavenly reward: 'For all of us must be made manifest before the tribunal of Christ, so that each one may receive what he has won through his body.'[9] The soul of each person should make provision for the rewards to be meted out for life in the world. Very aptly does he say: 'what each has won through his body,' that is, what the part of man which must be ruled has taken upon itself. If she [the soul] has ruled this part well, let her receive the reward for which she was subject in hope; if badly, punishment, since she did not hope in God or strive for that adoption of sons and the freedom of true glory.

The Apostle has taught us that created human nature is subject to vanity. What is so much a man as his soul? Of partnership with it, he says: 'When we are in the body, we sigh under our burden.'[10] But David also says: 'Man is like a breath of aid,'[11] and: 'All things are vanity: every man living.'[12] The life of man in this world is vanity. The soul is subject to this vanity. Therefore, when a saint does the things of the body, he does them, not by choice, not willingly, but by reason of Him who made him subject in hope so that he may obey Him. Let us proceed from this example of the soul to the rest of creation.

Consider that the sun, the moon, and the stars, the lights of the sky which, though they shine with brilliant splendor, are yet creatures, and, whether they rise or fall in their daily performance of duty, they serve the will of the eternal

---
8 Cf. Rom. 8.20.
9 2 Cor. 5.10.
10 2 Cor. 5.4.
11 Ps. 143.4.
12 Cf. Ps. 38.6.

Creator, bringing forth the beauty with which they are clothed and shining by day and by night. How often is the sun covered by clouds or taken from the gaze of the earth when the ray of its light is dispelled in the sky or an eclipse occurs, and as Scripture says: 'The moon knows its going down.'[13] It knows when it should shine in full light or weakened light. The stars, which are engaged in service to this world's advantage, disappear when they are covered by clouds, not willingly, surely, but in hope, because they hope for gratitude for their labor from Him who made them subject. Thus, they persevere for His sake, that is, for His will.

It is not strange that they persevere with patience, since they know that their Lord and the Creator of all that is in heaven or on earth has taken upon Himself the frailty of our body, the slavery of our state. Why should they not persevere patiently in the servitude of their corruption when the Lord of all humbled Himself to death for the whole world, and took the form of a servant,[14] and was made the sin of the world and a curse for our sakes? Although the heavenly creatures, who imitate Him, may groan because they are subject to the vanity of this world, they console themselves in the thought that they will be set free from the slavery of corruption into the liberty of glory, at the coming of the adoption of the sons of God, the redemption of all: 'When the fullness of the Gentiles comes, then will all Israel be saved.'[15] Will He not forgive those people, He who forgave His persecutor who had said: 'Crucify him! Crucify him!'[16] and 'His blood be on us and on our children'?[17] But, because even the heavenly creation is subject to vanity, in hope the

---

13 Ps. 103.19.
14 Cf. Phil. 2.7.
15 Rom. 11.25.
16 John 19.6.
17 Matt. 27.25.

devotion to truth and the redemption of all will allow even their treachery and intoxication to arrive at pardon, since creation was brought low by the vanity of this world.

To conclude, the sun, great as it is and such as it is, and the moon, which the shades of night do not cover, and the stars, which adorn the sky, all now endure the slavery of corruption because every body is a corruptible thing. Indeed, even the skies will perish and heaven and earth will pass.[18] At length the sun and the moon and the other lights of the stars will rest in the glory of the sons of God, since God will be all in all,[19] and will be in you and in us by His plenitude and mercy.

Do we not believe that the angels themselves groan in the performance of their various functions amid the toils of this world, as we read in the Apocalypse of John,[20] for they are made the ministers of penalties and destruction? They who enjoy the life of beatitude would surely prefer to return to that high state of peace rather than be involved in avenging the punishment of our sins. They who rejoice over the repentance of one sinner surely lament the hardships of so many sinners.

If even heavenly creatures and powers endure the slavery of corruption, but through hope, so as to rejoice later for us and with us, let us also comfort ourselves for the sufferings of this time with the hope and expectation of future glory.

Farewell, son, and love us, because we love you.

---
18 Cf. Matt. 24.35.
19 Cf. 1 Cor. 15.28.
20 Apoc. 3.1-22.

52. Ambrose to Horontianus (c. 387)

My last letter answered your inquiry; this letter is a part of my answer which will not destroy but will fulfill the former. For, while I considered the matter further, I was disturbed, I admit, because he [Paul] added: 'For we know that all creation groans,' although in an earlier verse he had said without any addition: 'For creation was made subject to vanity.' He said not that 'every creature' but 'creation' has been made subject. And again, he says: 'Since creation itself will be delivered from its slavery to corruption.' And, in the third place, he adds: 'every creature groans.'[1]

What does he wish to imply by this addition except, perhaps, that not every creature is subject to vanity, and, since not everyone is subject to vanity, not everyone will be freed from slavery to corruption? Why should that be set free which is unacquainted with and free from subjection to vanity and from slavery to corruption? Let everyone groan, not over his own labor but over ours, and give birth, perchance, to that spirit of adoption of the sons of God that he may have a share in the joy and happiness over the redemption of the human race. Everyone groans over our labor because of love for himself or for the member of his own body, of which the head is Christ. But, whether he meant this as we have said, or that every creature in subjection groans and gives birth, this understand as you wish.

Let us now consider what he adds: 'And not only it, but we ourselves also who have the first fruits of the spirit—we ourselves groan within ourselves, waiting for the adoption as sons, the redemption of our body.'[2] What adoption of sons does the previous page teach? To explain the meaning we must go back to the previous page.

---
1 Rom. 8.20-22.
2 Rom. 8.23.

He says that one who puts to death the deeds of the flesh will live.³ It is not strange that he lives, since one who has the spirit of God becomes a son of God. It is for this reason that he is the Son of God so that he may receive not the spirit of slavery but the spirit of the adoption of sons, inasmuch as the Holy Spirit gives proof to our spirit that we are the sons of God. The proof of this comes from the Holy Spirit, because it is He Himself who cries out in our hearts: 'Abba, Father,' as it was written to the Galatians.⁴ It is also a powerful proof that we are sons of God in that we are heirs of God, co-heirs with Christ, and He is co-heir of the one who glorifies Him, and He, too, glorifies him who by suffering for Him suffers with Him.⁵

In order to encourage us to suffer, he adds that all our suffering is less than and not to be compared to the great reward of the future blessing which will be revealed to us in return for these hardships, and that, when we have been formed to the image of God, we will deserve to see His glory face to face.

To enhance the greatness of the future revelation he adds that creation also awaits this revelation of the sons of God, being now subject to vanity, not by its own will but in hope, for it hopes for gratitude from Christ for the service which it rendered Him, and because it will itself be freed from slavery to corruption, that it may be taken up into the liberty of the glory of the sons of God, so that there will be a single liberty of creation and of the sons of God when their glory is revealed. But now, while the revelation is postponed, every creature groans, awaiting the glory of our adoption and redemption, giving birth to that spirit of salvation, and wishing to be freed from slavery to vanity.

---

3 Cf. Rom. 8.13.
4 Gal. 4.6.
5 Cf. Rom. 8.16,18.

To this the Apostle joins the groaning of the saints who have the first fruits of the Spirit. Even they groan. Although they are saved by their merits, they are compassionate because the redemption of the world is yet to come. For, while the members of their body suffer, how can the other members, although superior ones, not feel compassion for the distressed members of the one body?

For this reason, I think, the Apostle said that at that time even the Son Himself will be made subject, the one who subjected all things to Himself.[6] Those who still labor are not yet made subject, and in them, perhaps, Christ still thirsts, still hungers; in them He is naked because they still do not fulfill the word of God, they do not put on Christ, who is the garment of believers, the cloak of the faithful. But those in whom He is weak still need medicine, and they have not yet become His subjects. It is a subjection of strength, not of weakness. The Son of God is made subject in the strong and in those who do the will of God. He now works more in those who do not assist the laborers than He does in those who ask assistance for themselves. This is a holy and true interpretation of the subjection of the Lord Jesus, who will make Himself subject so that God may be all things to all men.

We are arriving at the Apostle's meaning. Let us now consider who those are who have the first-fruits of the Spirit.[7] Let us then ask the Old Law what it means by the word 'first-fruits' or 'firstlings.' It says: 'Thou shalt not hold back the first-fruits of the threshing floor and thy water,'[8] and further on: 'Thou shalt offer the first-fruits of thy first products to the house of the Lord thy God.'[9] Some are first-fruits; others are tithes. First-fruits have greater favor and

---

6 Cf. 1 Cor. 15.28.
7 Cf. Rom. 8.13.
8 Exod. 22.29.
9 Exod. 34.26.

are held in very great reverence. Abel was very pleasing since without holding back he offered his gift, a firstling of his flock.[10] Some may wish to distinguish between first-fruits and firstlings, that is, what is born first, because when the seed has been gathered it may be offered as the very first-fruits of the harvest; yet, what is taken first from the harvest is offered to the Lord, but that from the threshing floor [is offered] to others.[11] Indeed, the whole harvest of grain seems to become holy when the first-fruits are given as a gift, but the first-fruits themselves are holier still.

Likewise, the saints are the first-fruits of the Lord, particularly the Apostles. God first placed Apostles in the Church who prophesied many things and preached the Lord Jesus, for they first received Him.[12] Simeon the Prophet first received Him;[13] Zachary the Prophet received Him, and so did his son John; and Nathaniel in whom there was no guile,[14] who was reclining under a fig tree; and Joseph, who was called just, who buried Him.[15] These are the first-fruits of our faith, although the same nature but less grace may be in some first-fruits as in some seeds: 'God is able out of these stones to raise up children to Abraham.'[16]

Lo, you have an example from the Lord Jesus Himself. In the resurrection of the dead He is called the first-born from the dead.[17] Yet, the Apostle has shown that the same one is the first-fruit, in the words: 'In Christ all are made to live,

---

10 Cf. Gen. 4.4.
11 Ambrose makes a distinction between first-fruits (*primitia*) and firstlings (*initia*). First-fruits are taken from the harvest field; they consist of ears of corn and are to be used in asking favors. Firstlings are from the threshing floor; they are the pure seeds and are to be used in rendering thanks to God.
12 Cf. 1 Cor. 12.28.
13 Cf. Luke 2.28.
14 Cf. John 1.47.
15 Cf. Luke 23.53.
16 Matt. 3.9.
17 Cf. Col. 1.18.

but each in his own turn. Christ is the first-fruits; then, they who are Christ's, who have believed in His coming.'[18] The same reality of body is in Him as in us, but still He is called the first-born of the dead because He arose first, and He is called the first-fruits because He is holier than all fruits, since He sanctified the other fruits of His union. He is also the firstling of those who are in His image, just as He is the image of the invisible God,[19] in whom, in accord with the divinity, there is nothing corporeal, nothing temporal, for He is the splendor of the Father's glory, and the image of His substance. Our letter has run to the length of a sermon while we are endeavoring to show what are first-fruits.

Our first-fruits are the Apostles, who were chosen out of all the fruits of that time, to whom it was said: 'And greater than these you will do,'[20] since the grace of God poured itself out upon them. They, I say, groaned while they awaited the redemption of the whole body, and they still groan, because of the toil of many who still waver. If a man reaches the shore but is still buffetted by waves around his waist, he groans and travails until he emerges entirely. In the same way he groans who is still saying to us: 'Who is weak, and I am not weak?'[21]

Let us not be disturbed because it has been so written: 'We who have the first-fruits of the spirit—we ourselves groan within ourselves, waiting for the adoption as sons, the redemption of our body.'[22] The meaning is clear why those who have the first-fruits of the spirit groan while they await the adoption as sons. This adoption as sons is the redemption of the whole body. When it is face to face as a son of God it will see that divine and eternal good. The adoption as sons

---
18 1 Cor. 15.22.
19 Cf. Gal. 1.15.
20 John 14.12.
21 2 Cor. 11.29.
22 Rom. 8.23.

is in the Church of the Lord when the Spirit cries: 'Abba, Father,' as you have it said to the Galatians. But it [the adoption] will be perfect when all will rise in incorruption, in honor, and in glory, worthy to see the face of God. Then will humanity know that it is truly redeemed. So the Apostle boasts in the words: 'For in hope were we saved.'[23] Hope saves, as does faith, also, of which it is said: 'Thy faith has saved thee.'[24]

Thus the creature which is subject to vanity, not by its own will but in hope, is saved by hope, as was also Paul, for, although he knew that it was gain to die so that, freed from the body, he might be with Christ, he remained in the flesh for the sake of those whom he was gaining for Christ.[25] What is hope, if not the awaiting of things to come? So he says: 'Hope that is seen is not hope.'[26] Not things seen, but things unseen, are eternal. Does anyone hope for what he sees? We seem to have what we see; how, then, do we hope for what we have? So, none of the things which are hoped for are seen, for: 'Eye has not seen, nor ear heard, what God has prepared for those who love Him.'[27]

If the unseen cannot be hoped for, they do not say rightly: 'What one sees, that he also hopes,' unless they say: 'What one sees, why should he also hope for,' or what does he wait for? It is true that we hope for what we do not see, and, although it seems far removed from us, we hope for it in patience: 'Hoping I hoped in the Lord, and he looked down on me.'[28] For this reason we hope patiently, because 'The Lord is good to those who wait for him.'[29] This seems to

---

23 Rom. 8.24.
24 Luke 18.42.
25 Cf. Phil. 1.2.
26 Rom. 8.24.
27 1 Cor. 2.9.
28 Ps. 39.2.
29 Thren. 3.25.

mean that he returned by reason of our patience. We expect what we hope for and do not see. He does much who hopes and expects things which are not seen. And because he turns his attention to that which is everything, he continues steadfast.

It is aptly said, therefore, regarding the power and riches of this world: 'But hope that is seen is not hope.'[30] You see that, when one is renowned for power and chariots, he has no hope of chariots which he sees. We do not put our hope in the element of heaven, but in the Lord of heaven. A Chaldean astronomer has no hope in the stars which he studies, nor does the rich man in his possessions, nor the miser in his gain. But he has hope who puts his hope in Him whom he does not see, that is, in the Lord Jesus, who stands in our midst and is not seen.[31] Finally, 'Eye has not seen, nor ear heard, what the Lord has prepared for those who love Him.'[32]

53. Ambrose to Horontianus (c. 387)

Our letters are forming a chain and we seem to be letting the chips fly in the presence of one another. I get the material for my letter-writing from your questioning, and you get yours from my explanations.

You have pointed out that you wonder of what spirit it was said: 'Because he pleads for us with unutterable groaning.'[1] Let us go on, so that the reading will make clear what we are searching for: 'But in like manner the Spirit also helps the weakness of our prayer.' Does not this seem to be the Holy Spirit, for He is our helper, to whom it is said:

---
30 Rom. 8.24.
31 Cf. John 1.26.
32 1 Cor. 2.9.

---
1 Rom. 8.26.

'Thou art my help; cast me not off, and abandon me not, O God, my Saviour.'[2]

What other spirit could teach Paul what to pray for? The Spirit of Christ teaches, as Christ also teaches His disciples to pray.[3] And, after Christ, who would teach if not His Spirit whom He Himself sent to teach and direct our prayers? We pray with the Spirit; we pray, too, with the understanding.[4] In order that the understanding be able to pray well, the Spirit goes on ahead and leads it on to a level road,[5] so that things of the flesh or things less or greater than our strength may not surprise it: 'Now the manifestation of the Spirit is given to everyone for profit.'[6] Moreover, it has been written: 'Seek the great and the little will be given you. Seek heavenly things and those of earth will be given.'[7]

He wishes us to seek greater things, not to linger among earthly ones. He who allots to each according as He wills[8] knows what He will give. Sometimes, knowing our limitations of which we are ignorant, He says: 'You cannot now receive this.' I pray for the sufferings of a martyr for myself—the Holy Spirit is willing[9]—but when He sees the weakness of my flesh, fearing that while I seek too great things I may lose the smaller ones, He says: 'You cannot receive these.' What opportunities I have had, and have been called back almost from the goal![10] A good doctor knows what food is suitable for the state of illness, and at what stage in the

---

2 Ps. 26.9.
3 Cf. Luke 11.1.
4 Cf. 1 Cor. 14.15.
5 Cf. Ps. 142.10.
6 1 Cor. 12.7.
7 Matt. 6.35.
8 Cf. 1 Cor. 12.11.
9 Cf. Matt. 26.41.
10 The persecution of the Arian empress and Ambrose's embassy to the usurper Maximus show that Ambrose was not unwilling to be a martyr.

course of the recovery. Sometimes the taking of food brings back good health, but if one takes it at the wrong time or takes what is not suitable he is imperiled.

Therefore, since we do not know what we pray for, and how we should pray, the Holy Spirit asks for us.[11] He is the Spirit of Jesus, our Advocate. And He asks with unspeakable groanings, as Christ, too, grieves for us.[12] And God the Father says: 'My bowels are in pain.'[13] We read that He was often angry and grieved. He groans that He may take away our sins, that He may teach us to do penance. It is a reverent groan, filled with power, of which the Prophet says: 'My groaning is not hidden from thee.'[14] He did not hide like Adam, but He said: 'Behold, I am the shepherd. But as for this flock, in what has it been sinful? It is I that have sinned; punish thou me.'[15]

From this comes the groaning of the Spirit of God, and the groaning of the Prophet, well-nigh ineffable because it is heavenly. The things that Paul heard in heaven were ineffable. Thus, men should not utter what is hidden to men, although known to God. He, the searcher of our hearts, knows all things, but He searches what the Spirit has purified. Therefore, God knows what the Spirit is asking and what is the wisdom of the Spirit which pleads for the saints, as you read: 'The Spirit also pleads for us.'[16] It is those for whom Christ suffered and whom He cleansed with His blood for whom also the Spirit pleads.

Farewell, and as a son love us, because we love you.

---

11 Cf. Rom. 8.26.
12 Cf. Isa. 53.4.
13 Jer. 14.9.
14 Ps. 37.10.
15 1 Par. 21.17.
16 Rom. 8.27.

54. Ambrose to Simplicianus, greetings[1] (c. 386)

You remarked recently when we were chatting in a way characteristic of our long-standing affection that it pleased you to have me preach to my people on some of the writings of the Apostle Paul. Since his depth of meaning is understood only with difficulty, he should lead the one who hears him to lofty thoughts and should set on fire the commentator. In some instances, in fact, the speaker engages in exegesis and, having nothing of his own to add, being anxious to say something, fulfills the task of grammarian rather than exegete.

I realize in this complaint the result of our old friendship and, what is more, a tenderly fatherly love (for the passage of time brings intimacy, along with many benefits, but a father's love does not).[2] Then, too, because I feel that I have already done not without spirit what you are asking, I shall obey your wish, advised and instigated by my own pattern—by no means difficult for me. I will not be imitating some great personage, but myself, as I return to some of my own insignificant practices.

Now, as regards our plan, I think that when we express in our sermons the metaphor and representation of the happy life, we have reached a conclusion which most persons, and especially you, a friend, will not find unsuitable. Yet it is more difficult not to displease your judgment than that of most others, though, by your devotion, you lighten the weight of your judgment and render it much milder to me.

Yet the Epistle, which troubled you after you were gone, has to do with the meaning of Paul the Apostle, who says in calling us from slavery to liberty: 'You have been bought with a price; do not become the slaves of men.'[3] In this he

---

[1] The first of four letters to Simplicianus, Bishop of Milan after the death of Ambrose in 397. He was instrumental in the conversion of St. Augustine (*Conf.* 8.1,2,5).

[2] Cf. *Conf.* 8.2, where Augustine says that Ambrose loved Simplicianus 'truly as a father.'

[3] 1 Cor. 7.23.

shows that our liberty consists in the knowledge of wisdom. This passage has been pitched and tossed on a great mass of discussion by philosophers, who say that every wise man is free, every fool is a slave.

This was said long before by a son of David in the words: 'A fool is changed like the moon.'[4] A wise man is not shattered by fear, or changed by power, or elated by good fortune, or overwhelmed by sadness. Where there is wisdom there are strength of spirit and perseverance and fortitude. The wise man is constant in soul, not deflated or elated by changing events. He does not toss like a child, carried about by every wind of doctrine, but remains perfected in Christ, grounded by charity, rooted by faith. The wise man is never idle and experiences no changing states of mind. But he will shine like the Sun of justice that shines in the kingdom of His Father.[5]

Let us consider the source of that philosophy from which the patriarchs drew their wisdom and learning. Was not Noe the first to curse his son when he learned that Chanaan[6] had made fun of his nakedness: 'Cursed be Chanaan; meanest of slaves shall he be to his brethren,'[7] and he put as lords over him his brothers, who with wisdom knew that they should respect their father's years.

Did not Jacob, that source of all wisdom, who by reason of his wisdom was preferred to his elder brother,[8] pour an abundance of this reasoning into the hearts of all? Although the devoted father felt a father's affection for both his sons, he judged each differently (for love is not estranged from kinship, but judgments are formed according to merit). Hence, he gave favor to one, pity to the other, favoring the wise, but pitying the unwise because he could not rise to

---

4 Eccli. 27.12.
5 Cf. Matt. 13.43.
6 Chem.
7 Gen. 9.25.
8 Cf. Gen. 27.29.

valorous deeds by his own strength or advance his steps at will. Thus, he blessed him so that he would serve his brother and be his slave, revealing how the lack of wisdom is brought low by servitude, that his slavery may be a remedy for him, because the foolish man cannot rule himself, and if he is without a guide he is undone by his own desires.

After due deliberation, the devoted father made him his brother's slave so that he would be guided by the other's prudence. Thus, to indiscreet persons the wise become as rulers to guide by their power the foolishness of the crowd which they rule under the guise of power, when they bring unwilling subjects to obey those who are more wise and to submit to the laws. So he put a yoke on the foolish one as on an unruly man, and he denied liberty to one who he decreed must live by his sword. He put his brother over him so that he might not sin by his temerity, but that, being subject to his authority and limitations, he might come to repentance. Slavery, you see, draws a distinction (some are weak of necessity though strong of purpose, because that is more beautiful which is done not of necessity but willingly), and so he put on him the yoke of necessity and later secured for him the blessing of willing subjection.

Not nature but foolishness makes the slave. Not manumission but learning makes a man free. Esau was born free, but he became a slave; Joseph was sold into slavery,[9] but he was raised to power[10] that he might rule those who had purchased him. Yet he did not slight his obligation to work zealously; he clung to the heights of virtue; he preserved the liberty of innocence, the stronghold of blamelessness. So the Psalmist beautifully says: 'Joseph had been sold into slavery. They had bound his feet with fetters.'[11] 'He had been sold into

---
9 Cf. Gen. 37.28.
10 Cf. Gen. 41.41.
11 Ps. 104.17,18.

slavery,' he says; he did not become a slave. They had bound his feet, but not his soul.

How is his soul bound when he says: 'The iron pierced his soul'?[12] Although the souls of others were pierced with sin (iron is sin, because it pierces within), the soul of blessed Joseph did not lie open to sin, but pierced through sin. He was not swayed by the beauty of his mistress' charms and so he did not experience the flames of passion, for he was aflame with the greater flame of divine grace. Thus, it is said very aptly of him: 'Because the word of the Lord burned him,'[13] and with this he quenched the fiery darts of the Devil.

How was he a slave, the man who showed the princes of his people how to regulate the corn supply, so that they knew beforehand and made provision for the coming famine? Or was he a slave, the man who took possession of the whole country of Egypt and reduced its entire population to slavery?[14] This he did, not in order to put upon them the status of ignoble slavery, but to impose a tax, except upon the property of the priests, which remained free from tax because among the Egyptians the priestly caste was held in reverence.

A sale did not make a slave of him, though he was sold to traders. Thinking in terms of a price, you will find many who have purchased young girls of unusual beauty and being enamored of them, have reduced themselves to shameful slavery. The concubine of King Darius, Apene, appeared sitting on his right when she took the crown from his head and put it on her own, and struck his face with her left hand. The king gazed at her with delight and smiled whenever the woman smiled at him. But if she showed contempt for him he thought he was unhappy and distressed, and if he

---

12 Ps. 104.18.
13 Ps. 104.19.
14 Cf. Gen. 47.20.

lost his power over her he would speak soft words and beg her to be reconciled with him.[15]

But why do we take great pains to assert this? Do we not ordinarily see parents ransomed by their children when they have fallen into the power of pirates or savage barbarians? Are the laws of ransom stronger than the laws of nature? Is filial piety being forced into slavery? There are merchants of lions, yet they do not rule them, but when they see them angrily shake their shaggy masses from their neck[16] they flee and seek shelter. The money which purchased these masters for them makes no difference, nor do the auction tables on which the buyer is generally judged and sentenced. The agreement does not change his condition of birth or take away the freedom of wisdom. Many free men are servants of a wise slave and he is a wise slave who rules his foolish masters.[17]

Who do you think is more free? Only that wisdom is free which sets the poor over riches and makes slaves draw interest on their masters, not drawing money as interest, but wisdom. That talent draws interest from the Lord's eternal treasury which is never despoiled and whose gain is priceless. That knowledge draws as interest the silver of heavenly speech of which the Law says: 'Thou shalt lend to many nations and thou shalt never borrow.'[18] The Hebrew[19] loaned to the nations; he did not receive knowledge from the people, but, instead, gave it. To him the Lord opened His treasury to bedew the Gentiles with the water of His speech and make them the prince of nations having no prince above them.

The free man is the wise man who was bought with the price of heavenly speech, the gold and silver of God's word,

---

15 Cf. 3 Esd. 4.29,30.
16 Cf. Virgil, *Aeneid* 12.7.
17 Cf. Prov. 17.2.
18 Deut. 15.6.
19 I.e., Joseph.

bought with the price of blood (not least important is it to know the buyer), bought with the price of grace, for he heard and understood the one who said: 'All you who thirst, come to the waters; and you that have no money, make haste, buy and eat and drink.'[20]

The free man is the warrior who sees a woman of comely beauty and takes his enemy's wealth as booty; then, when he is beset with longing and finds her, he sells what he does not need, removes the cloak she wore when she was taken, and weds the woman who is no longer a slave, but free. He knows that his learning and wisdom will not make him subject to her slavedom. Therefore, the Law says: 'She may not be sold for money,'[21] since nothing precious deserves this. And Job says: 'Draw out wisdom in deeper places.'[22] The topaz of Ethiopia will not be compared to her, being reckoned more precious than gold and silver.

Not only is the person free who has not fallen to the buyer's bid, nor seen the finger raised,[23] but that man rather is free who is free within himself, free by the law of nature, knowing that the law of nature has been laid down by custom, not by conditions, and that the extent of man's duties harmonizes not with his choice but with the teachings of nature. Would that man only seem free to you who appeared as a censor and prefect of morals? Scripture says very truly that the poor will rule over riches, and the borrowers over creditors.[24]

Would that man seem free in your estimation who bought votes for himself with money, standing more in need of the approval of the populace than of the opinion of the wise? Is he free if he is swayed by popular opinion and dreads the

---
20 Isa. 55.1.
21 Cf. Deut. 21.10-14.
22 Job 28.18.
23 A reference to the ancient custom whereby one who had purchased a slave raised his finger as a guarantee of the sale.
24 Cf. Prov. 22.7.

whisper of the crowd? The freedman does not receive liberty when the hand of the lictor is laid on him.[25] I consider not wealth but virtue as liberty, for it does not bow to the wishes of the stronger, and it is laid hold of and possessed by one's own greatness of soul. The wise man is always free; he is always held in honor; he is always master of the laws. The law is not made for the just but for the unjust.[26] The just man is a law unto himself and he does not need to summon the law from afar, for he carries it enclosed in his heart, having the law written on the tablets of his heart, and it is said to him: 'Drink water out of thy own vessels and from the stream of thy own well.'[27] What is so close to us as the Word of God? This is the word on our heart and on our lips which we behold not but hold.

The wise man is free, since one who does as he wishes is free. Not every wish is good, but the wise man wishes only that which is good; he hates evil for he chooses what is good. Because he chooses what is good he is master of his choice and because he chooses his work is he free. Then, because he does what he wishes the free man is wise. The wise man does well everything that he does. One who does all things well does all things rightly. But one who does all things rightly does everything without offense, without blame, without loss and disturbance within himself. And one who does nearly everything without giving offense acts blamelessly and acts without disturbance to himself, without loss. He does not act unwisely but wisely in all things. One who acts with wisdom has nothing to fear, for fear lies in sin. Where there is no fear there is liberty; where there is liberty there is the power of doing what one wishes. Therefore, only the wise man is free.

---

25 A rod, called a *festuca*, was laid on the manumitted slave by a praetor or lictor.
26 Cf. 1 Tim. 1.9.
27 Prov. 5.15.

One who cannot be forced or held in check is by no means a slave; the wise man cannot be forced or forbidden; a slave, therefore, is not wise. One who does not enjoy what he desires is held in check. But what does the wise man desire except what belongs to virtue and learning, without which he cannot exist? These are in him and they cannot be torn from him. If they are torn away, then he is no longer a wise man, for he is without the habit of virtue and without learning, of which he defrauds himself if he is not a willing broker of virtue. If compulsion is used on him it is clear that he acts unwillingly. In all our deeds there are either corrections by virtue, missteps by malice, or that which is midway or lacking in distinction. The wise man is not forced to virtue but he is a willing follower of it, because in fleeing evil he drives out all that is pleasing [to the senses] and does not let sleep overtake him. In what is neither good nor evil he is not disturbed so as to be swayed to this side and that like the common crowd, but his mind hangs, as it were, in a perfectly balanced scale. Thus, he leans neither entirely toward pleasure nor in the direction of what he should reject, but, showing moderate interest, he remains fixed in purpose. Therefore, it appears that the wise man does nothing unwillingly nor by force. If he were a slave he would be forced; therefore, the wise man is free.

The Apostle, too, declares this to be true when he says: 'Am I not free? Am I not an apostle?'[28] Indeed, he is so free that when certain persons slipped in to spy on his liberty, as he himself says,[29] he would not yield in submission for one hour, that the truth of the Gospel might be preached. As one who did not cease he preached willingly. Where there is willingness there is the reward of willingness; where there is necessity, there is subservience to necessity. Willingness

---
28 1 Cor. 9.1.
29 Cf. Gal. 2.5.

is better, therefore, than necessity. The wise man must be willing, the foolish man must obey and serve.

This is the declaration of the Apostle, who says: 'If I do this willingly, I shall have a reward. But if unwillingly, it is a stewardship that has been entrusted to me.'[30] The wise man is given a reward, yet he acts willingly; therefore, according to the Apostle, the free man is wise. Hence, he himself cries out: 'For you have been called to liberty; only do not use liberty as an occasion for sensuality.'[31] He separates the Christian from the Law that he may not seem to fall under the Law unwillingly. He calls him to the Gospel which they who are willing preach and carry out. The Jew is under the Law, the Christian in the midst of the Gospel. There is slavery under the Law, liberty in the Gospel, for in it is the understanding of wisdom. Everyone who accepts Christ is wise; he who is wise is free; every Christian, then, is both free and wise.

The Apostle has taught me that beyond this liberty there is the liberty of being a slave: 'For free though I was,' he says, 'I made myself a slave of all that I might gain the more converts.'[32] What lies beyond that liberty except to have the spirit of grace, to have charity? Liberty makes us free before men, charity a friend before God. Therefore Christ said: 'But I have called you friends.'[33] Charity is good and of it is said: 'By the charity of the Spirit serve one another.'[34] Christ, too, was a servant so that He might make all men free. 'His hands have served in the basket.'[35] He who did not think it robbery to be equal with God took the nature of a slave,[36] and He

---
30 1 Cor. 9.17.
31 Gal. 5.13.
32 1 Cor. 8.19.
33 John 15.15.
34 Gal. 5.13.
35 Ps. 80.7.
36 Cf. Phil. 2.6.

became all things to all men to bring salvation to all.[37] Paul, an imitator of Him, as if he was under the Law and lived as if outside the Law, spent his life for the advantage of those whom He wished to gain. He willingly became weak for the weak in order to strengthen them; he ran the race to overtake them; he chastised his body to triumph in Christ over natures of bronze.[38]

A wise man, though he be a slave, is at liberty; and from this it follows that, though a fool rule, he is in slavery, and, what is worse, though he have care of a very few, he is slave to more and harsher masters. For he is slave to his passions; he is slave to his own wishes; he cannot escape his rulers night or day because he has these rulers within him; within he suffers unbearable slavery. Slavery is twofold, one of the body and the other of the soul, men being masters of the body, but sin and passion masters of the soul, and from these only liberty of spirit frees a man so that he is delivered from his servitude.

Let us look for that truly wise man, the truly free man, who, although he lives under the rule of many, says freely: 'Who is he that will plead against me? Do thou alone withdraw thy hand from me, and from thy face I will not be able to hide; and let not thy dread terrify me.'[39]

King David following him said: 'Against thee only have I sinned.'[40] In his regal position, like the lord of laws he was not subject to laws, but he was guilty before God who alone is Lord of hosts.

Listen to another free man: 'But with me it is a very small matter to be judged by you or by man's tribunal. Nay, I do not even judge my own self. For I have nothing on my

---

37 Cf. 1 Cor. 9.22.
38 See Plato, *Repub.* 3.415 A-C, for the allusion to men of gold, of silver, and of bronze.
39 Job 13.19-21.
40 Ps. 50.6.

conscience . . . but he who judges me is the Lord.'⁴¹ True liberty belongs to the spiritual man, for he judges all things, but is himself judged by no one,⁴² not by anyone who shares his created nature. He knows that he is subject to God alone, who alone is without sin, of whom Job says: 'God liveth, who so judges me,'⁴³ for He alone can judge the just man in whose sight the heavens are not pure, nor the lights of the stars shining and clear.

Who is he who puts into the midst of Sophocles' play those verses which say: 'Jupiter is over me but no man'? How much more ancient is Job, how much more aged is David? They should know that they have drawn their excellent sayings from our writers.⁴⁴

Is a man wise if he does not reach the secrets of the Godhead and learn the hidden things of wisdom revealed to him? He alone is wise, then, who uses as his guide God to search out the lair of truth, and although a mortal he becomes the heir of His immortal God, successor by grace and partaker of His joy, as it is written: 'Therefore God, thy God, has anointed thee with the oil of gladness above thy fellows.'⁴⁵

If one looks into this state of affairs more closely he will learn how great are the advantages to the wise and how great the hindrances to the unwise, because to the former liberty is a help, to the latter servitude is a hindrance. The wise man emerges as a victor over those who warred with him, triumphing over lust, fear, cowardice, gloom and other vices, until he puts them out of the hold of his mind and beats them back and shuts them from his boundaries and his lands. Like a careful leader he knows he should beware of the onrush of brigands and certain strategies of war by means

---
41 1 Cor. 4.3,4.
42 Cf. 1 Cor. 2.15.
43 Job 27.2.
44 Cf. Letter 81 for this same thought.
45 Ps. 44.8.

of which hostile enemies of the soul often throw flaming arrows.[46] For we have certain battles in time of peace and peace in time of war. So he also says: 'Conflicts without, anxieties within.'[47] 'But in all these we overcome because of him who loved us.'[48] And he says he is frightened neither by troubles, nor persecutions, nor hunger, nor danger, nor death.

Is a man not a slave if he shudders at these [trials] and is fearful of death? Surely he is a slave, and his state of slavery is pitiable. Nothing so reduces the soul to total slavery as does the fear of death. How will that mind raise itself which is cast down, poor and debased, if it has been given over to a whole whirlpool of weakness by its longing for this life? See how the slave says: 'I shall hide myself, and I shall be mourning and fearful on earth, and it will happen that whosoever finds me will kill me.'[49] Then, like a slave, he received a mark and he could not escape death. Thus is the sinner a slave to fear, a slave to desire, a slave to greed, a slave to lust, a slave to sin, a slave to anger, and, though such a man appears to himself free, he is more a slave than if he were under tyrants.

The free are those who abide by the laws. True law is a direct statement, true law is not carved on tablets, nor inscribed on bronze, but stamped on the mind and imprinted in the senses. Since a wise man is not under the law he is a law to himself, for he carries the law in his heart in a mode of expression natural to himself and embellished with a sort of heading. Is our blindness such that we do not see very evident declarations of ideas and examples of virtues? How degrading it is that respectable men obey human laws that they may share freedom, yet the wise cast aside and abandon

---

46 *furta belli*. Cf. Virgil, *Aen.* 11.515.
47 Cf. 2 Cor. 7.5.
48 Rom. 8.37.
49 Gen. 4.14.

the true law of nature, though they are made to the image of God and bear the true mark of freedom. So great is this freedom that as children we do not know how to be slaves to vice, we are strangers to anger, we are free from greed, unacquainted with lust. How sad it is that we who are born in freedom die in slavery!

This comes from inconstancy and weakness of character, for we are concerned over foolish worries and spend ourselves uselessly. The wise man's heart, his acts, his work must be deeply rooted and immovable. Moses gave this instruction when his hands became so heavy that Josue the son of Nun could scarcely hold them up.[50] Yet the people won a victory because, although the work they did was not important, it was full of meaning and courage, not done with a sense of wavering or unsteady purpose, but with the constancy of a well-grounded intention. The wise man stretches out his hands, the fool draws them in, as it is written: 'The fool foldeth his hands together, and eateth his own flesh,'[51] for he thinks more of the body than of the spirit. Was it not a daughter of Juda who called to the Lord with outstretched hands: 'Thou knowest that they have borne false witness against me.'[52] She thought it was better not to sin and to fall into the snare of her accusers rather than to sin under the cloak of impunity. By despising death she preserved her innocence. And was it not the daughter of Jephte who by her own encouraging words confirmed her father's vow to immolate her?[53]

For contempt of death I do not draw on the books of the philosophers, or the ascetics of India, and the highly praised answer which Calanus gave Alexander when he told him to

---

50 Cf. Exod. 17.12.
51 Eccle. 4.5.
52 Dan. 13.43.
53 Cf. Judges 11.36-38.

follow him: 'Of what kind of praise do I seem worthy, if you ask me to return to Greece and I can be compelled to do what I do not want to do? Your words are truly filled with authority, but my mind is more filled with liberty.' Then he wrote this letter.

Calanus to Alexander:[54] 'Friends who do not see our works in their visions are bidding you lay hands and force on the Indian philosophers. You will move their bodies from place to place, you will not force their souls to do what they do not wish any more than you will force rocks and trees to speak. A huge fire burns pain into living bodies and causes destruction; we are above this, we are consumed alive. There is no king or leader who can torture us to do what we have not planned. Unlike the philosophers of Greece who plan their pronouncements on events, looking to the fame of their opinion, we keep a relation between words and deeds. Events are swift; words are short-lived; our freedom is blessed in virtue.'

Famous words, but mere words! Brilliant firmness of purpose, but from a man! A brilliant letter, but from a philosopher! Among us, even maidens climb the steps of virtue mounting to the very sky with their longing for death. What need to mention Thecla, Agnes, and Pelagia, who produced noble offspring, rushing to their death as if to immortality? Amid lions the maidens frolicked and fearlessly gazed on roaring beasts. Let us compare our examples with those ascetics of India: blessed Lawrence proved by his deeds what he had boasted in words, that when he was being burned alive, surviving the flames, he said: 'Turn me and eat me.' Not unworthy of the daughter of Abraham was the struggle of the sons of the Machabees:[55] some chanted above the flames, others, while being burned alive, asked not to be

---

54 From Philo Judaeus: *Quod omnis probus liber sit* 14 (Loeb Class. Lib. *Philo* 9 [tr. F. H. Colson] 63-67, 516).
55 Cf. 2 Mach. 7.5-41.

spared, but they were so carried away that the persecutor was the more inflamed with anger. The wise man was free.

What example is more sublime than blessed Pelagia, who, when she was overwhelmed by her persecutors, said before she went into their presence: 'I die willingly, no one will lay a hand on me, no one will harm my virginity with his shameless glance, I shall take with me my purity and my modesty unsullied. These robbers will have no reward for their brazenness. Pelagia will follow Christ, no one will take away her freedom, no one will see her freedom of faith taken away, nor her remarkable purity, the product of wisdom. That which is servile will remain here, bound for no use.' Great was the freedom of that pious maiden who, though she was hedged in by lines of persecutors with utmost danger to her purity and life, was in no way shaken.

The man who is ruled by anger is also bound by the yoke of sin. The man who is easily stirred to wrath has dug up sin;[56] 'whoever commits sin is a slave of sin.'[57] He is not free who is a slave to greed, for he cannot possess his own vessel. He is not free who, serving his own needs and pleasures, wavers on straying bypaths. He is not free who is warped by ambition, for he is a slave to another's power. But he is free who can say: 'All things are lawful to me, but not all things are expedient. All things are lawful for me, but I will not be brought under the power of anyone. Food for the belly, and the belly for food.'[58] He is free who says: 'Why is our liberty judged by the unbeliever's knowledge?'

Liberty suits the wise, not the unwise, for one who wraps a stone in a hurling machine is like the man who gives honor to a fool. He hurts himself and brings more danger to himself as he throws the javelin. As the harm of a stone is increased

---

56 Prov. 29.22 (Septuagint).
57 John 8.34.
58 Cf. 1 Cor. 6.12,13.

by the engine of war and is doubled by its fall, so, too, is the downfall of the fool in freedom more violent. The power of the fool must be curtailed, his liberty should not be increased, because slavery fits him. Thus, Proverbs added: 'Thorns grow in the hand of a drunkard, so slavery in the hand of a fool.'[59] As the drunkard is hurt by his drinking, so is the fool by his deeds. The one plunges himself into sin by drinking, the other convicts himself by his work and is dragged into slavery by his deeds. Paul saw himself dragged into bondage by the law of sin,[60] but in order to be freed he took refuge in the grace of freedom.

Fools are not free; it is said to them: 'Be not like the horse and the mule, which have no understanding. Control with bridle and bit the jaws of those who come near thee. Many are the blows of the wicked.'[61] Many blows are necessary that their wickedness be controlled; training, not harshness, exacts this. Besides, 'He that spareth the rod hateth his son,'[62] since each one is punished more heavily for his sins. The weight of sin is heavy, the stripes for crimes are heavy; they weigh like a heavy burden; they leave scars upon the soul and make the wounds of the mind fester.[63]

Let us lay aside the heavy load of slavery, let us give up wantonness and pleasures which bind us with chains of desires and restrain us with their ties. Pleasures do not help the fool, and one who gives himself to pleasure from childhood will remain in slavery, so that, although alive, he is dead. Therefore, let wantonness be cut out, let pleasures be removed; if anyone has been wanton let him say farewell to the past. The pruned vine brings forth fruit, the half-pruned grows, the neglected grows wild. So it is written: 'like a man careless of

---

59 Cf. Prov. 26.8,9.
60 Cf. Rom. 7.23.
61 Ps. 31.9,10.
62 Prov. 13.24.
63 Cf. Ps. 37.5,6.

his field is the unwise man, like a man careless of his vineyard is the man bereft of reason; if you abandon it, it will be deserted.'[64] Let us cultivate this body of ours, let us chastise it, let us reduce it to slavery, let us not underestimate it.

Our limbs are means of righteousness; they are also the means of sin. If they are raised, they are the means of justice so that sin does not rule them; but, if the body is dead to sin, blame will not reign over it, and our limbs will be free from sin. Let us not obey its desires, nor give our limbs to sin as the weapons of injustice. If you look at a woman to covet her, your limbs are the weapons of sin. If you speak to her in order to harass her, your tongue and your mouth are the weapons of sin. If you remove the boundary stones laid down by your ancestors, your limbs are the weapons of sin. If you run with hurried steps to shed the blood of innocent people, your limbs are the weapons of evil.

On the contrary, if you see the needy and bring him home, your limbs are the weapons of justice. If you snatch up one who is being led to death, if you tear up the debtor's bond, your limbs are the weapons of justice. If you confess Christ (the lips of the wise are weapons of the intellect[65]), your lips are weapons of justice. Whoever can say: 'I was an eye to the blind, a foot to the lame, the father of the poor,'[66] his limbs are limbs of justice.

Let us who are free from sin, purchased, as it were, by the price of Christ's blood, let us not be subject to the slavery of men or of passion. Let us not be ashamed to confess our sin. See how free the man who could say: 'I have not been afraid of a very great multitude, so that I would not confess my sin in the sight of all.'[67] One who confesses to the Lord is freed

---

64 Prov. 24.30.
65 Cf. Prov. 14.7.
66 Job 29.15,16.
67 Job 31.34.

from his slavery: 'The just is tne accuser of himself in the beginning of his speech.'[68] He is not only free but just, for justice is in liberty, and liberty in confession, and as soon as one has confessed he is pardoned. To conclude: 'I said "I will confess my iniquity to the Lord," and thou didst forgive the guilt of my heart.'[69] The delay of absolution is in the confession, the remission of sin follows confession. He is wise who confesses, he is free whose sins are forgiven and he trails no clouds of sin.

Farewell, and love us as you do, because I also love you.

55. Ambrose to Simplicianus, greetings (c. 386)

We seem to have become involved in a philosophic debate when, taking the text of the Apostle Paul's Epistle, we discussed the statement: 'every wise man is free.' Later, however, when I was reading the Epistle of Peter the Apostle, I noticed that every wise man is also rich. And he does not exclude the other sex, for he says that women do not have all their wealth in jewels, but in the good dispositions of the heart: 'Let not theirs be the outward adornment of braiding the hair, or of wearing gold, or of putting on robes; but let it be the inner life of the heart.'[1]

Those two, namely, the man of inner life and the rich man, require no use of riches for themselves. He has mentioned very beautifully 'the inner life of the heart' because the whole man of wisdom is hidden, just as wisdom herself is unseen but understood. No one before Peter used such an expression in speaking of the man of inner life. The exterior

---

68 Prov. 18.17.
69 Ps. 31.5.

---

1 1 Peter 3.3,4.

man has many parts in him; the interior man is filled with wisdom, with favors, with beauty.

'In the imperishableness of a quiet and gentle spirit,' he says, 'which is of great price in the sight of God,'[2] he is truly rich who can appear rich in the sight of God, under whose gaze the earth is a miniature and the universe itself small. God alone knows the man of possessions, the one rich in immortality, the one storing up the fruit of virtues, not riches. What is so rich in God's sight as the peaceful and modest spirit which is never disturbed? Does not that man appear to be rich who has peace of soul, the tranquility of repose, so that he longs for nothing, is stirred by no storm of passion, tires not of the old, seeks the new, and always by desire becomes poor in the midst of the greatest riches?

Truly that is a rich peace which surpasses all understanding.[3] A rich peace, a rich dignity, a rich faith: 'The faithful man has the whole world for his possession';[4] it is a rich simplicity, for those are riches of a simplicity which nothing scatters, which entertain no despondent thought, or suspicious or fraudulent one, but pours itself out with pure affection.

There is a rich excellence upon which one feeds if he has saved the heavenly riches of his inheritance. To use the older examples from Scripture, he says: 'Blessed is the man whom the Lord correcteth: refuse not therefore the chastising of God. In famine he shall deliver thee from death; and in battle, from the hand of the sword. He shall hide thee from the scourge of the tongue. Thou shalt not be afraid of wild beasts and thou shalt know that thy house will be in peace.'[5] When you have subdued the body's sins and passions which war against the spirit, your habitation will be free from

---
2 *Ibid.*
3 Cf. Phil. 4.7.
4 Prov. 17.6 (Septuagint).
5 Job 5.17,20-24.

trouble, your house will have no stumbling block, your seed will not be fruitless, your descendants will be like the smell of a plentiful field,[6] your place of burial will be a harvest. Indeed, when others realize that their fruits have failed, then will the heap of your ripe grain be brought to the heavenly storerooms.

The righteous always gain rewards; the unjust go begging. The one gains righteousness; he gains God's command to the poor and needy. But the fool does not own even what he thinks he has. Does he possess riches, do you think, if he broods over his wealth day and night and is tormented by a wretched miser's worries? He is actually in need; although he appears wealthy in the opinion of others, he is poor in his own. He makes no use of what he has, but, while grasping one thing, he longs for another. What enjoyment of riches is there when there is no limit to one's longing? No one is rich if he cannot take from this life what he has, because what is left here is not ours but another's.

Henoch was rich, for he took away with him what he had and carried all his wealth of blessing in heavenly vessels,[7] and 'He was taken away lest wickedness should alter his heart.'[8] Elias was rich, for he drove aloft to the heavenly abodes carrying the treasury of his virtues in a fiery chariot.[9] Even he has left no small wealth to his heir, while he himself lost none of it. Would anyone call him a pauper either then or when he was sent to the widow to be fed by her, when he himself needed food for his daily sustenance? When at his prayer heaven was opened and shut? When at his word the pot of meal and cruet of oil did not fail for three years, but abounded, for it was not diminished but replenished by use?[10]

---
6 Cf. Gen. 27.27.
7 Cf. Gen. 5.21-24.
8 Wisd. 4.11.
9 Cf. 4 Kings 2.11.
10 Cf. 3 Kings 17.9-16.

Would anyone call him poor at whose wish fire came down [from heaven],[11] and rivers which he approached did not close in on him,[12] but went back to their source, letting the Prophet cross with dry feet?

An ancient story tells of the two neighbors,[13] King Achab and a poor man Naboth. Which of these do we consider the poorer, which the richer: the one who had been endowed with a king's measure of wealth, insatiable and unsatisfied with his wealth, who longed for the little vineyard of the poor man; or the other, heartily despising a 'king's fortune of much gold' and imperial wealth, who was satisfied with his vineyard? Does he not seem richer and more a king, since he had enough for himself and regulated his desires so that he wanted nothing which belonged to others? But was he not very poor whose gold was of no account, while he considered the other's vines of priceless value? Understand why he was so very poor: because riches amassed unjustly are disgorged,[14] but the root of the righteous remains,[15] and flourishes like a palm tree.[16]

Is he not more in need than the poor man who passes away like a shadow?[17] The wicked man is praised today; tomorrow he will not exist nor will any trace of him be found.[18] What does being rich mean except 'spreading out,' 'overflowing'? Is he rich who is depressed in soul? Is not one so depressed held in confinement? In confinement what overflowing is possible? He is not rich who does not overflow. So David very aptly says: 'The powerful have become poor and

---

11 Cf. 4 Kings 1.14.
12 Cf. 4 Kings 2.8.
13 Cf. 3 Kings 21.1-16.
14 Cf. Job 20.15.
15 Cf. Prov. 12.12.
16 Cf. Ps. 91.13.
17 Cf. Ps. 143.4.
18 Cf. Ps. 36.35,36.

have hungered,'[19] because, when men have the treasures of the heavenly Scriptures and do not have understanding, they become poor, they become hungry.

There is nothing richer than the wise man's condition, nothing poorer than the fool's. Since the kingdom of God belongs to the poor,[20] what can be richer than that? And the Apostle, too, says brilliantly: 'Oh, the depths of the riches of the wisdom and of the knowledge of God.'[21] Brilliantly, too, David rejoiced in the way of divine precepts as if he were amid all riches.[22] In definite terms, too, does Moses rejoice who says: 'Nephthali will be among those who receive abundance.'[23] Nephthali is interpreted in Latin as 'abundance' or 'diffusion.' Therefore, where there is abundance, there is a sufficiency; where there is the hunger of desire, there is unfulfilled longing; there, in fact, is poverty. Then, because there is scarcely a desire for money or things of this world which reaches satisfaction, he adds: 'And he will be filled with blessing.'[24]

In these terms the Apostle Peter showed that women's ornament consists not in gold and silver and garments, but in the inner and hidden life of the heart.[25] Let no woman, therefore, lay aside the garb of piety, the adornment of grace, the inheritance of everlasting life.

Farewell, and love us, because we love you.

---
19 Ps. 33.11.
20 Cf. Matt. 5.3.
21 Rom. 11.33.
22 Cf. Ps. 118.14.
23 Deut. 33.23.
24 *Ibid.*
25 1 Peter 3.3,4.

56. Ambrose to Simplicianus, greetings[1]

You tell me that you were perplexed over the meaning when you read that Moses, after offering sacrifice and immolating sacred victims to the Lord, put half of the blood into bowls and sprinkled the rest on the altar.[2] But what causes you to be perplexed and ask my help, when you have traveled the whole world to acquire faith and divine knowledge, and in constant reading day and night have spent the whole span of your life? With remarkably brilliant intellect you have embraced all objects of the understanding, so that you are able to show how the works of the philosophers have deviated from the truth, several being so futile that the words in their writings have perished in their lifetime.

Yet, because it is of great profit to exchange talk, as it is to exchange money, whereby great progress is made in furthering the common good of trade, I cannot refrain from saying how wonderful is the division of blood of which you speak. Part seems to signify the moral training, part the mystical training of wisdom. The part put into vessels is moral, that sprinkled upon the altar is mystical, because it is granted, by the favor and inspiration of heaven, that human minds conceive fitting ideas of God, ideas filled with faith.

Moreover, those who have spoken of His majesty and of heavenly matters, whether Apostles or holy Prophets, dared not utter anything unless it had been shown them by revelation. Hence, Paul bears witness in his Epistle that he was caught up to heaven and heard words which it is not lawful for man to utter.[3] Stephen also saw the heavens open and Jesus standing on the right hand of God;[4] and David the

[1] Undated.
[2] Cf. Exod. 24.6.
[3] Cf. 2 Cor. 12.4.
[4] Cf. Acts 7.55.

Prophet saw Him sitting.[5] What shall I say of Moses, of whom Scripture says that there has risen no greater Prophet in Israel, who saw the Lord face to face, in the many signs and prodigies which He performed in the land of Egypt?[6]

The mystical portion is offered to God, and by the brightness of divine Wisdom, whose Father and Parent He is, He quickens the vigor of the soul and illumines the mind. But the Wisdom of God is Christ, whose breast John reclined upon,[7] that from the secret source of Wisdom he may be said to have imbibed divine mysteries. John, who knew the gift [he had received], recorded this incident for he feared to claim for himself and to attribute to his own genius what he had received. Even the Lord Himself said to the Apostles, opening His mouth: 'Receive the Holy Spirit,'[8] declaring that He was the one who had said to Moses: 'I will open your mouth, and I will teach you what you are to speak.'[9] Thus does Wisdom divine, ineffable, untainted, incorruptible, pour her grace into the souls of the saints and reveal to them knowledge that they may behold her glory.

But training in moral wisdom is that which is put into bowls and taken therefrom and drunk. The bowls are the organs of the senses. The bowls are the two eyes, the ears, the nostrils, the mouth, and other parts suited to their function. For the eyes receive and minister to sight, the ears to hearing, nostrils to smell, mouths to taste, and so forth. The Word, who is the source of the priesthood and of prophecy, pours into these bowls part of His Blood that He may quicken and animate the irrational parts of our nature and make them rational.

Finally, when he [Moses] had numbered the command-

---

5 Cf. Ps. 109.1.
6 Cf. Deut. 34.10,11.
7 Cf. John 13.25.
8 John 20.22.
9 Exod. 4.12.

ments of the Law and had proclaimed them to the people, leaving to a later time his explanation of the meaning of the mystical Ark of the Testament, of the candlestick, and of the censer, he offered victims and poured a libation, sprinkling part of the blood on the sacred altars and putting part into bowls.

A division is made between a mystical, that is, divine wisdom, and moral wisdom. The Logos is the divider of souls and of virtues; but the Logos, the Word of God, is powerful and quick, for it pierces and penetrates even the division of the soul, and it discerns and divides virtues. Therefore, His servant Moses, by the division of blood, distinguished the kinds of virtues.

And because nothing is announced more emphatically in the Law than is Christ's coming and nothing prefigured more clearly than His passion, consider whether that is not the saving victim which God the Word offered in Himself and which He immolated in His own body. For, in the Gospel and in the Law, He first taught us moral instruction, and in His suffering and in His every act and deed, as though putting our senses and habits into bowls, pouring, as it were, the very substance and marrow of wisdom, He enlivened the minds of men to become a seed bed of virtues, the regulator of piety. Then, drawing near the altar, He poured out the Blood of His own victim.

If you choose to understand these incidents this way, the sense is pious; or, if you wish, Solomon's interpretation is equally agreeable; namely, that the Prophet Moses poured the blood into bowls, which you may understand to be the same blood of which it has been written that wisdom has mingled her wine in a bowl,[10] bidding men leave foolishness and seek wisdom. From the bowl we drink wisdom, instruction, knowledge, correction, amendment of life, control of

---

10 Cf. Prov. 9.2.

habits and thoughts, grace of devotion, increase of virtue, a fount of abundance.

You may also understand by the sprinkling of the blood upon the altar the cleansing of the world, the forgiveness of all sins. For, as a victim, He sprinkled that blood upon the altar to take away the sins of many. The lamb is a victim, but not a rational creature, although it has divine power, for it was said: 'Behold the lamb of God, behold him who takes away the sins of the world.'[11] For He has not only cleansed the sins of all with His Blood, but also bestowed a divine power. Does it not seem to you that He poured out His Blood, since water and blood from His side flowed over the altar of His passion?[12]

Farewell, and love us, as you do, with the affection of a father.

57. Ambrose to Simplicianus, greetings[1]

The reading which disturbs you ought to serve as proof of each man's greatness in his own task, for, although no one saw God more intimately than did Moses,[2] and no greater Prophet arose in Israel, seeing God face to face, as did Moses,[3] though he was with God continually for forty days and nights when receiving the Law on the mountain,[4] he, I say, to whom God gave the words which he was to speak,[5] he is found to have approved his brother Aaron's counsel more than his own. Was ever any one of mankind

---

11 John 1.29.
12 Cf. John 19.34.

1 Undated.
2 Cf. Num. 12.8.
3 Cf. Deut. 34.10.
4 Cf. Exod. 34.28.
5 Cf. Exod. 4.12.

wiser and more learned than Moses? Yet we read that Aaron and Miriam sinned later [by chiding Moses for his] Ethiopian wife.[6]

But distinguish carefully this very thing: at what time Moses rendered a decision with wisdom and when Aaron did so with counsel. Moses was the great Prophet who said of Christ: 'Him thou shalt hear like unto me.'[7] And of him the Lord Himself said: 'If they do not hearken to Moses and the Prophets, they will not believe even if someone goes to them from the dead.'[8] Therefore, in the matter of prophecy, Moses ranks first as a Prophet, but, in the concern and duty and task of the priesthood, Aaron ranks first as a priest. Let us, then, discuss this point.

A buck-goat had been immolated for sin and offered as a holocaust. Moses later went in search of it, but it had been burned. 'And Moses was angry with Eleazar and Ithamar the sons of Aaron that were left, and he spoke saying: "Why did you not eat the sacrifice for sin in the holy place? For these are the holy of holies; this I gave you to eat, that you may take away the sin of the synagogue, and you ought to have eaten it within, as was commanded me." When Aaron saw that he was angry, he answered calmly: "If this day hath been offered the victim for sin, the holocaust before the Lord: and to me such things have happened, shall I eat what was offered for sin today? Or shall it please the Lord?" And Moses heard and it pleased him.'[9] Let us consider what these things signify.

Only God does not sin. The wise man mends his way and corrects the man who is astray and does penance for sin. Yet, this is difficult in the life of men. For, what is so rare as

---

6 Cf. Num. 12.1.
7 Deut. 18.15.
8 Luke 16.31.
9 Lev. 10.16-20.

to find a man who convicts himself of sin and condemns his action? Rare, then, is the confession of sin, rare is penance, rare is a man's declaration of servitude. Nature rebels, shame rebels; nature does so because all are under sin, and he who is clothed in flesh is prone to evil. Therefore, nature rebels against the flesh, and the world's attraction fights against innocence and purity. Shame, too, rebels, for each one is ashamed to admit his own fault while he thinks of the present more than the future.

Moses was desirous of finding a soul free from sin that it might put off the covering of error and depart free from blame without any disgrace to himself. But he did not find such a soul; quickly, the force of unreason came into play and a sort of flame of impetuosity fed on the soul and consumed its innocence. Present considerations outweigh those that are to come, the violent the moderate, the many the better, the joyous the serious, the soft the harsh, the glad the sad, those full of charm those more unbending, and the speedy the slower ones. Swift is iniquity which heaps up opportunities for harm, because 'swift are his feet to shed blood.'[10] But every virtue is gentle and she delays a long time before she judges and studies what things are to come. So the mind of the good man is a watcher of his counsels, and examines beforehand what is comely and fair, but iniquity with labor sets herself before wisdom. Penance is sluggish and shameful, for it is overwhelmed and checked by regard for those present. It is intent on future things only, wherein hope is late, where enjoyment is slow, and slow, too, the search.

Amid these endeavors of hope and virtue shamelessness comes running, and, because of the type of persons present, penance is neglected, love for penance is destroyed, and introspection is at an end. The Law seeks and does not find

---
10 Ps. 13.3.

her, for she has been consumed by the heat and smoke of iniquity, and hatred of the Law is aroused. Moses says that penance should have been consumed in the holy of holies; he upbraids the priests for being sluggish. Aaron replies that the priestly judgments should be far-seeing, and this task is not easily assigned to a weak conscience. Let us not have this error worse than the first, for, by a foul-smelling vase, oil and wine are easily corrupted and deteriorated.

How could the sin be burned out when the fire was dangerous, and this in the sight of the Lord to whom even secrets are known? Can he please the Lord if, while he is still involved in iniquities and while he keeps injustice enclosed in his heart, he says that he is doing penance? In the same way, when a sick man pretends to be well he will grow more ill, because pretending good health is of no avail when he is falsified in his words and is not supported by any helping strength.

A dangerous fire is lust; a dangerous fire is every flame of unjust desire; a dangerous fire is all the heat of greed. With this fire no one is purified, he is burned. If one presents himself in the sight of the Lord, where there is that dangerous fire, fire from heaven then consumes him, as fire from heaven burned Abiad and Nadah along with offerings made at the sacred altars for sin. Let one who wishes to purify his sin remove from himself the dangerous fire. Let him offer himself only to that fire which consumes a fault, not a man.

Listen to one saying what that fire is, for 'Jesus baptizes with the Holy Spirit and with fire.'[11] This is the fire which dried up the blood of the woman suffering a hemorrhage for twelve years.[12] This fire forgave the sin of Zaccheus, who said that he gave half of his goods to the poor and, if he

---
11 Matt. 3.11.
12 Cf. Matt. 9.20.

defrauded anyone, he restored it fourfold.¹³ This is the fire which removed the thief's sin, for it is a consuming fire which said to him: 'This day thou shalt be with me in paradise.'¹⁴ Thus did He heal those in whom He found a simple and pure confession, not evil and not deceit.

In fine, Judas could not reach the remedy, although he said: 'I have sinned in betraying innocent blood,'¹⁵ for he wrapped a dangerous fire in his heart and this drove him in his madness to the noose. He was unworthy of a remedy because he did not groan, being converted in the inmost part of his heart, nor did he eagerly practice penance. The Lord Jesus is so loving that He would have given him pardon had he awaited Christ's mercy.

This fault, therefore, priests do not remove; nor do they remove the sin of one who presents himself in deceit and still is desirous of sinning, for they cannot feast on food which is full of cunning and gnaws within. The food of a priest is in the remission of sins. Therefore, the Prince of priests, Christ, says: 'My food is to do the will of my Father who is in heaven.'¹⁶ What is the will of God but this: 'When you turn and groan, then shall you be saved.'¹⁷ But in deceitfulness there is no food. Finally, he who has not a sincere and pure conscience cannot partake of the sweetness of feasting. The bitterness of deceit conceals the sweetness of feasting. Nor does an evil conscience make it possible for penance to refresh and nourish a wicked soul.

Such affection, such seeking, such penance, therefore, are of no use, no joy to priests. And rightfully was that goat burned, not being sacrificed for sin in a holocaust, since the

---

13 Cf. Luke 19.8.
14 Luke 23.43.
15 Matt. 27.4.
16 John 30.15.
17 Isa. 30.15.

victim was not sincere,¹⁸ for in its sacrifice was discovered a dangerous fire. Hence, it is not a pleasing or acceptable sacrifice to God, for it is not acceptable unless it has been proved amid the riches of sincerity and truth.

Thus, elsewhere you read of two goats, one in whom is the lot of the Lord, in the other the emissary [goat]; the one in which there is the lot of the Lord to be offered and immolated for sin, the one in whom is the lot of the emissary [goat] to be let go into the desert, that it may receive the iniquities of the people and of every sinner.¹⁹ For, as there are two in the field, but one shall be taken and the other shall be left,²⁰ so are there two goats: one for sacrifice, the other to be allowed to go into the desert. This last is of no use; he is neither to be eaten nor feasted upon by the sons of the priests. Just as, of those things that are used as food, the good part is eaten and the useless or bad is cast out, so do we consider good works as feasts because they are food.

The Lord will not be pleased if a priest consumes a sacrifice in which there is a deceitful offering, and not the sincerity of a careful confession. Indeed, that goat must be allowed to go into the desert where our fathers wandered, wherein they wandered and could not reach the land of the resurrection, and where their memory perished from the earth. Now, understand the works which are feasts: 'Your foods shall be sabbaths to the lands.'²¹ Feasts and banquets are that rest in God which brings about the tranquility of the soul. So let us rest also in our discourse.

Farewell, and love us as you do, for we love you.

---
18 Cf. Lev. 16.27.
19 Cf. Lev. 16.8-10.
20 Cf. Matt. 24.40.
21 Lev. 25.4.

58. Ambrose to his clergy[1]

Men's minds are frequently tempted to abandon their duty when they take offense lightly at things which do not fit in with their personal desires. I can tolerate this state in other classes of men, but it causes me great sorrow when it is found in those who are dedicated to the service of God.

In the ranks of the clergy there are some aggrieved in this way, into whom the Devil, being unable to find entrance otherwise, wishes to make his way and instill thoughts of this sort: 'What advantage is there for me to remain among the clergy, bear injuries, and endure hardships, as if my farm could not support me, or, lacking that, as if I could not get support some other way?' By thoughts like these [men of] good dispositions fail their duty, as though the only requirement for a cleric were to provide for his support, and not rather to win for himself the help of God after death. Yet, only that man will be rich after death who on earth has been able to contend unharmed against the wiles of his numerous enemies.

Therefore, Ecclesiastes says: 'It is best that there be two rather than one: for there is good advantage for their labor, since if one fall he shall lift up his companion.'[2] Where are two better than one, if not where Christ is, and he whom Christ guards? When a man falls who is with the Lord Jesus, Jesus raises him up.

Why did he say: 'For their labor'? Is Christ laboring? Yes, truly, for He says: 'I have labored calling.'[3] He labors, but He labors on us. Moreover, being weary, He sat at a well.[4] His mode of labor the Apostle has taught us by his own more

---
1 An undated letter to certain clergy of Milan who were discouraged over work and difficulties in the ministry.
2 Eccle. 4.9,10.
3 Ps. 68.4.
4 Cf. John 4.6.

lowly example: 'Who is weak, and I am not weak?'[5] And the Lord Himself taught us in the words: 'I was sick and you did not visit me: naked, and you did not clothe me.'[6] He labors to raise me when I fall.

Hence, in Eliseus the Lord is prefigured, for the Prophet threw himself upon the dead child to raise him up;[7] in this is the belief that Christ died with us so as to rise with us. Christ so placed Himself on a level with our weakness that He raised us up. He threw Himself down, He did not fall, and He raised His comrade. For He Himself made us His comrades, as it is written: 'He was anointed with the oil of gladness above his fellows.'[8]

Fittingly does Ecclesiastes say: 'For if one falls he raises up his companion.'[9] He himself is not raised up, for Christ was not raised up by another's help and power, but He Himself raised Himself. Indeed, He said: 'Destroy this temple, and in three days I will raise it up. This he said of the temple of his body.'[10] It is well that He who did not fall should not be raised by another, for one who is raised by another has fallen, and one who falls needs help to be raised up. Additional words also teach this when Scripture says: 'Woe to him that is alone: for when he falleth, he hath none to lift him up. And if two lie together, they shall warm one another.'[11] We have died with Christ and we live together with Him.[12] Christ died with us to warm us, and He said: 'I have come to cast fire upon the earth.'[13]

I was dead, but by dying with Christ in baptism I have received the light of life from Christ. One who dies in Christ,

---

5 2 Cor. 11.29.
6 Matt. 25.43.
7 Cf. 4 Kings 4.34.
8 Ps. 44. 8.
9 Eccle. 4.10.
10 John 2.19,21.
11 Eccle. 4.10,11.
12 Cf. Rom. 6.8.
13 Luke 12.48.

being warmed by Christ, receives the breath of life and of the resurrection. The child was cold; Eliseus warmed him with his breath; he gave him the warmth of life.[14] He lay with him so that, being buried with him in figure, the warmth of his repose might wake him up. He is cold who does not die in Christ, nor can he be warmed unless a glowing fire is applied to him; neither can he give warmth to another if he has not Christ with him.

For your understanding that this was said of the mystery, not of the number that 'two are better than one,' he adds mystically: 'A threefold cord it not easily broken.'[15] Threes which are not compounded are not broken. The Trinity of an uncompounded nature cannot be broken, because God is whatever is one and simple and not compounded, which continues to be what it is, and is not destroyed.

It is good to cling to one another and to wear the other's chain upon your neck, to lower your shoulders and carry him, and not to grow weary of his bonds, because he went from the house of bondsman to be king, that boy who is greater than an old and foolish king.[16] They who follow him are bound in chains; Paul [was] a prisoner of Jesus Christ;[17] and Jesus Himself led captivity captive.[18] He [Paul] thought it not enough to destroy the captivity which the Devil had imposed, so that he could not again attack those freely walking about, but he considered it perfect freedom to live subject to Christ, and to put his feet in the shackles of wisdom, to be His captive, so that you may be free of His adversary.[19]

Rightly is He called a child, 'For a Child is born to us,'[20] and truly is He a good Son, to whom it was said by God the

---
14 4 Kings 4.34.
15 Eccle. 4.12.
16 Cf. Eccle. 4.13.
17 Cf. Eph. 3.1.
18 Cf. Eph. 4.8.
19 This entire paragraph is omitted in the Benedictine edition.
20 Isa. 9.6.

Father: 'It is good for You to be called My Son.'[21] He is also wise as the Gospel teaches: 'He advanced in age and wisdom.'[22] Likewise, He is poor: 'Being rich, He became poor, that by His poverty He might make us rich.'[23] In His kingdom, therefore, He does not despise the poor man, but listens to him and frees him from his difficulties and troubles.

Let us live as His subjects so that the old foolish king[24] will have no power over us, for, while he wishes to reign as the lord of his own will and be not in the bonds of the Lord Jesus, being confirmed in sin, he falls into ugly foolishness. What is more foolish than to abandon things of heaven and become engaged in earthly ones, not to esteem those that endure and to choose those which are perishable and frail?

No one should say: Our portion is not in Jacob, nor our inheritance in Israel,[25] nor say: I am not in the lots, for it is written: 'Give to Levi his lots.'[26] Later, David said that one who rests among the lots flies aloft on wings of the spirit.[27] Do not say of your God: 'He is grievous to me,'[28] nor of your position: 'It is useless to me,' for it is written: 'Leave not thy place.'[29] The Devil wishes to take it from you, he wishes to carry you away, for he is jealous of your hope and jealous of your task.

But you who are in the lot of the Lord, His portion and possession, do not let go the Lord, so that you may say to Him: 'You have possessed my reins, you have received me from my mother's womb,'[30] and He will say to you as a good servant: 'Come and recline at table.'[31]

Farewell, sons, and serve the Lord because the Lord is good.

---

21 Isa. 49.6 (Septuagint).
22 Luke 2.52.
23 2 Cor. 8.9.
24 Cf. Eccle. 4.13.
25 Cf. 3 Kings 12.16.
26 Deut. 33.8 (Septuagint).
27 Cf. Ps. 67.14.
28 Wisd. 2.15.
29 Eccle. 10.4.
30 Ps. 138.13.
31 Luke 17.7.

59. Ambrose, servant of Christ, called bishop, to the Church at Vercelli and those who invoke the name of our Lord Jesus Christ. May grace be in you from God the Father and His only-begotten Son in the Holy Spirit (396)[1]

I am in sorrow that the Church of the Lord among you is still without a bishop and now alone of all the districts of Liguria and Aemelia and Venetia and other territories of Italy needs that service which other churches used to beg for themselves from her. What is more shameful—your contention, which causes the difficulty, is laid to my charge. Since dissensions exist among you, how can we make any decision, how can you make a choice, how can anyone agree to accept among dissenters the task which he could hardly endure among those who are united?

Is this the training of a confessor, is this the line of those upright fathers who, although they did not know blessed Eusebius[2] before, setting aside their fellow citizens, approved him as soon as they saw him? And so much more did they approve him when they observed him. Rightfully did he come forth, the man whom the entire Church elected; rightfully was it believed that he, whom all had demanded, was elected by God's judgment. You, then, should follow the example of your parents, especially since you have been much better instructed by a saintly confessor than were your fathers inasmuch as a better teacher has instructed and trained you,

---

[1] Written when the Church at Vercelli was unable to agree on a successor for their Bishop Limenius, who had died. As metropolitan bishop, Ambrose wrote what is the longest letter in his correspondence as well as bearing the latest exact date. However, it was without effect, and Ambrose eventually went in person to help choose the new bishop, Honoratus. The entire letter forms a treatise on the election of bishops and the duties of pastors and electors.

[2] Ambrose praises those people of Vercelli who formerly accepted Eusebius as the choice of God Himself.

and you must give evidence of your moderation and accord by agreeing in your request for a bishop.

We have our Lord's saying that 'when two agree upon anything on earth it will be done for them concerning whatever they ask,' as He says, 'by my Father who is in heaven, for where two or three are gathered together in my name, there am I in the midst of them.'[3] How much more true is it that when the full congregation is gathered in the name of the Lord, and when the demand of all is one in accord, we may not in any way doubt that the Lord Jesus will there be the judge—the source of their will, the presiding officer of the ordination, the giver of grace!

Therefore, make yourselves appear worthy of having Christ in your midst. Where there is peace, there is Christ, for Christ is our peace.[4] Where there is justice, there is Christ, for Christ is justice.[5] Let Him be in the midst of you, that you may see Him and that it may not be said of you, also: 'But in the midst of you there stands one whom you do not see.'[6] The Jews did not see Him in whom they did not believe; we behold Him with devotion; we gaze on Him with faith.

Let Him stand in the midst of you so that there may be opened for you the heavens which tell the glory of God,[7] that you may do His will and work His work. The heavens are opened to him who sees Jesus as they were opened to Stephen, who said: 'Behold I see the heavens opened and Jesus standing at the right hand of God.'[8] Jesus stood as a helpmate; He stood as if anxious to help Stephen, His athlete, in the struggle; He stood as though ready to crown His martyr.

---

3 Matt. 18.20.
4 Cf. Eph. 2.14.
5 Cf. 1 Cor. 1.30.
6 John 1.26.
7 Ps. 18.2.
8 Acts 7.56.

Let Him then stand for you that you may not fear Him sitting, for He sits when He judges, as Daniel says: 'Thrones were placed and the books were opened and the Ancient of days sat.'⁹ But in Psalm 81 it is written: 'God rises in the divine assembly, in the midst of the gods he gives judgment.'¹⁰ He sits to judge, He stands to give judgment, and He judges the imperfect, but gives judgment among the gods. Let Him like a good Shepherd stand as your defender, so that dreadful wolves may not attack you.

Not without reason do I advise you up to this point, because I hear that those foolish men, Sarmation and Barbatianus, have come to you, saying that there is no merit in fasting, no grace in frugality, and none in virginity; that all persons are of equal value, and that they are mad who chastise their body by fasting in order to make it subject to the spirit. If he had thought it madness, Paul would never have done so nor written to instruct others, but he glories in it, saying: 'I chastise my body and bring it into subjection, lest preaching to others, I myself should be found a castaway.'¹¹ Thus, those who do not chastise their body and yet wish to preach to others are themselves considered castaways.

How reprobate is that which prompts wantonness, bribery, and lewdness, namely, the incitement to lust, the enticement to sinful pleasure, the fuel of incontinency, the fire of greed! What new school has sent out those Epicureans? They who preach pleasure, urge delights, and think that purity is of no benefit are not followers of philosophy, as they assert, but ignorant men. They were with us, but they were not of us,¹² for we are not ashamed to say what John the Evangelist says. When they were first stationed here they fasted, they stayed

---
9 Dan. 7.9.
10 Ps. 81.1.
11 1 Cor. 9.27.
12 Cf. 1 John 2.19.

within the monastery; there was no room for wantonness and the chance to dispute in mockery was not allowed them.

But these dissolute men could not stand this. They went off, and when they wished to return they were not admitted, for I had heard several things which put me on my guard. I warned them, but accomplished nothing. In anger, therefore, they began scattering such seeds as made them the wretched instigators of all vices. So they have lost the benefit of having fasted, they have lost the benefit of having been self-controlled for a while. Now with a devilish purpose they envy the good deeds of others, since they themselves miss their enjoyment.

What maiden does not groan upon hearing that virginity has no reward? Far be it from her to believe this easily, or lay aside her efforts, or change her heart's intention. What widow, finding that there is no profit in her widowhood, would prefer to keep faith in her husband and spend her life in sadness rather than to enter upon a happier life? What woman bound by marriage ties, when she hears that there is no honor in chastity, will not needlessly be subject to temptation through levity of body or of soul? Therefore, the Church each day proclaims the praise of chastity and the glory of purity in the sacred lessons and in the sermons of her bishops.

In vain, then, did the Apostle say: 'I wrote to you in the letter not to associate with the immoral.'[13] And that they might not say, perhaps: 'We are not speaking of all the immoral persons of the world, but we say that one who has been baptized in Christ ought no longer be considered immoral, but be what it may, his life has become acceptable to God,' the Apostle added: 'Not meaning, of course, the immoral of this world'; and below: 'If a brother is called immoral, or covetous, or an idolator, or evil-tongued, or a drunkard, or greedy, with such a one not even to take food.

---

13 1 Cor. 4.9.

For what have I to do with judging those outside?'[14] And to the Ephesians he said: 'But immorality and every uncleanness or covetousness, let it not even be named among you, as becomes saints.' And immediately he adds below: 'For know this, that no shameless, or unclean person, or covetous one (for that is idolatry) has any inheritance in the kingdom of Christ and God.'[15] Certainly it is clear that he spoke of the baptized, for they receive the inheritance who are baptized in Christ's death and buried with Him so that they may rise with Him.[16] Indeed, they are heirs of God, joint-heirs of Christ, heirs of God because the grace of God is bestowed on them, joint-heirs of Christ because they are reborn to His life, heirs also of Christ because through His death the inheritance, like that of a testator, is given to them.

Wherefore, they who have what they may lose ought to be more solicitous for their needs than those who have not. They ought to act with greater care, to avoid the allurement of vices, the incitement to wrong, which arise chiefly from food and drink, for 'The people sat down to eat, and drink, and they rose up to play.'[17]

Moreover, the famous Epicurus, whom these persons think they should follow rather than the Apostles, that advocate of pleasure, although he denies that pleasure brings on evil, does not deny that certain things follow from it and from these spring evils; and he says also that the life of luxurious persons, which is filled with pleasure, does not seem blameworthy unless it is troubled by the fear of pain or death. But how much a stranger he is to the truth is seen from the fact that he says that pleasure was originally created in mankind by God, just as his follower Philomarus[18] argues in his

---
14 1 Cor. 5.11,12.
15 Eph. 5.3,5.
16 Cf. Rom. 6.3.
17 Exod. 32.6.
18 This is probably the philosopher Philodemus (*c.* 110-*c.* 40/35 B.C.).

Epitome, claiming that the Stoics are the originators of this opinion.

But holy Scripture refutes this, for it teaches us that pleasure was suggested to Adam and Eve by the crafty enticements of the serpent.[19] If the serpent itself is pleasure, then the passions of pleasure are changeable and slippery, and are infected, as it were, with the poison of corruption. It is certain, then, that Adam, deceived by the desire of pleasure, fell away from the command of God and from the enjoyment of grace. How, then, can pleasure call us back to paradise, when by itself it deprived us of paradise?

Therefore, the Lord Jesus, wishing to make us strong against the temptations of the Devil, fasted when He was about to struggle with him, so that we might know that we cannot otherwise overcome the enticement of evil. Further, the Devil himself hurled the first shaft of his temptations regarding pleasure, saying: 'If thou art the Son of God, command that these stones become loaves of bread.' Then the Lord said: 'Not by bread alone does man live, but by every word of God,'[20] and He would not [change stones to bread] although He could, but He taught us by a salutary precept to attend to the pursuit of our reading rather than to pleasure. Since they say we ought not to fast, let them show us why Christ fasted if not to make His fast an example for us. Then, in the words which He spoke later, He taught us that evil cannot easily be conquered except by our fasting, saying: 'This kind of devil is only cast out by prayer and fasting.'[21]

And what is the purpose of Scripture in teaching us that Peter fasted and that the mystery regarding the baptism of the Gentiles was revealed to him when he was fasting and praying,[22] if not to show that the saints themselves, when

---
19 Gen. 3.1-6.
20 Cf. Matt. 4.2-4.
21 Matt. 17.20.
22 Cf. Acts 10.10.

they fast, become more illustrious? Moses received the Law when he was fasting,[23] and so Peter, when he was fasting, was taught the grace of the New Testament. Daniel, too, by virtue of his fasting, stopped the jaws of the lions and saw the events of future times.[24] Or what salvation can we have unless by fasting we wipe out our sins, since Scripture says fasting and almsgiving purge away sin![25]

Who, then, are these new teachers who reject the merit of fasting? Is it not the voice of heathens who say: 'Let us eat and drink,' whom the Apostle ridicules, saying: 'If, as men do, I fought with beasts at Ephesus, what does it profit me? If the dead do not rise, "let us eat and drink for tomorrow we shall die" '?[26] That is to say, what did my struggle even unto death profit me, except that I might redeem my body? And it is redeemed in vain if there is no hope of a resurrection. And if all hope of the resurrection is lost, let us eat and drink and lose not the enjoyment of the things present, for we have none to come. They should indulge in food and drink who hope for nothing after death.[27]

Finally, the Epicureans say they are followers of pleasure because death means nothing to them, because that which is dissolved has no feeling, and that which has no feeling means nothing to us. Thus they show that they are living only carnally not spiritually, and they do not discharge the duty of the soul, but only of the flesh, thinking that all life's duty is ended with the separation of soul and body, that the merit of virtues and all the vigor of the soul come to an end, that they cease completely when the feeling of the body ceases, that there are no remains of the soul although even the body itself does not at once disintegrate. Does the soul,

---

23 Cf. Exod. 34.28.
24 Dan. 14.37,38; 9.2,3.
25 Cf. Tob. 12.8,9.
26 1 Cor. 15.32.
27 The Benedictine edition repeats this paragraph.

then, disintegrate before the body, although for their own satisfaction, they must see that flesh and bones survive after death, and in all truthfulness they may not disavow the grace of the resurrection?

Rightly, then, does the Apostle, arguing against such men, warn us not to be shaken by such opinions, saying: 'Do not be led astray, "evil companionships corrupt good morals." Be righteously sober, and do not sin; for some have no knowledge of God.'[28] Sobriety, then, is a good, for drunkenness is a sin.

But as to Epicurus himself, the champion of pleasure, whom we have frequently mentioned in order to prove that these men are either disciples of the heathen or followers of the Epicurean sect, whom the philosophers themselves exclude from their company as the patron of luxury—what if we show that he is more tolerable than these men? He declares, as Demarchus[29] asserts, that neither drinking, nor banquets, nor a line of sons, nor the embraces of women, nor abundance of fish, and other such things, which are prepared for splendid use at a banquet, make life sweet, but sober discussion does so. He adds, too, that those who do not yearn for the richness of banquets immoderately use them moderately. One who delights only in using the juice of plants or bread and water despises feasts of delicacies, for many inconveniences arise therefrom. Elsewhere, too, these [philosophers] say: 'It is not excessive banquets nor drinking but a life of temperance which occasions the sweetness of pleasure.'

Since, then, philosophy has disowned those men, is the Church not to exclude them, especially since by reason of the bad case which they have they frequently undo themselves

---

28 1 Cor. 15.33.
29 Demarchus is mentioned by no other writer besides Ambrose. The Benedictines suggest he may have meant Hermachus, successor and disciple of Epicurus, 267 B. C.

by their own assertions? For, although their principal tenet is that there is no enjoyment of pleasure except that which is derived from food and drink, yet, knowing that they cannot without the greatest shame cling to so disgraceful a definition, and that they are eschewed by all, they have tried to color it with a kind of stain—spurious argument. Thus, one of them has said: 'While we are desirous of pleasure through banquets and songs, we have lost that which is infused into us by the reception of the Word by which alone we can be saved.'

Do they not appear to us by these various arguments to differ and disagree? Scripture, too, condemns them, and did not fail to mention those whom the Apostle refuted, as did Luke, who wrote his book as a history telling us in the Acts of the Apostles: 'And some of the Epicurean and Stoic philosophers debated with him; and some said, "What is this babbler trying to say?" But others, "He seems to be a herald of strange gods." '[30]

Yet, the Apostle did not leave these people without favor, for even Dionysius the Areopagite believed along with his wife Damaris and many others. So that assembly of learned and eloquent men showed that they were themselves overcome in a simple discussion by the example of believers. What, then, do those men want who are trying to corrupt those whom the Apostle has gained, and whom Christ has redeemed with His Blood? They assert that baptized persons ought not to strive for training of the virtues, that reveling does them no harm, nor excess of pleasure, that they are foolish who go without these things. Virgins ought to marry, to bear children, and widows likewise should repeat that converse with man which they once experienced with bad results, and, even if they can restrain themselves, they are in error who do not wish to enter marriage again.

What then? Is it proper for us to put off the man, and put

---

30 Acts 17.18.

on the beast, and stripping ourselves of Christ to clothe ourselves or add to our clothing the garments of the Devil? The very teachers of the heathen did not think honor and pleasure could be joined together, because they would seem thus to class beasts with men, and shall we infuse the habits of beasts into the breast of man, and inscribe on the reasonable mind the unreasonable manner of wild beasts?

Yet, there are many kinds of animals which, having lost their mate, refrain from mating again and spend the time in a life of solitude; many, too, feed on simple herbs and will not learn how to slake their thirst except at a pure stream; one may also see dogs refrain from food forbidden them, closing their famishing mouths if restraint is put upon them. Are men to be warned against the practice which brute beasts have learned through man not to transgress?

What is more excellent than fasting which makes the years of youth grow aged so that there is an old age of character? For, as advanced age is stimulated by excess in food and by drunkenness, so the wildness of youth is subdued by scanty food and by the running stream. An external fire is extinguished by pouring on water, nor is it strange if the inner heat of the body is cooled by a drink from a stream, for the flame is fed with fuel or it fails. As things like hay and straw, wood and oil, are the nourishment of the fire by which it is fed, so, if you take them away or do not supply them, the fire dies. Likewise, by food the heat of the body is supported or lessened; it is aroused by food; by food it is tamed. Therefore is excess the mother of lust.

And is not temperance in harmony with nature and that divine law which in the beginning of all things gave the springs for drink and the fruits of trees for food? After the Flood, the just man found wine a source of temptation to him.[31] Let us, then, use the natural food of temperance, and

---

31 Cf. Gen. 9.20-21.

would that we all could do so! But, because all are not strong, the Apostle therefore says: 'Use a little wine for thy frequent infirmities.'[32] We must drink it not for our pleasure, but for our infirmity, sparingly as a remedy, not excessively as a gratification.

Lastly, Elias, whom the Lord was rearing to the perfection of virtue, found at his head a cake and a vessel of water, and in the strength of that food he fasted forty days.[33] Our fathers, when they crossed the sea on foot, drank water, not wine.[34] Daniel and the Hebrew youths were fed with their native food[35] and given water to drink; the one was victorious over the fury of lions,[36] the others saw the burning fire play around their limbs with harmless touch.[37]

And why should I speak of men? Judith, absolutely unmoved by the luxurious banquet of Holofernes, solely by virtue of her temperance carried off the triumph which men's strength despaired of; she lifted her country from siege; she slew the general of the army with her own hands.[38] This is clear proof that his luxury had enervated that warrior, terrible to the nations, and temperance in food had made this woman stronger than men. Here it was not in her sex that nature was overcome, but she overcame through her own food. Esther by her fasts won the favor of a proud king.[39] Anna, who for eighty-four years as a widow worshiped in the temple with fasts and prayers day and night, knew Christ whom John announced, he who was the teacher of abstinence and, as it were, a new angel on earth.[40]

---

32 1 Tim. 5.23.
33 Cf. 3 Kings 19.6-8.
34 Cf. Exod. 17.6.
35 Cf. Dan. 1.8,15.
36 Cf. Dan. 14.39.
37 Cf. Dan. 3.23,49,50.
38 Cf. Judith 13.
39 Cf. Esther 4.16.
40 Cf. Matt. 3.4.

O foolish Eliseus, feeding the Prophets with wild and bitter gourds![41] and Esdras, unmindful of the Scriptures, although he restored the Scriptures from memory![42] Foolish Paul, glorying in fasts,[43] if fasting profits nothing!

How are they of no profit, if they cleansed sins? If you make an offering with humility and with mercy, as Isaias said by the Spirit of God, your bones shall be fat and you shall be like a watered garden.[44] Then your soul and its virtues gleam through the spiritual richness of fasting, and your joys are manifold because of the richness of your mind, so there will be in you the ebriety of sobriety, like that cup of which the Prophet says: 'My brimming cup, how excellent it is!'[45]

Not only is that temperance praiseworthy which leaves aside food, but that, too, which leaves aside lust, for it is written: 'Go not after thy lusts: but say no to thy own will. If thou give to thy soul her desires, thou wilt be a joy to thy enemies,' and below: 'Wine and women make wise men fall off.'[46] Therefore, Paul teaches temperance even in marriage,[47] for one who is incontinent in marriage is like an adulterer and violates the Apostle's law.

Why should I tell of the great grace of virginity which was worthy of being chosen by Christ so that it might be the bodily temple of God, in which, as we read, dwelt the fullness of the Godhead bodily.[48] A virgin begot the salvation of the world, a virgin brought forth the life of all. Should virginity, then, be abandoned which was of benefit to all in Christ? A virgin carried Him whom this world cannot contain

---

41 Cf. 4 Kings 4.39.
42 Cf. 2 Esd. 8.2.
43 Cf. 2 Cor. 11.27.
44 Cf. Isa. 58.11.
45 Ps. 22.5.
46 Eccli. 18.30,31; 19.2.
47 Cf. 1 Cor. 7.2-6.
48 Cf. Col. 2.9.

or support. And when He was born of Mary's womb, He yet preserved the enclosure of her modesty, and the inviolate seal of her virginity. Thus, Christ found in the virgin that which He wanted to be His own, that which the Lord of all might take for Himself. Through a man and a woman flesh was cast out of paradise; it was joined to God [through a virgin].

What shall I say of that other Mary, the sister of Moses, who, as leader of a woman's band, went on foot over the waters of the sea?[49] By the same gift Thecla was reverenced by lions, so that the unfed beasts lying at the feet of their prey prolonged a holy fast and harmed the maiden neither by wanton glance nor claw, for the sacredness of virginity is harmed even by a glance.

Again, with what reverence for virginity did the holy Apostle speak: 'Now concerning virgins I have no commandment of the Lord, yet I give an opinion, as one having obtained mercy from the Lord.'[50] He has not a commandment, he has a counsel, for what is beyond the law is not made a precept, but is rather advised by way of counsel. Authority is not taken for granted, but grace is pointed out, nor is it pointed out by anyone whatsoever, but by one who has obtained the mercy of the Lord. Are the counsels of these men better than the Apostle's? Says the Apostle: 'I give an opinion'; but they think they have to dissuade one from striving for virginity.

We ought to realize what praise of it the Prophet, or, rather, Christ in the Prophet, has expressed in a short verse: 'My sister, my spouse, is a garden enclosed, a garden enclosed, a fountain sealed up.'[51] Christ says this to the Church which He wishes to be a virgin, without spot, without

---
49 Cf. Exod. 15.20.
50 1 Cor. 7.25.
51 Cant. 4.12.

wrinkle. A rich garden is virginity which brings forth many fruits of rich odor. 'A garden enclosed' [is virginity] because it is shut in on all sides by the wall of chastity. 'A fountain sealed up' is virginity for it is the fount and wellspring of modesty which keeps the seal of purity inviolate, in whose source there may shine the image of God, since the pureness of simplicity coincides with chastity of the body.

And no one can doubt that the Church is a virgin, which, also in Corinthians,[52] the Apostle Paul espoused to present as a chaste virgin to Christ. Thus, in the first Epistle he gives a counsel, and considers the gift of virginity good, since it is not disturbed by the troubles of the present world, nor polluted by any filthiness, nor shaken by any storm; in the later Epistle he becomes a godparent for Christ, because he is able to attest the virginity of the Church by the purity of its people.

Tell me now, Paul, in what way you will give counsel under the present distress? 'He who is unmarried,' he says, 'is concerned about the things of the Lord, how he may please God.' He adds, too: 'And the unmarried woman, and the virgin, thinks about the things of the Lord, that she may be holy in body and spirit.'[53] She has her wall, protecting her against the storms of this world, and, thus fortified by the enclosure of God's protection, she is disquieted by no winds of this world. Counsel is good, then, because in counsel there is advantage; in precept, fetters. Counsel attracts the willing; precept binds the unwilling. If anyone has followed counsel, and has not regretted it, she has reached an advantage. But if one has regretted it, she has no reason to blame the Apostle. She herself should have decided her own weakness, and she is responsible for her own will, since she bound herself by fetters and a knot too heavy to bear.

---

52 Cf. 1 Cor. 7.26.
53 1 Cor. 7.32,34.

Therefore, he gives to some counsel, to others he shows a remedy like a good physician desirous of preserving the steadfastness of virtue in the strong, and of giving health to the infirm: 'He who is weak, let him eat vegetables,'[54] let him take a wife; he who is stronger, let him seek the stronger meat of virtue. Rightly he adds: 'But he who stands firm in his heart, being under no constraint, but is free to carry out his own will, and has decided to keep his virgin—he does well. Therefore both he who gives his virgin in marriage does well, and he who does not give her does better. A woman is bound as long as her husband is alive, but if her husband dies, she is free. Let her marry whom she pleases, only let it be in the Lord. But she will be more blessed, in my judgment, if she remains as she is. And I think that I also have the Spirit of God.'[55] This is to have the counsel of God, to seek diligently into all things, and to advise those things that are better, to point out those that are safer.

A cautious guide points out many paths so that each one may proceed along that which he wishes and considers suitable for himself, provided he happens on one by which he can reach the camp. The path of virginity is good, but, being lofty and steep, it requires stronger wayfarers. Good also is that [path] of widowhood, not as difficult as the former, but being rocky and rough it demands more cautious wayfarers. Good, also, is that of marriage; being smooth and straight, it reaches the camp of the saints by a more roundabout way, it admits most persons. Virginity, therefore, has its rewards, widowhood has its merits, and there is place, too, for conjugal modesty. There are steps and progress in each and every virtue.

Stand firm, therefore, in your heart so that no one may undermine you, so that no one can overthrow you. The

---

54 Rom. 14.2.
55 1 Cor. 7.37-40.

Apostle has explained what it is 'to stand,' that is, what was said to Moses: 'The place whereon thou standest is holy ground;[56] for no one stands unless he stands by faith, unless he stands firm in the determination of his heart. Elsewhere, we also read: 'But stand thou here with me.'[57] Two things were said to Moses by the Lord: 'where thou standest is holy ground,' and 'stand thou here with me,' that is, you stand with me, if you stand in the Church. The very place is holy, the very ground is rich in sanctity, and abounding in a harvest of virtues.

Stand, therefore, in the Church, stand where I appeared to you, there I am with you. Where the Church is, there is the most solid lodging for your mind; there is the foundation for your soul, where I appeared to you in the bush. You are the bush, I am fire. Fire is in the bush, I in your flesh. Wherefore I am the fire so that I may give light to you, and that I may consume your thorns, that is, your sins, and that I may show you my grace.

Standing firm in your hearts, rout from the Church the wolves which are trying to carry off prey. Let there be no sloth in you, let not your mouth be evil, nor your tongue bitter. Sit not in the council of vanity, for it is written: 'I have not sat in the council of vanity.'[58] Listen not to those who disparage their neighbors, lest while you listen to others you be stirred up to dishonor your neighbors and it may be said to each one of you: 'Sitting thou didst disparage thy brother.'[59]

Men sit when they disparage, but they stand when they bless the Lord, to whom it is said: 'Behold, now bless ye the Lord, all ye servants of the Lord, who stand in the house of the Lord.'[60] One who sits (to speak of the bodily habit) is,

---

56 Exod. 3.5.
57 Deut. 5.31.
58 Ps. 25.4.
59 Ps. 49.20.
60 Ps. 133.1,2.

as it were, enervated, when the body is idle and when he relaxes the tension of his mind. But a cautious watchman, an active searcher, a wide-awake guard before the camp, stands. The soldier on duty, who wishes to anticipate the enemy's designs, stands in the battle line before he is expected.

'Let him who stands take heed lest he fall.'[61] One who stands knows not how to engage in detraction. For it is the tales of men in idleness wherein detraction is sown, malice is disclosed. Therefore the Prophet says: 'I have held in hatred the company of malicious men, and I will not sit with the wicked.'[62] And in Psalm 36, which he has filled with moral precepts, he has put right at the beginning: 'Do not be malicious among the malicious, nor envious of those who do iniquity.'[63] Malignity harms more than malice, for malignity has neither pure simplicity nor open malice, but a hidden ill-will. It is more difficult to guard against what is hidden than against what is known. So our Saviour warns us to beware of malignant spirits, because they would capture us under the guise of sweet pleasures and a show of other things, when they hold out honor to entice us to ambition, riches to entice us to greed and power, the charm of pride.

Therefore, not only in every act, but especially in the demand for a bishop, malignity should have no place, for in him the life of all is formed; so that he is a man preferred to all by a calm and peaceful decision, being chosen from among all, one who is to heal all, for: 'The meek man is the healer of the heart.'[64] And the Lord in the Gospel calls Himself this healer, saying: 'It is not the healthy who need a physician, but they who are sick.'[65]

He is the good Physician, who has taken upon Him our

---
61 1 Cor. 10.12.
62 Ps. 25.5.
63 Ps. 36.1.
64 Prov. 14.30.
65 Matt. 9.12.

infirmities, has healed our illnesses, and yet He, as it is written, did not glorify Himself becoming a high priest, but He who spoke to Him, the Father, said: 'Thou art my son, I this day have begotten thee.' And elsewhere He says: 'Thou art a priest forever according to the order of Melchisedech.' Since He was to be the type of all priests He took flesh, so that 'in the days of his flesh with a loud cry and tears he offered up prayers and supplications to God the Father: and from those things which he suffered, though the Son of God, he learned obedience which he taught to us so that he might be the cause of our eternal salvation.'[66] At last, when His sufferings were completed, as though completed Himself, He gave health to all, He bore the sin of all.

So He Himself also chose Aaron as priest,[67] in order that not man's will but the grace of God should have chief place in the election of a priest, not the voluntary offering of himself, nor the taking of it upon himself, but the heavenly call; thus he may offer gifts for sins who can compassionate sinners, since He Himself, he says, bears our weakness. No one ought take the honor to himself, but be called by God, as was Aaron. Thus, even Christ did not demand but received the priesthood.[68]

Lastly, when the succession, derived through family descent from Aaron, contained rather heirs of the family than sharers of righteousness, there came, in the type of that Melchisedech of whom we read in the Old Testament, the true Melchisedech, the true King of peace, the true King of justice, for his name is interpreted: 'Without father, without mother, without genealogy, having neither beginning of days nor end of life.'[69] This refers to the Son of God, who in His divine

---
66 Heb. 5.5-9.
67 Cf. Num. 17.8.
68 Cf. Heb. 5.2-4.
69 Heb. 7.3.

generation had no mother, and in His birth from the Virgin Mary had no father. Begotten of the Father alone before the ages, born of the Virgin alone in this age, surely He could have no beginning of days, since He was in the beginning. And how could He have an end of life, since He is the Author of life to all? 'He Himself [is] the beginning and the end of all.'⁷⁰ But this is also referred to Him as an example, that a priest ought to be without father and mother, since in Him is chosen not nobility of family, but holiness of character and pre-eminence in virtues.

Let there be in him faith and perfection of character, not one without the other, but let both meet in one with good works and deeds. Therefore the Apostle Paul wishes us to be imitators of those who through faith, he says, and patience, possess the promises made to Abraham, who by patience was worthy to receive and possess the grace of the blessing promised to him.⁷¹ The Prophet David bids us be imitators of holy Aaron, for he set him among the saints of the Lord to be imitated by us, saying: 'Moses and Aaron are among his priests, and Samuel among them who call upon his name.'⁷²

Plainly he is a man worthy of being set before all to be followed, for, when a dreadful plague spread among the people because of stubborn persons, he offered himself between the living and dead so that he might restrain the plague and that no more persons should perish.⁷³ Truly is he a man of priestly mind and spirit who with dutiful affection, like a good shepherd, offered himself for the flock of the Lord. Thus he broke the sting of death, checked its onslaught, refused it further course. Love assisted his merits, for he offered himself in behalf of those who were resisting him.

---

70 Apoc. 1.8.
71 Cf. Heb. 11.9.
72 Ps. 98.6.
73 Cf. Num. 16.46-48.

Let those who cause dissension learn to fear to rouse the Lord and to appease His priests. Why? Did not an earthquake swallow up Dathan and Abiron and Core because of their dissensions? For, when Core and Dathan and Abiron had stirred up 250 men against Moses and Aaron, to separate from them, they rose up saying: 'Let it be enough for you, that all the congregation are holy, and the Lord among them.'[74]

Then the Lord in anger spoke to all the congregation. The Lord considered and knew who were His[75] and He drew His saints to Himself. And those whom He did not choose He did not draw to Himself. And the Lord bade Core and all who had risen up with him against Moses and Aaron, the priests of the Lord, to take censers and put on incense, so that he who was chosen by the Lord might be established as holy among the Levites of the Lord.

And Moses said to Core: 'Hear ye sons of Levi. Is it a small thing unto you, that God has separated you from the congreation of Israel, and drawn you to himself, to minister the services of the tabernacle of the Lord?' And further on: 'Seek ye to perform your priesthood, as you and all the congregation are gathered against the Lord? For what is Aaron that you murmur against him?'[76]

Considering, then, what causes of offense existed, that unworthy persons desired to discharge the office of priest, and therefore were causing dissension, murmuring in censure of the judgment of God in the choice of His priest, the whole people were seized with great fear and dread of punishment came upon all. But when all implored that all should not perish through the insolence of a few, those guilty of crime were singled out, and 250 men with their leaders were

---
74 Cf. Num. 16.35,3.
75 Cf. 2 Tim. 2.19.
76 Num. 16.8-11.

separated from the people, the earth with a groan was rent in the midst of the people, a deep gulf opened, the guilty were swallowed up, and these were removed from all the elements of this world, so they might neither contaminate the air by inhaling it, the sky by beholding it, the sea by touching it, nor the earth by their entombment.

The punishment ended, but the wickedness did not end, for there arose in consequence of this very thing a great murmuring on the part of the people that these persons had perished through the priests. With what anger the Lord would have destroyed them all had He not been swayed first by the prayers of Moses and Aaron, and then by the intervention of His high priest Aaron, preferring to bestow on them, with greater humiliation to them, the grace which they had spurned!

Mary the prophetess, who with her brothers had crossed the waters of the sea on foot, and, because she did not yet know the mystery of the Ethiopian woman and had murmured against her brother Moses, broke out with leprous spots, so that she would hardly have been cured of the contagion had not Moses begged it.[77] Yet that murmuring refers to the type of the synagogue which does not know the mystery of the Ethiopian woman, that is, the Church, which is taken from the nations, and murmurs with daily reproach, and envies this people, by whose faith it shall be delivered from the leprosy of unbelief, in accord with what we read: that 'a partial blindness only has befallen Israel, until the full number of the Gentiles should enter, and thus all Israel should be saved.'[78]

And that we may observe how in priests divine grace works rather than human grace, of the many rods which Moses had received from tribes and had laid away, that of

---
77 Cf. Num. 12.10-15.
78 Rom. 11.25.

Aaron alone blossomed. Thus, the people saw that the gift of the divine call is to be looked for in a priest, and they ceased to claim equal favor for a human choice, although before they thought they had a similar privilege. What did that rod show except that the priestly grace never decays, and in the deepest lowliness it has in its office the flower of power entrusted to it, or that this also is referred to in mystery? Nor do we think this happened without purpose, toward the end of the life of Aaron the priest. It seems to be manifest that the ancient people, decaying by reason of the long-continued unfaithfulness of their priests, formed anew, at last, in zeal for the faith and devotion, by the example of the Church, will again send forth with renewed grace the flower dead for so many ages.

But what is meant by the fact that, after Aaron was dead, God commanded not all the people, but only Moses who is among the priests of the Lord, to clothe with the garments of Aaron the priest, his son Eleazar,[79] except that we should understand that a priest must consecrate a priest, and he himself clothe him with the vestments, that is, with priestly virtues; then, if he sees that he lacks none of the priestly garments, and all things are in good order, he admits him to the sacred altars. One who is to make supplication for the people should be chosen by the Lord and approved by the priests, so there may be nothing which may give serious offence in him whose duty it is to intercede for the offences of others. The priestly virtue is of no ordinary kind, for he has to beware of taking part not only in more serious faults, but even in the least. He must be prompt to show mercy, not regret a promise, recall the fallen, have sympathy with pain, preserve meekness, love piety, repel or quell anger; let him be like a trumpet urging the people to devotion, exalting them to tranquility.

---

79 Cf. Num. 20.26.

The old saying is: 'Accustom yourself to being consistent, so that your life will set forth as it were a picture, always preserving the same likeness which it received.' How can he be consistent who is at one time aflame with anger, at another seething with fierce indignation, now with face aglow, now changed to paleness, varying and changing color every moment? But, granted that it is natural to be angry, or that there generally is good reason therefor, it is man's duty to temper wrath; not to be carried away with the fury of a lion, not knowing how to be gentle; not spreading tales, nor engendering family quarrels, for it is written: 'A passionate man diggeth up sin.'[80] He that is double-minded is not consistent, nor is he consistent who knows not how to check himself in anger, of whom David aptly says: 'Be angry, and sin not.'[81] He does not control anger but gives way to nature, which man cannot prevent but can moderate. Therefore, although we are angry, let our passion give vent to natural emotion, not to unnatural sin. For who would permit one who cannot govern himself to receive others to govern?

Therefore, the Apostle has provided a pattern, saying that a bishop must be blameless,[82] and elsewhere he says: 'For a bishop must be blameless as being the steward of God, not proud, or ill-tempered, or a drinker, or a brawler, or greedy for base gain.'[83] How can the compassion of one who distributes alms and the greed of a covetous man agree with one another?

I have set down what I have learned to avoid, but the Apostle is the master of virtues who instructs us to refute those who gainsay us with patience, who lays down the rule that he be the husband of one wife,[84] not in order to exclude

---

80 Prov. 15.18.
81 Ps. 4.5.
82 Cf. 1 Tim. 3.2.
83 Titus 1.7.
84 Cf. Titus 1.6.

him from the privilege of marriage (for this is beyond the force of the precept), but that he may by conjugal chastity preserve the grace of his baptism; or, again, that he be induced by the Apostle's authority to beget children, for he speaks of having sons, not entering or repeating marriage.

I have not passed over this point, because many persons contend that the husband of one wife has reference to the time after baptism, so that any impediment which would ensue would be washed away in baptism. Indeed, all faults and sins are washed away, so that, if one has polluted his body by many whom he has not bound to himself by the marriage law, these are all forgiven him. But the marriages are not done away with if he has made a second contract, for sin, not the law, is loosed by the laver [of baptism]. There is no sin in marriage, but there is a law. Whatever is of law, therefore, is not remitted like a sin, but it is retained, like a law. Therefore, the Apostle laid down the law saying: 'If anyone is without reproach, the husband of one wife.'[85] Whoever, then, is without reproach, the husband of one wife, is included among those held by the law to be qualified for the priesthood, but he who entered a second marriage has not the guilt of pollution, though he is disqualified from the privilege of the priesthood.[86]

Having stated what is lawful, let us state in addition what is reasonable. Let us understand, first of all, that not only did the Apostle lay down rules covering a bishop and priest, but the Fathers, also, in the Council of Nicaea,[87] added the mandate that no one who has contracted a second marriage should be admitted to the clergy. How can he console or honor a widow, or urge her to preserve her widowhood, or

---

85 1 Tim. 3.2.
86 See Tertullian, *Ad uxorem* 2.7.
87 That a decree of the Council of Nicaea forbade clergy to be drawn from those who had contracted a second marriage is not among the canons.

the faith pledged to her husband, which he himself has not kept in regard to his first marriage? Or what would be the difference between priest and people if they were bound by the same laws? The life of a priest ought to surpass others as its grace surpasses, and he who binds others by his precepts ought himself to keep the precepts of the law in himself.

How I fought against being ordained! And, finally, when I was compelled, I tried at least to have the ordination deferred! But the prescribed rule did not avail, pressure prevailed. Yet the Western bishops approved my ordination by their decision, and the Eastern bishops, too, by their examples.[88] Yet the ordination of a new convert is prohibited lest he be lifted up by pride.[89] If the ordination was not postponed it was because of constraint, and if humility which is becoming to the priesthood is not wanting, where there is no cause, blame will not be imputed.

Now, if in other churches so much consideration attends the ordination of a bishop, how much care is needed in the church at Vercelli where two things seem to be equally demanded of the bishop, the restraint of the monastery and the discipline of the Church? These matters so different, Eusebius of holy memory was the first in the lands of the West to bring together, so that living in the city he observed the rules of the monks, and ruled the Church in the temperance of fasting.[90] For, one brings much support to the grace of the priesthood if he binds youth to the practice of abstinence and to the rule of purity, and forbids them, even though living in the city, the manners and mode of the city.

Hence came that procession of heroes—Elias, Eliseus, John, son of Elizabeth—who, clothed in sheepskins and goatskins,

---

88 In the election of Nectarius as Bishop of Constantinople. Cf. above, Letter 42 n. 3.
89 Cf. 1 Tim. 3.6.
90 Like Eusebius, Ambrose had the clergy living with him after the death of his brother Satyrus.

poor and needy, afflicted with distress and pain, wandered in deserts among steep and wooded mountains, pathless rocks, rough coves, marshy pitfalls, of whom the world was not worthy. Hence came Daniel, Ananias, Azarias, Misael, who were reared in a royal palace, were fed with fasting, as though in the desert, with coarse food and ordinary drink. Rightly did these royal slaves prevail over kingdoms, despise captivity, shaking off its yoke, subdue powers, overcome the elements, quench the nature of fire, dull the flames, blunt the edge of the sword, stop the mouths of lions. They were found most strong when they were esteemed most weak; they fled not from the mocking of men, for they hoped for heavenly rewards; they did not dread the darkness of prison, for on them shone the beauty of eternal light.

In imitation of these blessed Eusebius left his country and his family and preferred living in foreign lands to ease at home. For the faith, too, he preferred and chose the hardships of exile, and Dionysius of holy memory joined him, he who esteemed the emperor's friendship less than voluntary exile. Thus these illustrious men, when armed bands surrounded them and an army closed in on them, when they were torn from the great Church, triumphed over the imperial power, for by these hardships on earth they purchased fortitude of spirit and kingly power. Those from whom the band of soldiers and din of arms could not tear the faith subdued the raging of a bestial spirit which could not harm the saints. For, as you have in Proverbs: 'As the roaring of a lion, so also is the anger of a king.'[91]

He [the emperor] admitted he was beaten when he asked them to change their opinion, but they thought their pen was mightier than a sword of iron. Then was unbelief so damaged that it fell; the faith of the saints was undamaged. They desired no tomb in their native country, for a dwelling

---
91 Prov. 19.12.

in heaven was waiting for them. They wandered over the whole earth, as having nothing, and possessing all things.[92] Wherever they were sent they looked upon it as a place of delight, for, being rich in faith, they were in want of nothing. They even enriched others, being poor themselves in earthly means, but rich in grace. They were tried but not destroyed in fasting, in labors, in prisons, in watchings. From weakness they emerged strong.[93] They did not await the enticement of pleasures, for hunger fattened them; the parching heat of summer did not burn those whom the hope of everlasting grace refreshed; nor did the cold of icy lands break them whose devotion ever budded afresh with glowing fervor. They did not fear the chains of men, for Jesus had set them free; they wanted not to be rescued from death, for they expected to be raised again by Christ.

At last, blessed Dionysius begged in prayer that he might lay down his life in exile, fearing lest on his return home he would find the minds of people or clergy disturbed by the teaching practice of unbelievers, and he obtained this favor, so that he bore within him in a calm heart the peace of the Lord. Therefore, as blessed Eusebius first raised the standard of suffering, so blessed Dionysius in the land of exile gave up his life with higher honor than the martyrs.

This patience in blessed Eusebius was nourished by the discipline of the monastery, and from the custom of yet harsher observance he derived the power of enduring labors. Who doubts that in stricter Christian devotion these two qualities are the more excellent: the duties of clerics and the customs of monks? The one is a discipline which trains for courtesy and morality, the other for abstinence and patience; the one as on an open stage, the other in secrecy; the one is observed, the other is hidden from sight. So that good athlete

---
92 Cf. 2 Cor. 6.10.
93 Cf. Heb. 11.34.

says: 'We have been made a spectacle to this world and to angels.'[94] Surely he was worthy of being observed by angels, while he was striving to reach the goal of Christ, while he strove to lead the life of angels on earth and overcome the spiritual wickedness on high, for he wrestled with spiritual forces of wickedness.[95] He deserved to have the world gaze on him that the world might imitate him.

The one life, then, is in the arena, the other in a cave;[96] the one is opposed to the confusion of the world, the other to the desires of the flesh; the one subdues, the other flees the pleasures of the body; the one more agreeable, the other safer; the one ruling, the other reigning in self; yet each denying herself that she may be Christ's, because to the perfect it was said: 'If anyone wishes to come after me, let him deny himself, and take up his cross, and follow me.'[97] He follows Christ who can say: 'It is now no longer I that live, but Christ lives in me.'[98]

Paul denied himself when, aware that chains and great tribulations awaited him in Jerusalem, he willingly offered himself to danger, saying: 'Nor do I count my life more precious than myself, if only I may accomplish my course and the ministry of the word which I have received from the Lord Jesus.'[99] And finally, when many stood about weeping and entreating him, he did not change his mind, so rigid a judge of itself is ready faith.

The one, therefore, struggles, the other withdraws; the one overcomes enticements, the other flees them; for the one the world is a triumph, to the other a place of exile; to the one the world is crucified[100] and itself to the world, to the other

---

94 1 Cor. 4.9.
95 Cf. Eph. 6.12.
96 This and the next two paragraphs contain a beautifully written contrast of the active and contemplative life.
97 Matt. 16.24.
98 Gal. 2.20.
99 Acts 20.24.
100 Cf. Gal. 6.14.

it is unknown; the one has more trials, and so a greater victory; the other falls less often, and keeps guard more easily.

Elias himself, that the word of his lips might be confirmed, was sent by the Lord to hide himself near the torrent Carith.[101] Achab made threats; Jezabel made threats. Elias grew afraid and rose up, and in the strength of that spiritual food he walked for forty days and forty nights to the mount of God, Horeb, and he entered a cave and abode there.[102] Later he was sent to anoint kings, for he was inured to patience by dwelling in lonely places, and, as if supplied with the fatness of virtue by his rough food, he went on stronger.

John, too, grew up in the desert, and he baptized the Lord,[103] and there he first practiced that austerity that later he might rebuke the king.

Since in speaking of blessed Elias' dwelling in the desert we have idly passed over names of places not given without a purpose, it seems fitting to go back to what they mean. Elias was sent to the torrent of Horeb where ravens fed him, brought him bread in the morning and flesh in the evening.[104] Not without cause was bread brought in the morning, for it strenghtens man's heart.[105] And how was the Prophet fed if not with mystical food? At evening flesh was served him. Understand what you read, for Carith means 'understanding'; Horeb means 'every heart,' or 'as a heart'; Bersabee is interpreted 'of the seventh well' or, in Latin, 'of an oath.'

Elias went first to Bersabee, to the mysteries of the holy law, to the sacraments of divine justice; later he was sent to the torrent, to that river's stream which gladdens the city of God.[106] You have both Testaments of the one author, the old

---

101 Cf. 3 Kings 17.3.
102 Cf. 3 Kings 19.8,9.
103 Cf. Luke 3.2,19.
104 Cf. 3 Kings 17.6.
105 Cf. Ps. 103.15.
106 Cf. Ps. 45.5.

Scripture like a well, deep and obscure, whence you draw with difficulty, not full, because the one who was to fill it had not yet come. Then later he says: 'I have not come to destroy the Law, but to fulfill it.'[107] Thus the holy one is bidden by the Lord to cross over to the stream,[108] for he who has drunk of the New Testament not only is a river, but from his belly will flow rivers of living water,[109] rivers of understanding, rivers of meditation, spiritual rivers. However, these dried up in the time of unbelief, lest the sacrilegious would drink and lest unbelievers sup.

There the ravens recognized the Prophet of the Lord, whom the Jews did not recognize. Crows fed the one whom a royal and noble race was persecuting. What is Jezabel who persecuted[110] except the synagogue spreading in vain, in vain abounding in the Scriptures which she neither guards nor understands? What ravens fed him but those whose young call him, whose cattle he feeds, as we read: 'to the young ravens that cry to him?'[111] Those ravens knew whom they were feeding, for they were close to understanding and carried the food to that stream of sacred knowledge.

He feeds the Prophet who understands and guards that which was written. Our faith gives him sustenance; our progress gives him nourishment; he feeds upon our minds and thoughts; his speech is fed with our understanding. We give him bread in the morning, when, lying in the light of the Gospel, we bring him the strength of our hearts. By these he is fed, by these he grows strong, with these he fills the mouths of those who fast, to whom the faithlessness of the Jews served not the food of faith. There, every word of the Prophet is a

---

107 Matt. 5.17.
108 Cf. 3 Kings 17.3.
109 Cf. John 7.38.
110 Cf. 3 Kings 19.2.
111 Ps. 146.9.

fasting diet, for they do not see the interior fatness; it is empty and thin and cannot fatten their jaws.

Perhaps, too, they brought the flesh at night, as stronger food, such as the Corinthians, whose minds were weak, could not take, and were fed therefore with the milk of the Apostle.[112] Thus, stronger food was brought at the evening of this world, bread in the morning. And because the Lord commanded this food to be served, that prophetic saying may well suit him in this place: 'Thou wilt give joy at the going out of mornings and evenings,' and below: 'Thou hast prepared their food, for so is its preparation.'[113]

Enough, I think, has been said of our Master; let us now go to the life of the disciples who have engaged themselves in that praise, celebrating it with hymns day and night. This is the service of the angels, to be always occupied with the praises of God, to propitiate and beseech the Lord with frequent prayers. They devote themselves to reading, or busy their minds with continual labors, and, removed from women, they provide a safeguard for one another. What a life is this in which there is nothing to fear and much to imitate! The hardship of fasting is compensated by tranquility of mind, it is lightened by practice, it is aided by leisure, or beguiled by occupation; it is not burdened by the cares of the world, or occupied with others' troubles, or weighted down by the distractions of the city.

You realize what sort of teacher must be found for the preservation or teaching of this task, whom we can find if your unanimity shows us favor, if you forgive one another, if any one thinks he has been hurt by the other.[114] This is not the only pattern for righteousness, not to hurt one who has not hurt you, but also that of forgiving one who has hurt

---

112 Cf. 1 Cor. 3.2.
113 Ps. 64.9,10.
114 Cf. Eph. 4.32.

you. We are generally hurt by another's deceit, by our neighbor's guile. Shall we think it virtue to avenge guile with guile, to repay deceit with deceit? If righteousness is a virtue, it should be free from reproach; nor should it ward of wickedness by wickedness. What virtue is it for you to punish others for the same things you do? That is only spreading wickedness, not avenging it. It makes no difference whom you mistreat, a just man or an unjust one, since mistreatment is not permitted you. Nor is there a difference in how you are ill-willed, whether out of desire to avenge or a wish to injure, since in either case it is not without reproach. Being so, one is the same as unjust, so it is said to you: 'Be not ill-willed because of evildoers, nor envious of them that work iniquity,'[115] and above he says the same: 'I hate the company of them that do evil.'[116] Of course, he included everyone, he excepted no one; he mentioned ill-will, he asked not the cause.

What better pattern of righteousness is there than the divine, for the Son of God says: 'Love your enemies' and again: 'Pray for those who persecute and calumniate you.'[117] He so far removes from the perfect the desire for vengeance that He commands charity for those who do them harm. And since He had said in the old Scriptures: 'Revenge is mine and I will repay,'[118] He says in the Gospel that we must pray for those who have done us harm, so that He who said He will have to punish will not punish them; it is His wish to pardon by your consent with which He agrees according to His promise. For, if you seek revenge, you know that the unrighteous is punished more severely by his own convictions than by the severity of his judges.

Since no one can be without some trouble, let us strive not

---
115 Ps. 36.9.
116 Ps. 25.5.
117 Matt. 5.44.
118 Deut. 32.35.

to have our troubles caused by our sin. And no one is so severely condemned by another's judgment as the fool by his own, for he is the author of his own evils. Therefore, let us keep away from tasks which are troublesome and fraught with discord, having no advantage, producing only added weight. Yet, we should live so as not to regret our decisions or our actions. A wise man usually looks ahead, so he will not often have to repent, for only God never repents. What is the advantage of righteousness but peace of mind? What is the meaning of living righteously but living with peace? As the pattern of the master is, so is the condition of the whole house. If these are needed for a home, how much more for the Church, 'Where there is rich and poor, slave and freeman, Greek and Syrian, patrician and plebeian, we are all one in Christ.'[119]

Let no one think that he is to be paid more deference because he is rich.[120] In the Church a man is rich if he is rich in faith, for the faithful man has a whole world of riches. Is it strange that the faithful man owns the world, since he owns Christ's inheritance, which is more priceless than the world? 'You were redeemed with the precious blood' surely was said to all, not only to the rich. But, if you wish to be rich, follow Him who says: 'Be you also holy in all your behavior.' This He says not only to the rich but to all, because He judges without respect of persons as His faithful witness, the Apostle, says: 'Spend the time of your sojourning not in luxury, nor in fastidiousness, nor haughtiness of heart, but in fear.'[121] You have been given time on this earth, not eternity; use the time as those who know they are going to set out from here.

Trust not in riches, because they must all be left here;

---
119 Col. 3.11.
120 Cf. Prov. 17.5.
121 1 Peter 1.18,19,15,17.

only faith will go with you. Righteousness will be your companion if faith leads the way. Why do riches flatter you? 'You were not redeemed with gold or silver,' with possessions or silk garments, 'from your vain manner of life, but by the precious blood of Christ Jesus.'[122] He is rich who is an heir of God, a joint-heir of Christ. Despise not a poor man, for He made you rich. Despise not a man in want, for 'The poor man cried, and the Lord heard.'[123] Reject not the needy, for Christ even became poor although He was rich, but He became poor for you so that He might with His poverty enrich you. Exalt not yourself as rich; He sent forth His Apostles without money.

And the first of them said: 'Silver and gold I have none.'[124] He glories in poverty as if escaping contamination. 'Silver and gold,' says he, 'I have none,' not gold and silver. He does not know their order, for he does not know their use. 'Silver and gold I have none, but faith I do have. I am rich enough in the name of Jesus, which is above every name.'[125] I have not silver, neither do I desire it; I have not gold, neither do I want it. But I have what you rich men do not have, I have what even you consider of more value, and I give it to the poor, so that I say in the name of Jesus: 'Strengthen ye feeble hands, and weak knees.'[126]

But, if you wish to be rich, you must be poor. Then you will be rich in all things, if you are poor in spirit. Not property, but the spirit, makes one rich.

There are some who abase themselves amid many riches, and they do so rightly and wisely, for the law of nature is sufficiently rich to all, whereby one quickly finds what is more than enough, but for lust all the abundance of riches is

---
122 1 Peter 1.18,19.
123 Ps. 33.7.
124 Acts 3.6.
125 Cf. Phil. 2.9.
126 Isa. 35.3.

poverty. Finally, no one is born poor, he becomes so. Poverty is not in nature, but in our feelings; therefore it is easy for nature to be found rich, difficult for greed to be so. For, the more each one acquires, the more he thirsts and is parched by a certain intoxication of his desire.

Why do you seek for a heap of riches as if it were necessary? Nothing is so necessary as to know what is not necessary. Why do you turn the blame upon the flesh? It is not the belly of the body, but greed of mind that makes a man unsatisfied. Does the flesh take away the hope of the future? Does the flesh destroy the sweetness of spiritual grace? Does the flesh hinder faith? Does the flesh concede anything to vain opinions, as to harsh masters? Rather does the flesh love moderate frugality, by which it is stripped of a burden, and is clothed in good health, because it lays down its concern and takes on tranquility.

Riches themselves are not to be censured. 'The ransom of a man's life are his riches,'[127] for one who gives to the poor ransoms his soul. Therefore, even in riches there is scope for virtue. You are like helmsmen on a great sea. If one steers his course well, he passes quickly over the sea to reach harbor. But one who does not know how to manage his property is drowned by his load. Therefore it is written: 'The substance of the rich is a very strong city.'[128]

What is that city but Jerusalem which is in heaven where there is the kingdom of God? This is the good possession which produces everlasting fruit; the good possession which is not left here, but is possessed there. One who will have this possession says: 'The Lord is my portion.'[129] He says not: My portion extends from this boundary to that. He says not: My portion is among certain neighbors, except, perhaps,

---
127 Prov. 13.8.
128 Prov. 10.15.
129 Ps. 72.26.

among the Apostles, among the Prophets, among the Lord's saints. This is the righteous man's portion. He says not: My portion is in meadows, in forests, in plains, except perhaps in the plains of the forest where is found the Church of which it is written: 'We have found it in the fields of the forest.'[130] He says not: My portion consists of herds of horses, for 'Untrustworthy is the steed for safety.'[131] He says not: My portion consists of herds of oxen, asses, or sheep, except, perhaps, he counts himself among those herds which know their owner, and wishes to consort with that ass which does not shun the crib of Christ,[132] and that sheep is his portion which was led to the slaughter and the 'Lamb which was dumb before his shearer and did not open his mouth,'[133] in whose humiliation judgment has been exalted. Well does he say: 'Before his shearer,' because He laid on the cross what was superfluous, not His own essence; when He was stripped of His body, He did not lose His Godhead.

Not everyone, therefore, says: 'The Lord is my portion.' The greedy man does not say this, because greed comes and says: You are my portion; I have you under my sway, you are become my slave, you sold yourself to me in that gold of yours, you turned yourself over to me in that possession of yours. The luxury-loving man does not say: Christ is my portion, because luxury comes and says: You are my portion; I made you my slave in that banquet, I caught you in the net of those feasts, I have you bound to payment by the surety of your gluttony. Do you not know that you valued your table more than your life? I convict you by your own judgment. Deny it if you can, but you cannot. Finally, you kept nothing for life, you spent all for your table. The

---
130 Ps. 131.6.
131 Ps. 32.17.
132 Cf. Isa. 1.3.
133 Isa. 53.7.

adulterer cannot say: 'The Lord is my portion,' because passion comes and says: I am your portion; you bound yourself to me by your love for that maiden, by a night with a harlot you came under my laws and into my power. The traitor does not say: Christ is my portion, because at once the vileness of sin rushes upon him and says: He is deceiving you, Lord Jesus, he is mine.

This example we have,[134] that, when Judas had received the bread from Christ, the Devil entered his heart, as if claiming his possession, as if retaining his right to his portion, as if saying: 'He is not Yours, but mine; indeed he is my tool, Your betrayer; plainly he is mine. He reclines with You, and serves me; he dines with You, and eats with me; from You he took bread, from me money; he drinks with You, and sells me Your Blood.' And he proved how true were his words. Then Christ went out of him and Judas himself also abandoned Jesus, following the Devil.

How many masters he has who has run away from the One! But let us not run from Him. Who will run away from Him whom they follow bound in chains, but willing chains, which loose and do not bind, and those who are bound with these chains boast and say: 'Paul, a prisoner of Christ Jesus, and Timothy.'[135] It is more glorious for us to be bound by Him than to be set free and loosed from others. Who, then, will run from peace? Who will run from salvation? Who will run from mercy? Who will run from redemption?

You see, my sons, the kind of men who have escaped, who followed after such things, and how they work although they are dead? Let us strive to reach the diligence of those virtues whose glory we so admire, and what we praise in others let us silently behold in ourselves. Nothing tender,

---
134 Cf. John 13.2.
135 Philem. 1.1.

nothing weak attains to praise: 'The kingdom of heaven is taken by force, and the violent carry it away.'¹³⁶ The patriarchs ate the lamb in haste. Faith is hasty, devotion is quick, hope is nimble, it does not love contradictions of the soul, but the passage from fruitless leisure to fruitful labor. What are you putting off until tomorrow? You can gain only today. Be careful lest you have not that and lose this. The loss of one hour is not slight and one hour is a portion of a whole life.

There are young men who want to reach old age quickly so that they will no longer be subject to the will of their elders. There are old men who would like, if possible, to return to their youth. I approve of neither of these desires, because youths, tired of the present, as if ungrateful, seek a change of life, old men its lengthening; whereas youth can grow old in character, and old age fresh in action. Not age so much, but discipline, brings a betterment of habits. How much more, then, should we raise our hopes toward the kingdom of God where there will be newness of life, where there will be a change of grace, not of life.

The reward is not obtained by laziness or sleep. The sleeper does no work, leisure has no profit, but loss instead. Esau, by taking leisure, lost the primacy of blessing,¹³⁷ because he preferred to have food given him rather than to go in search of it. By his labor Jacob found favor with both his parents.

Yet, although Jacob surpassed his brother in virtue and favor, he yielded to his wrath when he grieved over the younger borther's being preferred to him. So it is written: 'Give place to the wrath,'¹³⁸ lest another's wrath draw you into sin when you wish to offer resistance, when you wish to

---
136 Matt. 11.12.
137 Cf. Gen. 27.35.
138 Rom. 12.19.

be avenged. You can take the fault from him and from yourself if you decide to yield [to the other]. Imitate the patriarch who went far away at his mother's advice. What mother's? Rebecca's; that is, patience's. Who but patience could have had this plan? The mother loved her son, but she preferred him to be an exile from her rather than from God. And so, because she was a good mother, she gave to both, but to the younger son she gave a blessing which he could keep. She did not prefer one son to another, but the nimble to the leisurely, the faithful to the faithless. And even to the older son she gave not a little by loving the younger son, lest she make him a murderer.

Since he[139] was exiled from his parents by reason of his piety, not for his wickedness, he spoke with God, he increased in wealth, in children, in favor. Nor was he puffed up by these things when he met his brother, but he humbly bowed down to him, not considering him as pitiless, as wrathful, as base-born, but reverencing Him whom he saw in his brother. So he bowed down seven times, which is the number of forgiveness, because he reverenced not the man, but Him who he saw in spirit would come in man's flesh to take away the sins of the world.[140] This mystery is disclosed to you in the response to Peter, when he says: 'How often shall my brother sin against me, and I forgive him? Up to seven times?'[141] You see that the forgiveness of sins is a type of that great sabbath, of that everlasting rest of grace, and it is granted by contemplation.

But what is meant by his arranging his wives and children and all servants and ordering them to bow down to the earth?[142] Surely it was not to that element which is generally

---
139 Cf. Gen. 27.43.
140 Cf. John 1.29.
141 Matt. 18.21.
142 Cf. Gen. 33.6.

filled with blood, on which is the workshop of crime, or which is often rough with huge crags, or steep cliffs of barren dry ground, but as to that flesh which will be our protection. Perhaps that is the mystery the Lord taught you when He says: 'Not only seven times, but seventy times seven.'[143]

Therefore, do you forgive your injuries that you may be the children of Jacob.[144] Do not be angry like Esau. Imitate blessed David who like a good master left us what to imitate, saying: 'In return for their loving me, they reproached me, but I gave myself to prayer,' and when he was cursed, he prayed. Prayer is a good shield by which insult is kept away; cursing is repelled and is thrown frequently back upon those who uttered the curse so that they are wounded with their own weapon: 'Let them curse,' he says, 'but mayst thou bless.'[145] One must solicit the curse of men, which brings the blessing of the Lord.

And for the rest, consider, dearly beloved, why Jesus suffered outside the gate,[146] and do you leave this earthly city, because your city is Jerusalem which is above. Live there so that you may say: 'Our abode is in heaven.'[147] Therefore, Jesus went forth from the city so that you, going forth from the world, might be above the world. Moses, the only one to see God, had his tabernacle outside the camp when he spoke with God,[148] and the blood of victims, which were offered for sin, was offered on altars,[149] but their bodies were burned outside the camp, because no one who is in the midst of the evils of this world can be rid of sin, nor is his blood acceptable to God unless he leaves the defilement of this body.

---

143 Matt. 18.22.
144 Cf. Col. 3.13.
145 Ps. 108.4,28.
146 Cf. Heb. 13.12.
147 Phil. 3.20.
148 Cf. Exod. 33.7-9.
149 Cf. Exod. 29.12,13.

Love hospitality, by which blessed Abraham found favor, and received Christ as his guest, and Sara already worn with age deserved to have a son. Lot also escaped the destructive fire of Sodom,[150] and you can entertain angels if you offer your hospitality to strangers. What shall I say of Rahob who by this means found salvation?[151]

Show compassion for those who are bound by chains, as if you yourself were bound with them. Console those who grieve: 'It is better to go to the house of mourning, than to the house of joy.'[152] From one is borne the merit of a good work; from the other, a lapse into sin. Lastly, from the one you hope for a reward; in the other you receive it. Suffer with those who are in trouble, as if being in trouble with them.

Let a woman show deference, not be a slave to her husband; let her show she is ready to be guided, not coerced. She is not worthy of wedlock who is worthy of chiding. Let the husband, too, manage his wife like a steersman, pay honor to her as his life partner, share with her as the co-heir of grace.

Mothers, wean your children, love them, but pray for them that they may be long-lived above the earth, not on it, but above it. Nothing is long-lived on this earth, and that which lasts long is brief and more hazardous. Warn them rather to take up the cross of the Lord than to love this life.

Mary the Mother of the Lord stood at the cross of her Son; no one told me this except St. John the Evangelist.[153] Others described how the earth was shaken during the Lord's passion, how the sky was covered with darkness,[154] that the sun was darkened, that the thief was received into paradise after a confession of faith.[155] John taught what the others did

---

150 Cf. Gen. 18.1,2; 19.2,3,13-22.
151 Cf. Josue 2.1-19.
152 Eccle. 7.3.
153 Cf. John 19.25.
154 Cf. Matt. 27.45.
155 Cf. Luke 23.43.

not, how when He hung on the cross He called his Mother by name, thinking it of more import that the Victor over suffering showed His Mother the marks of piety than that He gave a heavenly gift. For, if it is pious to give pardon to a thief, it is a sign of richer devotion for a mother to be so honored with affection by her Son: 'Behold,' he says, 'thy son. . . . Behold, thy mother.' Christ made His will from the cross and apportioned the duties of piety between mother and disciple. The Lord made not only a public, but also a private will, and this will of His John sealed, a worthy witness of so great a Testator—a good testament not of money, but of life eternal, which was written not with ink, but with the Spirit of the living God, who says: 'My tongue is the pen of a ready scribe.'[156]

Nor was Mary less than was befitting the Mother of Christ. When the Apostles fled, she stood before the cross and with reverent gaze beheld her Son's wounds, for she awaited not her Child's death, but the world's salvation. Or perhaps that 'regal chamber' knew that through her Son's death would be the world's redemption, and she thought through her own death she would give herself for the common weal. But Jesus had no need of a helper in redeeming all, for He saved all without a helper. Therefore He says: 'I have become as a man without help, free among the dead.'[157] Indeed, He received the devotion of His Parent, but He did not seek another's aid.

Imitate her, holy mothers, who in her dearly loved only Son set forth such an example of motherly virtue; you do not have sweeter children, nor did the Virgin seek the consolation of being able to bear another son.

Masters, command your slaves not as if they are beneath you in rank, but remembering that they are sharers of the

---
156 Ps. 44.2.
157 Ps. 87.5,6.

same nature as yourselves.[158] Slaves, too, serve your masters with good-will, for each should patiently accept that to which he is born; obey not only good but also severe masters. For, what favor has your service if you zealously serve good masters? But, if you render favors also too harsh, [you gain merit]. For, free men have no reward if, being guilty, they are punished by judges, but this is merit if they suffer not being guilty. Therefore, if you serve your masters amid difficulties, contemplating the Lord Jesus, you will have a reward. Indeed, the Lord Himself, a just man, suffered from the unjust, and nailed our sins to His cross by His marvelous patience, so that whoever imitates Him may wipe away his sins with His Blood.

In conclusion, turn, all of you, to the Lord Jesus. Let the joy of this life be in you in a good conscience, in suffering death with the hope of immortality, the assurance of the resurrection through the grace of Christ, truth with simplicity, faith with confidence, fasting with holiness, diligence with soberness, living with modesty, learning without vainglory, soberness of doctrine, faith without the intoxication of heresy.

The grace of the Lord Jesus Christ be with you all. Amen.

---

158 Cf. 1 Peter 2.18.

LETTERS TO HIS SISTER

60. Ambrose, bishop, to Marcellina his sister (Easter, 386)

N MOST of your letters you make anxious inquiry about the church. Hear, then, what is going on: The day after I received your letter, in which you remarked that your dreams were troubling you, a great wave of serious disturbances began overwhelming us. This time it was not the Portian Basilica, that is, the one outside the walls,[1] which was being demanded [by the Arians], but the new basilica, that is, the one inside the walls, the larger one.

First, the military authorities,[2] imperial counts,[3] came with their command to me to hand over the [new] basilica[4] and also to see to it that the people caused no disturbance. I answered, as was proper, that a bishop could not hand over the temple of God.

On the following day in church this [statement of mine]

---
1 The so-called Basilica of St. Victor.
2 *principes virtutum.*
3 *comites consistoriani.*
4 The Ambrosian Basilica.

was loudly approved by the people; then the praetorian prefect arrived there and began to urge us to give up the Portian Basilica. The people protested again, whereupon he left, saying that he would make a report of matters to the emperor.

The following day, the Lord's day, after the lessons and sermon, I dismissed the catechumens and then went on giving an exposition of the Creed to several candidates for baptism in the baptistries of the basilica. There I was informed that some of the people were flocking over to the Portian Basilica since they had learned that officers[5] had been sent from the palace and were hanging up the imperial banners.[6] Yet I stayed at my duty and began to celebrate Mass.

While I was offering [Mass] I learned that a certain Castulus, whom the Arians declared to be a priest, had been seized by the people as they encountered him in the public square. I began to weep very bitterly and to pray God precisely at the Offertory that there would be no blood shed in a case involving the Church, or, at least, that it would be my blood which would be poured out, not alone for the salvation of my people but also for the unbelievers themselves. To be brief, I dispatched priests and deacons and rescued the man from harm.

Very severe penalties[7] were decreed then and there,[8] first on the entire class of merchants. Consequently, during the holy days of the last week [of Lent], when the bonds of debtors are customarily loosed, chains rattled and were put upon the necks of innocent people, and they were taxed 200 pounds' weight of gold[9] [to be paid] in three days' time. People said they would give that much, or double, if asked,

---
5 *decani.*
6 *vela.*
7 In the form of taxes and/or imprisonment.
8 These are the events of Monday of Holy Week.
9 This was subsequently returned to the merchants; cf. below.

provided that they might practice their faith. The prisons, too, were packed with tradesmen.

All the palace officials, the clerks, the agents of affairs, the attendants of various counts were ordered to avoid going out on the pretext that they were forbidden to take part in the rebellion. Men of high rank were threatened with many dire consequences unless they effected the surrender of the basilica. The persecution spread, and, had they opened their doors, the people seemed on the verge of breaking forth into every sort of abuse.

To effect a speedy surrender of the basilica I myself was approached[10] by counts and tribunes who said that the emperor[11] was using his rights inasmuch as all property was under his jurisdiction. I answered that if he were asking for what was mine—my estate, my money, or anything of this sort—I would not resist, even though all my property belongs to the poor; but sacred objects are not subject to the jurisdiction even of the emperor. If he wants my patrimony, come take it; my person, I am here; do you want to drag me off to prison, or to death? The pleasure is mine, I will not shelter myself with a throng of people, nor cling to the altars, begging for my life. Instead, I will more gladly be sacrificed before the altars.

Actually, in my heart I was frightened, since I knew that armed men had been sent to seize the basilica of the church; [I feared] that in defending the basilica bloodshed would occur and turn to the harm of the whole city. I kept praying that I would not live to see the ruin of this great city or, possibly, of all Italy. I dreaded the ill-will that would arise from the spilling of blood; I offered my own throat. Some tribunes of the Goths were there; I assailed them, saying: 'Is this why the Roman state has taken you in, to make you

---

10 These are the events of Tuesday.
11 Valentinian, under the direction of his mother Justina, who was an Arian.

agents of a public riot? Where will you go if these lands are destroyed?'

I was told to quiet the people. I retorted that it was in my power to arouse them, but to quell them rested with God. Then I said that if I was considered the trouble-maker I should be punished, or banished to any lonely spot on earth they wished. After these words, they went off, and I spent the entire day in the old basilica. Then I went home to sleep, so that, if anyone wanted to arrest me, he might find me ready.

Before dawn,[12] when I set foot out of doors, the basilica had been surrounded and was being occupied by soldiers. The soldiers were said to have told the emperor that if he wished to leave he would be given the opportunity; too, they would escort him if they saw him joining the Catholics; otherwise, they would join the meeting called by Ambrose.

No one of the Arians dared appear, for there were none among the citizens; they consisted of a few who belonged to the imperial household and several Goths. Just as formerly they had a wagon for a dwelling, so now the church is their wagon.[13] Wherever that woman[14] goes, she takes along with her all her retinue.

From the groaning populace I understood that the basilica was surrounded. But, while the lessons were being read, I was informed that even the new basilica was filled with the populace; the crowd seemed to be greater than when they were all free to go there, and they were clamoring for a reader. In short, the soldiers themselves, who appeared to be besieging the basilica, after learning that I had ordered them kept from membership in our communion, began coming over to our meeting. Some of the women were deeply troubled

---

12 On Wednesday.
13 A reference to the Scythian origin of the Arian Goths who formerly lived and held their religious meetings in wagons as they traveled about.
14 Empress Justina.

when they saw them and one rushed out. But the soldiers declared they had come to pray, not to fight. The people broke into some kind of shouting. With what restraint, with what steadfastness, with what reliance on God did they keep begging that we go to that basilica! It was said that in that basilica, too, the people were demanding my presence.

Then I began the following discourse:[15] Brethren, you have heard the Book of Job being read which we follow during this solemn service and season. Even the Devil knew from experience that this book would be made known where all the power of his temptation is revealed and set forth. On that account he hurled himself today with greater strength. But, thanks be to our God who so confirmed you in faith and patience. I mounted the pulpit to praise one man, Job; I have found all of you to be Jobs whom I admire. In each of you Job has lived again, in each the patience and virtue of that holy man has shone again. For, what more timely could be said by Christian men than what the Holy Spirit has said in you today? We beg, O Augustus, we do not battle. We are not afraid, but we are begging. It befits Christians to hope for the tranquility of peace and not to check the steadfastness of faith and truth when faced with danger of death. The Lord is our Head who will save those who hope in Him.[16]

But let us come to the lessons before us. You see, permission is granted to the Devil to be a tempter[17] in order that the good may be tried. The Devil envies the progress of the good; he tempts them in various ways. He tempted Job in his possessions; he tempted him in his children; he tempted him in pain of body. The strong man is tempted in his own body, the weak man in another's. And he wanted to take from me the riches which I have in you, and he desired to scatter this

---
15 The full text of Ambrose's sermon is here given in the six following paragraphs.
16 Cf. Ps. 16.7.
17 Cf. Job 1.12.

inheritance of your tranquility. He longed to snatch you away, too, my very good sons, for whom I daily renew the Sacrifice. He was trying to drag you into the ruins of public disorder. I have, therefore, experienced two kinds of temptations. And perhaps because the Lord God knows that I am weak, He still has not given him [the Devil] power over my body. Although I make it my will and make the offering, He judges me still unequal to this struggle, and He tries me with various labors. And Job did not begin but ended with this struggle.

Moreover, Job was tried by accumulated tidings of evils; he was even tried by his wife who said: 'Speak a word against God, and die.'[18] You see what great disturbances are suddenly at hand—Goths, armed men, heathens, fining of merchants, punishment of saints. You see what is asked when this command is given: Hand over the basilica—that is: 'Speak a word against God, and die,' do not merely speak a word opposing God, but make yourself an opponent of God. The order is: Hand over the altars of God.

We are hard-pressed by the royal edicts, but we are strengthened by the words of Scripture, which answered: 'You have spoken like one of the senseless.'[19] And that was no slight temptation, because we know that those temptations are more severe which are brought about through women. Indeed, through Eve Adam was deceived, and thus did it come about that he departed from the divine commands. When he learned his mistake and was conscious of the sin within himself, he wished to hide but could not. And so God said to him: 'Adam, where art thou?'[20] that is, what were you before? Where now have you begun to stay? Where did I put you? Whither have you wandered? You realize that you are naked because you have lost the robes of good faith.

---
18 Cf. Job 2.9; the Vulgate is 'Bless God, and die.'
19 Job 2.10.
20 Cf. Gen. 3.6,9.

Those are leaves with which you now seek to cover yourself. You have repudiated the fruit, wishing to hide under the leaves of the law, but you are betrayed. You desired to leave the Lord your God for one woman, and you are fleeing One whom formerly you wished to behold. With one woman you have preferred to hide yourself, to abandon the Mirror of the world, the abode of paradise, the grace of Christ.'

Why should I tell of how Jezabel severely persecuted Elias,[21] and Herodias caused John the Baptist to be put to death?[22] Individual women persecuted individual men, but in so far as my merits are far less, so are these trials of mine heavier. My strength is weaker, my danger greater. Women's fortune changes, their hatreds are replaced by others, their contrivances vary, they are following their elders and making a pretext [of protecting] the king from harm. What reason is there for such serious trials against a mere worm, except that they are persecuting not me but the Church?

Then the command is given: 'Hand over the basilica.' I answer: 'It is not lawful for me to hand it over, nor is it expedient for you, O Emperor, to receive it. If you cannot rightly violate the house of a private individual, do you think that the house of God can be appropriated?' It is alleged that all things are permitted the emperor, that everything is his. To this I reply: 'Do not burden yourself with thinking that you have imperial power over things which are divine. Do not exalt yourself, but, if you wish to be emperor for a long time, be subject to God. Scripture says: "What things are God's to God, what are Caesar's to Caesar."[23] Palaces belong to the emperor, churches to the bishop. You have been given authority over public edifices, not over sacred ones.' Again it is said the order came from the emperor: 'I, too, ought to have a basilica.' I answered: 'It is not lawful for you to have

---

21 Cf. 3 Kings 19.1,2.
22 Cf. Matt. 14.3-12.
23 Matt. 22.21.

one. What have you to do with an adulteress? She is an adulteress who is not joined to Christ by lawful union!'

While I was treating of these matters, word was brought to me that the royal hangings had been gathered up, the basilica was filling with people, and they were demanding my presence. At once I turned my discourse in that direction, saying: How lofty and deep are the sayings of the Holy Spirit! As you remember, brethren, we responded with great sorrow of soul to the words read at Matins: 'O God, the heathen have invaded thine inheritance.'[24] In reality, the heathen have invaded, and even more than the heathen have invaded. For the Goths have invaded, and men of different nations; they invaded with arms and surrounded and seized the basilica. We lamented this, being ignorant of your greatness, but our want of wisdom drew forth this [lament].

The heathen have invaded, and truly they have invaded your inheritance, for those who invaded as heathen have become Christians. Those who came to invade the inheritance became co-heirs of God. I have as defenders those whom I thought to be enemies; I possess as allies those whom I thought to be adversaries. That is fulfilled which David the Prophet sang of the Lord Jesus: 'His abode is in peace,' and 'There he has broken the sides of the bows, the shield, the sword and the war!'[25] Whose task is this, whose work but Yours, O Lord Jesus? You saw armed men coming to Your temple, people groaning for this reason and coming in crowds that they might not seem to be handing over God's basilica, and, on the other hand, the soldiers were under orders to do violence. Death was before my eyes, but that amid these events madness should be given no right You put Yourself in our midst, O Lord, and made both one.[26] You quieted the

---
24 Ps. 78.1.
25 Ps. 75.3,4.
26 Cf. Eph. 2.14.

armed men, saying, no doubt: 'If you rush to arms, if those shut up in my temple are disturbed, "What profit will be from my blood?"' Thanks be to You, Christ! Not a legate or messenger, but 'Thou, O Lord, hast made safe thy people.' Thou hast tossed away my sackcloth, and thou hast girt me with gladness.'[27]

These things I said and marveled that the feeling of the emperor could have grown gentle through the zeal of the soldiers, the entreaty of the counts, and the prayers of the people. Meanwhile the message came to me that an envoy had been sent to bring me a decree. I withdrew a little and he acquainted me with the decree. 'What,' he said, 'is your idea in acting contrary to the emperor's wish?' 'I do not know his wish,' I answered, 'nor am I certain of what I have done in disobedience.' 'Why,' he asked, 'did you assign priests[28] to the basilica? If you are a usurper, I want to know how to prepare myself against you.' I replied, saying that I had done nothing to harm the church, that when I had heard that the basilica was besieged by soldiers, I only gave free vent to my lament, and when many urged me to go there I stated: 'I cannot hand over the basilica, yet I cannot wage a fight.' And after I learned that the royal hangings had been taken away[29] when the people demanded that I go there, I sent some priests. I was unwilling to go myself, but I told them: In Christ I believe that the emperor himself will join us.

If these seem to be the acts of a usurper, I have weapons, but only in the name of Christ. I can offer my life. Why does he delay striking if he thinks I am a usurper. Under the Old Testament imperial power was bestowed by priests, not despotically claimed, and it is commonly said that emperors aspired to the priesthood rather than priests to the

---

[27] Ps. 29.10; 27.9; 29.12.
[28] *presbyteri*.
[29] By the emperor's soldiers.

imperial power. Christ fled lest He be made a king.³⁰ We have a power of our own. The power of the priest is weakness. He [St. Paul] said: 'When I am weak, then I am strong.'³¹ He should take care not to make himself a usurper, he against whom God has not raised up an adversary. Maximus does not say that I am a usurper of Valentinian, though he complained that through the intervention of my delegation he was unable to come to Italy. I said, too, that bishops were never usurpers but often had suffered from usurpers.

That whole day was spent in sorrow on our part. The royal hangings were torn by children in their play. I could not return home because soldiers were stationed around the basilica, keeping it under guard. We recited the Psalms with the brethren in the smaller chapel of the church.³²

The next day³³ the Book of Jonas was read according to custom, and when it was finished I began this sermon:³⁴ Brethren, a book has been read in which it is prophesied that sinners shall return to penance. It is understood to mean that they may hope for the future in the present. I added that the just man had been willing to receive even blame, so as not to see or prophesy destruction for the city. And because that sentence was mournful, he grew sad when the gourd withered. God said to the Prophet: 'Are you sad over the gourd?' Jonas answered: 'I am sad.'³⁵ The Lord said that if he was grieving because the gourd had withered, how much greater should his care be for the salvation of so many people! And, in fact, he did away with the destruction which had been prepared for all the city.

Word came promptly that the emperor had ordered the soldiers to withdraw from the basilica, and fines which had been levied on the merchants were being returned to them.

30 Cf. John 6.15.
31 2 Cor. 12.10.
32 This event is also described by St. Augustine (*Conf.* 9.7).
33 Thursday of Holy Week.
34 Another sermon is summarized here.
35 Cf. Jonas 4.7,10.

What, then, was the joy of all the people! What cheering from the whole crowd! What thanksgiving! It was the day on which the Lord had delivered Himself for us, the day when penance in the Church is ended. Soldiers vied with one another in spreading the good news; rushing to the altars, and kissing them, they gave token of peace. Then I knew that God had smitten the early worm so that the whole city might be saved.

These events took place, and would that they were now at an end! But the words of the emperor, full of turmoil, point to greater disturbances. I am called a usurper; even worse than a usurper. For when the counts begged the emperor to give in to the Church, and said that they did this at the request of the soldiers, he answered: 'If Ambrose ordered you, you will give me to him in chains.' After such a speech, just think what is coming! All were horrified at this statement, but some of his men are urging him on.

Finally, too, Calligonus, the grand chamberlain, dared to address me in this fashion: 'While I live, do you treat Valentinian with contempt? I will take your life!' I answered: 'May God grant you to fulfill what you threaten, for I shall suffer what bishops suffer, and you will act as eunuchs act.'[36] May God turn them from the Church and direct their weapons all on me, and slake their thirst with my blood.

---
36 The entire description of Ambrose's encounter with Valentinian is comparable to his later conduct before the tyrant Maximus at Trier. See Letter 10.

61. To the lady his sister, dearer than life and eyes, a brother (June 20, 386)

Ordinarily, I do not leave your Holiness unacquainted with the events taking place here in your absence. You should know, then, that we have found some holy martyrs. When I had consecrated the basilica, many persons with one accord began appealing to me, saying: 'Consecrate this as you did the Roman basilica.' 'I will,' I said, 'if I find relics of martyrs.' And at once I was seized, as it were, with a great presentiment of some sort of divine sign.[1]

In short, the Lord bestowed His favor. Even the clergy were afraid when I bade them clear away the ground in the spot before the grating of Sts. Felix and Nabor. I found encouraging signs. And when certain persons were brought forward to have my hands laid on them [in blessing], the holy martyrs began driving away [the evil spirit], so that before I had said anything one woman[2] was seized and thrown forward at the holy burial place. We found two men of wondrous stature, such as ancient ages bore. The bones were all intact and there was much blood.[3] A great throng of people was there during these two days. In short, we arranged everything in orderly fashion. As it was close to evening, we transferred them to the basilica of Fausta. All that night watch was kept and blessings were given. The next day we transferred them to that which is called the Ambrosian Basilica. While they were being transferred a blind man was cured. My sermon to the people was as follows:

When I consider the overflowing and unprecedented number in this gathering of yours, and the gift of divine grace

---
1 Augustine also describes this event (*Conf.* 9.7; *De civ. Dei* 22.8). See also Paulinus, *Vita Ambros.* 14.
2 The editors read *una*, not *urna* as in the mss.
3 Some rationalists maintain that Ambrose found prehistoric burials in which bones were often covered with red ochre. Cf. Dudden, *op. cit.* I 306-307.

which has shone forth in the holy martyrs, I confess I feel unequal to this task, nor can we express with words what we can scarcely understand with the mind or grasp with the eye. But when the regular reading of the holy Scriptures began, the Holy Spirit who spoke by the Prophets bestowed His gift so that we might utter something worthy of so great a throng and your hopes and the merits of the holy martyrs.

'The heavens declare the glory of God.'[4] When this psalm is read, the thought occurs that it is not the material elements but heavenly graces which seem to offer worthy praise to God. Yet, today, it is evident from the chance reading of the lesson what heavens declare the glory of God. See on my right hand, see on my left, these most sacred relics! See these men of heavenly manner of life! Look at the rewards of a great soul! These are the heavens which declare the glory of God; these are the works of His hands which the firmament proclaims. It was not the charm of the world but the grace of God at work which brought them to the firmament of the most holy passion. In fact, long ago, their characters and virtues were tested and bore witness of them because they remained firm against the hazards of this world.

Paul was a heaven when he said: 'Our citizenship is in heaven.' James and John were heavens, and for this reason they are called 'Sons of Thunder.'[6] In fact, John, like heaven, saw the Word with God.[7] The Lord Jesus Himself was a heaven of everlasting light when He revealed the glory of God, but a glory which no one had beheld before. And so He said: 'No one has at any time seen God. The only-begotten Son, who is in the bosom of the Father, he has revealed him.'[8] If you also are seeking for the works of God's hands, hear Job when he says: 'The spirit of God who made me.'[9] Thus

---
4 Ps. 18.2.
5 Phil. 3.20.
6 Mark 3.17.
7 Cf. John 1.1.
8 John 1.18.
9 Job 33.4.

strengthened against the temptations of the Devil, he held the path of constancy without stumbling. But let us proceed to the remaining verses.

'Day,' it is said, 'unto day heralds the message.'[10] See the true days which no mist of night makes false. See the true days of full light and brilliance everlasting which herald the work of God, not with foolish talk, but firm in the confession of Him from the innermost heart, persevering in martyrdom.

Another psalm which was read says:[11] 'Who is as the Lord our God who dwelleth on high, and looketh down on the low things in heaven and in earth?' God, no doubt, casts His eyes on the lowly, He who laid bare the relics of the holy martyrs of His Church, lying hid under the lowly turf, their souls in heaven, their bodies in the earth: 'Raising up the needy man out of the dust, lifting up the poor man out of the dunghill,' placing him, as you see, with the princes of his people. Whom are we to think of as the princes of his people if not the holy martyrs in whose number long ago the unknown Protase and Gervase were given place? They now cause the Church at Milan, barren of martyrs, now the mother of many children, to rejoice in the glory and examples of their suffering.

This should not be unlike the true faith: 'Day unto day heralds the message,'[12] soul unto soul, life unto life, resurrection unto resurrection. 'And night unto night makes it known,'—that is, flesh unto flesh whose suffering reveals to all its true knowledge of faith. Those nights are good, those nights are clear in which there are stars, 'For as star differs from star in glory, so also with the resurrection of the dead.'[13]

With good reason do people call this the resurrection of the martyrs. But I will see whether the martyrs arose for

---
10 Ps. 18.3.
11 Ps. 112.5-8.
12 Ps. 18.2.
13 1 Cor. 15.41,42.

their advantage or for ours. You know, and, in fact, have seen many persons cleansed of the evil spirits. And many who touched the clothing of the saints with their hands were rid of sicknesses which troubled them. Miracles from times past are beginning anew as when at the coming of the Lord Jesus great grace poured itself upon the earth. You have seen how many have been healed by the mere shadow of the bodies of the saints. How many handkerchiefs have been passed about! How many garments which were laid upon the sacred relics are now said to possess healing power in their very touch! Everyone is glad to touch the outer cloth and touching it he will be cured.

Thanks be to you, O Lord Jesus, for having aroused the spirit of the martyrs at this time when Your Church needs greater protection. Let everyone know the kind of defenders I need, those who can fight back but are not wont to attack. These I have secured for you, O holy people, so that they will bring help to all and harm to none. I am soliciting defenders like these, I do not have soldiers like these—soldiers, that is, who are not of the world, but soldiers of Christ.[14] With such as these, I fear no ill-will; the greater the number of them, the safer are my defenses. And I hope for the protection from them for the very ones who grudge them to me. Let them come and see my bodyguards. I do not deny that I am surrounded with such arms: 'Those are strong in chariots, these in horses, but we will be great in the name of the Lord our God.'[15]

The text of holy Scripture tells how Eliseus spoke to his servant who was afraid when he was surrounded by the army of the Syrians and bade him not to fear: 'Because,' he

---

14 St. Charles Borromeo inscribed Ambrose's words, '*Tales ego ambio defensores*,' on a banner of Sts. Gervase and Protase, which was carried through the streets of Milan during the great plague of 1576-1577. This is but one instance of many, illustrating Charles' devotion to his saintly predecessor in the see of Milan.
15 Ps. 19.8.

said, 'there are more with us than against us.'[16] To prove this he prayed that the eyes of Giezi be opened, and, when they were opened, he [Giezi] saw countless hosts of angels. Although we cannot see them, we feel that they are present. Our eyes were closed as long as the bodies of the saints lay hidden under cover. The Lord has opened our eyes; we have seen His troops which have so often protected us. Formerly, we did not see them, although we had them. Then, because we were afraid, the Lord said, as it were: 'Behold the great martyrs whom I have given you.' So with our eyes unsealed we look upon the glory of the Lord which took place in the past in the sufferings of the martyrs and is present in their works. Brethren, we have escaped no slight load of shame, for we had patrons and did not know it. We have found this one thing in which we appear to surpass our elders—we have regained the knowledge of the saintly martyrs which they had lost.

The glorious relics are rescued from an inglorious tomb; the trophies are exhibited to heaven; the tomb drips with blood; the marks of the bleeding triumph appear; the undisturbed relics are found on the spot in perfect order, with the head torn from the shoulders. Old men say now that they used to hear other names given to these martyrs and that they have read their inscription. The city which had carried off the martyrs of others had lost her own. Although this is the gift of God, I cannot deny the grace which the Lord Jesus has granted in the time of my bishopric. And because I myself am not worthy to be a martyr, I have secured these martyrs for you.

Let the triumphant victims take their place where Christ is the victim. Let Him be above the altar who suffered for all; let them be beneath the altar who were redeemed by His suffering. This is the spot that I had destined for myself, because it is fitting that a bishop rest where he was wont to

---

16 4 Kings 6.16.

offer the Holy Sacrifice. But I yield the right-hand portion to the sacred victims, that place is owed the martyrs. Let us therefore bury the sacred relics, carrying them to worthy resting places, and let us celebrate the entire day with the worship of faith.

The people shouted that the burial of the martyrs should be postponed to the Lord's day. Finally, however, it was agreed to have it take place the following day. On that day the sermon which I gave to the people was like this:

Yesterday I explained the verse: 'Day unto day heralds the message,' in so far as the range of my ability carried me. Today, holy Scripture seems not only to have prophesied in the past but also to be doing so in the present. For, when I see the throngs of your Holiness continuing day and night, the words of the Prophet's song declare that these days, yesterday and today, are those of which it is most fittingly said: 'Day unto day heralds the message,' and those nights of which it is very suitably calculated that 'night unto night makes it known.' For what except the Word of God have you heralded for two days from the bottom of your hearts and given proof that you have a knowledge of the faith?

Yet, the usual ones grudge you this celebration. And because they cannot understand your celebration with their envious minds they hate the reason for it. They reach such folly as to say that there are no merits in the martyrs, although even the evil spirits admit them. But this is not strange. Indeed, so great is the lack of faith of the unbelieving that the confession of the Devil is more tolerable. For the Devil said: 'Jesus, Son of the living God, why have you come to torment us before the time?'[17] And when the Jews heard this they still denied that He was the Son of God. Now, you have also heard the demons crying out and admitting to the martyrs that they cannot bear their punishment, saying: 'Why have you come to torment us so severely?' And the

---

17 Matt. 8.29.

Arians say: 'These are not martyrs, nor can they torment the Devil, nor free anyone,' although the torments are attested by the words of the demons themselves, and the benefits of the martyrs are disclosed by the cures of those who were healed and the testimony of those who were set free.

They say that the blind man has not been given his sight, but he does not say he was not healed. He says: 'I see, I who did not see.' He says: 'I have ceased to be blind,' and he proves it by the fact. They deny the benefit who cannot deny the fact. This man is well known,[18] for he was an employee of the state when he was well, a man named Severus, a butcher by trade. He gave up his employment when his affliction befell him. He calls to witness the men whose kindness formerly supported him; he summons those as witnesses of his healing whom he used to have as witnesses and judges of his blindness. He cries out, saying that when he touched the hem of the martyrs' garment in which the sacred relics were covered light was restored to him.

Does this not resemble the account we read in the Gospel? We praise the power of the one Author; it makes no difference whether it is a work or a gift, since He gives a gift in His work and He works in His gift. What He enjoins others to do, this His name works in the works of others. We read, therefore, in the Gospel that the Jews, when they saw the restoration of health in the blind man, asked proof from his parents. They asked them: 'How is it your son sees?' when he said: 'Whereas I was blind, now I see.'[19] In this case, too, the man says: 'I was blind and now I see. Ask others if you do not believe me. Ask strangers so that you will not think that my parents are under agreement to me.' Their obstinacy is more hateful than that of the Jews. When they were in

---
18 See Augustine, *De civ. Dei* 22.8; *Serm.* 381.1; *Retr.* 13.7.
19 John 9.25.

doubt, they asked the parents. These ask in secret and openly deny. No longer do they disbelieve the work, but the Author.

But what is it, I ask, which they do not believe? Is it whether persons can be healed by martyrs? This is to fail to believe in Christ, for He Himself said: 'And greater than these you will do.'[20] Or [do they ask whether persons can be healed] by those martyrs whose merits for a long time were vigorous, whose bodies were found long ago? Here now I ask: Do they grudge me or the holy martyrs? Can I perform any miracles? Can anything be done by my work, in my name? Why, then, do they grudge me what is not mine? If they grudge the martyrs (for it still remains that, if they do not grudge me, they seem to grudge the martyrs), they show that the martyrs were of another faith than what they believe. For no other reason would they envy their works unless they realized that the faith in them was other than their own, that faith which was established by the tradition of the fathers, which the devils themselves cannot deny, although the Arians do so.

We have heard those who had hands laid on them say today that no one can be saved unless he believes in the Father, the Son, and the Holy Spirit, that he is dead and buried who denies the Holy Spirit and does not believe in the omnipotence of the Trinity. The Devil admits this, but the Arians do not wish to profess it. The Devil says: 'Let him who denies the Godhead of the Holy Spirit be tormented as he was by the martyrs.'

I do not accept the Devil's testimony, but I do accept his confession. The Devil spoke unwillingly under duress and torment. Torture exacts that which wickedness suppresses. Although the Devil yielded to blows, the Arians do not know how to yield. How like Pharao have they suffered many

---
20 John 14.12.

misfortunes and are hardened by their misfortunes! The Devil said those words which we read: 'I know who thou art, thou art the Son of the living God.'[21] The Jews said: 'We do not know who he is.'[22] The devils said today and yesterday and last night: 'We know that you are martyrs.' And the Arians say: 'We do not know, we do not want to know, we do not want to believe.' The devils say to the martyrs: 'You have come to destroy us.' The Arians say: 'The torments of the devils are not real; they are feigned and empty mockery.' I have heard of many things being imagined, but no one could ever feign this and pretend that he was a devil. What is it which we see so disturbs them on whom a hand is laid? Where is there room for deceit? Where is there a trace of pretense?

Yet I do not make use of the statement of the demons as a support for the martyrs. Their holy suffering is proved by its benefits. It has judges, but they are those who have been cleansed; it has witnesses, but they are those who were set free. The proof of those who came here ill is worth more, for their healing attests it. The proof which blood sends forth is stronger, for blood has a piercing voice which reaches from earth to heaven, as you read that God said: 'The blood of your brother cries out to me.'[23] Here blood cries out by disclosing its color; blood cries out by publishing its work; blood cries out by the triumph of its suffering. Your petition has been granted to postpone until today yesterday's burial of relics.

---

21 Mark 1.24.
22 John 9.29.
23 Gen. 4.10.

62. A brother to his sister (December, 388)

You condescended to write me saying that your Holiness was still anxious because I had written that I was anxious. I am surprised that you did not receive my letter in which I wrote that peace had flowed back upon me. For, when the report came that the synagogue of the Jews and an assembly place of the Valentinians had been burned[1] at the instigation of a bishop, the order was made, while I was at Aquileia, for the bishop to rebuild the synagogue, and the monks who had burned the Valentinians' building to be punished. Thus, when I accomplished nothing by frequent attempts, I wrote and sent a letter to the emperor, and when he came to church[2] I delivered this sermon:

It is written in the book of the Prophet: 'Take to thyself a rod of a nut tree,'[3] so we must consider why the Lord said this to the Prophet, for it is not written without a purpose, since we also read in the Pentateuch that the nut tree of Aaron, the priest, blossomed after it had been laid away for a long while. By the rod he appears to point out that the prophetic or priestly power should be straightforward, so that it may counsel not what is pleasant but what is expedient.

Indeed, the Prophet is bidden to take a nut tree branch because the fruit of that aforesaid tree has a bitter rind and a hard shell, but a good fruit within; thus, in imitation of it, the Prophet also may utter bitter and hard sayings, and be unafraid to give voice to harsh teaching. The priest, too, may do the same, because his teaching, bitter though it may seem to some persons for a while and long laid away in the ears of hypocrites, yet, after a time, when it seems to have dried up, it blossoms forth like Aaron's rod.

---

1 At Callinicum, modern Ar-Rakka, on the Euphrates. Cf. above, Letter 2, to Theodosius.
2 Paulinus (*Vit.* 22-23) says that Ambrose wrote from Aquileia to Theodosius, who was at Milan, and then later preached the sermon in his own Cathedral at Milan.
3 Jer. 1.11.

Therefore the Apostle says: 'What is your wish? Shall I come to you with a rod, or in love, and in the spirit of meekness?'[4] He first mentioned the rod and, as it were, struck with the nut-tree rod those going astray, so that he might comfort them later in the spirit of meekness. Thus did meekness restore one whom the rod had deprived of the heavenly sacraments. He also gave similar commands to his disciple, saying: 'Reprove, entreat, rebuke.'[5] Two of these are harsh, one is mild; but they are harsh only that they may soften, as persons, suffering from an excess of gall, find the bitterness of food or drink sweet, and, on the other hand, sweet foods bitter; thus, when the soul is wounded, it grows worse under the warmth of pleasurable flattery, and is again put in order by the bitterness of correction.

These thoughts may be gathered from the reading of the Prophet. Let us also consider what is contained in the reading of the Gospel: 'One of the Pharisees asked the Lord Jesus to dine with him; so he went into the house of the Pharisee, and reclined at table. And behold, a woman in the town, who was a sinner, upon learning that Jesus was at table in the Pharisee's house, brought an alabaster jar of ointment; and standing behind him at his feet, she began to bathe his feet with her tears.' And then I read on to the words: 'Thy faith has saved thee; go in peace.'[6] How simple, I went on to say, in words, how deep in meaning is the reading of the Gospel! Therefore, since they are the words of the great Counselor,[7] let us consider their depth.

Our Lord Jesus Christ decided that men could be bound and won over to what is right more readily by love than by fear, and that love does more for correction than does fear. And so when He came, born of a virgin, He sent ahead His

---
4 1 Cor. 4.21.
5 2 Tim. 4.2.
6 Luke 7.36-38,50.
7 Isa. 9.6.

grace to forgive sin in baptism in order to make us more pleasing to Himself. Then, if we repay Him by services befitting grateful men, He declared in this woman that there shall be to all men the reward of grace itself. If He had forgiven only our first debts, He would have seemed more cautious than generous, more intent on our correction than magnanimous in His reward. It is only the cunning of a narrow mind which tries to entice, but it is fitting that God lead on with an increase of His grace those whom He has invited by grace. So He first bestows on us a gift in baptism, and later He is most generous with His gifts to those who serve Him well. These benefits of Christ, therefore, are both incentives and rewards of virtue.

Let no one be surprised if we use the word 'creditor.'[8] We were formerly under a harsh creditor who could not be satisfied or fully paid except by the death of the debtor. The Lord Jesus came; He saw us bound by a heavy debt. No one could pay his debt with his inheritance of innocence; I was able to take nothing of mine with which to free myself; He gave me a new kind of acquittal, enabling me to get another creditor, because I had not the means of discharging my debt. Yet, not nature, but sin, had made us debtors; by our sins we contracted heavy debts so that we who were free became bound, for a debtor is one who uses any of a creditor's money. Sin is from the Devil. That wicked one, as it were, has these treasures among his possessions, for as Christ's riches are virtues, so the Devil's possessions are crimes. He had reduced the human race to everlasting captivity under a heavy debt of inherited liability, which our forefather, being under debt, had transmitted by legacy to his posterity. The Lord Jesus came; He offered His death for the death of all; He poured out His blood for the blood of everyone.

---

8 A reference to Luke 7.41, which Ambrose has not quoted in full in this letter.

We, then, have changed our creditor; we have not entirely escaped, or, rather, we have escaped, but the debt remains, while the interest is canceled, the Lord Jesus saying: 'To them that are bound: Come forth. And to them that are in prison: Go forth,'[9] for your sins have been forgiven. He has forgiven all and there is no one whom He has not set free. For it is written that He forgave 'all your sins, canceling the decree against us.'[10] Why, then, do we hold decrees of others and wish to make exactions of others, while we enjoy our own freedom? He who forgave all required of all that each forgive others, remembering his own forgiveness.

See to it that you do not get into a worse state as creditor than you did as debtor, like the man in the Gospel whose master forgave his whole debt, but who began later to demand of his fellow servant what he had not paid, so that the master in anger exacted from him with great severity what he had forgiven him before. Let us beware of this happening to us, that by not forgiving what is owed to us we be held responsible for what we owe, for it is written in the words of the Lord Jesus: 'So also my heavenly Father will do to you, if you do not each forgive your brothers from your hearts.'[11] Let us who have been forgiven much forgive a little, and let us realize that we will be more acceptable to God the more we forgive, for we are more pleasing to God the more we have been forgiven.

Then, when the Pharisee was asked by the Lord: 'Which of them loved him more?' He answered: 'He, I suppose, to whom he forgave more.' And the Lord replied: 'Thou hast judged rightly.'[12]

The Pharisee's judgment is praised, but his affection is disapproved. He judges well of others, but he does not believe what he thinks of others. You hear a Jew praise the Church's

---

9 Isa. 49.8.
10 Col. 2.13,14.
11 Cf. Matt. 18.27-35.
12 Luke 7.42,43.

discipline, proclaim its true grace, honor the Church's priests; you ask him to believe, but he refuses, so that what he praises in us he himself does not follow. It was not ample praise he heard from Christ: 'Thou hast judged rightly,' for Cain also made his offerings rightly, but did not divide rightly, and so God said to him: 'If thou offerest rightly, but do not divide rightly, thou has sinned, be still.'[13] In like manner this man offered rightly, because he judged that Christ ought to be more loved by Christians, for He forgave us many sins, but he did not divide rightly, because he thought that the One who forgave men their sins could be ignorant of men's sins.

Therefore He says to Simon: 'Dost thou see this woman? I came into thy house; thou gavest me no water for my feet; but she has bathed my feet with tears.'[14] We are all the one body of Christ, whose head is God, whose members we are;[15] some perhaps are the eyes, like the Prophets; others, teeth, as the Apostles who passed the food of the Gospel teaching into our hearts, and so it is written: 'His eyes are bright with wine, his teeth whiter than milk.'[16] His hands are those who are seen carrying out good works. Those who bestow the strength of nourishment upon the poor are His belly. Some are His feet, and would that I were worthy to be His heel! He pours water on the feet of Christ who forgives the lowly their sins, and, in setting free the common man, he bathes the feet of Christ.

He pours water on Christ's feet who cleanses his conscience from the filth of sin, for Christ walks in the hearts of each and every one. Beware of having a soiled conscience and beginning to defile the feet of Christ. Beware of His stumbling on a thorn of wickedness in you, for this would hurt His heel as He walks in you. This is why the Pharisee poured no water on Christ's feet, because he had not a soul free from

---

13 Gen. 4.7.
14 Luke 7.44.
15 Cf. 1 Cor. 12.12.
16 Cf. Gen. 49.12.

the filth of unbelief. And how could he wash his conscience if he had not received the water of Christ? But the Church has this water and the Church has tears, the water of baptism, the tears of penance. Faith which weeps over former sins bewares of sinning anew. Therefore, Simon the Pharisee, who had no water, had, of course, no tears. How could he have tears if he did not do penance, for, not believing in Christ, he had no tears? If he had had them, he would have bathed his eyes so that he could see Christ whom he did not see although he was at table with Him. If he had seen Him, surely he would never have doubted His power.

The Pharisee had no hair, since he could not recognize the Nazarite, but the Church has it, for she sought the Nazarite. Hairs are considered among the superfluities of the body, but, if they are anointed, they give forth a good perfume and are an ornament to the head; if they are not anointed with oil, they are a burden. Thus riches are a burden if you do not know how to use them, if you do not sprinkle them with the perfume of Christ. But if you feed the poor, and wash their wounds, and cleanse their filth, you have indeed wiped the feet of Christ.

'Thou gavest me no kiss, but she, from the moment she entered, has not ceased to kiss my feet.'[17] A kiss is a mark of love. How, then, can a Jew have a kiss, who has not known peace, who has not received peace from Christ when He said: 'My peace I give you, my peace I leave unto you.'[18] The synagogue has no kiss, but the Church has, for she waited and loved and said: 'Let him kiss me with the kiss of his mouth.'[19] She wished with His kiss to quench gradually the burning of the long desire which had grown with longing for the Lord's coming; she wished to satisfy her thirst with this boon. Therefore, the holy Prophet says: 'Thou wilt open

---
17 Luke 7.45.
18 John 14.27.
19 Cant. 1.1.

my mouth, and it shall declare thy praise.'[20] One who praises the Lord Jesus gives Him a kiss; one who praises surely believes. David himself says: 'I trusted, even when I spoke,'[21] and above: 'Let my mouth be full of thy praise, and let me sing thy glory.'[22]

The same Scripture teaches you of the infusion of special grace, how he gives a kiss to Christ who receives the Spirit, the holy Prophet saying: 'I opened my mouth, and drew in the Spirit.'[23] He kisses Christ who confesses Him: 'For with the heart a man believes unto justice, and with the mouth profession is made unto salvation.'[24] He truly kisses Christ's feet who, in reading the Gospel, recognizes the acts of the Lord Jesus and admires them with holy affection, and so with a reverent kiss, as it were, he caresses the footprints of the Lord as He walks. We kiss Christ, therefore, in the kiss of Communion: 'Let him who reads understand.'[25]

How could a Jew have this kiss? For he who did not believe in His coming did not believe in His passion. How does he believe that He suffered whom he did not believe to have come? The Pharisee, therefore, had no kiss except perhaps that of the traitor Judas. But even Judas did not have a kiss, and when he wished to show the Jews the promised kiss as a sign of betrayal the Lord says to him: 'Judas, dost thou betray the Son of Man with a kiss?'[26] that is, you are offering Me a kiss, and you do not have the love of a kiss; you offer a kiss, and you know not the mystery of a kiss. It is not the kiss of the lips which is sought, but of the heart and soul.

But you say: He kissed the Lord. Yes, he kissed with his

---

20 Ps. 70.8.
21 Ps. 115.10.
22 Ps. 70.8.
23 Ps. 118.131.
24 Rom. 10.10.
25 Matt. 24.15.
26 Luke 22.48.

lips. This kiss the Jewish people have, and so it is written: 'This people honors me with their lips, but their heart is far from me.'[27] Therefore, one who has not faith and love has not a kiss, for with a kiss the strength of love is impressed. Where there is not love, there is not faith, there is not tenderness, and what sweetness of kisses can there be?

But the Church does not cease to kiss Christ's feet, and demands not one but many kisses in the Canticle of Canticles,[28] since like blessed Mary she listens to His every saying, she receives His every word, when the Gospel or the Prophets are read, and she keeps all these words in her heart.[29] The Church alone has kisses, like a bride, for a kiss is a pledge of nuptials and the privilege of wedlock. How could a Jew have kisses, since he does not believe in the Bridegroom? How could a Jew have kisses, if he still does not know that the Bridegroom has come?

He has not only no kisses, but neither does he have oil to anoint Christ's feet,[30] for if he had had oil, he would have, before now, softened his own neck. Therefore, Moses says: 'For it is a stiff-necked people,'[31] and the Lord says that the Levite and the priest passed by and neither of them poured oil or wine into the wounds of the man beaten by robbers,[32] for they had nothing to pour, but, if they had had oil, they would have poured it into their own wounds. But Isaias declares: 'They cannot apply ointment nor oil nor bandage.'[33]

But the Church has oil with which she dresses her children's wounds lest the severity of the wound work deep within. She has oil which she received secretly. With this oil Aser washed his feet, as it is written: 'A blessed son is Aser, and

---

27 Matt. 15.8, quoting Isa. 29.13.
28 Cf. Cant. 1.1.
29 Cf. Luke 2.51.
30 Cf. Luke 7.46.
31 Exod. 34.9.
32 Cf. Luke 10.31,32.
33 Isa. 1.6.

he shall be acceptable to his brethren, and shall dip his foot in oil.'³⁴ With this oil the Church anoints the necks of her children so that they may take the yoke of Christ; with this oil she anointed the martyrs so that they might wipe off the dust of this world; with this oil she anointed confessors lest they give way to toil, succumb, being weary, or be overcome by the heat of this world. Therefore did she anoint them so that she might cool them with the oil of the Spirit.

The synagogue has not this oil, for it has not the olive, not having known that dove which carried an olive branch after the flood.³⁵ That dove descended later when Christ was being baptized, and it remained over Him, as John testifies in the Gospel, saying: 'I beheld the Spirit descending as a dove from heaven, and it abode upon him.'³⁶ How did he see the dove who did not see Him over whom the Spirit descended as a dove?

The Church, therefore, washes the feet of Christ and wipes them with her hair and anoints them with oil and pours ointment upon them, since not only does she care for the wounded and fondle the weary, but she also bedews them with the sweet perfume of grace. And she pours this grace not only on the rich and powerful, but also on men of lowly birth. She weighs all in an equal balance; she receives all into the same bosom; she fondles all in the same embrace.

Christ died once; He was buried once; nevertheless, He wishes ointment poured upon His feet each day. What feet of Christ are they that we pour ointment upon? They are the feet of Christ of whom He Himself says: 'What you have done for one of the least of these, you have done to me.'³⁷ These feet the woman in the Gospel refreshes, these she bedews with her tears,³⁸ when sin is forgiven the lowest of

---

34 Deut. 33.24.
35 Cf. Gen. 7.11.
36 John 1.32.
37 Matt. 25.40.
38 Cf. Luke 7.38.

men, guilt washed away, and pardon granted. These feet he kisses who loves even the least of God's people. These feet he anoints with ointment who imparts the favor of his gentleness to those who are more frail. In these the martyrs, in these the Apostles, in these the Lord Jesus Himself declares He is honored.

You see how virtuous the Lord is, that He urges you to piety through His own example, for He is virtuous even when He offers reproof. Accusing the Jews, He says: 'O my people, what have I done to thee or in what have I grieved thee or in what have I molested thee? Answer thou me. For I brought thee out of the land of Egypt and I delivered thee out of the house of servitude.' And He adds: 'And I sent before thy face Moses and Aaron and Mary.'[39] Bear in mind what Balac plotted against you, that is, the one seeking the help of magical art; but still I did not permit him to harm you. As an exile in a foreign country, you were overwhelmed and hard pressed with burdensome trials; I sent before your face Moses and Aaron and Mary, and he, who had robbed the exile, was himself first robbed.[40] You who had lost your possessions gained those of others, being freed from the enemy who walled you in, and safely you saw the destruction of your enemies amid the waves, while the same water which surrounded and carried you forward flowed back and drowned the enemy. When you needed food, as you came through the desert, did I not provide a rain of food and provisions in abundance wherever you went?[41] Did I not bring you, after subduing all your enemies, into the country of the Botrys?[42] Did I not deliver to you Sehon, King of the Amorrhites[43] (that is, the proud, the king of those who provoke you), and did I not hand over to you the King of Hai alive, whom you, because of an ancient curse, fixed to the wood and hung

---
39 Mich. 6.3,4.
40 Cf. Exod. 14.29.
41 Cf. Exod. 16.4.
42 Cf. Num. 13.24,25 (Septuagint). Botrys is called Wady Eshcol in the Vulgate.
43 Cf. Num. 21.26.

upon a cross?⁴⁴ Why should I mention the slaughter of the troops of the five kings who endeavored to keep the land they owed you? And in return for all this, O man, what do I ask but that you do judgment and justice, and love mercy, and be prepared to walk with the Lord your God.

What was His reproach through the Prophet Nathan to King David himself,⁴⁵ that pious and gentle man? I chose you, He said, the youngest of your brethren; I filled you with the spirit of meekness; I anointed you king through Samuel in whom I and My name dwelt; I removed that former king⁴⁶ whom an evil spirit induced to persecute the Lord's priests, and from an exile I made you a conqueror. I raised up to your throne one of your seed, not an heir as much as partner; I made the strange nations subject to you, to serve you, whereas they had been your attackers. Will you draw those who serve Me into the power of My enemies? And will you take away what belonged to a servant of Mine, and thereby be branded with sin, and will you give My adversaries an occasion to boast?

Therefore, O Emperor—for I will speak not only about you, but to you—since you observe how seriously the Lord is wont to censure, take thought, now that you have become glorious, to submit all the more to your Maker. For it is written: 'Say not when the Lord your God has brought you into another's land and you have eaten another's fruit: "My virtue and my justice gave this to me, but the Lord God bestowed it, but Christ in His mercy brought it." '⁴⁷ Thus, in loving this body, that is, the Church, bring water for His feet, and kiss His feet,⁴⁸ not only pardoning those who have become enmeshed in sin, but by your peace giving them concord and putting them at peace. Pour ointment on His

---

44 Cf. Josue 8.23,29.
45 Cf. 2 Kings 12.7-12. Ambrose here makes the reproach of Nathan fall upon Theodosius.
46 Valens.
47 Deut. 9.4.
48 Cf. John 12.3.

feet, that the whole house wherein Christ reclines at table may be filled with the odor of your ointment, that all at table with Him may be pleased with your perfume; in other words, pay honor to the least [of men]. Thus, angels may be gladdened by the forgiveness of these, as over one sinner doing penance;[49] the Apostles may rejoice, the Prophets may delight! The eyes cannot say to the hand: 'We do not need thy help'; nor, again, the head to the feet: 'I have no need of you.'[50] But, because all are needed, guard the whole body of the Lord Jesus, that He also by His heavenly condescension may preserve your kingdom.

When I came down from the pulpit, he [the emperor] said to me: 'You spoke about me.' I answered: 'I preached what is intended to benefit you.' Then he said: 'I really made too harsh a decision about the bishop's repairing the synagogue. The monks do many outrageous things.' Then Timosius, general of the cavalry and infantry, began being abusive about the monks. I answered him: 'I am dealing with the emperor, as is fitting, for I know that he fears the Lord; but one must deal otherwise with you, for you speak so rudely.'

Then, when I had stood for some time, I said to the emperor: 'Let me confidently sacrifice in your behalf; set my mind at rest.' When he continued sitting and nodding, and made no promise openly, and I remained standing, he said he would correct the edict. I immediately went on to say that he should end the whole investigation, so that the count would not harm the Christians in any way on the pretext of an investigation. He promised. I said to him: 'I am acting on your promise,' and I repeated: 'I am acting on your promise.' 'Go ahead,' he said, 'on my promise.' So I went to the altar,

---
49 Cf. Luke 15.10.
50 1 Cor. 12.21.

but I would not have done so if he had not fully promised.[51] Indeed, so great was the grace of the Offering that I myself felt that the favor had been very pleasing to our God, and that we were in the presence of God. Thus, all was done as I wished.

51 This sentence reveals Ambrose's determination to establish very definite episcopal and imperial spheres of influence.

LETTERS TO LAYMEN

63. Ambrose to Alypius[1]

THE HONORABLE Antiochus[2] delivered to me your Excellency's letter, and I have not been remiss in sending a reply. I dispatched a letter to you by my own messengers, and, unless I am mistaken, sent another when a second opportunity arose.[3] Feeling as I do that we are to amass rather than carefully weigh out tokens of friendship, it became my duty to make some return of correspondence, especially since our friend upon returning put me under obligation by mentioning your letters. Only thus might I stand clear with each of you, and he with you, for he was bound to bring back to you what he had received from you.

Farewell, and love those who love you.

64. Ambrose to Antonius[1]

You are never unmentioned by me, nor shall I ever complain of being passed over in silence, for I know that I am not

---

[1] Undated; the addressee is undoubtedly Faltonius Probus Alypius, prefect of the city in 391.
[2] Antiochus was proconsul of Achaia in 395. He and Alypius are also both mentioned in the correspondence of Symmachus.
[3] Internal evidence of other letters of Ambrose to Alypius.

[1] Undated, to Claudius Antonius, consul in 382 (?).

absent from your heart. But, since you are concerned over what is precious, how can you refuse to give what others often receive, not as a token of love but as an exchange of civility?[2]

Indeed, from my own feelings I can in turn judge yours, believing I am never far from you nor you from me, so closely are we united in our souls. I should never feel I need your letters or you mine, for I talk with you each day, turning toward you my gaze, my attention, and all my respects.

Rivalry with you in acts like these gives me pleasure, for—to speak openly with one who is inseparable from my heart—your letters put me to shame. I beg you, then, cease expressing your gratitude, for my respects to you have their full reward if I know I have not failed in my duty toward you.

Farewell, and love us, because I also love you.

65. Ambrose to Atticus[1]

You sent a letter by my friend Priscus. He delivered it to me and I am doing the same to him. Continue to love Priscus as you do, and even more than you do; this I advise because I esteem my friend Priscus very highly. I feel toward him that pristine love of ours which from childhood on has grown with our years. But it was a long while since I had seen him, so that not only by his name but by the long interval of time he came to me as truly 'pristine.'

Farewell, and love us who cherish you, for we love you.

---
2 Viz., a letter.

1 Undated; it is probable that Atticus was the consul of 397.

66. Ambrose to Bellicius, greetings[1]

You tell me that while you lay very ill you believed in the Lord Jesus and soon began to grow better. This sickness was intended for your health and brought you more pain than peril, since you were long postponing the fulfillment of your promise.[2] This is the meaning of the words: 'I will strike, and I will heal.'[3] He struck you with illness; He healed you with faith. He saw the inward desire of your soul, not void of pious longing, but troubled by delays, and He chose to admonish you in such a way as not to harm your health and yet to incite your devotion.

How could He harm your health, He who is wont to say, as we read in the Gospel: 'I will come and cure him'?[4] In the same way, undoubtedly, when invited by your friends to visit your home, He said: 'I will come and cure him.' Although, perhaps, you did not hear Him, He as God spoke imperceptibly, and if you did not see Him, there is no possible doubt that He visited you though without a body.

You saw Him, for you believed in Him; you saw Him, for you received Him into the dwelling of your mind; you saw Him in spirit; you saw with inner eyes. Hold fast your new Guest, long awaited, but lately received, in whom 'we live and have our being and move.'[5] You have tasted the first fruits of faith; let not the word be hidden in your heart. This is all grace, this is every gift. No one appraises the secret recesses of a house from the entrance, since all the fruit is within;[6] the wise man will not look at a house

---

1 This and the following letter are undated.
2 Bellicius had evidently promised to become a Christian and delayed the fulfillment of the promise until stricken with illness.
3 Deut. 32.39.
4 Matt. 8.7.
5 Acts 17.28.
6 A reference to the sacraments of baptism, confirmation, and Holy Eucharist, all of which Bellicius must first learn about before he is allowed to receive them.

from a window and it is foolish for men to listen at the door.

The mysteries of the more perfect sacraments are of two kinds, as Scripture says: 'Eye has not seen nor ear heard, what things God has prepared for those who love Him.'[7] Of one kind are the things which the Prophets foretold about the future glory, for they were revealed to them, and the saints have preached the good tidings 'by the Spirit of God sent from heaven. Into these things angels desire to look,' as the Apostle Peter says.[8] Of still another kind are the mysteries wherein are the redemption of the world, remission of sin, division of graces, participation in the sacraments. On receiving these you will marvel that man has been given so transcendent a gift and you will know that even the manna, which we so wonder at for having been rained down from heaven upon the Jews,[9] did not have such grace or power to work our salvation. All who received the manna in the desert are dead, except Josue the son of Nun, and Caleb,[10] but one who tastes this sacrament will never die.

May the Lord Jesus give you health! Farewell.

67. Ambrose to Bellicius

You have heard, my brother, the reading of the Gospel where it is related that the Lord Jesus, as He was passing on His way, saw a man blind from birth. If the Lord Jesus, when He saw him, thought he should not be passed by, then we ought not pass by one whom the Lord did not pass by, especially since he had been blind from birth, a fact that is mentioned not without good reason.

There is a blindness resulting from sickness which obscures

---
7 1 Cor. 2.9.
8 1 Peter 1.12.
9 Cf. Exod. 16.15,16.
10 Cf. Num. 32.12.

the vision and is remedied by the passage of time. There is a blindness which is caused by flowing humors and this, also, when the trouble is removed, is generally cured by the skill of medicine. From this you may know that when one is cured who has been blind from birth it is not a case of skill but of power. The Lord gave health, and He used no medicine, for the Lord Jesus healed those whom no one else had cured.

How stupid of the Jews to ask: 'Did this man sin, or his parents?' attributing bodily weaknesses to punishment for sin. The Lord therefore said: 'Neither has this man sinned, nor his parents, but the works of God were to be made manifest in him.' What fell short of its náture, this the Creator, the Author of nature, was able to remedy. He then added: 'As long as I am in the world I am the light of the world,'[1] that is, all the blind can see if they search for me, the light. Come also you, and be enlightened that you may be able to see.[2]

What did He wish in that He who gave back life at His command bestowed health by His word, saying to the dead: 'Come forth'[3] and Lazarus came forth from the tomb; saying to the paralytic: 'Arise, take up thy pallet'[4] and the paralytic arose and began to take up the pallet on which he was carried when he was paralyzed in all his limbs; why, I say, did He spit and make clay and spread the clay over the eyes of the blind man and say to him: ' "Go, wash in the pool of Siloe" (which is interpreted "sent")? So he went away and washed and began to see.'[5] What is the reason for this? An important reason, unless I am mistaken, for he whom Jesus touches sees more.

Notice at the same time His divinity and His sanctity. As the Light He touched and shed light; as Priest He fulfilled in the figure of baptism the mysteries of spiritual grace. He spat

1 John 9.2,3,5.
2 Cf. Ps. 33.6.
3 John 11.44.
4 Mark 2.11.
5 John 9.6,7.

so that you might realize that the things within Christ are light. One who is cleansed by the means which Christ uses truly sees. His spittle cleanses and so does His word, as you have: 'You are already clean because of the word that I have spoken to you.'[6]

This making clay and spreading it on the eyes of the blind man, what does it signify to us but that He who made man from clay[7] restored man to health by smearing him with clay, and that this flesh of our clay may receive through the sacrament of baptism the light of eternal life? Do you, also, draw near to Siloe, to one who was sent by the Father, as you read: 'My teaching is not my own, but his who sent me.'[8] Let Christ wash you that you may see. Come to baptism; now is the time; come in haste that you may say: 'I went and washed, and I began to see';[9] that you may say: 'I was blind, and I began to see'; that you may say as he [Paul] said when the light had been shed upon him: 'The night is far advanced; the day is at hand.'[10]

The night was blindness. It was night when Judas received the morsel from Jesus and Satan entered into him.[11] For Judas, in whom was the Devil, it was night; for John, who reclined on Christ's breast, it was day. It was day, too, for Peter when he saw the light of Christ on the mountain.[12] For the others it was night, but for Peter it was day. But to that very same Peter it was night when he denied Christ. Then the cock crowed and he began to weep,[13] in order to mend his wrong, for now the day was at hand.

The Jews kept asking the blind man: 'How were your eyes

---

6 John 15.3.
7 Cf. Gen. 2.7.
8 John 7.16.
9 John 9.11.
10 Rom. 13.12.
11 Cf. John 13.27.
12 Cf. Matt. 16.2-6.
13 Cf. Matt. 26.75.

opened?"¹⁴ Great madness! They asked what they saw; they asked the reason when they saw the effect.

'And they heaped abuse on him, saying: "Thou art his disciple." '¹⁵ Their curse is a blessing, because their blessing is a curse. 'Thou art his disciple,' they said. They do good when they supposed they are doing harm.

Farewell, son, and love us as you do, for we love you.

68. To Clementianus¹

Today, my son, you heard the lesson in the Apostle that 'The Law has been our tutor unto Christ, that we might be justified by faith.'² It seems to me that by this one text those questions are resolved which ordinarily trouble many persons. There are those who say: 'Since God gave the Law to Moses, why is it that there are many things in the Law which seem made void now by the Gospel? And how can the Author of the two Testaments be one and the same, when a thing permitted in the Law was no longer permitted when the Gospel came, such as bodily circumcision, though it was then given only as a sign, in order that the reality of spiritual circumcision might be retained? But why was it given even for a sign? Why is there such a difference of opinion, so that circumcision, being then considered piety, is now thought an impiety? Further, according to the Law it was ordained that the Sabbath be kept as a holiday, and if one carried a bundle of sticks he was guilty of death,³ but now we see that very day devoted to carrying burdens and conducting

---

14 John 9.10.
15 John 9.28.

---

1 An undated letter, attributed to Irenaeus in the mss., although its contents connect it with the following letter to Clementianus.
2 Gal. 3.24.
3 Cf. Num. 15.32-35.

business without any penalty being attached. There are many commandments of the Law which seem to have ceased at the present time.'

Let us consider the reason for this, for not unintentionally did the Apostle say that 'The Law has been our tutor unto Christ.' Who has a tutor, an older person or a youth? Undoubtedly, a youth or child, that is, one of tender age, for *pedagogus,* as the word is rendered in Latin, means a child's teacher; he cannot impart perfect precepts to an imperfect age, because it cannot bear them. Then, through the Prophet, the God of the Law says: 'I shall give you statutes that are not good,'[4] that is, not perfect, for perfect is surely what is good. But the same God has preserved the most perfect things for the Gospel, as He says: 'I have not come to destroy the Law, but to fulfill it.'[5]

What, then, was the cause of this diversity if not man's changeableness? He knew that the Jewish people were stiff-necked, prone to fall, base, inclined to unbelief, who heard with their ears and did not heed, who saw with their eyes and did not see, being fickle with the instability of infancy, heedless of commands. And so He provided the Law as a tutor for the unstable disposition and weak mind of His people, and moderating the very precepts of the Law, He desired one to be read, the other to be understood. Thus, the fool would at least keep watch over what he was reading and not depart from the instruction of the letter, while the wise would understand the thought of God's mind which the letter did not convey; the man lacking judgment would keep the command of the Law, the man of judgment its mystery. Thus does the Law hold a sword's severity, as the tutor does his rod, in order to awe by threatening punishment of the weakness of an imperfect people. Yet, the Gospel has a gentleness by which sins are forgiven.

---

4 Ezech. 20.25.
5 Matt. 5.17.

Rightly, then, does Paul say that 'the letter kills, but the spirit gives life.'[6] The letter circumcised a small part of the body, the understanding spirit keeps the circumcision of the entire soul and body, so that chastity might be preserved, frugality loved, with the unnecessary parts cut off (for nothing is so unnecessary as the vices of greed, the sins of lust, which did not belong to nature but which sin has caused). Bodily circumcision is the symbol, but the reality is the spiritual circumcision; the one cuts off a member, the other sin. Nature has created nothing imperfect in man, nor has she bade it be removed as unnecessary. However, in order that those who cut off part of their body might realize that there is more need for their sins to be cut off, and those persons cut down who led them to sin, even though they are joined by a certain bodily union, you have the words: 'If thy right hand is an occasion of sin to thee, cut it off and cast it from thee; for it is better for thee that one of thy members should be lost than that thy whole body should go into hell.'[7] To the Jews, therefore, like children, precepts are not given in full but only in part, and they who could not keep the whole body clean are bidden to keep clean, as it were, only one part of it.

They were also commanded to keep the Sabbath holiday one day of the week,[8] so that they would be laden with no burden, having escaped and been released from worldly tasks, so as to carry with them to that everlasting sabbath of future ages no burdens of grievous sins. Yet, because He knew that His people were fickle, God demanded that the weak ones observe but one day; He reserved for the stronger ones the full observance. The synagogue observes the day; the Church, immortality. In the Law is a part; in the Gospel is perfection.

The Jewish people are forbidden to carry wood,[9] that is,

---
6 2 Cor. 3.6.
7 Matt. 5.30.
8 Cf. Exod. 31.15.
9 Cf. Num. 15.33.

such things as are consumed by fire. One who keeps out of the sun has shade. The Sun of Justice does not allow the shade to hinder you; pouring forth the full light of His grace He says to you: 'Go thy way, and from now on sin no more.'[10] The imitator of that everlasting Sun says: 'But if anyone builds upon this foundation, gold, silver, and precious stones, wood, hay, straw—the work of each will be made manifest, for the day of the Lord will declare it, since the day is to be revealed in fire. The fire will assay the quality of everyone's work.'[11] And so let us build upon Christ (for Christ is our foundation) that which is not burned but improved. Gold is improved by fire, so is silver improved.

You heard gold and silver mentioned and you think of the material; you want to accumulate it. You are wasting my effort. This gold and silver bring a burden, but no enjoyment. The burden of the man who searches for it is the profit of his heir. This gold is burnt like wood, not kept forever. This silver will bring loss to your life in that day, not gain. Another kind of gold and silver is required of you, that is, a good thought, a fine word; from these God says He gives vessels of gold and silver. These are God's gifts: 'The words of the Lord are sincere, silver tried by fire, refined of the earth, purified seven-fold.'[12] The beauty of your mind, the brilliance of chaste speech, are asked of you; the brightness of faith, not the tinkling of silver. The one remains; the other perishes. The one includes a reward and we carry it with us; the other entails loss because we leave it here.

If any rich man thinks that the gold and silver which he has hoarded and stored away can avail for his life, he is carrying a worthless burden which the fire of judgment will destroy. Rich men, leave here your pieces of wood so that your burden will not add fuel to the fire which is to come.

---
10 John 8.11-13.
11 1 Cor. 3.12,13.
12 Ps. 11.7.

Your burden will be lightened if you give away some of your load, and what remains will be no burden. Miser, do not bury your treasure, lest you be a Christian in name only, a Jew in practice, realizing that your burdens are your punishment. For it has been said to you, not in the shade, but in the sun: 'If his work abides he will receive reward; if his work burns he will suffer loss.'[13]

Accordingly, like a perfect man learned in the Law and made firm in the Gospel, accept the faith of both Testaments, for, as we read today: 'Blessed is he who sows upon every water, where the ox and the ass tread,'[14] that is, who sows upon the people who follow the teaching of both Testaments; this is the ploughman's ox, wearing the yoke of the Law, of which the Law says: 'Thou shalt not muzzle the ox that treadeth out thy corn,'[15] for this ox has the horns of holy Scripture. But in the Gospel the Lord, representing the people of the Gentiles, mounts the colt of an ass.[16]

But I think that, since the word of God is rich in meaning, we should also understand that an ox has horns that fill one with terror, that a bull is fierce, an ass gentle. This thought is suited to our purpose, because that man who is both severe and gentle is blessed: his severity, by striking terror maintains discipline; his gentleness does not crush innocence; for excessive severity often prompts a lie. God prefers being loved to being feared, for the Lord exacts love, a servant fear, although fear cannot last forever in man because it has been written, as we read today: 'Behold, in fear of you they will fear whom you feared.'[17]

Farewell, son, and love us, because we love you.

---

13 1 Cor. 3.14.
14 Isa. 32.20.
15 Deut. 25.4.
16 Cf. Luke 19.30-37.
17 Source unknown.

69. Ambrose to Clementianus[1]

I am well aware that nothing is more difficult than treating properly the Apostle's meaning, for even Origen's exposition of the New Testament is far inferior to his exposition of the Old. Yet, because you feel that in my previous letter I have not explained amiss the reason why the Law is a tutor, I shall, in what I say today, plan to unfold the full force of the Apostle's meaning.

Now, the first part of this discourse declares that no one is justified by the works of the Law, but by faith, 'Since those who rely on the works of the Law are under a curse,' but 'Christ redeemed us from the curse of the Law, becoming a curse for us.' The inheritance is not given by the Law, but by promise, for 'The promises were made to Abraham and to his offspring . . . who is Christ.' The Law, therefore, 'was enacted on account of transgressions, until the offspring should come to whom the promise was made,' and so 'All things were shut up under sin, that by the faith of Jesus Christ the promise might be given to those who believe. . . . But now that faith has come, we are no longer under the Law,' that is, under a tutor.[2] And, because we are sons of God, we all are also in Christ Jesus. But, if we are in Christ Jesus, then we are the seed of Abraham, the heirs according to the promise. This is the conclusion which the Apostle reaches in his thought.

Yet, he meets the objection even of the Jew who can say: 'I also am an heir, for I am under the Law.' The Law is called the Old Testament, and where there is a testament there is an inheritance, although the Apostle himself told the Hebrews that a testament is of no force while the testator lives, but is confirmed by his death.[3] But, because the Lord

---
1 Undated.
2 Gal. 3.10-16,22-24.
3 Cf. Heb. 9.17.

said of the Jews in Jeremias: 'My inheritance has become to me like a lion,'[4] he [Paul] would not say they were not heirs. But there are heirs without property, and those with property, and while the testator lives those who are mentioned in the will are called heirs, though they are without property.

Little children are also heirs, no different from slaves, since they are under guardians and stewards: 'So,' says he, 'we, too, were Jews enslaved under the elements of this world. But when the fullness of time came, Christ also came,'[5] and now we are no longer servants, but sons, if we believe in Christ. Thus, He gave them the semblance of an inheritance, but withheld its possession; they have the name of heir, but not its advantage, for, like children who are heirs, they possess the bare name of heirship but not its privilege, having no right of command or use, awaiting the fullness of their age that they may be released from their guardians.

Just like children, so are the Jews also under a tutor. The Law is our tutor; a tutor brings us to the master; Christ is our only master: 'Do not say lord and master to yourselves, for one only is your master, the Christ.'[6] A tutor is feared, the master points out the way to salvation. Fear brings us to liberty, liberty to faith, faith to love, love obtains adoption, adoption an inheritance. Therefore, where there is faith, there is freedom, for a slave acts in fear, a free man through faith. The one is under the letter, the other under grace; the one in slavery, the other in the spirit; for 'Where the Spirit of the Lord is, there is freedom.'[7] If, where there is faith, there is freedom; where freedom, grace; where grace, an inheritance—then one who is a Jew in the letter but not in spirit is in slavery. One who has not faith has not liberty of spirit. Where there is no freedom, there is no grace; where

---

4 Jer. 12.8.
5 Gal. 4.1-3.
6 Matt. 23.10.
7 2 Cor. 3.17.

no grace, no adoption; where no adoption, no right of succession.

Thus, he beholds his inheritance as though on sealed tablets, he does not possess it, and he has not the right of choice. How can he say 'Our Father'[8] if he denies the true Son of God by whom our adoption is obtained? How can he draw up a will if he denies the death of the Testator? How can he obtain freedom if he denies the Blood by which he was redeemed? For, it is the price of our freedom, as Peter says: 'You were redeemed with the precious blood,'[9] not of a lamb, but of Him who came in meekness and humility like a lamb, and freed the whole world with the single offering of His body, as He Himself said: 'I was led like a lamb to be sacrificed,'[10] and John also says: 'Behold, the lamb of God, behold the one who takes away the sins of the world.'[11]

Hence, the Jew is an heir in the letter, not in the spirit; he is like a child under guardians and stewards. But the Christian who knows the fullness of time when Christ came, made of a woman, made under the Law, to redeem all who were under the Law, the Christian, I say, through the unity of faith and the knowledge of the Son of God, rises to perfect manhood, to the measure of the age of the fullness of Christ.[12]

Farewell, son, and love us, for we love you.

---

8 Matt. 6.9.
9 1 Peter 1.19.
10 Isa. 53.7.
11 John 1.29.
12 Cf. Eph. 4.13.

70. Ambrose to Cynegius[1]

How you have ennobled yourself by consulting me on a matter you did not approve, desiring only to suit your conduct to your father's wishes, so that you might not lessen your affection, feeling sure that I would make no reply but what benefited holy relationships.

I willingly took your burdens upon myself and reconciled, I hope, the niece to her uncle. I truly do not know why he wanted you to become his son-in-law, changing his status of uncle to that of father-in-law.[2] I need say no more for fear that this, too, would lead to confusion.

Farewell, son, and love us, because we also love you.

71. Ambrose to Eusebius[1] (c. 392)

The secretary of the prefecture, who got into trouble by his work at Portus,[2] is now sailing into port.[3] He came most opportunely, for as soon as I received your letter I saw the prefect and interceded for him. He immediately pardoned him and ordered withdrawn the letter which he had dictated for the sale of his property. Even if the secretary's arrival had been delayed, no one would have admitted the difficulty of rebuilding the port more than one who would have suffered shipwreck there, had you not been his pilot. Under the conditions he would barely have escaped alive.

---

1 Palanque dates this letter at the beginning of 393, associated with the letter to Paternus.
2 Marriage with a niece was forbidden by a law of Constantine in 339. Cf. *Cod. Theod.* 3.12.1.

1 Eusebius was a distinguished layman of Bologna, whose son, Faustinus, was spending some time in Milan.
2 Situated on the harbor of Ostia. Eusebius was probably a superintendent of some work being done there.
3 One of the many puns of Ambrose.

Little Faustinus is suffering from a cough, and he has come to his saintly sister to be cured, and come willingly, for he has found that his stomach ailment is better cared for here. He thinks, too, that I am a doctor and looks to me for his meals. So he gets his medicine here twice a day and has begun feeling fairly well, but when, out of excessive love, they hold off the doses, his stomach cough begins worse than before, and if he does not return to his medicines he will continue to suffer.

Farewell, and love us, for we also love you.

72. Ambrose to Eusebius (c. 395)

The two Faustinuses[1] have returned to you, the two little Ambroses[2] are staying with me. In the father you have what is most distinguished, in the son what is most agreeable, for you have the height of virtue and you yourself show the grace of humility. I have what is midway between father and young son. With you is the head of the whole house, and the uninterrupted succession of a name handed down; with me remains the frugal mean which depends upon the head and shares the nature of what follows. You have the one who is the peace of both of us, who, when he is given me in turn, smoothes away all the concerns of my soul. You have the one who by his life and deeds and progeny has found favor with our Lord. You have the one who amid the storms of this world has fostered a spiritual dove[3] to bring him the fruits of peace,[4] for she is anointed with the oil of chastity. With you is one who built an altar to God, whom God

---
1 Eusebius' son and grandson.
2 Ambrose and Ambrosia; for the latter he wrote his *Inst. Virg.* (PL 16.305-334).
3 A reference to Ambrosia.
4 Cf. Gen. 8.11.

blessed with his sons, saying: 'Increase and multiply,'[5] with whom He established the covenant of His peace which would endure for him and his children for everlasting generations.

You have the heir of the divine benediction, a partner of grace, a sharer of righteousness. Be careful, I beg you, that this Noe, our husbandman, the good planter of a fruitful vineyard, when he is inebriated with the cup of your love and grace, does not become like a man drunk with wine, who after indulging too long in rest, happens to fall asleep and is awakened by the longing for our Chem.

Japhet is there, too, the youngest of the brothers, who with reverential piety covers his father, whom his father sees even while he sleeps and never puts out of his thoughts, but keeps always in his sight and in his embrace, and upon awaking will know what his youngest son has done for him. In Latin his name signifies 'richness of expression,' because grace is poured out upon his lips and in his life. God therefore has blessed him because, going backwards, so to speak, to Bologna, he covered his father with the pious cloak of charity[6] and showed honor to piety. Of him his father says: 'May God make Japhet rejoice in the houses of Chanaan.'[7] For this reason, too, in the story of this generation he is preferred to his elder brother, he is given the blessing in his stead, he is preferred out of honor to his name, he is ranked above the privilege of elder birth and the honor due to nature.

In Latin Chanaan signifies a 'name.' Truly is this Ambrose of ours a good name, in whose houses Japhet may rejoice, because 'A good name is better than a great abundance of riches.'[8] Let him be blessed and let his favor be above gold and silver, let this seed of Abraham be in his inheritance, let every blessing be upon his posterity and on the household

---

5 Gen. 9.9.
6 Cf. Gen. 9.23.
7 Gen. 9.27.
8 Prov. 22.1.

of the just man. But no one is accursed, all are blessed, for blessed is the fruit of Sara.

The Ambroses greet you, dear Parthenius greets you, so does Valentinian, now humbly disposed, greet you, for in Hebrew he is called 'Chanaan,' being, as it were, his brother's servant, yielding to him and to his name. He is like mighty Nembroth who had a double name, the famous hunter upon earth, of whom it is said: 'Even as Nembroth the great hunter before the Lord.'[9] He is rude by nature and of great bodily strength, and in his prowess he surpasses those whose genius he cannot match; he seems to carry with him the Comacine cliffs and to resemble them in expression, being a sort of bull,[10] enraged because he has been set aside, deprived of his paternal title, made subject to a man from Bologna, though he is an inhabitant of the capital. You see, he knows not the charming ways of infancy, and when he is hurt he shakes off his nurse's embrace.

Farewell; love us, for we love you.

73. *Ambrose to Faustinus, greetings (late 394)*

I knew very well that you would lament with bitter grief the death of your sister, yet not in such a way as to estrange yourself from us, but to come back to us. Although mourners have not joyous consolations, they are always necessary ones. But you have gone off to a mountain retreat, to a cave amid the haunts of beasts, spurning all part in the affairs of men and, what is more serious, disregarding even your own good judgment.

Did your sister deserve that a human relationship which gave you a woman so remarkable and which should have exerted its influence on you, should have but little privilege?

---

9 Gen. 10.9.
10 Cf. Virgil, *Georg.* 3.58.

Indeed, when she was departing from life she comforted herself with the consolation that she was leaving you as her survivor to be a parent to your nephews, a mentor for her children, a help to the bereaved. You are keeping yourself from your nephews and us, so that we do not have the enjoyment of that consolation. Her dear children bid you not grieve but comfort them, so that when they see you they will think that their mother has not died; in you they will know her again; in you they will cling to her presence; in you they will feel that her life remains for them.

You are sad because she who was in good health for a long time died unexpectedly. This is an experience which we share not only with men but even with cities and countries.[1] As you left Claterna behind, coming from Bologna, and then Bologna, Modena, and Reggio, Brescello was on your right, and ahead Piacenza meets you, still echoing its ancient nobility in its name. You were moved with pity for the ruined areas of the Apennines to the left, and you pondered the towns of once-prosperous peoples and parted from them with sorrowful thoughts. Do not the empty remains of so many half-ruined cities and the destruction of so many lands set before your gaze counsel you to consider the death of one, although she is a holy and admirable lady, to be more consoling, since they have fallen and have been ruined forever, but she, who has been taken from us for a time, lives a better life beyond.

I think that she should not be mourned but, rather, followed with prayer. I believe that you should not lament for her with tears, but commend her soul to the Lord by your prayers.

Of course, you may say that she is saved through her

---

1 An extensive imitation of Servius Sulpicius' letter of consolation to Cicero on the death of Tullia, Cicero *Epist. ad Fam.* 4.5. For interesting remarks on this letter, see addendum to commentary in R. Y. Tyrell-L. C. Purser, *Correspondence of M. Tullius Cicero*, Vol. 5 (2nd ed., 1915) xc-xci, where the editors say that 'the language [of Ambrose] may, perhaps, be inferior to that of Sulpicius, but the hope is higher.'

merits and her faith, yet that you cannot bear the longing for her, no longer seeing her in the body, and this causes you terrible grief. Does not the saying of the Apostle touch you: 'So that henceforth we know no one according to the flesh. And even though we have known Christ according to the flesh, yet now we know him so no longer'?[2] Our body cannot be everlasting and enduring. It must fall that it may rise; it must be broken apart that it may rest and experience the end of sin. Indeed, we have known many in the flesh, but we know them now no longer. We knew our Lord Jesus Himself, says the Apostle, according to the flesh, 'and now we know him so no longer.' For He had already laid away the body's covering; He was seen no more in the guise of man; now He had died for all and all have died in Him. But that they may be made anew through Him, and made alive in spirit, they live now not for themselves, they live for Christ. Elsewhere the same Apostle says: 'It is now no longer I that live but Christ lives in me.'[3]

It is but just that before he knew Christ according to the flesh he already knew His works, though not seeing them. He studied now not His flesh but His power, and, as a persecutor, with hostile animosity overwhelmed the disciples of the Man, His followers in the flesh. Yet, later, he became the teacher of the Gentiles and began to teach and rear for the preaching of the Gospel those who venerated His majesty. In fact, he adds: 'If any man is in Christ, he is a new creature,'[4] that is, one perfect in Christ is a new creature, because one who is in the flesh is imperfect. The Lord Jesus Himself says: 'My spirit shall not remain in man forever, because he is flesh.'[5] A man in the flesh is not in Christ, but if one is in Christ he is a new creature, formed in the newness not of nature, but of grace. The old things according to the flesh

---
2 2 Cor. 5.16.
3 Gal. 2.20.
4 2 Cor. 5.17.
5 Gen. 6.3.

have passed away, all have become new. If the scribe instructed in the kingdom of heaven knows not these things,[6] he is like the householder who brings from his treasure new things and old, not old without new, or new without old. So the Church says: 'The new and the old I have kept for thee.'[7] The old have passed away, that is, the hidden mysteries of the Law have all been made new in Christ.

This is the new creature of whom the Apostle speaks to the Galatians: 'For in Christ Jesus neither circumcision is of any avail, nor uncircumcision, but a new creature,'[8] through which the flesh now renewed flourishes and, having borne the thorns of inveterate sin in the past, finds now the fruit of grace. What need is there for us to grieve if now it is said to the soul: 'Thy youth is renewed like the eagle's'?[9] Why do we lament the dead when the reconciliation of the world with God the Father has already been made through the Lord Jesus?[10]

Having the blessings of Christ, we act as ambassadors for Christ, not only to all, but also to you, that you may know that His gifts are irrevocable, that you may believe what you have always believed, and not bring your understanding into doubt owing to your exceedingly great grief. For our Lord Jesus became sin to take away the sin of the world,[11] and that we might all be made in Him the justice of God,[12] no longer entangled in sin but sure of a reward for justice.

Farewell, and love us, for we love you.

---

6 Matt. 13.52.
7 Cant. 7.13.
8 Gal. 5.6.
9 Ps. 102.5.
10 Cf. 2 Cor. 5.18.
11 Cf. John 1.29.
12 Cf. 2 Cor. 5.21.

74. Ambrose to Irenaeus, greetings (c. 387)

You have made a wise decision to seek an answer to the question whether there is some difference in God's love of those who have had the faith since childhood and of those who have believed only in the course of youth or later manhood. Holy Scripture has not failed to note this problem, nor has it left the matter untouched. Indeed, the Lord our God said meaningfully to the Prophet Joel: 'Lament with me over my spouse in sackcloth and for the husband of her youth,'[1] while He wept either for the synagogue that formerly, in her virginity, had been espoused to the Word of God, or perhaps for a soul that had fallen from grace. Her offense had led her into serious crimes so that she became hated and, having been cast aside because of her stain of impurity and the foul marks of wickedness and the stains of unbelief, she became an object of pity and a person despised, far removed from the grace of that spouse who had been worthy to hear the words: 'I will espouse thee to me in faith and justice and mercy.'[2]

There is good cause to consider her an object of pity since she has lost her claim to a reward and experienced so heavy a loss of the dowry of virtue that she has been deprived of the spouse of her virginity. According to our merits the Word of God either lives or dies in us. If our desires and works are good, the Word of God lives and works in us; if our thoughts and deeds are dark, the Sun of Justice goes down.[3] He teaches us to lament for such a soul. For, as those who have the bridegroom must rejoice and feast, so must that soul mourn when the spouse has been taken away, as it is said of the Apostles in the Gospel: 'for when the bridegroom shall be taken away from them, then will they fast in those days.'[4]

---

1 Joel 1.8.
2 Osee 2.19,20.
3 Cf. Mal. 4.2.
4 Matt. 9.15.

This soul, therefore, formerly experienced joy and gladness, when she had the Virgin Word. She did not fast, since those were the days for feasting and banqueting; the Bridegroom was present, lavishing on all the riches of plenty, the stores of heavenly food, and the flow of wine which gladdens the hearts of men.[6] But, after she had lost the Bridegroom through her deeds, she was ordered to do penance in sackcloth for her sins and to weep for herself because Christ who is the Virgin Word died and was crucified for her.

Sometimes a soul is espoused at an early age and never bears any other yoke, but from the beginning vows the virginal flower of her faith to Christ and is united to Him from the first in mysteries of piety, receiving a training in holiness as the heifer does the yoke. This is the soul of Jewish stock, from the race of ancient patriarchs, who, if she had kept her course of faith unstumbling, would have been counted worthy of great merit, the virginal spouse of the Word, as the woman who took hold of justice and went to meet him like a mother, and will receive him like a wife married of a virgin.[6]

The other, too, has been taken from the Gentiles; each is spouse of the one Word, and this is a great mystery. This is shown you in the Book of Kings:[7] David had two wives, Achinaa the Jezrahelite, and Abigail whom he took later. The first was somewhat severe, the other full of mercy and graciousness, a kindly and generous soul who saw the Father with face unveiled, gazing on His glory. She received that heavenly dew of the grace of the Father, as her name is interpreted. What is the dew of the Father but the Word of God, which fills the hearts of all with the waters of faith and justice?

Beautifully does the true David say to this soul what was said to Abigail: 'Blessed be the Lord God of Israel, who

---
5 Cf. Ps. 103.15.
6 Cf. Eccli. 15.2.
7 Cf. 1 Kings 25.39.

sent thee this day to meet me, and blessed be thy customs.' And again He says to her: 'Go in peace into thy house, behold now I have heard thy voice and have honored thy face.'[8] In the Canticles, too, these are the words of the bridegroom to his bride: 'Show me thy face and let me hear thy voice.'[9]

Then she was sent away, since she had another husband who was called, in Hebrew, Nabal, which, in Latin, means foolish, harsh, unkind, ungentle, ungrateful, for he did not know how to show gratitude. Later, when her husband died, David the Prophet took her as his wife, since she was set free from the law of her husband. Through this union is signified the mystery of the Church of the Gentiles which would believe, for, after losing her husband to whom she was at first united, she made her way to Christ, bringing a dowry of piety, of humility, and of faith, and enriched with the heritage of mercy.

But here it is not this wife who is deplored, but Achinaa who was hostile to her brother, so that her brother made trouble for her. And in their persons it is said: 'Thou hast made us a byword among the heathens, a shaking of the head among the people.'[10] And the Devil, finding her off guard, tore her like a lion and took away her beauty, and overturned her vineyard and fig tree[11] where everyone used to rest, and he made her harvest wither.

God had pity when they were parched and white with drought, and He said to the Prophet: 'Lament with me over my spouse wearing a sackcloth, over the husband of her youth,'[12] that is to say, over the dead husband of a soul of this sort, or over the synagogue. In another place, too, He

---

8 1 Kings 25.32,35.
9 Cant. 2.14.
10 Ps. 43.15.
11 Cf. Mich. 4.4.
12 Joel 1.8.

shows His disapproval[13] because she had forgotten her promise, forgotten her love, was unmindful of grace, strayed from obedience, and had lost her former affection as a wife. He reproves her with His words, recalling to her mind and repeating to her her tenderness, her expressions of devotion: 'Did you not call me one of your household, the parent and pattern of your virginity?'

For that soul the Virgin Word is dead when the Word of God has died through unbelief. He suffers grief, He appoints an intercessor, so that she will be called to penance whereby she may earn compassion. She who is prudent in understanding and beautiful to look upon, like Abigail, was won for Him in battle. Her adversaries were conquered, and her husband, who in the midst of spiritual wickedness struggled and fought so as not to lose his beautiful wife, is dead. So, like a victorious and loving spouse, he gives her sweetness and grace, cleansing from her all that might obscure her beauty. He takes off the garments of her captivity, laying aside even the hair of her head, that is, the curls of sin which seem to be superfluous parts of our person, because 'for a man to wear his hair long is degrading.'[14] Thus, in oneness of faith she may strive to reach to perfect manhood, to the mature measure of the fullness of Christ,[15] and, laying aside all the troubles of the soul, be grounded in love, and may grow up in the Lord Jesus, bringing growth to the whole body.

This is the soul which the Law shows you in the guise of a good woman, for if you see her among the prizes of war and desire to have her as your wife: 'Thou shalt bring her,' he says, 'into thy house.'[16] And in order that you may give her the whole interior of your house, the possession of all your body, you may take away her raiment, you may cut off her transgressions, and with a razor which is not too sharp, lest

---

13 Cf. Osee 4.6.
14 1 Cor. 11.14.
15 Cf. Eph. 4.13.
16 Deut. 21.12.

it come to evil, you may pare off the slough of your passion and your idle feelings. Therefore, 'You will shave her head,' he says, 'so that the eyes of the wise man, which are in his head, will suffer no harm.'[17] 'And she will sit,' he says, 'thirty days in thy house,'[18] lamenting the sins of her generation, the lies of her wicked father, the Devil, who wishes to gather what he has not sown.[19] Then, being cleansed by the purification of this mystical number, she may get possession of the keys of marriage.

Very aptly he says: 'And after that thou shalt go into her,' to enter completely into your soul, and recollect yourself within her, and dwell in her, and stay with her, letting all your life be in her. So you will be not in the flesh but in the spirit, and endeavor to bring her to share your life, knowing she will give you of her goods. Enjoying her favor, may you say: 'And I was a witty child and had received a good soul.'[20] And she will answer: 'I will take you, and bring you into my mother's house, into the chamber of her that bore me.' The good mother of souls is that Jerusalem which is in heaven.

She will be your wife and, finding you, she will kiss you. And if afterwards she please you not,[21] because she chastises her body and brings it into subjection, you will not allow her to be a slave, that is, to the pleasures of the body, nor will you make her a subject of the flesh, but let her remain free. You will not let her go, for that is to sell her; you will not despise her, but you will allow her to serve her God in purity of faith and in the sobriety of good works.

Farewell, and love us, because we love you.

---

17 Eccle. 2.14.
18 Deut. 21.13.
19 Cf. Jer. 17.11.
20 Cant. 3.4.
21 Cf. Deut. 21.14.

75. Ambrose to Irenaeus, greetings (c. 387)[1]

'The partridge has spoken, she has fostered a brood which is not hers.'[2] I should like to borrow the beginning of this letter from the close of my last. It has been frequently discussed, so, in order that we may be able to solve it, let us consider what natural history tells us regarding the nature of this bird.[3] It is the part of no small wisdom to ponder this, for Solomon understood the nature of animals and discoursed on flocks, birds, reptiles, and fish.[4]

This bird is said to be full of craft, fraud, and guile, expert in deceiving a fowler, and experienced in turning him aside from her own brood, since she omits no trial of any action to draw off the hunter from her nest and hiding place. Indeed, if she sees him approach, she sports about long enough to give the young the signal and the opportunity of getting away. When she knows they are gone, she, too, takes herself off, leaving her enemy tricked by her crafty wiles.[5]

It is also said that she is a promiscuous bird, and the males rush on the females with great force and burn with unrestrained desires. Therefore it is thought suitable to compare this unclean, evil-minded, deceptive animal to the adversary and deceitful circumventor of the human race, the author of uncleanness.[6]

---

1 Waghorn has been followed here in assigning this letter to Irenaeus rather than to Sabinus, as does Palanque. Although the opening words do follow the concluding text of Letter 27, to Sabinus, the testimony of the mss., Ambrose's tone of instruction to a disciple, and the presence in Letter 74 of the Scripture passage from Jeremias from which this letter stems—all of these arguments have been carefully weighed by Waghorn (7-9).
2 Jer. 17.11.
3 Several ancient authors, e.g., Aristotle *Hist. Anim.* 9.8,613B-614A, describe the cleverness of the partridge with hunters.
4 Cf. 3 Kings 4.33.
5 Cf. Virgil, *Aen.* 11.716.
6 The Benedictine editors give the number 3 to this and the following paragraph.

The partridge, which derives its name from perdition,⁷ is called Satan; in Latin, the Devil. He spoke first in Eve,⁸ he spoke in Cain, he spoke in Pharao,⁹ in Dathan, Abiron, and Core.¹⁰ He spoke in the Jews when they asked that gods be made for them while Moses was receiving the Law. He spoke again when they said of the Saviour: 'Let him be crucified, let him be crucified'; and 'His blood be on us and on our children.'¹¹ He spoke when they wanted Him to be made king so that they might not walk with the Lord God their king.¹² He spoke in every vain and wicked man.

With these words he has fostered a people who are not his creation, for God made man to His own image and likeness,¹³ and the Devil formed a fellowship with man by the cunning of his words. He has fostered the people of the Gentiles, acquiring riches without judgment. Therefore in the proverb it is said of the greedy rich man that the partridge fostered riches without judgment. But my Jesus, like a good judge, does all with judgment, for He comes, as it is written, saying: 'I speak justice and the judgment of salvation.'¹⁴

Therefore, He has robbed that partridge, the Devil, of favor; He has taken from him the riches of the multitude which evil fostered; He has called back the souls of the Gentiles from error and the hearts of nations which were going astray. And because He knew that they were deceived by the words of the Devil, He Himself, to loosen the chains and bonds of long-standing error, spoke first in Abel, whose voice of blood cried out.¹⁵ He spoke in Moses to whom He said:

---

7 Ambrose here draws a false etymology for the word *perdix* from *perdo*; the latter comes from *per* and *do*.
8 Cf. Gen. 3.4,5.
9 Cf. Exod. 5.2.
10 Cf. Num. 16.2.
11 Matt. 27.23,25.
12 Cf. 1 Kings 8.5.
13 Cf. Gen. 1.27.
14 Isa. 63.1.
15 Cf. Gen. 4.10.

'Why criest thou to me?'[16] He spoke in Josue son of Nun.[17] He spoke in David, who said: 'I cried to thee; save me.'[18] He spoke in all the Prophets. So He says to Isaias: 'Cry'; and he said: 'What shall I cry?'[19] He spoke in Solomon, calling to him with a mighty prophecy and wisdom: 'Come, eat my bread, and drink the wine which I have mingled for you.'[20] He spoke in His own body like the beetle in the wood.[21] He spoke to undo the Devil and overthrow him, saying: 'My God, my God, why hast thou forsaken me?'[22] He spoke to strip him of his spoil when He said to the thief: 'Amen, Amen, I say to thee, this day thou shalt be with me in paradise.'[23] Thus, when Jesus spoke, that partridge was abandoned by his brood in the midst of his days.

Some persons have thought they should adopt that custom of the partridge whereby she takes another's eggs, warms them with her body, and tries by this false means to get the offspring of others. But (as they say to deceive the wary, for even birds have certain tricks) when [the true mother] notices either that the eggs have been seized, or the nest entered, or the young harassed, deceived by false pretenses or deceptive appearances, although she is the weaker one, she clothes and arms herself with cunning. Then, when all the labor expended on food has exhausted the one who is rearing them, when the chicks begin to grow, she [the true mother] utters a cry and with a sort of trumpet of love calls her brood to her. They, roused with certain natural feelings, recognize their parent and abandon her who had played them false. So, when the one wishes to foster those who are not her brood, she loses those whom she thought she would feed.

16 Exod. 14.15.
17 Cf. Josue 1.1.
18 Ps. 118.146.
19 Isa. 40.6.
20 Prov. 9.5.
21 Cf. Hab. 2.11.
22 Matt. 27.46.
23 Luke 23.43.

Not without profit has Jesus spoken, since the people of the world, deceived by the words of the partridge, by his charms, skill, and appearance, had strayed from their origin, following deceitful ways.[24] Yet, called back by the words of their true parent, they will abandon the deceiver and desert his fraudulent practice in the midst of his days, that is, before the end of the world, whither our Lord is drawing us, calling us to eternal life. Now, dead to the world, we live to God.[25]

As the partridge will be utterly abandoned by her false children, then will the foolish man be saved whom God chose, and confounded the wise, for God chooses the foolish things of the world. So, if anyone seems to be wise in this world, let him become foolish, that he may be wise.[26]

Farewell, son, and love us as you do, since we love you.

76. Ambrose to Irenaeus, greetings (c. 387)

In our last letter we wrote that we should set our soul free from its enemies and form with it a bond of unbreakable living. And since this discourse caused us to use an example from Deuteronomy[1] where it treats of the man who had two wives, the one lovable, the other hateful, you seem rightly disturbed lest someone think he has received two souls, for this cannot be.

Indeed, you know very well that sometimes, when Scripture uses an allegory, it may refer at one time to the type of the synagogue, and at another to the type of the Church; some-

---
24 Cf. Virgil, *Aeneid* 11.716.
25 Cf. Rom. 6.8.
26 Cf. 1 Cor. 1.27.

---
1 Cf. Deut. 21.16.

times to the soul, at another time to the mystery of the Word, and at other times to different types and kinds of souls. He who judges by the spirit makes this distinction. Thus, in the following chapter of the Law, I think that not two souls but different qualities of the one soul are meant. For, that type of soul is lovable which desires pleasures, flees hardships, shies away from penance, and heeds not the judgment of God. Indeed, the lovable one, because she seems sweet and pleasing on occasion, does not influence the heart but merely gives pleasure. The other is more serious, for she is consumed with zeal for God, and like an earnest wife would not wish to prostitute her partner; she makes no allowances for her body, does not permit or grant it any indulgence, gives no rein to pleasure and delight, flees the hiding places of shameful deeds, engages in hard labor and dire dangers.

If, in these circumstances, each bears him a child, he will be unable in establishing his will, he says, to show preference to the eldest son of the lovable wife in place of the eldest son of the hateful wife, since he knows the son of the hateful one is the eldest. In this I think it is not meant to typify simply a case of preference between the two eldest as much as to express the fact that the son of the hated one has the rights of the eldest. For, the eldest is the first-born, and the saints are the first-born, because 'every male that opens the womb shall be called holy to the Lord.'[2] Yet, not every first-born is holy, for Esau was not holy although he was the first-born.

But the saints are the first-born, for you have in Numbers: 'Lo, I have taken the Levites from the midst of the children of Israel in place of every first-born who opens the womb among the children of Israel. Every first-born of Israel is mine since the day when I struck every first-born of Egypt.'[3] Accordingly, He receives the Levites instead of the first-born,

---
2 Exod. 13.2; Luke 2.23.
3 Num. 3.12,13.

just as He does the saints. We know from the Epistle to the Hebrews that the saints are first-born, for there you have: 'But you have come to Mount Sion, and to the city of Jerusalem, and to the company of ten thousands of angels and to the church of the first-born.'[4] Thus, as the first-born of the Church are the saints, so also are the Levites, since they also are first-born. They are not holy through their order of birth, but by reason of their duty of holiness. For Levi was the third son of Lia, not the first.[5]

One who is sanctified opens the womb. What womb? Hear the words: 'The wicked have departed from the womb.'[6] In fact, you know that the first-born is one who opens the womb; understand the womb of the good mother from whom the holy do not depart, but sinners do. But the Levites are taken from the midst of Israel, for they have nothing in common with the people whose worldly first-born are destroyed. The first-born of the world are of another mother, from whose womb Paul was separated when he was called to the grace of God.[7] Thus separated from the midst of the people, he received the Word, which is in the midst of our heart. So it is said: 'But in the midst of you there stands one whom you do not see.'[8]

That was not a purposeless digression which we made from one Law to another in order to demonstrate that the first-born is not the son of the lovable one, that is, of relaxation and pleasure, although the words of the chapter express this when Scripture says: 'He will be unable to prefer the eldest son of the loving wife since he knows the son of the hateful one is the eldest.'[9] He is truly the eldest who is the holy offspring of a holy mother, like the true mother from whose womb true sons do not depart, but sinners do. So, he

---

4 Heb. 12.22,23.
5 Cf. Gen. 29.34.
6 Ps. 57.4.
7 Cf. Gal. 1.15.
8 John 1.26.
9 Deut. 21.17.

who is son not of a true mother is not true eldest, but like an eldest son he is helped by riches so that he will not be in need; he is not honored that he may be rich. The other is given twice as much from all so that he will abound. For this reason, you have in Genesis the patriarchs each given two robes by their brother Joseph when they were sent back to their father, to signify to the father that Joseph was found whom the father believed to be dead.

The first-born, therefore, received the right of inheritance when Scripture said: 'This is the beginning of his children, and to him are due the first birthrights.'[10] The first-born saints are of the first-born Son of God; from that beginning, because He is the beginning and the end,[11] the saint takes his beginning; the son to whom is due the privilege of the first-fruits takes his beginning according to the saying of Abraham: 'Cast out the slave-girl with her son; for the son of this slave-girl shall not be heir with my son Isaac.'[12]

This is meant by divine Revelation to refer more to the inheriting of virtues than of money, when the Lord says: 'Heed all that Sara says to you; for through Isaac shall your descendants be called.'[13] What other thing was there in Isaac which ennobled his father if not the inheriting of sanctity? Indeed, he put the son of the slave-girl over nations, handing over, as it were, the full amount of his patrimony. But he gave double the amount to the son of Sara, on whom were conferred not only temporal but heavenly and everlasting blessings.

Farewell, and love us, because we love you.

---
10 *Ibid.*
11 Cf. Apoc. 1.8.
12 Gen. 21.10.
13 Gen. 21.12.

77. Ambrose to Irenaeus, greetings[1]

You asked me why the Lord God does not now rain down manna as He did on our fathers' people. If you reflect, you will realize that He does, even daily, rain down manna from heaven upon His servants. In fact, a corporeal manna is found today in many places, but it is not now a matter of such great wonder, because that which is perfect has come.[2] That which is perfect is the Bread from heaven, the Body from a virgin, of which the Gospel tells us with sufficiency. How much more excellent this is than what went before! Those who ate that manna, or bread, are dead, but he who eats this Bread will live forever.[3]

But there is also a spiritual manna, the dew of spiritual wisdom, which is shed from heaven upon those who are resourceful and in search of it. This waters the minds of the pious and puts sweetness into their mouths. Whoever experiences this downpour of divine Wisdom is delighted, and, needing no other food, lives not on bread alone but on every word of God.[4] One who is more diligent seeks that which is sweeter than honey. God's servant says to him: 'This is the bread which God gave you to eat.' Hear what that bread is: 'The word,' he says, 'which God hath commanded.'[5] This food, the command of God, nourishes the soul of the wise man, illumining and sweetening, shining with the gleam of truth, blending, as with honeycomb, the sweetness of many virtues and the word of Wisdom, for 'Well ordered words are as a honeycomb,'[6] as it is written in Proverbs.

Now, hear why it was small: because the grain of mustard seed which is compared to the kingdom of heaven[7] is very

---

1 Undated.
2 Cf. 1 Cor. 13.10.
3 Cf. John 6.5.
4 Cf. Matt. 4.4.
5 Exod. 16.15,16.
6 Prov. 16.24.
7 Cf. Luke 13.19.

small, and faith, which is like a grain of mustard seed, can move mountains and cast them into the sea.[8] Again, 'The kingdom of heaven is like leaven, which a woman took and buried in three measures of flour, until all of it was leavened.'[9] Likewise, Moses ground the head of the golden calf into powder and strewed it in the water and gave it to the people to drink,[10] for their heart had been fattened with the great mass of wickedness, and he did this so that it might be softened and refined by faith. Lastly, the woman who grinds well will be taken, but she who grinds ill will be left.

Do you, therefore, grind your faith so that you may be like the soul which excites in itself the love of Christ, which the powers of heaven admire as it mounts up, that it may rise easily and soar above this world with joy and gladness. Like the vine, put forth branches, and like smoke, rise on high, shedding the odor of a holy resurrection and the sweetness of faith, as you have it written: 'Who is she that goeth up by the desert like a branch of the vine burning with smoke, fragrant with myrrh and frankincense, and with all the powders of the perfumer?'[11]

Very aptly has the sacred writer described its refined nature, comparing it with powder or perfume, for we read in Exodus that thyme, a prophetic incense, was very refined and compounded of many things, for it was the prayer of the saints. Thus, it may be directed into the sight of the Lord, as David says: 'Let my prayer arise like incense unto thee.'[12] And in the Greek also says the same.[13] And in the Apocalypse of John we read that 'An angel stood before the altar, having a golden censer, and there was given to him much incense, from the prayers of all the saints. And,' he says, 'the incense,

---

8 Cf. Luke 17.6.
9 Luke 13.21.
10 Cf. Exod. 32.20.
11 Cant. 3.6.
12 Ps. 140.2.
13 Ambrose here quotes the passage in Greek.

the smoke of the prayers of the saints, went from the hand of the angel before the sight of God.'[14]

Small, too, are the navel and belly of the soul which ascends to Christ. Therefore, it is praised in the words of the spouse who says: 'Thy navel is like a round bowl never wanting wine, thy belly is like a heap of tiny wheat among lilies.'[15] It is polished by all kinds of learning and it is a spiritual draught never failing in fullness and in the knowledge of heavenly secrets. The belly of the soul is mystic, like the navel, and it receives not only strong food to strengthen hearts, but sweet and fragrant food by which it is delighted. Perhaps Moses meant that this sacrilege[16] needs to be atoned for by many and pious prayers.

In the Book of Kings, also, when the Lord revealed Himself to holy Elias, the whistling of a gentle breeze first came and then the Lord revealed Himself to him.[17] Thus we may learn that bodily things are fat and gross, spiritual things are tender and fine and cannot be perceived with the eye. The Spirit of Wisdom is described in the Book of Wisdom as subtle and lively,[18] because in her is the spirit of understanding, holy, one, manifold, subtle, lively; and she grinds her words before speaking so that she may not offend in any mode or meaning. Finally, it will be said to Babylon when she is about to be destroyed: 'And sound of millstone will not be heard in thee any more.'[19]

This manna, therefore, was fine and it was gathered each day, not kept for the day following, because what wisdom finds in a moment is more pleasing, nor is that more admirable for being found in leisure time than what is struck at once from the spark of genius. It may be that future mysteries are revealed: the manna kept until sunrise is unfit to be eaten—

---
14 Apoc. 8.2-4.
15 Cant. 7.2.
16 I. e., the making and adoring of the golden calf.
17 Cf. 3 Kings 19.21.
18 Cf. Wisd. 7.22.
19 Apoc. 18.22.

that is, it had grace only until the coming of Christ. When the Sun of Justice arose, and the more resplendent sacraments of Christ's Body and Blood gleamed, lesser things came to an end and the people were to take that which is more perfect.

Farewell, and love us, because we also love you.

78. Ambrose to Irenaeus, greetings[1]

As if you were my son, you have referred to me the question others have asked of you, why the Law was so severe in pronouncing unclean those persons who wear garments of the other sex, whether men or women, for it is written: 'Let not men's apparel cover a woman, neither shall a man be clothed with a woman's garment, for he that doeth these things is abominable before God.'[2]

If you investigate the matter well, what nature herself abhors must be unsuitable, for why do you want to seem not a man when you were born one? Why do you assume an appearance not yours? Why play the woman, or you, woman, the man? Nature clothes each sex in its proper raiment. Moreover, in men and women there are different customs, different complexion, different gestures, gait, and strength, different qualities of voice.

In the animals of the rest of creation, too, the form, strength, and roar of the lion and lioness, of bull and heifer, are different. Among deer, also, the stag and hind differ as much in sex as in appearance, so that one can distinguish them from a distance. Between birds and men there is an even closer comparison regarding their clothing, for their natural covering distinguishes the sex in them. The peacock is very beautiful, but his mate does not have feathers so

---
1 Undated.
2 Deut. 22.5.

variegated in color. Pheasants also have different colors to mark the distinction of sex. The same is true of chickens. How shrill is the cock's crow night after night performing its appointed task of rousing us and crowing!³ They do not change their appearance. Why do we want to change ours?

The custom prevailed in Greece for women to wear men's tunics because they were shorter. Let it be their custom to appear to imitate the nature of the better sex, but why should men want to assume the appearance of the inferior sex?⁴ A falsehood in words is degrading, and so is it also in dress. That is why in heathen temples where falsification of faith abides, there is also falsification of nature. There it is considered holy for men to assume women's clothing and female gestures. For this reason the Law declares that every man who puts on a woman's garment is an abomination to the Lord.

I think it refers not so much to clothing as to manners and to our habits and actions, since one act is becoming to a man, another to a woman. Therefore, the Apostle, as the interpreter of the Law, says: 'Let your women keep silence in the churches, for it is not permitted them to speak, but to be submissive, as the Law says. But if they wish to learn anything let them ask their husbands at home.'⁵ And to Timothy he says: 'Let a woman learn in silence with all submission. For I do not allow a woman to teach, or to exercise authority over men.'⁶

How unsightly it is for a man to act like a woman! Let

---

3 Cf. Ambrose's *Hymn at Matins* (*Hymnus* 1, *PL* 17.1409); translated by W. J. Copeland and others, in Dom Matthew Britt, O.S.B., *The Hymns of the Breviary and Missal* (New York 1948) 21.
4 Many early Councils forbade women to wear men's clothing and men to wear women's. For an example of the first prohibition, cf. *Summa Gangrensis Concilii*, Cap. 13: '*Ne mulieres virilem habitum usurpent*,' *Summa Conciliorum* (Venice 1781) 75.
5 1 Cor. 14.34,35.
6 1 Tim. 2.11,12.

those who curl their hair like women also conceive and bear children. The one sex is veiled; the other engages in war. There is an excuse for those who follow their native customs, barbarous as they are, the Persians, the Goths, the Armenians. But nature is greater than one's native land.

What shall we say of those who consider it a sign of luxury to have in their service slaves wearing curls and ornaments, while they themselves have long beards and the slaves have streaming hair? It is to be expected that chastity will be lost where the distinction of the sexes is not observed, and where nature lays down definite instruction, as the Apostle says: 'Does it become a woman to pray to God uncovered? Does not nature itself teach you that for a man to wear his hair long is degrading; but for a woman to wear her hair long is a glory to her? Because her hair has been given her as a covering.'[7] You must thus answer those who make inquiries.

Farewell, and love us as a son, because we as a parent love you.

79. Ambrose to Irenaeus, greetings (Summer, 393)[1]

After resting my mind a while during my reading, turning from my intensive study, I began thinking of the versicle which we had used at first Vespers: 'Thou art beautiful above the sons of men,'[2] and also: 'How beautiful are the feet of those who bring good tidings.'[3] Truly, nothing is more beautiful than that Highest Good which is exceedingly beautiful to preach, the setting forth of a continuous dis-

---
7 1 Cor. 11.13-15.

1 Dudden dates this 387.
2 Ps. 44.3; this is quoted in Greek.
3 Isa. 52.7.

course, and the footsteps, as it were, of the preaching of the Apostles. Who is capable of this? Those to whom God gave the power not only to announce Christ but also to suffer for Him.

As far as we are able, let us give our attention to that which is beautiful, comely, and good; let us be occupied with it, let us hold it in mind, so that by its glow and light our souls may become lovely and our minds transparent. For, if our eyes are refreshed with green fields and beautiful groves, after being clouded by mist, or if grassy hills take away the blur of the sick man's gaze, while his pupils and eye-balls seem to take on color, how much more does the eye of the mind, when it gazes upon the Highest Good, turning to It and feeding on It, become bright and shining, and so fulfill the words of Scripture: 'My soul shall be filled as with marrow and richness.'[4] One who wisely understands the souls of his flock cares for the grass of his field so that he will have large pastures, for the sweet grasses make the lambs fatter, and their milk is more healthful. The rich use these pastures, they who 'have eaten and adored,'[5] for it is the saint of God who is placed in these good pastures of faith.

The flocks of sheep are also nourished with that hay which makes them produce fleeces of wisdom and provides them the mantle of prudence. Perhaps, too, this is the mountain hay[6] upon which the Prophet's words distilled 'like snow upon the hay.'[7] The wise man diligently seeks this so that his sheep may be a covering for him, a sort of spiritual cloak. Thus the soul which clings to the Highest Good, which is divine, has its own food and clothing. This is what the Apostle Peter urged us to search for, so that by acquiring this knowledge we may become partakers of the divine nature.[8]

The good God discloses a knowledge of this to His saints,

---
4 Ps. 62.6.
5 Ps. 21.30.
6 Cf. Prov. 27.35.
7 Deut. 32.2.
8 2 Peter 1.4.

bringing it forth from His good treasures as the sacred writing proves: 'The Lord swore to your fathers to give and open his excellent treasure.'[9] From this heavenly treasure He gives rain to His earth in order to bless all the works of your hands. The rain signifies the utterance of the Scripture which bedews the soul which is rich and plentiful in good works so that it may have the rain of grace.[10]

David went in search of the knowledge of this Good, as he himself declares: 'One thing I have asked of the Lord; this will I seek: that I may dwell in the house of the Lord all the days of my life, to enjoy the sweetness of the Lord and to behold his temple.' And he immediately adds in this psalm that this is the Highest Good: 'I believe that I shall see the good things of the Lord in the land of the living.'[11] Here [on earth] He is sought; there [in heaven] he will be fully seen face to face. This Good is in the house of God, in His secret abode and sanctuary. Again he says: 'We shall be filled with the good things of thy house.'[12] In another place, too, he shows that this is the fullness of blessings: 'May the Lord bless thee out of Sion, that thou mayest see the welfare of Jerusalem.'[13] Blessed is he, therefore, who lives there in the entrance of faith, in the abode of the spirit, in the dwelling of devotion, in the life of virtue.

Let us abide there and remain in Him of whom Isaias says: 'How beautiful are the feet of those who preach peace and preach good tidings!'[14] Who are those who preach except Peter, Paul, and all the Apostles? What do they preach to us except the Lord Jesus?[15] He is our peace, He is our Highest Good, for He is the Good from Good, and from a good tree is gathered good fruit.[16] Then, too, His spirit is

---

9 Deut. 28.11,12.
10 Cf. Deut. 32.2.
11 Ps. 26.4,13.
12 Ps. 64.5.
13 Ps. 127.5.
14 Isa. 52.7.
15 Cf. 1 Cor. 1.1.
16 Cf. Matt. 7.18.

good, that Spirit which receives the servants of God from Him and brings them into the right way.[17] Let no one who has the Spirit of God in him deny that He is good, since He says Himself: 'Is thy eye evil because I am good?'[18] May there come into our soul, into our innermost heart, this Good which the kind God gives to those who ask Him. He is our Treasure; He is our Way; He is our Wisdom, our Righteousness, our Shepherd and the Good Shepherd; He is our Life. See the number of good things in the one Good!

The Evangelists preach these good things to us. David in search of these good things said: 'Who will show us good things?' And he shows that the Lord Himself is our Good, saying: 'The light of thy countenance is signed upon us.'[19] Who is the light of the Father's countenance except the brightness of His glory, the image of the invisible God,[20] in whom the Father is both seen and glorified, as He also glorifies His Son?[21]

The Lord Jesus Himself, therefore, is the Highest Good whom the Prophets announced, the angels made known, the Father promised, and the Apostles preached.[22] He came to us like ripeness, and not only as ripeness but as ripeness in the mountains, so that in our counsels there would be no bitterness or unripeness, and in our actions and our manners there would be no harshness or hardness. He Himself was the first to preach good tidings to us and said: 'I myself who spoke am here';[23] that is, I who spoke in the Prophets, I am present in the body which I took of a virgin; I am present, the inward likeness of God, the express image of His person; and I am present as man. But who knows Me? They saw a man,

---

17 Cf. Ps. 142.10.
18 Matt. 20.15.
19 Osee 4.6.
20 Heb. 1.3.
21 Cf. John 17.5.
22 Cf. 1 Tim. 3.16.
23 Heb. 1.1,2.

yet they believed that His works were greater than man. Was it not as man that He wept for Lazarus,[24] and greater than man that He raised him from the dead? Again, was it not as man that He was scourged, and greater than man that He took away the sins of all the world?[25]

Let us hurry to Him in whom is that Highest Good, since He is Goodness Itself. He is the patience of Israel calling you to penance, so you will not come to judgment but may receive the remission of sins. 'Do penance,' he says.[26] He is the one of whom the Prophet Amos cries: 'Seek ye good.'[27] He is the Highest Good, for He needs nothing and abounds in all things. Well may He abound, for in Him dwells bodily the fullness of divinity.[28] Well may He abound, of whose fullness we have all received, and in whom we have been filled, as the Evangelist says.[29]

If the soul, with its capacity for pleasure and delight, has tasted this True and Highest Good and has adhered to both with the means at her disposal, putting away sorrow and fear, then is she wonderfully inflamed. Having embraced the Word of God, she knows no bounds, she knows no satiety, and says: 'Thou art sweet, O Lord, and in thy joy teach me thy laws.'[30] Having embraced the Word of God, she desires Him above every beauty; she loves Him above every joy; she is delighted with Him above every perfume; she wishes often to see, often to gaze, often to be drawn to Him that she may follow. 'Thy name,' she says, 'is as oil poured out,'[31] and that is why we maidens love Thee, and vie with one another but cannot attain to Thee. Draw us that we

---

24 Cf. John 11.35.
25 Cf. John 1.29.
26 Matt. 4.17.
27 Amos 5.14.
28 Cf. Col. 2.9.
29 Cf. John 1.16.
30 Ps. 118.68.
31 Cant. 1.2.

may run after Thee, that from the odor of ointments we may receive the power to follow Thee.

The soul presses forward for a glimpse of hidden mysteries, to the very abode of the Word, to the very dwelling place of that Highest Good, and His light and brightness. In that bosom and secret dwelling place of the Father she hastens to hear His words, and having heard them she finds them sweeter than all things. Let the Prophet who has tasted this sweetness teach you, when he says: 'How sweet are thy words to my lips, above honeycomb to my mouth.'[32] What else can a soul desire when she has once tasted the sweetness of the Word, when she has once seen its brightness? When Moses remained on the mountain forty days to receive the Law, he had no need of food for the body.[33] Elias, going to that rest, asked that his soul be taken away from him.[34] Even Peter himself, foreseeing on the mountain the glory of the Lord's Resurrection, did not wish to come down, and said: 'Lord, it is good for us to be here.'[35] How great is the glory of that Divine Essence, how great the graces of the Word at which even angels wish to gaze![36]

The soul which beholds this Highest Good needs not the body, and, knowing that she should have very little familiarity with it, she shuns the world, she withdraws herself from the chains of the flesh, she casts off all the bonds of earthly pleasure. Thus Stephen beheld Jesus and had no fear of being stoned; in fact, while he was being stoned he prayed, not for himself, but for those by whom he was being murdered.[37] Paul, too, caught up into the third heaven, did not know whether he was in the body or out of it; caught, I say, into paradise, he no longer had need of the body, and after hear-

---

32 Ps. 118.103.
33 Cf. Exod. 34.28.
34 Cf. 3 Kings 19.4.
35 Matt. 17.4.
36 Cf. 1 Peter 1.12.
37 Cf. Acts 7.55-60.

ing the word of God he was ashamed to descend to the infirmities of the body.[38]

With the knowledge of what he had seen and heard in paradise, he cried out saying: 'Why, as if still viewing from the world do you lay down rules: "Do not touch; nor handle; nor taste!"—things which must all perish in their very use!'[39] He wished us to be in the world in figure, not in actual possession and use of it; so to use the world as if we did not use it, as if we were but passing through,[40] not residing in it, walking through as in a dream, not with desire, so that with the speed of thought we might pass through the shadow of this world. He himself, too, walking by faith, not by sight, was a pilgrim from the body and present with the Lord, and although he was on earth, his conversation was not on earth, but in heaven.

Therefore, let the soul which wishes to approach God raise herself from the body and cling always to that Highest Good which is divine, and lasts forever, and which was from the beginning and which was with God,[40] that is, the Word of God. This is the Divine Being 'in which we live and are and move.'[42] This was in the beginning, this is: 'The Son of God, Jesus Christ in you,' he says, 'in whom there was not Yes and No, but only Yes was in him.'[43] He Himself told Moses to say: 'HE WHO IS hath sent me.'[44]

Let our soul be with this Good, and, if possible, let it be there always, so that it can be said of us: 'My soul is always in thy hands.'[45] Such will be the case if it is not in the body, but in the spirit, if it does not entangle itself with things of earth. When it is concerned with the flesh, then the charms

---
38 Cf. 2 Cor. 12.2-5.
39 Col. 2.20-22.
40 Cf. 1 Cor. 7.31.
41 Cf. John 1.1.
42 Acts 17.28.
43 2 Cor. 1.19.
44 Exod. 3.14.
45 Ps. 118.109.

of the body creep over it, it tosses with anger and indignation, it is afflicted with sadness, it is cast down through arrogance, it is troubled with sorrow.

These are the dangerous illnesses of the soul by which it is often brought near death and its eyes are so blinded that they do not see the light of true glory and the richness of the eternal inheritance. But, if it keeps them always fixed on God, it will receive from Christ the splendor of wisdom, so that it will have its gaze illumined by the knowledge of God, and look upon the hope of our calling, and gaze on that which is good, well-pleasing, and perfect. The good is well-pleasing to the Father. That which is well-pleasing is perfect, as you read in the Gospel where the Lord says: 'Love your enemies, so that you may imitate your Father, who sends rain on the just and the unjust.' This proves what constitutes goodness. Later He concludes, saying: 'Be ye perfect, as your Father who is in heaven is perfect.'[46] Charity is perfect; it is the fulfilling of the law. 'For what is so good' as charity which thinks no evil?

Flee the regions where enmity, ambition, and contention have their dwelling. Let your soul open itself to grasp this good so that it may fly above the clouds, that it may be renewed like the eagle, and like the eagle spreading its wings with new vigor in its pinions, it may not fear to soar aloft,[47] to leave this earth, because an earthly habitation weighs down the soul.[48] Let it put off the old, let it lay aside the desire for evil, let it wash clean its eyes so that it may see the fount of true wisdom, the fount of eternal life, which flows and pours itself upon all and has no needs. Who has ever given Him anything, since 'from Him, and through Him, and in Him'[49] are all things?

---
46 Matt. 5.44,45,48.
47 Cf. Virgil, *Aeneid* 5.508,618.
48 Wisd. 9.15.
49 Rom. 11.36.

The fount of life is that Highest Good which bestows the substance of life on all, because it has life abiding in itself. It receives from no one as though it were needy; it lavishes goods upon all and borrows from others nothing for itself, for it has no need of us. It says, too, in the person of mankind: 'You do not need my goods.'[50] What is more lovely than to approach Him and cling to Him? What pleasure can be greater? What else can he desire who sees and tastes freely of this fount of living water?—what realms? what powers? what riches? when he sees how pitiable are the conditions of kings, how changeable the status of their power, how short the span of this life, in how great bondage even sovereigns must live, since they live at the will of others and not their own.

Does any rich man make his way to eternal life unless he is provided with money, the riches of virtue, the portion of all, the only thing a rich man cannot have? Happiness does not consist in using, but in seeing how you may despise these riches, how you may consider them void of truth, judge them vain and useless,[51] and love, instead, the beauty of naked truth which discloses the utterly false vanities of the world.

Lift up your eyes, then, my soul, those eyes of which the Word of God says to you: 'Thou hast wounded me in the heart, O my sister, my spouse, thou hast wounded me in the heart with one of thine eyes.'[52] Go up to the palm, overcome the world so that you may reach the height of the Word. Leave aside the vain show of this world, leave aside its wickedness. Bring, rather, goodness of heart which possesses grace in the tree of life, provided she will wash her robes and enter the city which is the true grace of the saints. There is the tabernacle of God, around which the scribes of the Lord are encamped, where neither day nor sun nor moon provide light, but the Lord Himself is the light illuminating that whole

---
50 Ps. 15.2.
51 Cf. Virgil, *Aeneid* 10.630.
52 Cant. 4.8.

city,⁵³ for He is the Light of the world.⁵⁴ Surely, He is not a visible light, but He is the brilliance of the mind in the souls of men, upon whom He pours Himself with the radiant light of wisdom and reason, which the Gospel says inspires the inmost soul with the warmth of His spiritual power.⁵⁵

If a man has taken up his residence in that heavenly city, let him not leave its life and customs, since he is an inhabitant. Let him not again depart, nor retrace the steps, I do not say, of the body, but of the heart. Let him not come back from there. Behind him is wantonness; behind is impurity. When Lot went to the mountains, he left behind the sins of Sodom, but the woman who looked back could not reach the higher ground.⁵⁶ Your feet should not turn back, neither should your actions turn back. Your hands should not hang idle, nor should the knees of your devotion and faith become weak. Let no weakness cause your will to backslide, nor evil deeds recur. You have made your entrance, now remain. You have reached this place, stand firm. 'Being safe, save thy life.'⁵⁷

In your ascent, take the straight path; it is not safe to turn back. Here is the road; there is downfall. Here is the path upward; there, a precipice. There is work in ascending, danger in descending. The Lord who is powerful will protect you if you are grounded and hedged round with the ramparts of the Prophets and the bulwarks of the Apostles. For this reason, the Lord says to you: 'Enter and tread the grape, for the vintage time is here.'⁵⁸ Let us be found within, not out of doors. In the Gospel, too, the Son of God says: 'Let him who is on the housetop not go down to take his vessels.'⁵⁹

---

53 Cf. Apoc. 21.23.
54 Cf. John 8.12.
55 Cf. Luke 24.32.
56 Gen. 19.30.
57 Gen. 19.17.
58 Joel 3.13.
59 Luke 17.31.

Surely, He does not mean our present dwelling but that one of which 'He has spread the sky like a roof.'⁶⁰

Remain within, therefore, within Jerusalem, within your soul which is peaceful, meek, and tranquil. Do not leave it or go down to take your vessels with honors or riches or pride. Remain within, so that strangers may not pass through you, so that neither sins nor vain works nor useless thoughts may pass through your soul. This will not happen if you wage a holy war against the snare of the passions in behalf of devotion and faith and in the pursuit of truth, if you will put on the armor of God in your fight against spiritual diseases and the cunning of the Devil who tempts our senses with cunning and fraud. Yet, he is easily crushed by the gentle warrior who does not sow discord, but, as befits the servant of God, teaches faith with moderation and refutes those who are his adversaries. Of this man Scripture says: 'Let the warrior who is gentle arise,'⁶¹ and the weak man says: 'I can do all things in him who strengthens me.'⁶²

Supported by this faith, even the weak man will prevail, his soul will be holy, and this mountain of the Prophets and the Apostles will drop down sweetness upon him.⁶³ The hills, too, will pour out milk as did that hill which gave milk to the Corinthians to drink.⁶⁴ And waters will flow upon him from his vessels and the depths of his wells, or from his belly will flow living waters, spiritual waters which the Holy Spirit gives to the faithful. May He deign to water your soul, too, so that in you there may abound the fount of water springing up into life everlasting.⁶⁵

Farewell, and love us as a son, because we love you as a father.

---

60 Ps. 103.2; 4 Esd. 16.60.
61 Joel 3.9.
62 Phil. 4.13.
63 Cf. Joel 3.18.
64 Cf. 1 Cor. 3.2.
65 Cf. John 4.14.

80. Ambrose to Irenaeus, greetings (c. 387)

When I had finished my last letter and directed it to be delivered to you, the words which the Lord spoke by the prophet Aggeus came to my mind: 'Is it time for you to dwell in carved houses?' What is the meaning of this except that we should dwell on high, not in cavernous dwelling places or beneath the earth. Those who dwell below the earth cannot build the temple of God, and their saying is: 'The time has not yet come for building the house of the Lord.'[1] It is a mark of sensual people to seek underground dwellings, longing for summer's coolness because, enervated by indulgences and requiring shady depths, they cannot otherwise bear the heat. Again, the slothful carry on low pursuits beneath the earth. And, finally, dark and shady places suit them best wherein they feel that their sins are concealed, according to the saying: 'Darkness compasseth me about like walls. Whom shall I fear?'[2] Their hope of this is vain, since God sees the hidden depths of the abyss and discovers all things before they take place.[3]

Neither Elias nor Eliseus lived in underground dwellings. The one carried the dead son of the widow into an upper chamber where he abode and there restored him to life.[4] The other had a chamber prepared for him in the upper part of the house by that great woman, the Sunamitess, as Scripture bears witness. There she won the privilege of conceiving a son,[5] for she was barren, and there also she saw the miracle of her child's restoration to life. What should I say of Peter, who went up to the roof at the sixth hour and learned there the mystery of the baptism of the Gentiles?[6] On the other hand, the murderer Absalom set up a pillar to himself in the

---

1 Agg. 1.4,2.
2 Eccli. 23.26.
3 Cf. Wisd. 8.8.
4 Cf. 3 Kings 17.22.
5 Cf. 4 Kings 4.15-37.
6 Cf. Acts 10.9.

valley of the king, and was thrown into a ditch when he was slain.⁷ Thus the saints go up to the Lord, the wicked go down to sin; the saints are on the mountains, the guilty in the valleys, 'For he is the God of the mountains and not the God of the valleys.'⁸

Those who dwelt in the houses of the plain where God does not dwell could not have the house of God within them, for this is the house which God sought from them so that they might build up themselves and rear within themselves the temple of God from living stones of faith. He did not want buildings made with earthen walls or wooden roofs, for the hand of an enemy would have been able to overthrow them. He wanted that temple which is built in the hearts of men, to whom it may be said: 'You are the temple of God,'⁹ in which the Lord Jesus might dwell and from there set out to redeem all mankind. There also could be prepared a sacred chamber in the womb of the Virgin where the King of heaven might live and a human body become the temple of God, which though it was destroyed, might yet be restored to life on the third day.

Sensual persons who dwell in vaulted houses¹⁰ and take delight in coffered silver ceilings do not build a house like this. As they despise plain silver, so do they despise a simple dwelling place.¹¹ They add to the site of their homes; adding more and more, they join one house with another, one estate with another; they dig up the ground so that the very earth itself gives way for their dwelling, and, like children of the earth, they are laid up within her womb and hidden within her flesh. Plainly it was of them that Jeremias said: 'Woe to them who build their house by injustice!'¹² The man who builds with justice builds not on earth but in heaven.

---
7 Cf. 2 Kings 18.17.
8 3 Kings 20.28.
9 1 Cor. 3.16.
10 Cf. Agg. 1.4.
11 Cf. Isa. 5.8.
12 Jer. 22.13.

'You have built,' says the Prophet, 'a house, to measure its upper storey, airy and marked with windows, roofed with cedar and painted with vermilion.'[13] That man measures the upper storey who has contemplated the judgment of God and judges the judgment of the humble and of the poor. But the man who goes in search of gain and of the blood of the innocent does not build his roofs with judgment, nor keep a due measure, because he has not Christ. He does not try to inhale the breath of divine grace, nor does he look for the brightness of the full light. He does not have his chambers painted with vermilion and it cannot be said to him: 'Thy lips are like scarlet lace.'[14]

'One of this sort,' it is said, 'will not be buried,'[15] for he has entrenched himself in the earth and buried himself in a tomb when alive, as it were, depriving himself of repose in a tomb when he is dead. Having laid himself away in the pit of bodily pleasure, he has not found that tomb from which one can rise. A man of this sort does not build a temple to God, because he does not know the time of his correction. How can such men build a temple, since like wild beasts and animals they have taken themselves into the caves and lairs of beasts[16] and wild animals, burying themselves like serpents in pits, digging into the earth in the manner of a cunning fox?

The man who dies before his time does not build his tomb, for, although he lives, he is dead.[17] He does not hear the words of Aggeus, interpreted the banqueteer, for he does not enter the tabernacle of God 'with the voice of joy and praise: the noise of one feasting.'[18] How does he hear His voice if he does not see His works? If he saw them he would hear the Word which was put within his grasp, he would rejoice in

---
13 Jer. 22.14.
14 Cant. 4.3.
15 Jer. 22.19.
16 Cf. Virgil, *Ecl.* 10.52.
17 Cf. 1 Tim. 5.6.
18 Ps. 41.5.

His acts, whereby 'he knocked and it was opened to him,'[19] and he would have gone down into his soul that he might feed therein upon the food of sincerity and truth.

Because he has failed to hear, the word of Aggeus again comes, saying: 'Rise from houses embossed and carved with wickedness, and go up to the mount of heavenly Scriptures and hew the tree of wisdom, the tree of life, the tree of knowledge. Make straight your ways, order your actions so that they may have the due order which is necessary and useful for building the house of God.'[20]

Unless you do this, heaven will not give her rain,[21] that is to say, the heavenly message which comes down on the hay like dew will not cool the fevered motions of the passions of your body, nor extinguish the fiery darts of your various desires, and the earth, the soul, will not bear its fruit, for it dries up unless it is well-watered with the Word of God and sprinkled with heavenly dew, the fullness of spiritual grace.

And because he knew how slothful they are who dwell beneath the earth in the dark abodes of pleasure, he said: 'I will stir up for them the spirit of Zorobabel of the tribe of Juda, and Josue the son of Josadec, the high priest,'[22] so that they will be encouraged to build the house of God, for, 'Unless the Lord build the house, they labor in vain who build it.'[23] Zorobabel means that 'overflowing fountain' on the hilltop; it is like the fountain of life and the Word of God, 'through which are all things, and from which are all things, and all things in it.'[24] This 'overflowing fountain' says: 'If anyone thirst, let him come to me and drink,'[25] drink, that is, from the stream of an unfailing flood. We read, too,

---

19 Matt. 7.7.
20 Agg. 1.8.
21 Cf. Agg. 1.10.
22 Agg. 1.14.
23 Ps. 126.1.
24 Col. 1.16,17.
25 John 7.37.

of Zabulon, 'a stream by night,' that is to say, 'prophetic.'[26] It is made clear now by the mingling of the waters in which was swallowed up the vanity typified by Jezabel, who was opposed to the truth and hostile to the utterances of the Prophets. She herself was so torn by the teeth of dogs that no trace of her remained, but her whole frame along with every mark of her posterity was blotted out.[27] Zorobabel himself, of the tribe of Juda, and Josue the high priest, both designated by a tribe and name, seem to represent two persons, although mention is made of only one. He who is almighty is born from the Almighty, as Redeemer is born of the Virgin, being the same in the diversity of His two divisible natures, and He, like the Giant of Salvation,[28] has fulfilled the verity of the one Son of God.

When He was on the point of calling from the dead the saintly Zorobabel, He said: 'Once more I will move heaven and earth, and seas and desert.'[29] He had moved them before when He delivered His people from Egypt,[30] when there was a pillar of fire in the sky,[31] a path through the waves, a wall on the sea, a road in the water, and in the desert a harvest of heavenly food provided each day, and a rock melted into streams of water. He moved these, too, during the Passion of the Lord Jesus,[32] when the sky was covered with darkness, the sun was veiled in shadows, rocks were rent, graves opened, the dead rose again, and the dragon vanquished on its own waters saw the fishers of men not only sailing, but even walking without peril, on the sea.

The dry land was moved, too, when the barren Gentile nations began to ripen with the harvest of devotion and faith. There was a movement of the desert and the Gentiles,

---

26 *profluvium nocturnum.*
27 Cf. 4 Kings 9.33-37.
28 Cf. Ps. 19.5.
29 Agg. 2.22.
30 Cf. Exod. 14.22-30.
31 Cf. Exod. 13.21.
32 Cf. Luke 23.44.

and so great and so powerful was the preaching of the Apostles whom He had sent to call the Gentiles that 'their sound went forth unto all the earth and their strains unto the farthest bounds of the world.'[33] So great was the movement of the desert, I say, that more were the children of the desolate than of her who had a husband;[34] it made the desert flower like a lily;[35] and the elect of the Gentiles entered into the places left by the people where the remnants were saved through election to grace.[36]

'I will fill this house,' he says, 'with my silver and gold,'[37] with the word of God which is like silver tried by fire,[38] and by the brilliance of the true light, shining like spiritual gold, in the secret hearts of the saints. These riches He confers on His Church, the riches by which the treasures of her heart are filled and the glory of her house is become greater than the glory which in times past the chosen people enjoyed.[39]

Peace and tranquility of soul are more than all the glory of the house, for peace surpasses all understanding.[40] This is that peace beyond all peace which will be given after the third moving of heaven, sea, earth, and dry land, when He will destroy all the Powers and Principalities. 'Heaven and earth will pass away,'[41] and the whole figure of this world. Every man will rise up against his brother with the sword, that is, with the word which penetrates the marrow of his soul,[42] to destroy what is opposed, namely, the chariot of Ephraim and the horse from Jerusalem, as Zacharias says.[43] And such will be the peace over all the passions of the body

---

33 Ps. 18.5.
34 Cf. Isa. 54.1.
35 Cf. Isa. 35.1.
36 Cf. Rom. 11.5.
37 Cf. Agg. 2.8,9.
38 Cf. Ps. 11.7.
39 Cf. Agg. 2.10.
40 Cf. Phil. 4.7.
41 Matt. 24.35.
42 Cf. Heb. 4.12.
43 Cf. Zach. 9.10.

which are not in opposition, and over the minds of unbelievers, who are not a hindrance, that Christ will be formed in all, and will make an offering of the hearts of all men in submission to His Father.[44]

So it is mystically said to Him alone: 'I will take thee, O Zorobabel, and I will make thee as a signet ring, for I have chosen thee.'[45] For, when our soul becomes so peaceful that it is said to her: 'Return, return, O Sulamitess,'[46] which means 'peaceful,' or to your own name 'Irenic,' then she will receive Christ like a signet ring upon her, for He is the image of God. Then she will be according to that image, because heavenly is the heavenly man.[47] And we need to bear the image of the heavenly one, that is, peace.

And that we may know that this is true you have in the Canticles to the soul, now fully perfect, what I wish the Lord Jesus may say to you: 'Put me as a seal upon thy arm.'[48] May peace glow in your heart, Christ in your works, and may there be formed in you wisdom and justice and redemption.

Farewell, son, and love us, because we love you.

81. *Ambrose to Irenaeus, greetings (c. 387)*

In the writings of some teachers we find the doctrine of Pythagoras in which he forbade his disciples to enter upon the common path trodden by ordinary people. It is well known whence he drew this principle. According to the opinion of most persons, he was a Jew by birth and therefore drew the teachings of his school from the learning of this

---
44 Cf. 1 Cor. 15.28.
45 Agg. 2.24.
46 Cant. 6.12.
47 Cf. 1 Cor. 15.48.
48 Cant. 8.6.

people.¹ Further, he is so highly esteemed among philosophers that they say he has scarcely met his equal. He had read in Exodus that Moses was bidden by God's command: 'Put off the shoes from thy feet.'² The same bidding was given to Josue the son of Nun—namely, that they who desired to walk the way of the Lord should shake off the dust of the road trampled by men.³ He had also read the command given to Moses to ascend the mountain with the priests while the people stayed behind.⁴ God first separated the priests from the people and then commanded Moses to enter the cloud.

You see, then, the separation. See how among priests one looks for nothing of a vulgar nature, nothing ordinary, nothing in common with the interests and practice and character of the undisciplined multitude. The priestly dignity demands a prudent demeanor, different from that of the crowd, a serious mode of life, an especial sense of gravity. How can the priest expect the people to honor him if he possesses no quality different from the people? Why should a man admire you if he sees his own qualities in you; if he sees nothing in you which he does not discover first in himself; if he finds in you, whom he thinks he should respect, the very thing of which he is ashamed in himself?

Let us tread beyond the opinions of the common herd, and let us avoid the thoroughfares of ordinary living, and the routes of the beaten road, and the footpath of the crowd where he travels whose day is swifter than the courier, of whom it is said: 'He fled away and did not see.'⁵ Let us find for ourselves the road where the conversations of the proud

---

1 Ambrose frequently maintained that pagan authors were not to be credited with originality or true wisdom. He finds many occasions to connect their sayings with those of Scripture; for example, the famous words of Pythian Apollo, 'Know thyself' are found in Cant. 1.7, whence, says Ambrose, the heathens took such sayings and put them into their works. Cf. *De off.* 1.31; *Expos. Ps.* 118 2.13.
2 Exod. 3.5.
3 Cf. Josue 5.16.
4 Cf. Exod. 24.13,14.
5 Job 9.25.

cannot approach, where the works of the wicked are not encountered, the road which no polluted person spoils, defiling it with the stain of his own sloth, smeared with the smoke of wickedness, his soul darkened and falling into ruin, while he has no taste for virtue, since he thinks he should look at it askance and not receive it with direct regard and wide open arms. And (as many do, who seem to themselves witty and polite, transforming the beauty of wisdom into the ugliness of guile) such a person does not look upon true grace, but, lying in darkness, even in the light of day he does not put his trust in those who live, for he is among the people of Thema and Saba who fall and turn from truth, as Job says: 'See the paths of Thema and Saba, they will fall into confusion if they have their hope in cities and riches. You have risen up against me without mercy, but seeing my wounds you are afraid.'[6]

Let us abandon the devious paths of those who wander, the dust of those that fail, who have often fallen in the desert while they searched. Let us turn and follow the road of wisdom, the way which the children of those who boast and glorify themselves have not trodden, the way which is unacquainted with destruction and knows not death. God has marked this: 'The depth saith: It is not in me. And the sea saith: It is not with me.'[7] But if you seek the path of wisdom and discipline, love of God and submission to Him is wisdom; to keep from sin is discipline.

What is the advantage for us of this way of the world where there is trial, for the life of man is a trial. It is more empty than vain tales to live in houses of clay, to spend our days and nights in quest of wealth, to think always of wealth, and, like hired servants, to want our wages each day, and, as they say crickets do, to live on the winds of pleasure. Living from day to day, they give vent to their complaints

---

6 Job 6.19-21.
7 Job 28.14.

like crickets in the springtime.⁸ To what else can we compare men of no gravity or discipline except to say that they are like crickets born for death each day, complaining rather than speaking? Under the heat of burning desires they lull themselves with songs that do them harm, and they soon die, bearing no fruit, possessed of no grace. Their paths are dangerous and intertwined like the paths of serpents which drag their bodies along in poisonous folds,⁹ coiling themselves into a knot of wickedness, unable to raise themselves to heavenly things.

Let us enter the gates of the Lord, the gates of justice, where the just man enters and gives thanks to the Lord.¹⁰ Few enter here, so the Lord said: 'Narrow the gate and close the way that leads to life! And few there are who find it.'¹¹ But wide is the gate and broad the way which many take leading to death and carrying there its travelers.

Let our road be more narrow, our virtues more abundant, our path more sure, our faith more lofty, our line more restricted, our strength of soul overflowing, our ways straight, because the course of virtue is unswerving. Thus, Solomon says: 'Oh, you who leave the right way.'¹²

Let our course take us to regions above, because it is better to ascend. Finally, as was read today: 'Woe to them that go down to Egypt.'¹³ Surely, it is not wrong to go to Egypt, but to change to the ways of the Egyptians, to change to the violence of their treachery and to the ugliness of their wantonness—this is wrong. He that changes in this way descends, and one who descends falls. Let us keep away, then, from the Egyptian who is a man, but [let us] not [keep away] from God. Even the king of Egypt himself fell under the

---

8 Cf. Virgil *Georg*. 3.328.
9 Cf. *Ibid*. 2.154.
10 Cf. Ps. 117.19.
11 Matt. 7.14.
12 Prov. 2.13.
13 Isa. 31.1.

dominion of his own vices and in comparison with him Moses was accounted a god, ruling over kingdoms and subjecting powers to himself. So we read that it was said to Moses: 'I shall make thee a God to Pharao.'[14]

Farewell, and love us, as you do, with the affection of a son.

82. Ambrose to Irenaeus, greetings (c. 387)

You have intimated that you find difficulty with the text: 'Let us sacrifice the abominations of the Egyptians to God.'[1] The solution of your difficulty is to be found in the words of Genesis that the Egyptians abominated the shepherd of the flock,[2] not so much because of the shepherd as because of the flock. The Egyptians, you know, were tillers of the land, but Abraham and Jacob and, later, Moses and David, were shepherds, who put a sort of royal stamp upon this occupation.

The Egyptians, consequently, abominated the offerings of sacrifice, that is, the perfect pursuit of the virtues and the full pursuit of obedience. The very thing which they viciously hated, good persons regard as a sincere and pious act. A person given to sensual pleasure hates the work of virtue; the glutton shuns it. The body of the Egyptian, given to pleasure, has an aversion for the virtues of the soul, abominates restrictions, and shuns the exercise of virtue and all works of this kind.

The very things which the Egyptian shuns—he who is an Egyptian rather than a mere man—embrace these, knowing what befits a man. Keep away from the things which they

---

14 Exod. 7.1.

1 Exod. 8.26.
2 Cf. Gen. 46.34.

follow and choose, because wisdom and foolishness cannot blend. And just as wisdom eludes those who are in the ranks of the foolish and intemperate, so does chastity elude them. The foolish and the unchaste man is alienated from the goods and inheritance which belong to the wise and the chaste.

The two holy daughters of that union, Lia and Rachel, the one meaning 'labored,' the other 'strong in desire,' tried to avoid not the tie of blood but the difference of their manners. When they learned from their conversation with the much-tried Jacob that he wished them to part from their country in order to escape the enmity and anger of Laban and his sons, they answered: 'Have we anything left among the goods and inheritance of our father's house? Hath he not counted us as strangers and sold us, and eaten up the price of us?'[3] Notice, first of all, how the foolish and envious man estranges himself and wants to part from the hard-working woman who practices a close discipline over herself. Realizing that they will be a burden to him, he considers it an advantage to part from them and he looks upon this leave-taking as his reward and the enjoyment of his desire.

Let us hear how foolishness has not the possessions of virtue, for they say: 'All the riches and glory which the Lord gave our fathers will belong to us and our sons.'[4] Rightly do they say that they were taken, God being their judge, since He is the Author of all good, and the foolish lose His favor. Because wicked and weak men cannot grasp the beauty of the divine inheritance, the man who is strong and brave, having a courageous spirit within himself, becomes the heir. Yet, who is strong except God alone who rules and guides all things?

The possession of God is owed to such as these, as Isaias says: 'This is the inheritance of those who believe in the

---
3 Gen. 31.14,15.
4 Gen. 31.16.

Lord.'⁵ Very aptly does he say: 'This is the inheritance,' for that alone is the inheritance; there is no other. The inheritance is not a treasure which men stumble upon blindly, and passing things have not the quality of an inheritance. The only inheritance is that in which God is the portion, as the Lord's holy one says: 'God is my inheritance,' and again: 'I have become an heir of thy precepts.'⁶ You see what are the possessions of the just man: God's commandments, His words, His precepts. In these he is rich; on these he feeds; with these he is delighted as if by all riches.

Lia and Rachel, possessing these, did not need their father's riches, his base coins, foolish outward show, and lack of spiritual vigor. Being rich and free themselves, they thought their father not rich, but in dire need. Those who partake of good and liberal training think that the foolish are not rich, but needy and poor—in fact, in dire distress—all the while the rich man abounds in the wealth of kings and proudly boasts of his power over gold.

We must flee the company of such men even though they are united to us by ties of blood. Association with the foolish is harmful, for it corrupts and darkens the prudent mind. Just as a holy man will associate with a holy man, so will the wicked associate with the wicked.⁷ It is a frequent occurrence for one who hears his own ideas attacked with rage—much as he wishes to cling to his way of continence—to be yet tinged with the dye of foolishness, for rightly do discipline and insolence prove contrary and repugnant to one another.

When the much-tried [Jacob] asked their opinion, they [the daughters of Laban] gave responses prompted by virtue tried by long practice, saying: 'Have we anything left among the goods and inheritance of our father's house?'⁸ that is to say, 'Are you asking whether we wish to part from him? Do

---

5 Isa. 54.17.
6 Ps. 118.57,111.
7 Cf. Ps. 17.26,27.
8 Gen. 31.14.

you really not understand that we can have no desire for his company, and we are not held by the desire for riches or delight in luxury which is sweet to worldlings. These we consider pitiable and alien to us; these we think are full of want and need.'

They add still another reason for their departure, the fact that Laban had lost the true glory and store of good treasure into which they were born. We were given strength of mind, a good coinage, a spiritual money, stamped with the image and likeness of God. He lost these because he chose the splendid things of this world rather than those which are true and useful for his life. The beauty of these escapes the man who is ignorant of the goods of heaven, since he has tricked himself and deceived himself in his judgment of what is beautiful. Now hear his [Laban's] words and be the judge.

He pursued blessed Jacob and his daughters, thinking he would find his same sin in them and thereby have the right to detain them. He chided the just man, and all along reason within him chided him so that he could find no answer nor give a reason why he should detain him. 'If you had told me,' he said, 'I would have let you go.'[9] In this he disclosed why it was that the just man was fleeing, so that he would not follow him or detain him, or so that he would not leave surrounded by such a retinue. First, he was unwilling to put himself at the service of so many masters and to have to be set free by Laban, like a servant. Then, because he was a man intent on virtue and endeavoring to find the true road to virtue, he wanted no one to lead him because the word of God sufficed. 'These,' he said, 'have instructed me to depart and accompany me on my way.'

'But how,' he said, 'would you have dismissed me? With that joy of yours which is full of sadness? With timbrels and instruments of poorly modulated harmony and the soft notes

---
9 Gen. 31.27.

of flutes sounding discordant strains? With mute voices and cymbals jarring the senses? Did you think that these could please me or call me back? It is these which I have fled, fearless before your words of scorn. I fled that these might not follow me, so that in leaving I would take along none of your gifts.'

With guides like these one does not reach the Church of Christ whither Jacob was directing his way, in order to lead there the wealth of the nations, to bring in the riches of the heathens, to transplant his posterity, fleeing the shadows of vain things, preferring to senseless images of virtue the breathing beauty of virtue, preferring serious matters to those that bring applause. You see how the heathens adorn their banquets and announce their feasts. These practices are distasteful to devout minds. By these many are deceived, being captivated by pleasant banquets, choruses of dancers, and at the same time they fly from fasts, think they are hard, and believe that they are dangerous and bad for the body.

'Did you think that I wanted your gold? You do not possess the gold tried by the fire with which the just are tried.[10] Did I want your silver? You do not possess the silver, for you have not the brightness of heavenly conversation. Perhaps I hoped that you would give me some of your slaves to serve me? I am looking for free men; I am fleeing the slaves of sin. Perhaps I needed comrades for the journey and guides for the road? Would that they could follow me! I would show them the paths of the Lord. You who do not know the Lord, how can you know His paths? Not everyone who enters, but those who have been chosen by the Lord, walk His paths, although no one is excluded.

'Let him who is prepared follow me; let him take the road which leads to Mesopotamia. Let him who seeks that country pass through the waters of the Tigris and Euphrates, the waters of fortitude and justice, the tears of penance and the

---
10 Cf. Ps. 11.7.

baptism of grace. Here is the path of the army of God, since all who belong to the Church are soldiers of God. Here is the flock marked with all kinds of virtues, the flock which Jacob chose for himself. Every soul that is unmarked is unwise and untaught, knowing no discipline. Those that are marked are rich in good works and wealthy in grace.

'Let him who comes first be reconciled with his angry brother. Let him who comes here dwell in Sichem, the precious and real storehouse of virtues where wounded chastity receives full revenge. Let him who comes here wrestle with God so that he may strive to imitate Him, coming close to Christ's humility and Passion. Let him take up his cross and follow Christ.[11] Lastly, a good combatant is not envious or puffed up. He even blesses his combatant by giving him a reward.'

Let us follow blessed Jacob and his paths so that we may reach these sufferings, these contests, his shoulder.[12] Let us reach patience, the mother of the faithful, and Isaac, the father, that is, one capable of joy who abounds in happiness.[13] Where there is patience there is happiness, because after tribulation comes patience, and patience works experience in which there is hope, in which we are not confounded.[14] Christ will not be ashamed of one who is not ashamed of the cross of Christ.

Farewell, my son, and do not be ashamed to ask questions of your father, as you are not ashamed to glory in the sufferings of Christ.

---

11 Cf. Matt. 16.24.
12 Sichem means 'shoulder' in Hebrew.
13 Isaac means 'laughter' in Hebrew.
14 Cf. Rom. 5.5.

83. Ambrose to Irenaeus[1]

You seem greatly disturbed over the Apostle's lesson, hearing it read today: 'For the Law works wrath; for where there is no law, neither is there transgression.'[2] For this reason you determined to ask why the Law was promulgated if it profited nothing, in fact, was injurious by working wrath and causing transgression.

Indeed, according to your inquiry, it is certain that the Law given to Moses was not necessary. For, if men had been able to keep the natural law which God the Creator planted in the breast of each one, there would have been no need of that Law, which, written on stone tablets, rather enmeshed and entangled the weakness of human nature than freed and liberated it. Moreover, that there is a natural law written in our hearts the Apostle also teaches when he writes that for the most part 'The Gentiles do by nature what the Law prescribes, and since they do not read the Law, they yet have the work of the Law written in their hearts.'[3]

This law is not written, but inborn; it is not acquired by reading, but springs up in each one as from the flowing font of nature, and men's minds drink from it. This law we should have kept even through fear of future judgment, which our conscience witnesses, revealing itself by silent thoughts before God, whereby our sin is reproved or our innocence justified. Therefore, that which has always been apparent to the Lord will be clearly revealed on the day of judgment, when the secrets of the heart, which were thought to be hidden, will be called to an account. The discovery of these things, these secrets, I mean, would do no harm if the natural laws were implanted in the human breast, for it is in itself holy,

---

1 Undated.
2 Rom. 4.15.
3 Rom. 2.14,15.

guileless, without craftiness, the companion of justice free from wickedness.

Accordingly, let us pose the question to childhood, let us see if any crime can be found therein, if greed, ambition, guile, rage, and insolence are there. It claims nothing for its own, assumes no honors for itself, knows not how to prefer itself to another, knows no guile, does not wish to and cannot avenge itself. Its pure and simple mind cannot comprehend the meaning of insolence.

This law Adam broke,[4] seeking to take for himself what he had not received, so that he might be like his own Creator and Maker, so that he might claim divine honor. Through disobedience he incurred guilt, and through arrogance he fell into sin. Had he not broken the command and had he been obedient to the heavenly precepts, he would have preserved for his heirs the prerogative of nature and of innocence which was his from birth. But because the authority of the natural law was corrupted and blotted out by disobedience, the written Law was determined necessary, that man who had lost all might regain at least a part, and he who had lost what was his at birth might know and guard at least a part. Since the cause of his fall was pride, and pride sprang from the privilege of his innocence, it was necessary for some law to be passed which would subdue and subject him to God. Now, without the Law he was ignorant of sin, and his fault was less when he was ignorant of his fault.[5] Thus, also, says the Lord: 'If I had not come and spoken to them, they would have no sin. But now they have no excuse for their sin.'[6]

The Law was passed, first, to remove all excuse for sin, lest any man might say: 'I knew no sin, for I received no rule as to what to avoid.' Next, that it might make all men

---
4 Cf. Gen. 3.6.
5 Cf. Rom. 7.8.
6 John 15.22.

subject to God through their recognition of sin.⁷ It made all subject, for it was given not only to the Jews, but it reached also the Gentiles, and converts from the Gentiles became their associates. Nor can that man possibly seem exempt who, being called, was found wanting, for the Law bound those whom she called. Thus, the sin of all men caused subjection, subjection humility, humility obedience. And as pride drew after her sin, so sin, on the contrary, begot obedience. Thus, the written Law, which seemed superfluous, was needed to redeem sin from sin.

Lest anyone again be alarmed and say that the Law caused an increase of sin, and that the Law was not only unprofitable but even injurious, he has at his disposal words which can relieve his concern, that 'although by the Law sin abounded, grace has also abounded.'⁸ Now, let us understand the meaning of this.

Sin abounded by the Law because through the Law came knowledge of sin⁹ and it became harmful for me to know what through my weakness I could not avoid. It is good to know beforehand what one is to avoid, but, if I cannot avoid something, it is harmful to have known about it. Thus was the Law changed to its opposite, yet it became useful to me by the very increase of sin, for I was humbled. And David therefore says: 'It is good for me that I have been humbled.'¹⁰ By humbling myself I have broken the bonds of that ancient transgression by which Adam and Eve had bound the whole line of their succession. Hence, too, the Lord came as an obedient man to loose the knot of man's disobedience and deception. And as through disobedience sin entered, so through obedience sin was remitted. Therefore, the Apostle says: 'For just as by the disobedience of one man the many

---

7 Cf. Rom. 3.9.
8 Rom. 5.20.
9 Cf. Rom. 7.7.
10 Ps. 118.71.

were constituted sinners, so also by the obedience of the one the many will be constituted just.'[11]

Here is one reason that the Law was unnecessary and became necessary, unnecessary in that it would not have been needed if we had been able to keep the natural law; but, as we did not keep it, the Law of Moses became needful to teach me obedience and loosen that bond of Adam's deception which had ensnared his whole posterity. Yes, guilt grew by the Law, but pride, the source of guilt, was loosed, and this was an advantage to me. Pride discovered the guilt and the guilt brought grace.

Consider another reason. The Law of Moses was not needful; hence, it entered secretly. Its entrance seems not of an ordinary kind, but like something clandestine because it entered secretly into the place of the natural law. Thus, if she had but kept her place, this written Law would never have entered in, but, since deception had banished that law and nearly blotted it out of the human breast, pride reigned and disobedience was rampant. Therefore, that other took its place so that by its written expression it might challenge us and shut our mouth, in order to make the whole world subject to God.[12] The world, however, became subject to Him through the Law, because all are brought to trial by the prescript of the Law, and no one is justified without the works of the Law; in other words, because the knowledge of sin comes from the Law, but guilt is not remitted, the Law, therefore, which has made all men sinners, seems to have caused harm.

But, when the Lord Jesus came He forgave all men the sin they could not escape, and canceled the decree against us by shedding His Blood.[13] This is what He says: 'By the Law sin abounded, but grace abounded by Jesus,'[14] since after

---
11 Rom. 5.19.
12 Cf. Rom. 3.19.
13 Cf. Col. 2.14.
14 Cf. Rom. 5.20.

the whole world became subject He took away the sins of the whole world, as John bears witness, saying: 'Behold the lamb of God, who takes away the sin of the world!'[15] Let no one glory, then, in his works, since no one is justified by his deeds, but one who is just has received a gift, being justified by baptism. It is faith, therefore, which sets us free by the Blood of Christ, for he is blessed whose sin is forgiven and to whom pardon is granted.

Farewell, son, and love us, because we love you.

84. To Irenaeus[1]

Although in a previous letter I have already disposed of the little question you proposed, I will not refuse your request, my son, to set forth and develop my meaning at greater length.

Numerous times the question has been raised, and well known, too, is the acquittal of the woman who in the Gospel according to John was brought to Christ, accused of adultery. The Jews had devised this stratagem so that, in case she was set free contrary to the Law, the sentence of the Lord Jesus might be charged with being contrary to the Law, but, if she were condemned according to the Law, the grace of Christ might seem void.

The question became more pressing after bishops began accusing criminals before public tribunals, some urging the sword and the death penalty, while other approved accusations of this sort and the bloody triumphs of bishops. What do these say except what the Jews said, namely, that the

---

15 John 1.29.

1 Written between 385 and 387. It is ascribed to Studius in the mss. since its contents closely follow those of the letter to Studius referred to in the opening sentence.

guilty should be punished by the laws of the state and those should be accused by bishops in state courts whom they say should have been punished by law? The case is the same, although the number is less, that is, the case of judgment is the same, but the odium of the penalty is not the same. Christ would not allow one woman to be punished according to the Law; these declare that too small a number has been punished.

But, where did Christ pass this judgment? He generally thought fit to shape His discourse in accordance with the characteristics of the place where He was teaching His disciples. For example, while walking in the porch of Solomon, that is, of the wise man, He said: 'I and the Father are one.' And when He was in the Temple of God He said: 'My teaching is not my own, but his who sent me.' While He stood in the Temple, too, He gave the sentence of which we are speaking, for in the following verses you have: 'Jesus spoke these words in the treasury while teaching in the Temple. And no one seized Him.'[2] What is the treasury? The contribution of the faithful, the bank of the poor, the refuge of the needy, and Christ sat near this and, according to Luke, gave the opinion that the two mites of the widow were preferable to the gifts of the rich,[3] preferring on God's word love joined with zeal and generosity rather than the lavish gifts of munificence.

Let us see what comparison He made when He passed such judgment there near the treasury, for with good reason He preferred the widow who contributed the two mites. That precious poverty of hers was rich in the mystery of faith. So are the two coins which the Samaritan of the Gospels left at the inn to care for the wounds of the man who had fallen among robbers.[4] The widow mystically representing the Church thought it right to put into the sacred treasury the

---
2 John 10.30; 7.16; 8.20.
3 Cf. Luke 21.2-4.
4 Cf. Luke 10.35.

gift with which the wounds of the poor are healed and the hunger of wayfarers is satisfied.

Therefore, what Christ now bestows you must spend spiritually. He gave to the people the silver of heavenly eloquence tried by fire and to satisfy the desires of the people He marked the coin with the royal image.[5] No one contributed more than He who gave all. He filled the hungry, supplied the needy, gave light to the blind; He ransomed the captives, He made the paralytic rise, He gave life to the dead; and, what is more, He brought pardon to sinners and forgave their sins. These are the two coins which the Church has contributed after having received them from Christ. What are the two coins but the price of the New and Old Testament? The price of Scripture is our faith, for we value what we read in proportion to our will and intellect. Remission of sins, then, is the price of each Testament and is announced in type by the lamb and fulfilled in reality by Christ.

Understand, then, that there was no purification of seven days without the purification of three days. The purification of seven days is according to the Law which foretold under the appearance of the present sabbath a spiritual sabbath. The purification of three days is according to grace which is sealed by the witness of the Gospel,[6] because the Lord arose on the third day. Where punishment for sins is prescribed there ought to be penance; where remission is given to sinners there also is grace. Penance precedes; grace follows. There is neither penance without grace nor grace without penance, for penance should first condemn the sin so that grace can do away with it. John fulfilled the type of the Law and baptized to penance; Christ, to grace.[7]

The seventh day symbolizes the mystery of the Law, the eighth that of the resurrection, as you have in Ecclesiastes:

---
5 Cf. Ps. 11.7.
6 Luke 24.7.
7 Cf. Matt. 3.11.

'Give a portion to those seven and to the eight.'[8] And in the prophet Osee you read that it was said to him: 'Get an adulteress for fifteen denarii,'[9] so that by the twofold price of the Old and New Testament, that is, by the full price of faith, he procures the woman who is attended by a wandering and adulterous crowd of heathen strangers.

'And I bought her for an omer of barley, and half an omer of barley and a measure of wine.' By barley is meant that he has called the imperfect to faith, to make them perfect; by the omer is understood a full measure, by the half-omer a half-measure. The full measure is in the Gospel; the half-measure is in the Law whose fulfillment is the New Testament. Indeed, the Lord Himself said: 'I have not come to destroy the Law, but to fulfill it.'[10]

We read the significant words in the Psalms of David regarding the fifteen degrees and that the sun had arisen fifteen steps when Ezekias, the just king, received additional years to his life.[11] The Sun of Justice is represented about to come to illumine with the light of His presence the fifteen steps of the Old and New Testament by which our faith mounts up to eternal life. I believe that today's reading in the Apostle[12] is a mystery, the fact that he [Paul] stayed fifteen days with Peter. It seems to me that, while the holy Apostles talked with one another about the interpretation of holy Scripture, the brilliance of the full light shone upon them and the shades of ignorance were dispersed. But let us go on to discuss the forgiveness of the woman charged with adultery.

A woman guilty of adultery was brought by the Scribes and Pharisees to the Lord Jesus and the malicious charge was laid on her so that if He forgave her He might seem to

---
8 Eccle. 11.2.
9 Osee 3.1,2.
10 Matt. 5.17.
11 Cf. Isa. 38.8.
12 Cf. Gal. 1.18.

destroy the Law, but if He condemned her He would seem to have changed the purpose for which He had come, for He had come to forgive the sins of all men. He said earlier: 'I judge no one.'[13] Presenting her, they said: 'We have found this woman openly in adultery. And in the Law[14] Moses commanded every adulterer to be stoned. What then do you say about her?'[15]

While they were saying this, Jesus, bending His head, wrote with His finger on the ground. And when they waited to hear Him, He raised His head and said: 'Let him who is without sin be the first to cast a stone at her.'[16] Is anything so godlike as that sentence that he should punish sin who himself is free from sin? For, how could we tolerate a person who condemned another for his sin and excused his own evil deeds? Does he not prove that he is more guilty by condemning in another what he himself commits?

He spoke these words and wrote on the ground. Why? As if He said: 'You see the speck which is in your brother's eye, but you do not see the beam which is in your eye.'[17] Lust is like a speck, quickly enkindled, speedily consumed. The sacrilegious affrontery with which the Jews refused to acknowledge the Author of their salvation indicates the greatness of their crimes.

He wrote on the ground with the finger with which He had written the Law.[18] Sinners are written on the ground,[19] the just in heaven, as you have it said to the disciples: 'Rejoice that your names are written in heaven.'[20] But He wrote a second time, so that you may know that the Jews were condemned by both Testaments.

---

13 Cf. John 8.3-11,15.
14 Lev. 20.10.
15 John 8.4,5.
16 John 8.7.
17 Matt. 7.3.
18 Cf. Exod. 31.18.
19 Cf. Jer. 17.13.
20 Luke 10.20.

When they heard these words they went out, one by one, beginning with the eldest, and they sat down thinking about themselves. And Jesus remained alone and the woman standing in the midst.[21] It is well said that they went out, for they did not wish to be with Christ. The letter is outside; the mysteries, within. In the divine teachings they wanted, as it were, the leaves of the tree and not its fruit, and they lived in the shadow of the Law and were unable to see the Sun of Justice.

When they had gone, Jesus remained alone and the woman standing in the midst. Jesus who was about to forgive sin remains alone, as He Himself says: 'Behold the hour is coming, and has already come, for you to be scattered, each one to his own house, and to leave me alone,'[22] because no herald or messenger, but the Lord Himself, saved His people.[23] He remains alone because no one can share with Christ the task of forgiving sins. This is the task of Christ alone who took away the sin of the world.[24] The woman deserved to be forgiven, since she remained alone with Jesus when the Jews withdrew.

Then Jesus, raising His head, said to the woman: 'Where are they who accused thee? Has no one stoned thee?' And she answered, 'No one, Lord.' And Jesus said to her: 'Neither will I condemn thee. Go thy way and now see that you sin no more.'[25] See, reader, the divine mystery and the mercy of Christ. When the woman is accused, Christ bows His head, but He raises it when an accuser is no longer there. Thus, He wishes no one to be condemned, but all to be forgiven.

By saying 'Has no one stoned thee?' He quickly destroys all the quibbling of the heretics. They say that Christ does not know the day of judgment because He said: 'As for sitting

---
21 Cf. John 8.9.
22 John 16.32.
23 Cf. Isa. 63.8.
24 Cf. John 1.29.
25 John 8.10,11.

at my right hand and at my left, that is not mine to give you.'[26] But see, He also says here: 'Has no one stoned thee?' How is it that He asks about what He saw? He is putting the question for our advantage that we may know that she was not stoned. Besides, it is a custom of man's nature that we often question what we see. And the woman answered: 'No one, Lord.' In other words, she said: 'Who can stone a woman whom You Yourself do not condemn? Who can punish another under such conditions?'

The Lord answered her: 'Neither will I condemn thee.' Notice how He softened His judgments, so that the Jews might not be able to accuse Him of forgiving the woman, but, rather, turn the insult against themselves if they had a mind to complain. The woman is sent away; she is not forgiven. Inasmuch as no accuser was at hand, her innocence was not for this reason proven. Why should they complain, since they were the first to discontinue the charge and fail to exact the penalty?

He adds these words to the one gone astray: 'Go, and see now that you sin no more.' He reformed the guilty one; He did not forgive the crime. A person receives a heavier penalty when he hates his fault and begins to condemn sin in himself. When a guilty man is put to death, the person rather than the fault is punished. But, when the fault is forsaken, the forgiveness of the person is the punishment of the sin. What do those words mean: 'Go, and now see that you sin no more'? It is this: Since Christ has redeemed you, let grace correct you, for a penalty would not reform you, but only punish you.

Farewell, son, and as a son love us, because we love you as a father.

---

[26] Matt. 20.23.

85. Ambrose to Irenaeus[1]

You have asked me to expound for you the full thought of the Epistle to the Ephesians, an epistle which seems somewhat obscure unless one draws the distinctions which made the Apostle realize he had to persuade us not to despair of the kingdom of God.

In the first place, he points out that for good men the greatest motive for the pursuit of virtue is the hope of rewards and the inheritance of heavenly promises which are brought within reach in the Passion and Resurrection of Christ.

Then he adds that not only has a way to paradise been made anew for us through Christ, but also there has been won for us the honor of a throne in heaven through our partnership with the flesh of Christ's Body. You need no longer doubt the possibility of your ascension, knowing that your partnership with the flesh of Christ continues in the kingdom of heaven, knowing that through His Blood reconcilation was made for all things, those on earth and in heaven (for He came down in order to fulfill all things), and by His Apostles, Prophets, and priests establishing the whole world and drawing together the Gentiles. Now, the purpose of our hope is the love of Him, that we may grow up to Him in all things, because He is the Head of all things, and by the building up of love we all rise up to Him into one body,[2] according to the measure of our work.

We ought not despair of the members being united to their Head, especially since from the beginning we have been predestined in Him through Jesus Christ to be the adopted sons of God, and He has ratified this predestination, maintaining that which was foretold from the beginning, that 'A man shall leave his father and mother, and cleave to his

---
1 Undated.
2 Cf. Eph. 4.15,16.

wife; and the two shall become one flesh,'³ for it is a mystery of Christ and of the Church. Therefore, if the union of Adam and Eve is a great mystery in Christ and in the Church, it is certain that as Eve was bone of the bones of her husband, and flesh of his flesh, we also are members of Christ's Body, bone of His bones and flesh of His flesh.

No other epistle has given utterance to so great a blessing upon the people of God as this in which the great witness of divine grace signified not only that we were blessed by God, but blessed with all blessing in the spirit and in the heavens, and predestined to the adoption of sons, endowed also with grace in the Son of God; by this [grace] we have been filled with the knowledge of the mystery of the eternal will. Especially, then, in the fullness of time when all things were made peaceful in Christ—those of earth, and those of heaven—we have been established in this possession, so that what is of the Law and what is of grace might be fulfilled in us. And although according to the Law we seemed chosen, even in that season of youth which signifies a holy life, without the wantonness of youth or the weakness of age, we have also been taught to battle with lively virtues not only against flesh and blood, but also against every force of spiritual wickedness on high.⁴

As they [the men of the Old Testament] by drawing lots entered into possession of lands taken from the enemy, so has the lot of grace fallen to us, so that we may be the possession of God, who possesses our reins, the seed-bed of chastity and temperance. Do you wish to have information regarding this lot? Recall that which fell upon Matthias with the result that he was included in the number of the twelve Apostles.⁵ The Prophet David also says: 'If you sleep among the lots,'⁶ because one who is in the middle, between the lot of the Old

---

3 Gen. 2.24; Eph. 5.31.
4 Cf. Eph. 6.12.
5 Cf. Acts 1.26.
6 Ps. 67.14.

and the New Testament reclining on both, attains the peace of the kingdom of heaven. This lot, their father's possession, the daughters of Salphaad sought and by God's judgment their petition was granted.[7] Yet they sought it in the shade, for Salphaad means 'the shade of the mouth'; they sought it in shady words and spoke what was not revealed. Hence, the request for their inheritance by the daughters of Salphaad was couched in obscure words, but by us the request is made in the light of the Gospel and by the revelation of grace.

Let us therefore be the possession of God, let Him be our portion, for in Him are the riches of His glory and of His inheritance. Who but God alone is rich, for He created all things? But He is even richer in mercy, for He redeemed all men, and as the Author of nature He changed us, who were by nature children of wrath and liable to harm, so that we are the children of peace and charity. Who can change nature but He who created it? Therefore, He raised the dead and made those who were brought to life in Christ sit in heaven in the Lord Jesus Himself.[8]

No one among men has earned the privilege of sitting on that seat of God of which the Father said only to the Son: 'Sit thou at my right hand,'[9] but in the flesh of Christ, through fellowship in the same nature, the flesh of the whole human race has been honored. For, as He is said to have been made subject in our flesh[10] by unity with the flesh and obedience of the body in which He was obedient even to death,[11] so have we, in His flesh, sat down in heavenly places. We have not sat of ourselves, but in Christ who alone sits at the right hand of God, the Son of Man, as He Himself said: 'Hereafter you shall see the Son of Man sitting at the right hand of God.'[12] The grace in Him and His goodness have

---
7 Cf. Num. 27.1-6.
8 Cf. Eph. 2.4-6.
9 Ps. 109.1.
10 Cf. Luke 2.51.
11 Cf. Phil. 2.8.
12 Matt. 26.64.

flowed upon us in Christ Jesus that, although we were dead by works, yet, having been redeemed by faith and saved by grace, He might give us the gift of deliverance, by which our very nature, as though raised from the dead, experiences the grace of a new vesture, and we, who were created in Christ, but fell away through the corruption of our guilty lineage, may walk doing good.

With the removal of those enmities which formerly existed in the flesh, peace with the universe has been made in heaven,[13] that men might be like angels on earth, that Gentiles and Jews might be made one, that in one man might dwell the old and the new man, with the middle wall of partition removed, which once stood between them like a hostile barrier. Now, since the nature of our flesh has stirred up anger and discord and dissension, and the Law has bound us with the chains of guilt, Christ Jesus has by mortification subdued the wantonness and intemperance of the flesh, has made void the commandments contained in ordinances, declaring that the decrees of the spiritual law are not to be interpreted according to the letter, putting an end to the slothful rest of the sabbath and the superfluous rite of bodily circumcision, and laying open to all an approach to the Father in one spirit. How, then, can there be discord where there is one calling, one body, one spirit?

What else did Christ effect by His coming down except to deliver us from captivity into liberty, and to make that captivity captive which had been fettered by the bonds of unbelief, restrained now by the fetters of wisdom, every wise man putting his feet into its bonds? So it is written that, when He had descended, He ascended to fill all things,[14] that we might all receive of His fullness.[15]

First, He placed in the Church Apostles, who were filled

---

13 Cf. Eph. 2.14.
14 Cf. Eph. 4.10.
15 Cf. John 1.16.

with the Holy Spirit, and some Prophets, some Evangelists, but others pastors and teachers, that by their exhortations the progress of believers might be accomplished, and the work of the faithful ministry increase.[16] Everyone by building up virtue is built into the measure of the inward life, and this more perfect measure of a holy life, that is, of perfect manhood,[17] partaking of the fullness of Christ, receives the fullness of grace.

Who is perfect save him who has been freed from the infancy of a childish mind, from the uncertain and slippery ways of youth, and from the unbounded fervor of young manhood, and has attained to that sureness of perfect manhood, and grown up to maturity of character so that he is not easily swayed by the words of a wily arguer, nor cast on the rocks, at it were, by the violent storm of foolish teaching. He makes use of the remedies for error. He follows truth in words and in works, and he undertakes to build in himself the edifice of love, that he may attain to a unity of faith and of knowledge.[18] As a member he does not neglect his Head, that is, Christ, who is the head of all, through whom the whole body of the faithful and the wise is joined together, knitted together, and united together through the reasonable harmony of the Word—that is, through every joint of the system, according to the functioning of each part—thereby increasing the body in order to build up himself in love. This he does so that one temple of God may arise in all, and one dwelling of the heavenly mansion be in the spirit of all men.

In this I think we are to understand not only the union in faith and in the spirit of holy men, but of all believers, of all the heavenly spiritual hosts and powers, that by a certain concord of powers and ministers the one body of all the spirits of an intelligent nature may cling to Christ their

---
16 Cf. Eph. 4.11.
17 Cf. Eph. 4.13.
18 *Ibid.*

Head, being so united to the framework of the building that there seems to be no trace even of the point where the several members are joined together. This, then, is the meaning of the Greek;[19] and it will not be difficult for so great an architect to unite each one to Himself according to the measure of each one's merits and faith, for the edifice of love closes and blocks up every crevice whereby offense may enter. We must not doubt that in the building of this temple the company of heavenly hosts will join with us, for it is unbecoming that human love can build up a temple of God, so that there is formed a dwelling of God in us, while this is not possible among the powers of heaven.

It is in order that this kind of building may rise more speedily in us that the Apostle urges us to open the eyes of our heart, raise them to things above, earnestly seek the knowledge of God, investigate the truth, store in our hearts the commandments of God, put aside the desire for evil and the hidden deeds of shame, be renewed through the grace of the sacraments, control anger, be reconciled before sunset, beware lest the Devil get the uppermost of you—that spirit who was able to plunge into the heart of Judas and break asunder the gates of his soul so that he was unable to resist, or shut out the thief, or eschew falsehood, or rise from the dead, or put on soberness. He says, too, that a wife should be subject to her husband, as the Church is to Christ; the husband is to offer his life for his wife, as Christ delivered Himself up for the Church.[20] Lastly, like good warriors we are to put on the armor of God, and strive ever, not only against flesh and blood, but against the spiritual forces of wickedness.[21] Nor should we be weakened by friends or vanquished by the enemy. This brief summary I have drawn up to the best of my ability.

Farewell, son, and love us, because we also love you.

---
19 Ambrose here quotes the Greek.
20 Cf. Eph. 5.25.
21 Cf. Eph. 6.12.

86. Ambrose to Paternus[1] (early 393)

I have read the greetings of my Paternus, one soul with me, but the problem arising from your wish to have your son marry your daughter's daughter is by no means paternal; rather, it is unbecoming you as a grandfather and father.[2] Take thought of what you are suggesting, for in all that we wish to do we should first ask its name and then determine whether it is praiseworthy or blameworthy. For example, carnal intercourse with women is a pleasure to some persons and even physicians say it is healthful. But we must consider whether it is done with one's wife or a stranger, a married or unmarried woman. Intercourse with one's wedded spouse he calls marriage, but one who assails the honor of another's wife commits adultery, whose very name generally checks so daring an attempt. To slay an enemy is a victory; to slay a criminal is justice; to slay an innocent man is murder, and the man who takes thought of this stays his hand. For this reason I beg you to consider what you are planning.

You wish to arrange a marriage between our children. I ask you, should those be wed who are alike or unlike? If I am not mistaken, they are generally called partners. In yoking oxen to the plow or horses to the chariot, one chooses co-partners of like age and appearance, that dispositions may not contrast too much or dissimilarity be a blemish. You are planning to have your son and your daughter's child wed, that is, to have him marry his sister's daughter, granted that he is of a different mother than she who will be his mother-in-law. Consider how the very names have a sanction: he is called her uncle, she his niece. Does not the very sound of the words check your resolve? When he mentions her

---
[1] Probably Aemilius Florus Paternus, proconsul of Africa in 393.
[2] Marriage with a niece was forbidden by a law of Constantius; cf. *Cod. Theod.* 3.12.1.

grandfather, she may refer this name to her uncle, which he refers to her grandfather.³ How much confusion is there in the other terms? You will be called grandfather and father-in-law; she will be called by different terms, niece and daughter-in-law. Brother and sister will be addressed by other names; one will be the mother-in-law of her brother, the other, the son-in-law of his sister. Your niece will marry her uncle and the affection of these pure children will be supplanted by an irregular love.

You tell me that your saintly bishop is awaiting my opinion on this. I do not think or believe this is so. If it were true, he would have felt the need of writing, but, by not doing so, he intimates that he thinks there is no doubt on this point. Where is there room for doubt when divine law which forbids marriage between first cousins extends to those related within the fourth degree? This is the third degree to which, even by civil law, the marriage union appears to be forbidden.

Let us first inquire what are the decrees of the divine law, for in your letters you allege that such a marriage is permitted by divine law in that it is not forbidden. But, I say, it is actually forbidden. For, if these privileges are forbidden first cousins, much more do I think this closer bond of union is not allowed. One who attaches censure to slight matters does not forgive, but condemns more serious ones.

Now, if you think it is permitted because it is not specifically forbidden, you also will find no expression in the law forbidding a father to take his daughter as a wife. Surely it is not allowed just because it is not forbidden? By reason of the near relationship it is forbidden by the law of nature, by the law in the hearts of each of us, by the unsullied rule of piety. How many things of this sort will you find, not

---

3 *Neptis* means both granddaughter and niece.

forbidden by the Law which was promulgated through Moses, yet forbidden by the voice of nature!

There are also many lawful things which it is not expedient to do, for 'all things are lawful but they are not expedient';[4] all things are lawful but they do not edify. If the Apostle also restrains our doing what does not edify, how can we imagine we can do what is not permitted by the word of the Law, and does not edify, since it is out of harmony with the right order of piety. Yet, the former things which were too harsh have been mitigated by the Gospel of the Lord Jesus: 'The former things have passed away; behold, they are made new!'[5]

What is so formal as a kiss between a niece and uncle, which he owes her as to a daughter, she as to a parent? You will bring suspicion upon this kiss of unoffending piety by proposing such a marriage, and you will deprive your dear children of this most holy token.

If the divine commands do not touch you, at least you should regard the laws of the emperors from whom you have received most lavish honors. Emperor Theodosius forbade the children of either brothers or sisters to unite in marriage, and he enjoined a very severe penalty on the union of brothers' children. Yet, they are on an equal basis, and he has wished those who are bound by ties of relationship and brotherly union to owe their birth to love.

You will say this rule has been relaxed for some. Yet, the law is not thereby prejudiced, for, when that which is decreed for the common good is relaxed for an individual, it profits only one individual and spreads envy far and wide. Although we read in the Old Testament of a man calling his wife his sister, it is unheard of for anyone to marry his niece and call her his wife.

---
4 1 Cor. 6.12.
5 2 Cor. 5.17.

It is very curious for you to say that your granddaughter can marry her uncle, your son, merely because they have no paternal relationship, as if half-brothers, born of the same father by a different mother, could be wed if of a different sex, in so far as they are not related on the father's side,[6] but only on the mother's side.[7]

You had better abandon your intention which, even if it were lawful, would not enlarge your family, for your son owes you grandchildren, your dear granddaughter owes you great-grandchildren.

Farewell to you and yours.

87. Ambrose to Romulus[1]

There is no doubt that letter-writing was devised that the absent may converse with those far away, and this improves in service and in form when many pleasant words are exchanged between father and sons, for then truly there is conveyed to those far removed in the body a seeming likeness of the other's presence. By these exchanges love is strengthened, as it is increased by your letters to me and mine to you. But I began a richer experience of this by the recent expressions of your affection whereby you determined to consult me [asking] what Aaron intended by taking gold from the people when they requested gods to be made for them, and was it because the head of the calf was shaped out of the gold or because Moses was so severely angry that he bade each man to rise with his sword and kill his neighbor.[2] It is important that those far away suffer no loss of elegant style,

---

6 *agnatio.*
7 *cognatio.*

1 Undated, to a distinguished layman of Aemelia, identified with Flavius Pisidius Romulus, consular of Aemelia-Liguria in 385.
2 Cf. Exod. 32.2-7.

or of the discussion and free investigation. Since you made the demand, I shall speak, more from a desire of a discussion than of interpretation.

While Moses was receiving the Law on Mount Sinai, the people were with Aaron the priest. And though they are said to have frequently wavered in sin, yet, while the Law was being given, it is not said they fell into sacrilege. In fact, when God's word was silent, sin stole upon them, so that they asked for gods to be made for them. Under compulsion, Aaron demanded their rings and the earrings of the women. Having received these, he consigned them to the fire and the head of a calf was molded.

We cannot excuse this great priest nor dare we condemn him. Yet, he was not unwise in taking the rings and earrings from the Jews, for those who were committing sacrilege could have no mark of faith or ornaments for their ears. In fact, even the patriarch Jacob buried the earrings of the Gentiles, along with their statues of gods, when he buried them at Sichem, so that no one might hear of the superstition of the Gentiles. Moreover, he aptly said: 'Take off your rings and the golden earrings which are the earrings of your wives,'[3] not to leave the earrings to the men, but to show that men do not have them. Fittingly, too, are earrings taken from women, lest Eve again hear the voice of the serpent.

And because they had listened to sacrilege, having fashioned their earrings, the image of sacrilege was made, for one who hears poorly usually fashions a sacrilege. Events that followed show why the calf's head was made: it signified that which would occur—either this nation would at a later time bring Jeroboa among them and the Hebrew people would adore golden calves,[4] or else all faithlessness is in the likeness of a monster and of the foolishness of beasts.

---
3 Exod. 32.2.
4 Cf. 3 Kings 12.30.

Stricken by the indecency of this act, Moses broke the tablets and shattered the head of the calf and beat it to powder in order to destroy all traces of impiety. The first tablets were broken so that the second ones might be repaired whereon, through the teaching of the Gospel, faithlessness, now utterly destroyed, vanished. Thus Moses shattered that Egyptian pride, and by the authority of the eternal law checked that loftiness overreaching itself. Therefore, David says: 'And the Lord will break the cedars of Libanus, and shatter them like the calf of Libanus.'[5]

Therefore, the people swallowed all faithlessness and pride, so that impiety and haughtiness might not swallow them. For it is better that each man be master of his flesh and its vices, that it may not be said of him that all-powerful death has devoured him,[6] but, rather: 'Death is swallowed up in victory! O death, where is thy victory? O death, where is thy sting?'[7] And it was said of the Lord: 'He shall drink of the torrent in the way,'[8] for He received vinegar in order to swallow the temptations of all men.

However, his making neighbors be killed by neighbors, sons by parents, brothers by brothers is evident proof that religion is to be preferred to friendship, piety to kinship. That is a true piety which prefers divine things to human ones, everlasting to temporal ones. Therefore, Moses himself said to the sons of Levi: 'Let him who has been prepared by the Lord come to me. And he said to them: The Lord God of Israel has said this; each one of you put his sword into his thigh, and pass through,'[9] in order that by contemplation and love of divine fear all affection for friends might be checked. Indeed, 3,000 men are recorded slain and we are not stirred with outrage over the number, for it is better that by the

---
5 Ps. 28.5,6.
6 Cf. Isa. 25.8.
7 1 Cor. 15.54,55.
8 Ps. 109.7.
9 Exod. 32.27.

punishment of a few all be exonerated than that all be punished. Nor does it seem a harsh act, for it was the punishment of a wrong against heaven.

Finally, for these tasks which are holier than others, Levites, whose portion is God, are chosen. They know not how to spare their possessions, knowing nothing as their own, since to the saints God is their all. Indeed, he is that Levite, the true avenger and defender, who slays the flesh that he may save the spirit, as was the man who said: 'I chastise my body, and bring it into subjection.'[10] What is so near as the flesh to the soul? What is so near as are the passions of the body? These the good Levite slays in himself with the spiritual sword which is the word of God, two-edged and strong.

It is the sword of the spirit which pierces the soul, as it was said to Mary: 'Thy own soul a sword shall pierce, that the thoughts of many hearts may be revealed.'[11] Is not the flesh joined to the soul by a certain fraternal union? Is not speech akin to and close to our mind? When we check our speech so as not to fall into sin by much speaking, we break the law of relationship and dissolve the ties of fraternal association. With the strength of reason the soul estranges its irrational parts, like a kinsman.

Thus did Moses teach the people to rise up against their neighbors through whom their faith was being lost and virtue hindered, so as to cut off in us whatever strays from virtue, is confounded by errors, is enmeshed in vice. By this instruction to the people he deserved not only to describe the anger of God and turn it aside when offended, but also to win grace.

In proportion to our ability we have expressed what we feel, for you sought our counsel. If you have anything better, share it with us, that from you and from ourselves we may learn what we are to choose and follow the more.

Farewell, and as a son love us, since we also love you.

---
10 1 Cor. 9.27.
11 Luke 2.35.

88. Ambrose to Romulus[1]

I am surprised at you, a country dweller, deciding to ask me why God said: 'I shall fashion a heaven of brass, an earth of iron.'[2] The very appearance of the country and its ready fertility can teach us how mild is the air, how genial the climate when God condescends to bestow fruitfulness. But, when He does not do so, its bareness makes everything tightly closed and the air so dense that it seems hardened into stiff brass. For this reason you have elsewhere that in the days of Elias heaven was shut for three and six months.[3]

The heaven being brass means that it was shut up and refused to let earth have the use of it. The earth, too, is of iron when it yields no crop, and, although seeds are cast upon it, with the harshness, so to speak, of an enemy, it shuts out of its fruitful ground the very seeds it is wont to nourish as in the bosom of a tender mother. When does iron bear fruit? When does brass send forth showers?

He threatens dreadful famine to those wicked men who know not how to manifest the devotion of children to the common Lord and Father of all; thus, they may be deprived of the support of His paternal mildness, the heaven will be of brass to them, and the air hard and solid in the consistency of metal; but the earth will be of iron bearing no fruit, sowing strife, as poverty is wont to do. They who are in need of food commit robbery, that at the expense of others they may alleviate their own hunger.

If the offense of the inhabitants is such that by God's design wars overtake them, truly their land is of iron, bristling with crops of spears, and stripped of its own fruit, rampant with punishment, barren of nourishment. Where is abun-

---
1 Undated.
2 Deut. 28.23.
3 Cf. 3 Kings 17.1.

dance? 'Behold I will rain bread from heaven for you,'[4] says the Lord.

Farewell, and love us, because we love you.

89. Ambrose to Sisinnius[1]

I attribute to your sense of duty more than to your regard for me your forgiving your son at my request for his having married without your consent. It is more significant that your sense of duty rather than anyone's request should have gained this from you. Assuredly, a priest's request makes greater gains when virtue triumphs, for his petition is merely dictated by his sense of duty. Nature gained and so did your son, and more fully so in that the consideration of a request is only temporary while the habit of virtue is lasting and natural affection is permanent.

The affair happened quite fittingly that you might regard yourself as a father at the same time as you had just cause for indignation. I prefer to admit the wrongdoing that your forgiving as a father may be praised the more. As a father you were offended because you were entitled to choose, in accord with your own judgment, the one who was to become a daughter, to whom you were to become a father. We obtain children by nature or adoption, by nature through chance, by adoption through choice. And we can be blamed for those we adopt more than for our natural children, for if natural children are degenerate, nature is blamed, but if children by adoption or marriage prove unworthy, it is said to be our own mistake. This was your reason for being angry with your son and for forgiving him, too, for choosing his

---
4 Exod. 16.4.

---
1 Undated.

wife by himself. You have obtained a daughter at no risk of choice, for if he has married well he has obtained an advantage for you; if he has made a mistake, you will improve the couple by taking them back; make them worse by disowning them.

A father chooses a girl for his son with more mature judgment, but she is introduced to her father by the son and enters her father's house at the choice of his son with a stronger intention of being obedient, since the son fears that his choice will be displeasing, while the daughter-in-law fears lest her role will be displeasing. The right of the father to make a choice ennobles and elevates his daughter-in-law; fear of giving offense humbles the daughter otherwise chosen and respect makes her submissive. The son will be unable to throw blame on his wife, as one free from blame may do, when any difficulty arises, as usually happens. In fact, he will work very hard to have his choice of wife win approval and have her show obedience to him.

As good parents do, you have readily granted pardon after being asked. Had you forgiven before being asked, it would have been not forgiveness but approval of their conduct. To delay pardon longer would have been painful to you, useless to them; your paternal affection could hold out no longer.

Through motives of high devotion and in obedience to the word of God, Abraham offered his son as a holocaust, and like a man devoid of natural feeling he drew his sword that no delay might dim the brightness of his offering. Yet, when he was ordered to spare his son, he gladly sheathed his sword, and he who with the intention of faith had hastened to sacrifice his only-begotten son hurried with greater zeal for piety to put a ram in place of the sacrifice.[2]

---

[2] Cf. Gen. 22.6-13. This entire paragraph is omitted in the Benedictine edition.

And Joseph, in order to keep his young brother, pretended he was angry with his other brothers for a concerted act of fraud. But when one of his brothers, Juda, unable to bear the affront, fell at his knees and when the others wept, Joseph was moved and won over by brotherly love and could no longer maintain his assumed air of hostility. Sending away the onlookers, he disclosed to his brothers that they were his kin, and he himself that Joseph whom they had sold. He said he no longer remembered their wrong, and he made a brother's excuse for their selling of a brother, referring what was blameworthy to deeper reasons: It must have been by God's design that he went to Egypt in order to feed his own needy people with grain from another country and in time of dearth to assist in supporting his father and his father's sons.[3]

What shall I say of blessed David, who at one woman's request permitted his heart to be softened, and then received back into his house his depraved son, who was stained with the blood of his brother?[4]

Moreover, that father in the Gospel, although his younger son had spent in riotous living all the substance he had received from his father, yet, when he returned, confessing that he had sinned against him, was moved with pity at his one sentence and ran to meet him with tenderness and embraced him. Then he fell upon his neck and ordered the best robe and ring and shoes brought for him; honoring him with a kiss and loading him with gifts, he entertained him with a great banquet.[5]

You have shown that you are an imitator of these men by your fatherly affection, whereby we approach every closely to God. Hence, I at once urged your daughter, despite the winter, to undertake the toilsome journey, for she will spend

---
3 Cf. Gen. 44.15-45.2.
4 Cf. 2 Kings 14.12.
5 Cf. Luke 15.22-24.

the winter more comfortably in her father's mansion and in his affection now that pardon has followed wrath. Furthermore, in order to attain fully to the likeness and pattern of the saints, you have censured those who contrived falsehoods and attempted to arouse your feelings against your son.

Farewell, and love us, because we love you.

90. Ambrose to Studius[1]

I know well the love in your pure soul, your zeal for the faith, and the fear of our Lord Jesus Christ. Yet I fear to send you an answer on this matter, being restricted on the one hand by what is enjoined on you as a guardian of the law, and on the other by mercy and grace, unless you follow the Apostle's authority on this matter: 'For not without reason does he carry a sword, who gives judgment,'[2] for he is the avenger of God against those who do evil.

Although you understand this, you have determined to make diligent inquiry. There are some persons—outside the Church, however—who do not admit to communion in the divine sacraments those who believe in capital punishment. Some stay away on their own accord.[3] They are praised and cannot be admonished in so far as we observe the authority of the Apostle and do not refuse them Communion.

You see, then, what authority permits and what mercy encourages. You will have no excuse, if you have taken action, and praise, if you have not done so. But, if you have been prevented from acting, I nevertheless approve of your not letting the guilty languish in prison, but, more in the manner

---

1 Written between 385 and 387, to a magistrate.
2 Rom. 13.4.
3 It was customary in the early years of Christianity for persons to refrain from Holy Communion after putting another to death by enforcement of the law.

of a priest, absolving them. For it can happen that, when a case has been studied, a prisoner will be sentenced who later wins pardon, or at least lives without great hardships, as they say, in prison. Yet, I have heard some heathens say that they returned from governing their province with ax unstained by blood. If heathens say this, what should Christians do?

In answer to all their questions hear the response of the Saviour.[4] When the Jews had found an adulteress they brought her to the Saviour, seeking to entrap Him, so that if He freed her He might appear to destroy the Law, He who had said: 'I have not come to destroy the Law, but to fulfill it.'[5] And if He would condemn her He would seem to have come against the purpose of His plan. The Lord Jesus, foreseeing this, bent His head and wrote on the ground. What did He write except the prophetic saying: 'Earth, earth, write that these men have been disowned,'[6] that which is written in the Prophet Jeremias concerning Jechonias?

When the Jews demand payment, the names of the Jews are written on the ground; when Christians come forward, the names of the faithful are written, not on the ground, but in heaven. Those who have been disowned by their Father are written on the ground, for they tempt their Father and flood the Author of salvation with insults. When the Jews demand payment Jesus bows His head. And because He has nowhere to lay His head,[7] He raises it again as if to pronounce sentence and says: 'Let him who is without sin be the first to cast a stone at her!' And again He inclined His head and wrote on the ground.

Those who were listening to Him began to go away, one by one, beginning with the eldest, either because they who had lived longer had more sins, or because, being older and

---
4 Cf. John 8.3-11.
5 Matt. 5.17.
6 Jer. 22.29.
7 Cf. Matt. 8.20.

supposedly wiser, they knew the righteousness of His sentence. They even began to weep more for their sins, since they had been the accusers of another's sin.

When they went away, Jesus remained alone and, raising His head to the woman, He said: 'Where are they who accused thee? Has no one stoned thee?' And she said: 'No one.' Jesus said to her: 'Neither will I condemn thee. Go and see that from now on you sin no more.' He does not condemn, as if purchasing her back; He as life restores her; like a fountain He washes her clean. And because when Jesus inclines His head He does so that He may raise up those who have fallen, He, the redemption of sins, says: 'Neither will I condemn thee.'[8]

You have this model to follow. It is possible for the guilty one to have hope of correction; if he is unbaptized, that he can receive forgiveness; if he has been baptized, that he can do penance and offer his body to Christ. How numerous are the paths of salvation!

Thus, our predecessors preferred to be rather indulgent toward judges, so that, while their sword was feared, the madness of crime was checked and not aroused. But, if Communion is refused, the punishment of the guilty seems avenged. Our elders preferred that there be more tempering of the will than need of the law.

Farewell, and love us, for we also love you.

91. Ambrose to Titianus (October, 392)

You have achieved a harmless victory, enjoying a guarantee of victory without the bitterness of begging. Rufinus in his consulate has been raised from master of the offices[1] to

---

8 John 8.7-11.

---

1 A secretary of state in domestic and foreign affairs. This is the Rufinus who had driven Theodosius to the massacre of the Thessalonicans.

praetorian prefect. Thus, he enters upon a more influential position and, at the same time, he can no longer be a hindrance to you, being prefect in another district. I am happy for him, as for a friend, in that he is receiving an increase in honor and is relieved of odium; and for you, as for a son, in that you have been set free from one who you thought would be too severe a judge for you. Now, if you arrange the business with your granddaughter, it will be through affection, not through fear.

Be prompt, therefore, in making your arrangements, for both hope and enjoyment of it are now grown greater: hope, because your granddaughter's father, who anticipated much from Rufinus' decision, no longer has anything to hope for from him. Rufinus has other concerns; he has forgotten the past or has laid it aside, along with the office he then held. The father now looks to the substance of his case, not to the supporter of his opinons. Enjoyment, too, is more pleasing in that the decison will be favorable to you, who could have scorned it and did not, satisfying the dutiful claims of kindred, the angry promptings of injury.

Farewell, and love us as a son, for as a parent we love you.

INDEX

INDEX

Aaron, 104, 312, 314, 338, 339, 342, 385, 394, 484, 485; rod of, type of Church, 342
Abel, 280, 426
Abigail, 421
Abiron, 340, 426
Abraham, 4, 71, 148, 241, 251, 253, 339, 361, 431, 458, 490
Absolom, 448
Achab, 306, 349
Achaia, 205; council proposed in, 224
Achaz, 232
Achinaa, 421, 422
Acholius, Bishop, 67-69, 200-205, 222
active life, and contemplative, compared, 347, 348
actors, 145
Adam, 130, 132, 135, 136, 243, 244, 326, 370, 465-467, 476
adoption, 412, 489
adornment, 437
Adragathius, 15 n.

adultery, woman taken in, 468-471, 493, 494
Aemelia, bishops of, 189
Aeons, 13
Africa, Church in, 219, 223
Africanus, 39
Agar, 245
age, old, 40, 69, 358
agnatio, 484 n.
Agnes, St., martyr, 299
aition, quality of rhetoric, 115
Alexander, Bishop, 230
Alexander the Great, 298, 299
Alexandria, Church at, 192, 220; Council at, 216, 218, 220 n.
Altaner, B., vii n.
Alypius, Faltonius Probus, 399
Ambrose, St., 102, 105, 152 n., 204, 214 n., 401, 402, 416-419; advice to priests of, 120-124, 151, 317, 438; baptism of, 318, 319; as bishop, vii, ix, 53, 321; desire for martyrdom of, 284, 366, 373, 375, 380; and em-

perors, 8-10, 16-21, 26, 27, 30, 31, 34, 35, 38, 56-67, 200, 201, 373, 374, 385, 396, 397, *see also* Gratian, *et. al.;* exhortations of, to bishops, 76-80, 102-105, 153-163, 174-177, 239-241; and friends, 67, 68, 102, 204, 286; and Greek Fathers, vi; and heretics, 89, 137, 365; and Jews, 10-17; as judge in legal affairs, 120, 161-163, 413, 481-484, 489-494; as letter writer, 24, 76, 101, 124, 127-129, 283; mention of prayer and of Mass, 24, 25, 29, 374; proposes Church councils, 221-224; sermons of, 377-396; relatives of, 414, 416; virtues of, 53, 54, 367, 368; works of: *Cons. Val.,* 37 n.; *De fide,* 5 n., 216 n.; *De off.,* vii, 455 n.; *Expos. Ps. 118,* 455 n.; *Hex.,* 129; *Hymn.,* 436 n.
Ambrosia, 414 n.
Ammianus, Bishop, 200
Ananias, 112, 346
Anatolius, Bishop, 200
angels, 276; power of, 453, 479
anger, 360
animals, 262, 263, 330, 435
Anna, widow, 228, 331
Antioch, Church at, 19, 172, 173, 212 n., 217, 218, 220-222
Antiochus, 399
Antonius, Claudius, 339

Anysius, Bishop, 67, 203, 204
Aper, priest, 230
Apollinaris, heretic, 126, 136, 139, 140, 224
apostasy, 9, 32
Apostles, 264, 280, 281, 439, 453, 478; *see also* Creed.
apotélesma, quality of rhetoric, 115
Aquila, 99
Aquileia, Councils of, 207, 208, 216-218, 220 n.
Aratus, of Cilicia, 259 n.
Arcadius, Emperor, 19 n.
Arians, 53 n., 55, 56, 89, 126, 207, 209-212, 216-218, 221, 223, 365, 382-384
Ariminium, Council of, 55
Aristotle, 272, 435 n.
Arius, 209, 210
Ascalon, 12
Athanaric, 15 n.
Athanasius, St., 216 n., 221, 225
athletes, 255-257
Attalus, heretic, 211
Atticus, consul, 400 n.
Attilius; *see* Regulus
Augustine, St., xii n., xiii, 286 n., 374 n., 376, 382 n.
Auxentius, heretic, 52, 53, 55, 230
avarice, 83
Azarias, 112, 346

Balaam, soothsayer, 71-75

500

Balak, 73, 394
banquets, 462
baptism, 73, 96, 240, 401 n., 404, 448, 463; of desire, 27
baptistry, 366
barbarians, 15, 39, 60, 149, 150, 202, 224, 368, 417; *see also* Goths
Barbatianus, heretic, 323
basilicas, 12, 365-368, 372, 376
Bassianus, Bishop, 103, 225
Bauton, 58, 59, 63
Beirut, 12
belief, 252-254
Bellicius, 401-402
Benjamin, tribe of, 163
Bersabee, mystically considered, 349
Bethany, 242-243
Bethlehem, 234, 236, 241
Bethphage, 241
bishops, rights and duties of, 6-8, 18, 20, 21, 35, 52, 53, 172, 173, 365, 380, 381, 468; succession of, 203, 204, 218, 321 n., 322 n., 337; virtues of, 208, 211, 212, 343, 345
blindness, of soul, 402
blood, mystical separation of, 308; of Christ, 467, 468
Bologna, 417
boundary stones, 89, 302
burning, of buildings by enemy sects, 11, 12

Cain, 80, 426
Calanus, 298, 299
Caleb, 402
calf, golden, 484
Calligonus, 375
Callinicum, synagogue at, 9-11, 385
calumny, 163 n.
Camillus, 39
Campania, 149
Candidianus, 70
Capharnaum, 242
Capua, Council of, 172, 173
Carthaginians, 39
catechumens, 63, 366
Cato, 134 n.
Chanaan, mystically considered, 415, 416
charity, 252-254, 390, 393, 394
Charles Borromeo, St., 379 n.
chastity, 171, 225-227, 344
Chem, mystically considered, 415
childhood, 465
children, 489
Christ, 78, 88, 100, 109, 111, 118, 132, 235, 236, 242, 249, 268, 278-281, 284, 285, 295, 315, 317-319, 322, 352, 356, 357, 361-363, 377, 393, 408, 418, 419, 421, 439-441, 444, 454, 463, 475, 478, *et passim*; as Architect, 480; Blood of, 467, 468; as

Bridegroom, 421; as Exemplar of virtue, 16, 84, 86, 95, 226, 275, 279, 326, 463, 466, 477; as Head of Mystical Body, 132, 277, 279, 389-390, 475, 479; Incarnation of, 4, 87, 126, 138, 139, 226, 227, 234, 235, 386, 449; as Judge, 249, 250, 322, 469; miracles of, 401-405, 470; nature of, 55, 137, 139-143, 210, 338, 339; Obedience of, 477; Passion of, 92, 93, 100, 191, 192, 311, 361, 362, 452, 463; as Physician, 253, 337, 338, 401-405; as Priest, 271, 272, 315; as Redeemer, 41, 84, 92, 93, 109, 110, 138, 139, 310, 387, 388, 435, 478; and sinners, 241-244, 386, 387, 471-474, 493, 494; as Teacher, 468-469
Christians, beliefs of, 40-42; conduct of, 42, 80, 81, 412; in public office, 34, 37, 49
Chromatius, Bishop, 70
Church, 48, 333, 334, 336, 390, 392, 393, 395, 422, 428, 453, 462
Cicero, 76 n., 125 n., 134 n., 272 n., 417 n.
circumcision, 90-100, 251, 252, 405-407
Clarus, Bishop, 200
Claterna, 417
Clementianus, 405, 410
clergy, 43, 317, 318, 347, 348; second marriage of, 344 n.

Coelestis, 48
cognatio, 484 n.
comets, 25 n.
compassion, 361
confirmation, 401 n.
conscience, 33, 80
consolation, letters of, xi, 417-419; of sick, 401, 402
Constantine, Emperor, 55
Constantinople, Council of, 217 n.; Church at, 221; imperial residence, 11
Constantius, Bishop, 76, 230
Constantius, Emperor, 49, 55 n., 207, 220 n., 481 n.
conversion, 89, 231, 244
Core, 340, 426
correction, 386, 387
counsel, 334, 335
Count of East, 9, 10
creation, 46-48, 133, 134, 254-265, 274-278, 282
Creed, 366; Nicene, 216 n.
Crescens, Bishop, 230
Curia, altar in, 34
Cybele, 48
Cynegius, 413
Cyrus, king, 50

dancing, of David, mystically considered, 145, 146
Dalmatius, notary, 52
Damaris, 329
Damasus, Pope, 34, 214 n.
Darius, king, 289
Dathan, 340

David, 22, 23, 31, 68, 87, 142, 145, 146, 295, 308, 309, 320, 339, 360, 395, 421, 422, 427, 439, 458, 466, 471, 491
death, contempt of, 298
Deferrari, R. J., 26 n., 27 n., 37 n.
Delila, 185-187
Delphinus, Bishop, 101
Demarchus, 328
Demophilus, heretic, 216
Devil, 317, 320, 326, 357, 370, 381-384, 426
didrachma, mystically considered, 105, 109, 111-113
Diocletian, era of, 195
Dionysius, Bishop, 346, 347
Dionysius, the Areopagite, 329
discipline, 234, 456
disobedience, 466
Dissertatio Maximini contra Ambrosium, 208 n.
drachma, mystically considered, 106, 107, 113, 114
dreams, 24
drunkenness, 132
Dudden, F. H., vii n., 15 n., 150 n., 217 n., 376 n., 437 n.
dwellings, lofty, 448

earrings, 485
Easter, date of, 189-200
Egypt, 197-199, 457, 458
eight, number, 266-267
eighth day, 471
Eleazar, 342

Elias, 145, 203, 264, 305, 331, 345, 349, 350, 371, 442, 448
Eliseus, 202, 203, 318, 319, 332, 345, 379, 380, 448
Elizabeth, 158
emperors, rights and duties of, 7, 8, 17, 18, 33, 52-54, 64, 65, 208, 212, 373, 374; *see also* Gratian, Theodosius, etc.
enneakaidekaetēris, 190 n.
enteléchia, 272
Ephraim, 241, 242
Ephrata, 234, 236
Epicureans, 323, 327, 328
Epicurus, 325
epistolography, in antiquity, xi-xii
Esau, 246, 247, 287-289, 358, 360
Ethiopians, practiced circumcision, 92
Eucharist, Holy, 236, 401 n., 492, 494
Eugenius, usurper, viii, 62, 65, 66
Euphrates, mystically considered, 462
Eusebius, Bishop, 200
Eusebius, Bishop of Vercelli, 321, 345-348, 413
Eustasius, Bishop, 230
Eustathius, 217 n.
Eutropius, 200
Euzoius, Bishop, 220 n.
Evagrius, of Antioch, 172, 173, 216 n.
Eve, 326, 370, 426, 466, 476

Eventius, Bishop, 230
excommunication, 62 n., 163 n.
extravagance, 149
Ezekias, 232, 471

faith, 253, 254, 358, 411, 433
famine, 38, 44
fasting, 228, 229, 323, 326, 327, 330, 351
father, of prodigal son, 491
Faustinus, 414, 416; the younger, 414
Favez, C., xi n.
Fegadius, 101
Felix, Bishop, 102
Felix, deacon, 30
Felix, heretic, 230
Felix, martyr, 376
festuca, 292 n.
fields, mystically considered, 438, 439
fifteen, number, 471
first-born, 430, 431
first-fruits, 277, 280
firstlings, 280
fish, Greek symbol of Christ, 110 n.
Figueroa, G., 9 n.
Flavian, of Antioch, 172, 173, 217 n.
forgiveness, of others, 351; of sin, 240, 359, 388

Gabanites, 165-170
Gallican bishops, 22
Gangrance, Council of, 436 n.

garments, of opposite sex not to be worn, 435
Gaul, Church in, 219, 223
Gauls, beliefs of, 55
Gaza, basilica at, burned, 12
Geminianus, Bishop, 230
Genesis, mystically considered, 135
Genial, heretic, 230
Germinator, heretic, 230
Gervase and Protase, martyrs, x, 378
gluttony, 132, 458
goat, as emissary, 316
God, 5, 24, 31, 32, 40, 65, 70, 71, 114, 118, 131, 133, 135, 136, 210, 211, 255, 409, 448, 449, 452, 459, 465, 477, 488; addressed as our Father, 412; benefits of, to man, 259; law of, 54; subordination of emperors to, 18
gold, 408, 462
Golgotha, 241, 244
Good, Highest, 437-441, 445
goose, sacred, 39
Goths, 15 n., 202 n.
grace, 109, 411, 470
Grata, 28 n.
Gratian, Emperor, viii, 3, 208, 212 n., 216; Ambrose pleads for body of, 56 n.; edicts of, on religion, 32; letter of, to Ambrose, 4; virtues of, 4, 5
greed, 80

Greek, Ambrose's knowledge of, vi; customs of women, 436
Gregory, of Nazianzen, 220 n.
grief, 416
growth, in Christ, 249

Hamilcar, 50, 51
Hannibal, 39
harlot, mystically considered, 81, 82
heaven, 201, 202, 257, 258, 360
Hebrews, laws of, 85
Henoch, 305
heretics, 211, 212 n., 223, 323, 329
Hermachus, 328 n.
hermits, 346
Herod, 235
Herodias, 371
Herodotus, 91 n.
Hexaemeron, 254
Hippocrates, 269
Honorius, Emperor, viii
hope, 282-283
Horeb, 349
Horontianus, 231, 241, 245, 251, 254, 272, 277, 283
hospitality, 176, 361
house, of God, 449, 450; of rich, 449, 450
hulë, quality of rhetoric, 115
humility, 84
husband, duty of, 480
Hyginus, Bishop, 62
hymns, 351
hypostásis, 220 n.

Indicia, 160, 163
indiction, 196
Ingeniosus, heretic, 230
inheritance, denied to priests, 42; of God, 459, 460
Innocents, Holy, 235, 269 n.
Irenaeus, 405 n., 420, 425, 428, 432, 435, 437, 448, 454, 458, 464, 468, 475
iron, magnet of, mystically considered, 132, 133
Isaac, 115, 245, 246, 251, 431, 463 n.
Isis, rites of, 144
Italy, 223, 417

Jacob, 68, 69, 287, 288, 320, 358, 458-463, 485
James, priest, 149
Januarius, heretic, 230
Japhet, mystically considered, 415
Jason, king, 65
Jeroboa, 485
Jerome, St., 232 n.
Jerusalem, Temple of, 11; heavenly, 424
Jews, 10, 11, 13-15, 100, 148, 250, 251, 390-392, 404-407, 410-412, 426, 466, 485, 486
Jezabel, 349, 350, 371, 451, 452
Joathan, 232
John the Baptist, St., 280, 331, 345, 349, 371, 470
Joseph, of Arimethea, 280

Joseph, son of Jacob, 84-87, 147, 148, 288, 289, 431, 491
Joseph, spouse of Mary, 158
Josephus, Flavian, 130, 178
Jovinian, heretic, 225 n., 230
Judas, 315, 357, 391, 404, 480
Julian, the Apostate, 11-14, 32, 51
Justa, sister of Valentinian, 28 n.
justice, 302, 303
Justina, Empress, x, 284 n., 367 n., 368 n.
Justus, Bishop, 105, 115
Julian Valens, 211

kiss, mystically considered, 390-392

Laban, 358, 459
labarum, 10
Lacy, J. A., xii n.
Laetus, 122, 124
law, given to Moses, 464, 465, 467; of God, 54; natural, 464, 467; a tutor, 248, 251, 405, 410
Lawrence, St., martyr, 299
lawsuits, 494, 495
Lazarus, 441
Leontius, 161-163
Leopardus, 230
Levite, of tribe of Benjamin, 164-168
Levites, 320, 340, 429, 430, 487
Lia, 459
Liberius, Pope, 213 n.
liberty, 286, 287, 411

Limenius, Bishop, 321 n.
Lot, 446
Lucius, heretic, 216
lust, 131, 132, 314, 315
luxury, 356
lying, impossible for God, 70

Macedonia, 200, 202, 203
Macedonius, Bishop, 200
Machabees, feast of, 13
Magdalen, Mary, 386, 390, 392
malignity, 337
man, ages of, 269; creation of, 114, 132, 254, 255, 258, 259, 264, 465; foolish, 406, 459, 460; free, 290, 291; perfection in, 259, 260, 479; powers of, 259-262; in rest of creation, 133, 255-257, 263; wise, 287, 292-301, 307, 312
Manasse, 75
manhood, 479
Mani, 93, 190
Manichaeans, 75, 229, 230
manna, 107, 138, 402, 432, 434
Marcellina, sister of Ambrose, vi, x, 20 n., 162, 365, 376, 385
Marcellinus, brother of Maximus, 60 n.
Marcellus, Bishop, 120
Marcion, heretic, 93
Mark, of Arethusa, 13 n.
Mark, of Pettau, 212
marriage, 174-176, 225, 226, 344, 345, 413, 481, 483, 489
Martian, heretic, 230

Martroge, F., 152 n.
martyr, 9; Ambrose's desire to be, 284, 366, 373, 375, 380
martyrdom, 94, 95
martyrs, 299, 300, 376, 379, 380, 383, 384
Mary, Virgin, 126, 134, 135, 158, 159, 226-228, 333, 339, 361, 362, 487
Mary, sister of Moses (Miriam), 312, 333, 341, 394
Mass, Sacrifice of, 6, 24, 25, 29, 190, 366, 370, 396, 397
masters, duties of, 362
Maximian, Emperor, 28, 36
Maximus, Bishop, 230
Maximus, of Alexandria, 217 n., 220, 221
Maximus, of Verona, 153, 154, 159-163
Maximus, usurper, viii, 16, 19 n., 56, 57, 59-61, 284 n., 374, 375 n.
McGuire, M., 20 n., 25 n., 48 n., 150 n.
Melchisedech, 338
Meletius, of Antioch, 217 n., 220
Mercurius, of Verona, 161
Michol, 145
midwives, 154-157
Milan, Church at, 190 n., Synod of, 212 n., 225 n.
miracles, 376, 379, 382
Misael, 112, 346
miser, 305, 408

Mithra, 48
Modena, 417
monastery, in Achaia, 205
monks, and clerics, compared, 347-349
Moses, 31, 117, 118, 144, 145, 264, 298, 308-314, 327, 336, 339-341, 360, 394, 433-435, 455, 458, 464, 484, 486, 487
mothers, duties of, 361, 362
Mystical Body. See Christ, Head of

Nabal, 422
Nabor, 376
Naboth, 306
Nabuchodonosor, 14
Narbonne, Bishops of, 207
Nathan, 22, 395
Nathaniel, 280
nature, described, 274; gifts of, to man, 263; progress of, 47, 48
Nectarius, 220, 222, 345 n.
neighbors, 89
Nembroth, 416
neptis, 482 n.
Nicaea, Council of, 55, 173, 189, 190, 196, 209, 344
Nicensis, 152 n., 155
Nicholaites, 75
nineteen years' cycle, 190
Noe, 147, 287
noûs, 111
nudity, 148
Numerius, Bishop, 200

oaths, of senators, 34
obedience, of Christ, 477
Origen, 236 n., 410
orphans, 80
Osiris, 195 n.
ousia, 220 n.

pagans, 33, 34, 38, 39, 45, 49; temple revenues of, 63-65
Palanque, J. R., v, ix n., 11 n., 20 n., 25 n., 150 n., 152 n., 220 n., 231 n., 425 n.
Palladius, heretic, 207, 208
paradise, 130, 244
parents, choosing of children's partners, 490
partridge, mystically considered, 109, 425-428
Paschasius, 215
Passover, 189, 190, 193, 194
paterfamilias, 90
Paternus, 162, 413 n., 481
patience, 463
Paul, St., 8, 128, 129, 235, 236, 252, 286, 303, 308, 319, 323, 332, 334, 339, 346, 357, 377, 430, 442
Paulinus of Antioch, Bishop, 217-220
Paulinus, of Milan, 385 n., *see also*: *Vita Ambrosii*
Paulinus, of Nola, 144
Paulus, Bishop of Constantinople, 224
peace, 304, 305, 454-476
pedagogus, 406

Pelagia, virgin, 299, 300
penance, 313-315, 462, 470
Pentateuch, 385
perfection, in man, 259, 260, 479
persecution, 14, 44, 366-369
Peter, St., 16, 77, 135, 137, 138, 244, 258, 303, 307, 326, 327, 359, 404, 448, 471
Peter, Bishop of Alexandria, 216 n., 220
Phamenoth, 195, 196
Pharao, 14, 157, 171, 426
Pharisee, mystically considered, 388-391
Pharmuth, 195-197
Philippus, Bishop, 200
Philo Judaeus, 269 n.
Philodemus, 325 n.
Philomarus, 325
philosophers, 328, 329
Photinus, heretic, 126, 212 n.
pirates, 290
plague, 203
planets, 261
Plato, 272, 295 n.
pleasure, 131, 134, 148, 149, 328
Plutarch, 299 n.
Polybius, 101
Pompey, Gnaeus, 50
Pope, entitled 'Good Shepherd,' 225
Portus, 413
poverty, 80, 81, 208, 354, 355, 469
prayer, 3, 25, 29, 103, 351, 417
pride, 83, 467

priesthood, 174, 177
priests, in lawsuits, 52, 120-124; persecution of, 43; qualifications of, 315, 316, 339, 342, 374, 455, 456
Priscus, 152, 400
prison, conditions in, 493
Proculus, 207
propitiatory (mercy seat), 104
prosperity, in Roman provinces, 46
psalms, singing of, 13, 374
punishment, capital, 492
purity, 171
Pythagoras, 454
Pythagoreans, 265
Pythian Apollo, 455 n.

Rachel, 156, 235, 236, 269, 459
Rahab, 361
ram, mystically considered, 115, 116
ransom, 290
Rebecca, 76, 359
Reggio, 417
Regulus, Attilius, 39
Renatus, of Verona, 161-163
resurrection, 327
revenues, for pagan temples, 62-67
rhetoric, rules of, 115
rich, the, 304, 408, 409, 460
riches, 80, 81, 83, 88, 303, 304, 353-355, 390
rights, civil *vs.* ecclesiastical, 371, 372

rites, foreign, in Rome, 48
Rome, Church at, 192, 222; Council of, 204 n.; primacy of, 174, 215, 221; Senate house at, 38-40, 49
Romulus, 484, 488
Rufinus, 494, 495
Rumoridus, 63

Sabbath, 407
Sabellians, 126
Sabinus, 124, 127, 129, 134, 136, 144, 225, 425 n.
sacraments, 73, 402
sacrifice, pagan, 32, 458
saints, 429-431, 449, 477
Samaritan, Good, 469
Samson, 176-189
Samuel, 31, 339
Sara, 148, 171, 245, 361, 431
Sarmatian, heretic, 323
Satan, 426
Satyrus, vi, 345 n.
Saul (Paul), 78
Scripture, Holy, 77, 78, 134, 135, 210, 236, 267, 350, 470, 471, 483; quotations from, or reference to, individual Books:

Acts, 64, 78, 90, 115, 122, 135, 138, 148, 257, 259, 273, 308, 322, 326, 329, 348, 354, 401, 442, 443, 448, 476
Aggeus, 448, 449, 451-454
Amos, 441

Apocalypse, 75, 114, 137, 138, 232, 255, 269, 272, 276, 339, 431, 434, 446

Baruch, 202

Canticle of Canticles, 68, 130, 231, 333, 390, 392, 419, 422, 424, 433, 434, 441, 445, 450, 454

Colossians, 104, 114, 200, 229, 280, 332, 353, 360, 388, 441, 443, 451, 467

1 Corinthians, 71, 73, 78, 87, 95, 98, 100, 108, 119-122, 126, 129, 132, 138, 150, 197, 199, 226, 229, 236, 239, 246, 248, 252-254, 256-258, 263, 268, 276, 279-284, 286, 293-296, 300, 322-325, 327, 328, 332, 335, 337, 348, 351, 378, 386, 389, 396, 402, 408, 409, 423, 428, 432, 436, 437, 439, 443, 449, 454, 483, 486, 487

2 Corinthians, 5, 68, 83, 97, 117, 126, 130, 137, 138, 192, 238, 252, 257, 264, 271, 273, 274, 281, 297, 308, 318, 320, 332, 347, 374, 406, 411, 418, 419, 443, 483

Daniel, 64, 112, 130, 153, 159, 161, 256, 264, 298, 323, 327, 331, 346

Deuteronomy, 71, 89, 104, 113, 114, 135, 175, 195, 205, 247, 252, 258, 290, 291, 307, 309, 311, 312, 320, 336, 352, 393, 395, 401, 409, 423, 424, 428, 430, 431, 435, 438, 439, 488

Ecclesiastes, 25, 38, 78, 107, 132, 137, 146, 192, 266, 298, 317-320, 361, 424, 471

Ecclesiasticus, 25, 84, 205, 234, 248, 287, 332, 421, 448

Ephesians, 79, 86, 238, 246, 257, 270, 319, 322, 325, 348, 351, 372, 412, 423, 475-480

2 Esdras, 332

3 Esdras, 290

4 Esdras, 272, 447

Esther, 331

Exodus, 103-105, 107, 111, 116-118, 138, 149, 157, 193, 197-199, 228, 252, 264, 268, 279, 298, 308, 309, 311, 325, 327, 331, 333, 336, 360, 392, 394, 402, 407, 426, 427, 429, 432, 433, 442, 443, 452, 455, 458, 472, 484-486, 489

Ezechiel, 7, 21, 142, 145, 227, 250, 406

Galatians, x, 113, 123, 128, 138, 143, 173, 191, 245, 246, 248, 249, 251, 252, 278, 281, 293, 294, 348, 405, 410, 411, 418, 419, 430, 471

Genesis, 4, 68, 76, 79, 80, 84, 87, 90, 92, 97-100, 115, 118, 119, 130-132, 135, 136, 147, 148, 156-158, 170, 174, 176, 229, 236, 241, 245-247, 251, 254, 257, 259, 261, 264, 265, 268, 280, 287-289, 297, 305, 326, 330, 358, 359, 361, 370,

384, 389, 393, 404, 414-416, 419, 426, 431, 446, 458-461, 465, 476, 490, 491
Habacuc, 80, 150, 264, 427
Hebrews, 74, 104, 126, 135, 145, 268, 271, 338, 339, 347, 360, 410, 430, 440, 453
Isaias, 58, 69, 77, 79, 81, 98, 139, 141, 143, 146-148, 158, 192, 226-228, 232, 237, 245, 250, 257, 265, 268, 285, 291, 315, 319, 320, 332, 354, 356, 386, 388, 392, 409, 412, 426, 427, 437, 439, 449, 453, 457, 460, 471, 473, 486
Jeremias, 12, 140, 143, 151, 192, 261, 262, 269, 271, 285, 385, 411, 424, 425, 449, 450, 472, 493
Job, 23, 291, 295, 296, 302, 304, 306, 369, 370, 377, 455, 456
Joel, 420, 422, 446, 447
John, 5, 71, 77, 90, 96, 109, 112, 136, 140, 141, 192-194, 235, 243, 250, 258, 261, 264, 275, 280, 281, 283, 294, 300, 309, 311, 315, 317, 318, 322, 350, 357, 359, 361, 374, 377, 382-384, 390, 393, 395, 403-405, 408, 412, 419, 430, 432, 440, 441, 443, 446, 447, 451, 465, 468, 469, 472, 473, 478, 493, 494
1 John, 198, 253, 271, 323
2 John, 214

Jonas, 229, 374
Josue, 31, 361, 395, 402, 427, 451, 455
Judges, 17, 164, 167, 169, 176-181, 184-188, 298
Judith, 331
1 Kings, 23, 87, 421, 422, 426
2 Kings, 15, 22, 23, 145, 395, 449, 491
3 Kings, 161, 204, 242, 305, 306, 320, 331, 349, 350, 371, 425, 434, 442, 448, 449, 485, 488
4 Kings, 17, 202, 203, 228, 263, 264, 305, 306, 318, 319, 332, 380, 448, 452
Leviticus, 100, 119, 175, 312, 316, 472
Luke, 16, 20, 82, 88, 98, 106, 110, 124, 134, 135, 158, 159, 170, 190, 192, 227, 228, 233-235, 244, 254, 269, 280, 282, 284, 312, 315, 318, 320, 349, 361, 386-393, 396, 409, 427, 432, 433, 446, 452, 469-470, 472, 477, 487, 491
1 Machabees, 19
2 Machabees, 65, 299
Malachias, 267, 420
Mark, 377, 384, 403
Matthew, 4, 8, 9, 24, 25, 36, 68, 77, 82, 93, 96-98, 100, 106, 109-111, 113, 118, 126, 135, 137, 140, 144, 146, 151, 153, 158, 193, 204, 226-229, 232, 235, 236, 238, 241-244, 250,

254, 255, 258, 263, 267, 276, 280, 284, 287, 307, 314-316, 318, 322, 326, 331, 337, 348, 350, 352, 358-361, 371, 381, 388, 391-393, 401, 404, 406, 407, 411, 412, 419, 420, 426, 427, 432, 439-442, 444, 451, 453, 457, 463, 470-472, 474, 477, 493

Micheas, 231-234, 237-240, 268, 394, 422

Numbers, 72-74, 76, 104, 161, 176, 228, 311, 312, 338-342, 394, 402, 405, 407, 426, 429, 477

Osee, 267, 420, 423, 440, 471

1 Paralipomenon, 285

2 Paralipomenon, 68, 69

1 Peter, 93, 253, 303, 304, 307, 353, 354, 363, 402, 412, 442

2 Peter, 258, 438

Philemon, 101, 357

Philippians, 86-88, 109, 126, 136, 138-140, 143, 201, 242, 271, 275, 282, 294, 304, 354, 360, 377, 447, 453, 477

Proverbs, 25, 38, 41, 78-82, 106-108, 234, 250, 290-292, 300-304, 306, 310, 337, 343, 346, 353, 355, 415, 427, 432, 438, 457

Psalms, 7, 22, 25, 31, 58, 64, 68, 76-80, 84, 87, 104-106, 108-110, 116, 124, 128, 133, 137-139, 141, 145-147, 150, 175, 191, 192, 194, 200, 201, 209, 228, 229, 234-237, 240, 246, 258, 260, 262, 264-266, 268, 269, 271, 274, 275, 282, 284, 285, 288, 289, 294-296, 301, 303, 306, 307, 309, 313, 317, 318, 320, 322, 323, 332, 336, 337, 339, 343, 349-352, 354-356, 360, 362, 369, 372, 373, 377-379, 391, 403, 408, 419, 421, 422, 427, 430, 433, 437-443, 445, 447, 450-453, 455, 457, 460, 462, 466, 470, 476, 477, 486

Romans, 8, 16, 65, 70, 84, 88, 93, 97, 110, 113, 133, 233, 237, 241, 248, 249, 251, 256, 260, 263, 268, 273-275, 277-279, 281-283, 285, 297, 301, 307, 318, 326, 335, 340, 358, 391, 404, 428, 444, 453, 463-467, 492

1 Thessalonians, 79

1 Timothy, 83, 104, 140, 215, 292, 331, 343-345, 436, 440, 450

2 Timothy, 8, 105, 109, 255, 340, 386

Titus, 214, 229, 343

Tobias, 175, 327

Wisdom, 40, 69, 248, 273, 305, 320, 434, 444, 448

Zacharias, 83, 142, 453

Secundianus, heretic, 207, 208
seers, 44, 48
senators, Christian, 34

Senones, 39
senses, mystically considered, 309
servitude, 111 n., 287, 288
seven, number, 265-269, 271, 470
Severus, Bishop, 149, 200
Severus, layman, of Milan, 382
sexes, differences in, 435
sheep, 68, 69, 358
silver, 408, 462
Simeon, 280
Simplicianus, vi, vii, 286, 303, 308, 311
sin, 24, 232, 233, 238-240, 295, 300, 301, 311-314; forgiveness of, 388, 389, 465-467
sinners, 276
Siricius, Pope, 151, 152, 225
Sirmium, Synod of, 212 n.
Sisinnius, 489
six, days of creation, 264, 265
slavery, 288-295, 301, 302, 363, 411; spiritual, 247, 248; to sin, 297-298
Socrates, 216 n.
Solon, 269
Sophocles, 296
soul, 237, 272, 273, 313, 421, 432, 433, 441, 443, 444, 446, 454, 480; mystically considered, 241-244, 420-424, 428, 434
Sozomen, 13 n., 15 n., 120 n.
speech, 79, 83, 84, 487; deceitful, 82; freedom of, 6, 7; rules of, 118, 119

Spirit, Holy, 5, 6, 107, 108, 278, 283-285, 314, 393, 434, 440
stars, 265, 269
stater, 109, 110
Stephen, St., 148, 308, 322, 442
Stoics, 326
stoning, 473, 474
strangers, hospitality to, 176
Studius, 468 n., 492
suffering, 278, 346, 347
Sunamitess, 448
Susanna, 130, 159
Syagrius, Bishop, 152, 163
Symmachus, prefect of Rome, 37, 63; *Relatio* of, 31 n., 37 n.
synagogue, 10-12, 341, 350, 385, 393, 423
Syrus, priest, 151

tablets, of Law, 486
temperance, 332
temptation, 237-240
ten, stages of life, 269, 270
Tertullian, 344 n.
Thecla, virgin, 299, 333
Theodoret, 13 n., 26 n., 172 n., 216 n., 217 n.
Theodorus, Bishop, 230
Theodosian Code, 43 n., 413 n., 481 n., 483
Theodosius, Bishop, 200
Theodosius, Emperor, viii, 6, 16, 17, 19-22, 24-26, 28-32, 35, 43 n., 55, 59-61, 63, 64, 202 n., 208, 213, 216, 219, 223; and affair at Callinicum, 10-12,

513

385; Thessalonian massacre, 395, 396, 494 n.
Theophilus, Bishop, 172
Therasia, 144 n.
Thessalonian massacre, 20 n., 22 200, 494 n.
thief, on cross, 243, 244, 315, 427
Thomar, 156
three, days, mystically considered, 470
Tigris, mystically considered, 462
Timosius, 396
Timotheus, Bishop, 200
Timothy, Bishop, 217
Titianus, 494
travel, 68, 172, 173
Trier, Ambrose's mission to, 57-62
Trinity, 5, 6, 126, 265, 278, 319, 383

uncle, marriage with, 481
Ursinus, anti-pope, 213-215
usury, 175

Valens, Emperor, 214, 216 n., 395 n.
Valentinian I, Emperor, vii, viii
Valentinian II, Emperor, viii, x, 26, 27, 31, 37, 52, 53, 57, 59, 60, 63, 64, 208, 216; Ambrose's embassy in behalf of, 56 n., 57-63; asking basilica, 367 n., 371, 374, 375 n.; death and burial of, 26-28; delegating state revenues to pagan temples, 32-33, 35; desire of, for baptism, 27
Valentinians, sect, 13, 17, 385
Vallio, 61
vengeance, 352
Venus, 48
Vercelli, Church of, 321, 345-348, 413
Vestal virgins, 35, 36, 38, 41, 42
vices, 352
Victor, son of Maximus, 19 n., 59
Victory, altar of, 34, 36, 37, 40, 49
Vienne, Bishops of, 207
Vigilius, Bishop, 174
vigils, 216-217
Virgil, 44-47, 87, 90, 191, 262, 266, 269, 290, 297, 416, 425, 428, 444, 445, 450, 457
virgin, trial of, 152, 153, 155, 156
virginity, 42, 225-228, 323, 332-335; of Mary, 226-228
virgins, 324, 332-333
virtues, 352, 353, 363, 408, 445-447, 475; of a Christian, 253, 342, 343, 351, 352
Vita Ambrosii, 62 n., 152 n.

Wady Eschcol, 394 n.
wages, defrauding of, 81, 82, 175
Waghorn, W. R., 425 n.
widows, 43, 80, 228, 324, 335; mystically considered, 469;

mite, mystically considered, 470
wisdom, 292-301, 459; divine, 309, 310
witnesses, from hearsay, 160 n.
wives, duties of, 361
women, clothing of, in pagan rites, 436; subject to husband, 480

Wytzes, J., 31 n., 32 n., 63 n.

Zabulon, 241, 452
Zaccheus, 314
Zachary, 280
Zeller, J., 208
Zeno, Bishop, 152, 153
Zorobabel, 451

www.ingramcontent.com/pod-product-compliance
Lightning Source LLC
Chambersburg PA
CBHW032021290426
44110CB00012B/619